Ireland and the Crimean War

And now, as he looked and saw the whole Hellespont
covered with the vessels of his fleet, and all the shore and
every plain about Abydos as full as possible of
men, Xerxes congratulated himself on his good fortune;
but after a little while he wept.

Herodotus, *The Histories*, VII, 45

23/5/02.

IRELAND AND THE CRIMEAN WAR

D̶A̶V̶I̶D̶ ̶M̶U̶R̶P̶H̶Y̶

To: Veronica Sentry.

May thanks for your support
--- and keeping me on my
toes in class!

Best regards,

David Murphy.

FOUR COURTS PRESS

Set in 10.5pt on 13pt Times by
Carrigboy Typesetting Services, County Cork for
FOUR COURTS PRESS LTD
Fumbally Lane, Dublin 8, Ireland
e-mail: info@four-courts-press.ie
http://www.four-courts-press.ie
and in North America for
FOUR COURTS PRESS
c/o ISBS, 5824 N.E. Hassalo Street, Portland, OR 97213.

ISBN 1–85182–639–4

Printed in Ireland
by MPG Books, Bodmin, Great Britain

Contents

Illustrations and maps

MAPS

Acknowledgements

I would like to extend my grateful acknowledgement first and foremost to Dr W.E. Vaughan of Trinity College, Dublin, who supervised my PhD thesis on the Irish in the Crimean war. His advice, assistance and support throughout the course of my researches has proved invaluable while his untiring patience in correcting earlier drafts of my work has served to eliminate many errors and inconsistencies. I would also like to thank Dr David Dickson for the help and advice he gave me when I first registered as a student in Trinity College, Dublin, in 1996. Special thanks are due to James McGuire of University College, Dublin, for the help and encouragement he has given me over many years.

I would like to acknowledge the help of Charles Benson and the staff of the Early Printed Books Department in Trinity College, Dublin, especially Shane Mawe and Rose Reddy. The assistance of Dr Noel Kissane of the National Library of Ireland, Gregory O'Connor of the National Archives, and Bríd Leahy of the Dublin City Archives, is gratefully acknowledged. I would like to extend my gratitude to Commandant Victor Laing and the staff at the Military Archives in Dublin. The help and encouragement offered by the late Commandant Peter Young of the Military Archives is also acknowledged.

Fergus O'Donoghue SJ, Helen Hewson and Orna Somerville of the Jesuit Archives in Dublin, and David Sheehy of the Dublin Diocesan Archives, were also most helpful during the course of my researches. The assistance of Siobhán O'Rafferty, and the staff at the Royal Irish Academy Library, is gratefully acknowledged, especially Bernadette Cunningham, Petra Schnabel, Marcus Browne, Dymphna Moore and Patrick Kelly.

I would also like to acknowledge the assistance of Michael Ball of the National Army Museum, Chelsea, and Lieutenant-Colonel R.J. Binks of the Royal Scots Dragoon Guards Museum in Edinburgh. Colonel Enrico Pino and Warrant Officer Luigi Diana of the Biblioteca Militare Centrale in Rome were most helpful during my researches as was Professor Angelo Tamborra of the University of Rome.

Special thanks are due to Rod Robinson, chairman of the Crimean War Research Society (CWRS), for his help and advice. Major Colin Robins OBE, and Keith Smith, also of the CWRS, were very helpful during the course of my researches. I would like to thank Brigadier-General Allan Mallinson, formerly of the Regiment of Light Dragoons and currently British Defence Attaché in Rome, for his support and also sending me books that I could not obtain in Dublin. The assistance of Lucia Sergienko of the Hermitage Museum in St Petersburg is gratefully acknowledged.

I am grateful to John Farrell and Liam Lawlor of Hardwicke Properties Ltd for allowing me to visit Stack A, venue of the Crimean banquet in 1856. Special thanks are due to Commandant Martin Lenihan for obtaining permission for me, and other CWRS members, to visit Clancy Barracks and Cathal Brugha Barracks in Dublin to view the Russian cannons in those barracks. Thanks are also due to Dr Des McCabe, Vivian Igoe, Jim Herlihy, Inspector John Duffy of the Garda Museum, Mrs Dymphna Moore, Tom Burke and Nick Broughall of the Royal Dublin Fusiliers Association, Derval O'Carroll of the Chester Beatty Library, Nigel Andrews, Assistant British Defence Attaché in Dublin, and Commandant Joseph Gallagher of the Military History Society of Ireland, all of whom provided me with further information.

I owe a special debt of gratitude to my good friend, Philip Lecane of the Royal Dublin Fusiliers Association. In the course of his own researches, Philip came across several pieces of information relating to the Crimean war and very kindly sent them to me.

I would like to acknowledge the help of Dr Tony Gaynor who took time out from his own very busy schedule to read early drafts of this book. His assistance and advice were much appreciated. I also wish to thank Lynn Pierce of Pierce Design who prepared the maps for this book. The financial assistance of the Royal Irish Academy is also gratefully acknowledged. In 2001 I received funds from the RIA's Eoin O'Mahoney fund which facilitated further research. I would also like to thank Michael Adams, Martin Fanning and Anthony Tierney of Four Courts Press for the help and advice they gave in preparing this book for publication.

Finally, I would like to thank my parents and sister for their support and patience during the past number of years. It is to them that this work is dedicated.

Author's note

Throughout this book I have used the modern form of spelling for proper-names and place-names. For example I spell Malakov with a 'v' rather than the double 'f' used in contemporary books and manuscripts. Also Sevastapol is usually referred to as 'Sebastapol' in contemporary sources. This was due to a misreading of the spelling of the town's name in the Cyrillic alphabet and I have therefore, with the exception of some contemporary book titles, adopted the correct form of 'Sevastapol'.

Introduction

The Crimean war of 1854–6 was one of the most important events of the nineteenth century.[1] Developments in weaponry, especially in the area of rifle technology, resulted in a new kind of warfare. The terrible effects of massed rifle-fire on large formations of infantry would be repeated later in the century, especially in the American Civil war. In the same way, the trench warfare that developed around Sevastapol forshadowed events in World War I.

The war also finally proved to the governments of the European powers that the 'Concert of Europe' had ceased to work. The war had different consequences for the countries involved; strengthening Britain's and France's position while both Turkey and Russia ultimatley experienced a further reduction of their prestige and power, marking yet another phase in the decline of both their empires. Conversely, the war resulted in the improvement of the position of Sardinia-Piedmont and marked another stage on the road to Italian unification.

While there has been a renewed interest in the Crimean war during recent years, there are several aspects of the war that have remained unexplored. For decades historians have been content to tell the stories of the charge of the Light Brigade and the 'Lady of the Lamp', focusing their research on events that have been written about almost constantly since the end of the war in 1856. While these aspects were significant, many major features of the war have been overlooked. The Crimean war is often portrayed as a 'cavalry war', yet it was the infantry, artillery and engineers who did the real fighting. The war had a global impact but the extensive nature of the Royal Navy's campaign is often totally overlooked and no one has yet written a full account of the naval war. The long-term effects of the Crimean war undermined Russia's position in Europe and Russia had still not recovered by the 1870s. The importance of the Crimean war in terms of nineteenth-century European history has been greatly underestimated. The roles played by various countries involved in the war have not been the subject of modern research. There have been no recent studies of the armies of Turkey, Sardinia and France. Research has only really begun again into the involvement of Polish Cossack regiments in the Turkish army.[2]

1 While Russia and Turkey were at war from 1853, France and Britain did not enter the war until 1854 while Sardinia-Piedmont did not declare war until 1855. 2 The last books on the Polish

The Irish aspect of the war is yet another area that has been largely ignored by historians. Ireland was involved in the war in a major way and the time for an assessment of the involvement of Irish men and women in the Crimean war of 1854–6 is long overdue. Studies of the British army in the Crimea usually treat it as a large homogenous body, totally disregarding the role played by its Scottish, Irish and Welsh soldiers. It can be shown that Irishmen constituted a large part of the British army in this period, and that they played a significant part in the war. Twenty-eight Irishmen were awarded the Victoria Cross for acts of bravery they carried out during the war, yet the Irish contribution has been totally forgotten over the past 150 years. There were also large numbers of Irishmen in the Royal Navy at this time, and in the medical and chaplaincy services. Irish nuns, engineers and railway navvies also served in the Crimea.

Despite the size of the Irish contingent, the Crimean war has not been studied by Irish historians. While there are several references to the war in *A new history of Ireland*, v, many standard texts, such as F.S.L. Lyons' *Ireland since the Famine* (London, 1971), do not contain a single reference.[3] The contribution of Irish men and women in the war has never been comprehensively dealt with. Evelyn Bolster's *The Irish Sisters of Mercy in the Crimean war* (Cork, 1964), remains the only piece of Irish research based on a specifically Crimean theme. Some articles on Irish Crimean topics appeared in the *Irish Sword*, the journal of the Irish Military History Society. These were mostly published in the 1960s but did not seem to generate any serious interest. It is also interesting to note that the comprehensive *Military history of Ireland* (1996), edited by Thomas Bartlett and Keith Jeffery, contains few references to the Crimean war.

The Channel 4 documentary series on the Crimean war, screened in 1997, did not refer to Ireland. When illustrating the ports where the transport ships assembled to carry the army to the East, Dublin and Cork, two of the most important points for the embarkation of troops, were not included on the map. This is perhaps not surprising due to the lack of interest in the war in Ireland. I gave a paper discussing the role of the Irish in the war at the CWRS's AGM in London in May 1998. The society's members later admitted that they had never even considered this aspect of the war as there was simply no literature on the subject.

This omission is perhaps even more significant given the massive revival of interest in the Crimean war. Collectors have been showing a renewed interest in Crimean war medals and documents over the last two to three years, and several significant items have come up for auction. In April 1996 a record price

contingent in the Crimean war were W. Dziewanowski, *Mundury Wojska Polskiego* (Lwow, 1938),W. Dziewanowski and A. Minkiewicz, *Polish armed forces through the ages* (London, 1944). The Norwegian historian, Knut Erik Ström, is currently researching Polish involvement in the Crimea.   **3** W.E. Vaughan (ed.), *A new history of Ireland*, v (Oxford, 1989).

was paid for the Crimean medal of a survivor of the charge of the Light Brigade, with Balaclava, Sevastapol and Alma clasps. Admittedly the medals of members of the Light Brigade have always fetched high amounts but Sotheby's initially expected the medal to fetch between £800 and £1,000, and were amazed when it fetched £5,290. Coincidentally, the medal had been awarded to an Irish trooper, Patrick Doolan from Nenagh, Co. Tipperary.[4] The Crimean war auction sensation of 1998 was a lot of about seventy letters written by Lieutenant Henry Fitzhardinge Maxe, Lord Cardigan's Brigade ADC, and his brother, Lieutenant Frederick Augustus Maxe RN. This significant collection had not been consulted for historical purposes before and drew the attention of both private collectors and military museums.

There have also been numerous books on the Crimean war published recently. One of the most significant of these was Andrew Lambert and Stephen Badsey's *The war correspondents: the Crimean war* (2nd edn, London, 1997). Lambert and Badsey's work, while focusing on the reportage of the Irish correspondent, William Howard Russell, tried to illustrate the part played by the Royal Navy in the war and also considered the role of France and Sardinia. In their introductory chapter Lambert and Badsey posed several questions which focused on the absence of modern studies on certain aspects of this most significant of nineteenth-century conflicts. The opinions of nineteenth-century authors continue to influence the modern historiography of the war. As Lambert and Badsey have put it:

> The popular image of the Crimea, however unsatisfactory it might be, is still the basis for modern studies. This version of the 'Crimean war' is long overdue for revision. In the absence of any study of British strategy, existing accounts fall back on the old standards, the charge of the Light Brigade, Florence Nightingale and the horrors of the Crimean winter. These were real enough, but had almost no impact on the outcome of the war and serve only to mislead.[5]

A close scrutiny of the modern historiography of the Crimean war reveals that only a limited number of topics are still being addressed. One of the most highly publicised books to be published in 1997 was Saul David's *The homicidal earl*, yet another biography of James Thomas Brudenell, 7th earl of Cardigan. First one must ask why the author felt that another biography of Cardigan was necessary. P. Compton's *Cardigan of Balaclava* (London, 1972) and D. Thomas's *Charge! Hurrah! Hurrah! A life of Lord Cardigan* (London, 1974) were both comprehensive biographies. Also Cecil Woodham-Smith had previously published *The reason why* (London, 1953), an insightful look at both the characters of Cardigan and Lucan, and at the reasons that contributed to the men's volatile

---

4 The *Irish Times*,12 April 1996; *Daily Telegraph*, 12 April 1996.   **5** Andrew Lambert and Stephen Badsey, *The war correspondents: the Crimean war* (2nd edn, London, 1997), p. 2.

relationship. Saul David's research provided no new information on Cardigan's violent nature, his relationship with his men, his women or the part he played in the Crimean war.

Similarly, Mark Adkin's *The charge: why the Light Brigade was lost* (London, 1996), goes over some well-covered ground. There have been numerous accounts of the charge of the Light Brigade, far too numerous, in fact, to be mentioned here. No one can satisfactorily explain the events of 25 October 1854 due to the differing accounts of those who survived. Again Cecil Woodham-Smith's *The reason why* provides a more than adequate account of 'the charge'. The most concise account of the action is contained in Paget's *History of the British cavalry,* ii (London, 1975).[6]

Perhaps the most comprehensive study of the war to be published recently was Trevor Royle's *Crimea: the great Crimean war, 1854–1856* (London, 1999). This is a massive study and, while it is comprehensive in its coverage of all aspects of the Crimean war, Royle has relied heavily on texts published in the nineteenth century, especially A.W. Kinglake's *The invasion of the Crimea* (8 volumes, London, 1863–87). Sue M. Goldie's *Florence Nightingale: letters from the Crimea* (1997) is also a useful and historically accurate work. While there are numerous biographies of Florence Nightingale, Goldie's book is helpful to historians of the period as it provides for the first time an extensive collection of Nightingale's correspondence in a single volume. The explanatory text that she provides is also not only accurate, but non-intrusive.

Some of the major engagements of the war have recently been the subject of new publications. John Sweetman, who previously published a life of Lord Raglan, has written *Balaclava 1854* (London, 1990), while Patrick Mercer has written *Inkerman 1854* (London, 1998) and, a more in-depth study of the battle, *Give them a volley and charge* (London, 2000). The producer of the Channel 4 series, Paul Kerr, also brought out a companion volume to the television series, *The Crimean war* (1998).

Finally, one should mention new works of fiction based on Crimean subjects. Beryl Bainbridge's *Master Georgie* (1998), based on the experiences of a group of British soldiers and camp-followers in the Crimea, was shortlisted for the Booker Prize in 1998. Garry Douglas has published two new fictional works, *The devil's own* (1998) and *Into the valley of death* (1998), based on the experiences of a gentleman ranker serving in the Connaught Rangers in the Crimea. Douglas' books are written in the style of Bernard Cornwell's *Sharpe* series, and contain quite a large amount of period detail. Perhaps the most refreshing aspect of the current glut of Crimea-related books, is the originality of the fictional pieces.

---

6 George Charles Henry Victor Paget (7th marquess of Anglesey), *History of the British cavalry*, ii (London, 1975).

It should also be mentioned that several books, published in the nineteenth century, and considered as being standard texts, are now being reprinted. While such books do not constitute new publications in a strict sense, it is interesting that, in the absence of original modern research, contemporary works are being republished. Such books include Lieutenant-Colonel Anthony Sterling's *The Highland Brigade in the Crimea*, first published in 1895.[7]

While this new interest in the Crimean war is encouraging, one cannot help but be disappointed by the lack of original research. Most of the volumes mentioned above do not cover original subjects or make use of any of the newly discovered manuscript sources. The lack of a study on Irish involvement in the Crimean war stands as a glaring historical omission. This would be understandable if the Irish had only played a small part in the war. Yet it will be shown in this book that the Irish formed a large part of the British army and the Royal Navy during the Crimean war. The involvement of Irish men and women in the support services, and in various other capacities, was also significant. It is the purpose of this book to assess the role played by Irish men and women during the Crimean war and an effort will also be made to try and ascertain the level of Irish public interest in the war.

It will also be shown that, while there are not a great number of Crimean war manuscript collections in the National Library of Ireland, the National Archives and the Public Record Office of Northern Ireland, several of the Irish collections that do exist are of major historical importance. In the same way, some of Irish participants later published accounts of the war and these are also important sources in their own right. The Irish in the Crimean war have been ignored by Irish historians in the same way that Irish involvement in World War I was ignored until recently. The extent of the Irish involvement in the Crimean war would suggest that the war had a major effect on Irish society in the 1850s and it is one of the purposes of this book to assess the impact of this European war on Ireland.

---

7 Lieutenant-Colonel Anthony Sterling, *The Highland Brigade in the Crimea* (Absinthe Press, 1995). Sterling was born in Dundalk, Co. Louth, in 1805.

A chronology of the major events of the Crimean war

1853

28 February: Prince Menshikov arrives in Constaninople on a diplomatic mission.

21 May: Menshikov leaves Constantinople, signalling the end of negotiations with Turkey.

8 June: British fleet leaves Malta and heads for eastern Mediterranean.

2 July: A Russian army crosses the Pruth river and occupies Turkey's Danubian Principalities (Moldavia and Wallachia).

14 October: British and French fleets anchor in the Dardanelles.

23 October: Turkey declares war on Russia.

30 November: Battle of Sinope. Russian Black Sea Fleet attacks Turkish fleet at anchor: Over 4,000 Turkish sailors killed. Battle portrayed in the British press as a massacre.

24 December: Sir James Graham, first lord of the admiralty, proposes an expedition to Sevastapol.

1854

3 January: Allied fleets ordered to the Black Sea.

11 January: Russia warned that her warships in the Black Sea must return to Sevastapol.

13 February: Lord Raglan appointed as commander of the British expeditionary force.

22 February: First troops sail from England, initially destined for Gibraltar and Malta.

24 February: First regiment leaves Ireland, the 50th Foot, sailing from Kingstown (Dun Laoghaire).

27 February: British ultimatum sent to the tsar, demanding a Russian withdrawal from Turkey's Danubian Principalities. An answer is required within six days.

11 March: British Fleet sails for the Baltic to establish a blockade of Russian ports.

26 March: First French troops leave for Turkey.

27 March: France declares war on Russia.

28 March: Britain declares war on Russia.

30 March: British force in Malta ordered to Gallipoli.

8 April: British troops land at Gallipoli.

10 April: Britain and France sign formal alliance.

15 April: Turkey joins Anglo-French Alliance.

22 April: Allied fleet bombards Odessa.

19 May: Russian army crosses south of the Danube and lays siege to Silistria.

23 May: Britain, France, Austria and Prussia guarantee Turkish independence.

25–29 May: Allied troops concentrate at Varna, to prevent further Russian advance.

21 June: Bombardment of the Bomarsund Fortress in the Baltic. For his bravery during this attack an Irishman, Charles Davis Lucas, was later awarded the first-ever Victoria Cross.

23 June: Turkish army, under Omar Pasha, raises siege of Silistria, without Anglo-French help.

16 July: Lord Raglan ordered to invade the Crimea.

19 July: Cholera breaks out in allied camp.

10 August: Fire in Varna destroys military stores. Landing in Crimea delayed as a result.

7 September: Allied fleet departs for the Crimea.

14–18 September: Landings at Calamita Bay.

19 September: Advance on Sevastapol begins. Minor skirmish at the Bulganek river.

20 September: Battle of the Alma. Sergeant (later General Sir) Luke O'Connor awarded the Victoria Cross for his bravery in the battle. Becomes the first man in the British army to be awarded the VC.

23 September: Russians sink warships in Sevastapol harbour, blocking the entrance.

24 September: Allies begin their flank march on Sevastapol.

25 September: Skirmish at McKenzie's Farm.

26 September: British take Balaclava and allied army establishes itself on the heights above Sevastapol.

27 September: Siege of Sevastapol begins.

17 October: First bombardment of Sevastapol. French magazine explodes and bombardment ends on 20 October.

25 October: Battle of Balaclava. Russian attempt to re-take Balaclava fails due to the defence of 93rd Highlanders ('the Thin Red Line') and the charges of the Heavy and Light Brigades.

26 October: Battle of Little Inkerman. Russian troops attack allied right wing on the Chersonese Uplands. The attack fails due to the 2nd Division's tenacious defence of Mount Inkerman.

5 November: Battle of Inkerman. A more powerful Russian attack on the allied right wing. Attack repulsed primarily by 2nd Division with French reinforcements.

6 November: Allied commanders decide to continue siege of Sevastapol.

14 November: A hurricane causes serious damage to allied shipping in Balaclava.

24 November: Twenty-seven men of the Irish Constabulary arrive in the Crimea to serve in the Mounted Staff Corps. More Irish constables later arrive to serve with the Commissariat Department.

1855

1 January: The forty-five regiments of the Militia of Ireland are embodied.

2 January: Sardinia-Piedmont joins the allies.

5 January: Omar Pasha lands in the Crimea with Turkish reinforcements.

19 January: The Enniskillen-born railway engineer, James Beatty, arrives in the Crimea to begin building the Balaclava-Sevastapol railroad.

25 January: John Arthur Roebuck's proposal that a select committee be set up to investigate the conduct of the war introduced in the Commons. Ultimately leads to resignation of Lord Aberdeen's administration.

5 February: Lord Palmerston new prime minister.

17 February: Unsuccessful Russian attack on Eupatoria.

24 February: Russians sink more blockships in Sevastapol harbour.

2 March: Tsar Nicholas I dies. Succeeded by Alexander II.

5 March: Sevastapol select committee begins its investigations.

9 April: Second bombardment of Sevastapol begins and continues for eight days.

3–5 May: Abortive Allied expedition to Kertch, on the Sea of Azov.

22–24 May: Allied forces occupy Kertch.

6 June: Third bombardment precedes allied attacks.

7 June: French capture Mamelon battery while British capture the quarries on the left of the allied line.

17 June: Fourth bombardment of Sevastapol.

18 June: Unsuccessful allied attack on Sevastapol. French fail to take the Malakov Bastion while the British fail to take the Redan. Sevastapol select committee reports to Parliament.

28 June: Death of Lord Raglan. Succeeded as British commander-in-chief by Sir James Simpson.

16 August: Battle of the Tchernaya. Russian attack repulsed by Sardinian and French troops.

17 August: Fifth bombardment of Sevastapol begins and lasts for a week.

5 September: Sixth bombardment begins.

8 September: Final assault on Sevastapol. French capture crucial Malakov Bastion but the British fail again at the Redan.

9 September: Russians abandon Sevastapol south of the bay during the night of 8–9 September and the allies take possession.

17 October: Fort Kinburn, on the confluence of the Dnieper and Bug rivers, attacked and captured by allied naval and land forces.

11 November: Sir William Codrington appointed as British commander-in-chief.

15 November: Ammunition explosion in French lines.

25 November: General William Fenwick Williams agrees to Russian conditions and surrenders the town of Kars in eastern Turkey.

16 December: An Austrian peace plan sent to Alexander II.

1856

16 January: Alexander II accepts peace terms.

29 January: Last Russian bombardment of the south side of Sevastapol.

28 February: Armistice signed in Paris.

29 February: Allied and Russian officers meet near Tractir Bridge to discuss armistice arrangements. They organize reviews of each other's troops.

30 March: Treaty of Paris signed.

27 April: Treaty of Paris formally ratified.

7 July: Mutiny of North Tipperary Militia in Nenagh. Mutiny breaks out due to plans to disembody the militia following the end of the war.

12 July: Last British troops leave the Crimea.

22 October: Grand Crimean Banquet in Dublin.

Map 1: The Baltic Sea area of operations

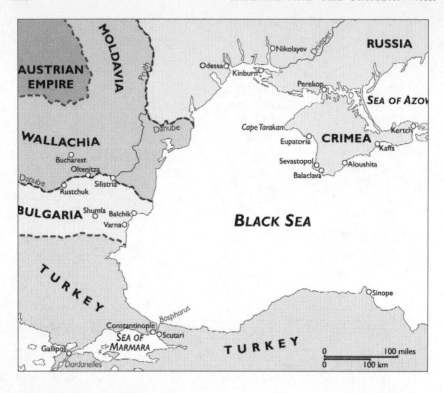

Map 2: The Black Sea area of operations

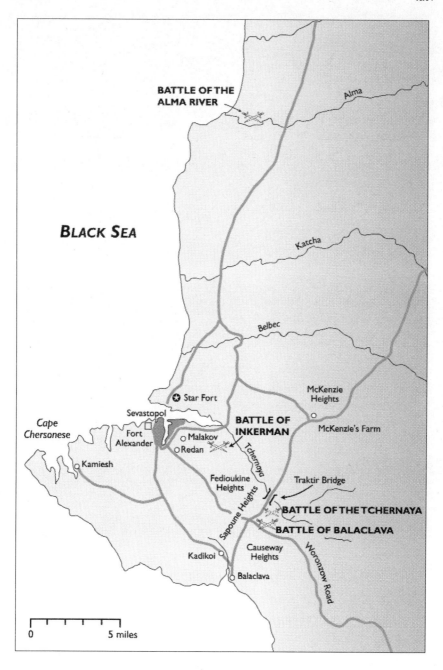

BLACK SEA

BATTLE OF THE
ALMA RIVER

Alma

Katcha

Belbec

McKenzie
Heights

Star Fort

Sevastopol   BATTLE OF
                          INKERMAN   McKenzie's Farm

Cape
Chersonese   Fort
                Alexander   Malakov
                         Redan   Tchernaya

Kamiesh   Traktir Bridge

                Fedioukine
                Heights   BATTLE OF THE TCHERNAYA

                              Sapoune Heights   BATTLE OF BALACLAVA

                                Causeway
                Kadikoi   Heights   Woronzow Road

                      Balaclava

0   5 miles

Map 3: The Crimean Peninsula

Ireland and the outbreak of the war

The origins of the war

It is not the intention of this book to examine the causes which led to the outbreak of the Crimean war in detail. Several comprehensive studies have dealt with this subject and there is no need to rehearse them here.[1] The Crimean war was caused by the long-term tensions which had developed in Europe after the end of the Napoleonic wars. These problems had been exacerbated by the European revolutions of 1848. Russia, under Tsar Nicholas I, was increasingly seen as the main threat to the European *status quo*. The Ottoman empire, perceived as being weak by Nicholas I, became the focus of Russia's territorial ambitions. Since the eighteenth century Russia had expanded and annexed new territories in the Ukraine and the Crimea. Further expansion had followed in the Caucasus region and, by the mid-nineteenth century, the tsar was considering invading Turkey's Balkan possessions. There were a series of dangerous clashes in the region. By the outbreak of the Crimean war Russia and Turkey had been at war three times (1806–7, 1810–11 and 1828–9). During the Greek war of independence (1821–9), a Russian army had invaded the Balkans and advanced close to Constantinople. The Russo-Turkish war of 1828–9 had resulted in a further weakening of Turkey's position. In the Egyptian-Turkish dispute of 1831–41 the sultan had received military aid from Russia and had promised to close the Bosphorus Straits to foreign warships on Russian demand.[2]

Both Britain and France shared fears of Russian expansion in the eastern Mediterranean and their governments viewed these events with alarm, fearing Russian control of the eastern end of the Mediterranean. The French also feared that Russia would advance through seized Turkish territory towards their possessions in North Africa. The British were concerned that the collapse of the Ottoman empire would clear the way for Russia to expand into India via Persia

1 For an in-depth analysis of the causes of the Crimean war see David M. Goldfrank, *The origins of the Crimean war* (London, 1994). See also Trevor Royle, *Crimea: the great Crimean war, 1854–1856* (London, 1999). There is a detailed account of the various diplomatic efforts to prevent the war in A.J.P. Taylor's, *The struggle for mastery in Europe, 1848–1918* (Oxford, 1971).
2 David M. Goldfrank, *The origins of the Crimean war* (London, 1994).

and Afghanistan. Throughout the 1840s, therefore, relations between these powers worsened. War became increasingly likely and by 1853 Sir James Graham, first lord of the admiralty, had drawn up two strategic plans to be implemented in the event of a war with Russia.

The event which eventually caused the outbreak of the war was somewhat bizarre. During the summer of 1850 Orthodox and Roman Catholic monks clashed in Bethlehem over the question of who should control the church of the Nativity. These clashes resulted in the death of several Orthodox monks. Tsar Nicholas demanded that he should be appointed as protector of the Orthodox Christians in the Ottoman empire. The sultan could not, of course, agree to Nicholas' terms and a Russian army was sent to occupy Turkey's Danubian principalities in July 1853. Britain and France sent fleets to the Dardanelles in a show of support, and even entered the Dardanelles, breaking the London Straits Convention of 1841.[3] By October 1853, Turkey had declared war on Russia, quickly followed by a Russian attack on Silistria and, on 30 November 1853, the destruction of a squadron of Turkish ships at Sinope. War was now a certainty as, by destroying the Turkish fleet at Sinope, Russia had become the main naval threat to France and Britain in the Black Sea and, potentially, the Mediterranean. In January 1854 an allied naval squadron entered the Black Sea, while the first British troops left for the East in February. War was finally declared on 28 March 1854.

Yet while the allies were mobilizing their armies, there seemed little agreement as to what the aims of the war were. The British, French, Austrians and Prussians spent months in ponderous discussions, which finally resulted in a plan that became known as the 'Four Points'. The Four Points stated that normal diplomatic relations between Russia and Turkey could not resume unless (1) the Russian 'protectorate' of the Danubian Principalities was replaced by a European guarantee; (2) the Danube was declared to be a free river; (3) the London Straits Convention of 1841was revised 'in the interests of the balance of Power in Europe'; (4) the Russians should abandon their claim to a protectorate over the Christian subjects in Turkey while the other European powers should obtain assurances of their protection. Russia refused to accept these terms and, while Austria and Prussia remained neutral, France and Britain became embroiled in a war.[4] Sardinia-Piedmont later entered the way on the allied side in 1855.

One must question the wisdom of this rush to war and even the whole concept of a Russian threat. There is no doubt the both France and Britain had allowed themselves to be influenced by a degree of 'Russophobia'. One could argue that the Russian threat to the allies' position was totally illusory. If Russia

---

3 The London Straits Convention of 1841 decreed that only Turkish ships could use the Straits. The treaty of Unkiar-Skelessi in 1833 had closed the Straits to French and British warships; this ban was extended to Russian warships under the terms of the 1841 Convention.   4 Goldfrank,

could not control recently acquired territory in the Caucasus, how could it then invade Central Asia and Afghanistan?[5] The Russian army, while large, was out-moded and generally badly led. Russia had a poor railway system, with not one mile of railway to the south or east of Moscow. How was this large Russian army to mobilize and fight other European powers? Also, while the Russian navy was large, it was still sail-powered and was no real threat to the now predominantly steam-powered ships of the Royal Navy.[6] The Russian threat was, therefore, more imagined than real. Indeed the Turks, whom the allies were rushing to help, did well after initial setbacks and, ably led by Omar Pasha, forced Russia to raise the siege of Silistria in June 1854.[7] By July 1854 the Russians had been driven from the Danubian Principalities. The Crimean war could have remained a local affair, another of the numerous disagreements that occurred between Russia and Turkey during the nineteenth century. Indeed the two countries were at war again in 1877. Perhaps the ultimate irony of the whole affair was that the Ottoman empire, described by Nicholas I as 'the sick man of Europe', would not finally collapse until 1919, outliving the Romanov dynasty by two years.

The reaction of Irish MPs

The early months of 1854 were ones of great international turmoil and one of the diplomats who tried to negotiate a peace settlement between Russia and Turkey was Lord Strangford, then serving with the diplomatic service in Constantinople.[8] Russia's refusal to withdraw from the Danubian Principalities and Turkey's declaration of war in October 1853 increased international tensions still further. The Sinope incident of 30 November 1853 increased the clamour for war, as the public became more intolerant of Lord Aberdeen's inaction. The strength of British public opinion in late 1853 and early 1854 cannot be underestimated for, whipped up into near-frenzy by newspaper reports of Russian atrocities in the Principalities, writers and MPs called for action. Lord Aberdeen faced the problem of leading a divided cabinet. His faction in the cabinet opposed an aggressive policy against Russia and were portrayed in the newspapers as being, at best, lukewarm on the whole Turkish issue. Lord Palmerston became the leader of the faction calling for decisive action against Russia.

Supported by Russell, Landsdowne and Clarendon he used, perhaps unfairly, his influence with the *Morning Post* to whip up anti-Russian felling and also to

---

Origins of the Crimean war (London, 1994). **5** In the early 1850s, Russian troops were engaged in a war with Chechen rebels in the Caucasus. **6** Andrew Lambert and Stephen Badsey, *The war correspondents*, pp 4–5. **7** Omar Pasha was the *nom de guerre* of Michael Lattas, a Croatian general in the Turkish service. **8** Percy Ellen Frederick William Smythe, 8th Viscount Strangford. It is ironic that his father, Percy Clinton Sydney Smythe, 6th Viscount Strangford, had

attack Aberdeen. Newspaper attacks on Aberdeen became increasingly virulent and *Punch* even published a cartoon depicting Aberdeen polishing the Tsar's boots! Yet it was a short passage in the *Westminster Review* which mentioned the risk to 'our passage to India and our commerce with all free nations' which created the most general public discontent with Aberdeen and his ministers.[9] To a great extent, this criticism of Aberdeen was unjustified as the country was not prepared for a major European war. It was still hoped that combined French and British pressure would force the tsar to see sense. Members of both the Commons and the Lords began to express doubts regarding the government's actions. In February 1854, the earl of Clanricarde, who had previously served as the British ambassador to St Petersburg (1838–41), urged the government to exercise caution:

> I beg to assure you that no person can be more anxious than I am at all times to preserve peace, if peace can be preserved consistently with the interests and, still more, with the honour of this country, and that any quarrel that I may have with Her Majesty's Government upon this subject at the present moment, is not that they have not earlier engaged us in a war, but that they have adopted measures (although I doubt not sincerely animated with a desire for peace) which have necessarily brought us into hostilities, and on the brink of, if not actually engaged in a great war. We do not see of that vigour and determination of purpose which I think might, in the first place, have avoided any such catastrophe, and which alone, I think, will be able to restore peace and bring that war to a satisfactory and early conclusion.[10]

There was also some debate as to where any resulting military campaign should take place. Some suggested the Black Sea, in order to be of immediate help to Turkey, while others advocated attacking Russia itself through the Baltic. In an effort to convince the public that a tough line was being taken certain measures were adopted which, considering that war had not been declared, seemed dangerous in the extreme. By January 1854 there was a combined French and British naval squadron in the Black Sea and in February troops began to leave for the eastern Mediterranean, initially being sent to Malta. By the end of February 1854, such actions were causing major debate in the press and in the House of Commons. Matters finally came to a head when Lord Aberdeen requested the members of the Commons to vote for increased funds without declaring his intentions.

The most vocal Irish MP during these debates was Isaac Butt, and he participated in the major Commons debate of 20 February 1854. Butt initially

---

also been a diplomat and had worked hard to prevent the Russo-Turkish war of 1828–9.   **9** John Sweetman, *Balaclava 1854* (London, 1990), p. 8. See also Kingsley Martin, *The triumph of Lord Palmerston: a study of public opinion before the Crimean war* (London, 1963).   **10** *The Times*, 15 Feb. 1854. Ulick John de Burgh, 14th earl and 1st marquess of Clanricarde (1802–74). His rose to reply to the speech of Henry Drummond who opposed sending troops to the Black Sea area and giving promises of support to the Turks.[11] Drummond felt that if Britain supported 'the infidel Turk', then Prussia and Austria would not support them. He concluded his speech thus:

> Strike your blow at the heart of Russia, and don't go wasting your shots in the Black Sea. Proclaim the re-establishment of the Kingdom of Poland and this will effect more to bring the continental Sovereigns to their senses than all your guards and fleets.[12]

Butt rose to his feet to refute many aspects of Drummond's speech. He felt that if Britain engaged in a war against Russia, it should not be a religious war or 'about such ridiculous matters as the Holy Places', but it should be a war against the establishment of a Russian protectorate in the Danubian Principalities that would have the effect of 'virtually withdrawing from the sultan 12,000,000 of his subjects'. He then addressed the more pressing point of Aberdeen's request for more funds to send naval expeditions to the Baltic and Black Sea:

> This is the first time since the revolution that a Ministry has come down to the House and asked for a war supply without stating distinctly and fully the grounds for such a proposition.[13]

Butt demanded that Aberdeen clarify just what the administration's intentions were. Was Britain, in light of the mobilization of troops and the dispatch of warships to the Baltic and Black Sea, at war? Should war not be declared immediately? He asked these questions, he stated, due to his own doubts regarding Britain's status in international law. Butt went on to ask:

> In what position is our Fleet at the Black Sea? Admiral Dundas has orders to send back Russian vessels to Russian ports. What, if in the execution of these orders, he destroys a Russian ship, while being at peace with Russia. Are the Ministers prepared to justify such a state of things.[14]

He finished his speech with a provocative statement on the inaction of the Government:

---

eldest son, Ulick Canning de Burgh, Lord Dunkellin, served in the Crimea with the Coldstream Guards and was ADC to Lord Lucan. Lord Dunkellin was also a Liberal MP for Galway. Brian M. Walker, *Parliamentary election results in Ireland, 1801–1922* (Dublin, 1978), p. 83. **11** Henry Drummond, Conservative MP for West Surrey (1847–60). Michael Stenton and Stephen Lees, *Who's who of the British Members of Parliament*, i, 1832–1885 (London, 1976), p. 114. **12** *The Times*, 21 Feb. 1854. It is worth noting that Drummond's suggestion regarding the re-establishment of the kingdom of Poland was met with cheers in the Commons. Butt would also seem to be referring to the Glorious Revolution of 1688, after which measures were introduced in an effort to ensure that funds could only be appropriated after the prime minister stated specifically what they were to be used for. **13** Ibid. **14** Ibid. Butt had apparently forgotten the

If her Majesty's Ministers are now prepared to defend the cause of liberty in
Turkey, and throughout the world, against the aggression with which it has been
threatened, I am confident that they would receive from the people of the United
Kingdom an ardent and unanimous support; but if, on the other hand, they now
falter with this great crisis, if they do not intend to maintain the independence of
Turkey, if they are merely making a parade of those military preparations for the
purpose of arriving at a dishonourable peace, then they will not only have
betrayed the honour and character of England, but the case of liberty and
civilisation throughout the world, and history will record their crime as that of
men who, in a crisis of State, betrayed their country and their Queen.[15]

Later in the same day Lord Palmerston and Disraeli made speeches along
similar lines. Butt supported Palmerston and the opponents of Aberdeen in an
effort to force the government's hand. The parliamentary debates of February,
March and April 1854 were dominated by political heavyweights such as
Palmerston, Clarendon, Russell, Disraeli and, of course, Aberdeen. With the
exception of Isaac Butt, the Irish MPs were not prominent in these debates, yet
some of them raised questions regarding the state of the army and navy. In
February 1854, Dr John Brady, Independent MP for Co. Leitrim, referred to the
shortage of surgeons in the army and navy. Brady stated that this shortage was
not surprising due to the poor pay and conditions which made army and navy
surgeons feel 'degraded in a social and professional point of view'.[16] It was
common for Irish MPs to raise such issues in the Commons during the war.
One can find instances of Irish MPs such as John D. Fitzgerald QC, and
William Keogh QC, commenting on the state of the medial services or the
Commissariat Department in the Crimea.[17]

The Commons debate of 20 February 1854 forced Aberdeen's administration
to take definite action. On 27 February 1854 an ultimatum was sent to the tsar
with the stipulation that a refusal to withdraw from the disputed areas, or the
failure to reply, would be taken as being the equivalent of a declaration of war.
The tsar, perhaps assuming that this was yet another bluff on Aberdeen's part,
did not even reply to this ultimatum and Britain declared war on Russia on
28 March 1854. An alliance was signed with France on 10 April and with
Turkey on 15 April 1854. It seems obvious from the wording of Isaac Butt's
speech during the critical Commons debate of 20 February 1854, that he was
very much a supporter of Palmerston. The emotive tone, and even some of the

battle of Navarino (20 October 1827) which occurred due to the efforts of Britain, France and
Russia to impose a settlement on Turkey and end the war for Greek independence. Despite the
fact that the allies had not declared war on Turkey, an allied fleet confronted a numerically
superior Turkish fleet in Navarino Bay on the west coast of the Peloponnese. The Turks refused
to withdraw and a naval battle began resulting in 8,000 Turkish casualties. Despite the allied
success the affair demonstrated the inherent danger of using powerful naval forces to influence
supposedly diplomatic negotiations. **15** Ibid. **16** Ibid. 18 Feb. 1854. **17** William Keogh QC,
Independent MP for Athlone. John David Fitzgerald QC, Independent MP for Ennis. Brian M.

issues raised, were the same as those used by Palmerston and were similar to the editorial outbursts in the *Morning Post*. In this way he played a significant part in forcing Aberdeen to send an ultimatum to the tsar, bringing Britain a step further to war.

Irish public reaction to the outbreak of the war

The outbreak of the Crimean war had an immediate effect in Ireland and newspaper accounts of this period show that young men rushed to join up with an almost unseemly haste. There were near hysterical scenes in the cities and towns of the British Isles as the troops departed for the East. In the immediate build-up to the war, recruiting for the army was brisk all over the British Isles. Ireland was no exception and the enthusiasm for the war was reflected in the number of young men who rushed to join the colours in the early months of 1854. The Dublin correspondent of *The Times* wrote on 14 February 1854:

> Recruiting continues brisk in Dublin, and, although the 'bounty' falls very short of the actual war standard, there seems to be no difficulty here in obtaining the requisite supply of able-bodied young men to complete the required augmentation of the land forces. The Royal Artillery, in Portobello Barracks have, it is said, been already extremely successful in procuring men for the 'right arm' of the service. The Linen-hall barracks, situated in the north east of the city are crowded with recruits for the regiment (the 63rd) stationed there, and the same may be said of nearly all the other recruiting depots in the garrison of Dublin. Up to Saturday it was calculated that the number of enlistment's in this city alone amounted to at least 500, and this in the space of one brief week.[18]

On 20 February 1854 the same newspaper reported not only the continued enthusiasm to enlist, but also commented on the different kinds of men so doing:

> Recruiting is being vigorously prosecuted throughout the south of Ireland. The *Leinster Express*, alluding to the military ardour evinced by the Dubliners says 'Nothing can exceed the enthusiasm with which the recruiting parties are met in Dublin; wherever they go; and the alacrity with which the initiatory shilling is taken exhibits something more than the ordinary "red fever" among the people. Those who are enlisting in Ireland just now have among them not only those who may have nothing to do, but actually men of substance in their own class of life, who are urged by a sort of humble chivalry in taking arms. A few days ago a number of car drivers, men whose worldly means are certainly superior to a common soldiers, threw down their whips with one accord and followed the ribands'.[19]

Walker, *Parliamentary election results in Ireland, 1801–1922* (Dublin, 1978), pp. 82–3. **18** *The Times*, 14 Feb. 1854. **19** *The Times*, 20 Feb. 1854.

The story of the Dublin car drivers enlisting en masse was also recounted by E.H. Nolan is his *Illustrated history of the war against Russia* (2 volumes, London, 1856–7). He wrote that a spokesman for the group asked the recruiting sergeant, 'D'ye think we'd ever get a prod at the Imperor of Roosha?' When the sergeant replied in the affirmative, the carmen joined as a body and 'Her Majesty had twenty additional soldiers'.[20] Yet not all of these potential soldiers were financially well-off. The Dublin correspondent for *The Times* had also noted:

> The recruiting parties from the several infantry regiments forming the garrison of Dublin have been plying their trades these few days with, it is said, no small amount of success. One corps (the 50th) has picked up several young men, ragged idlers about the streets of the metropolis, but who will doubtless, after a few weeks drill, reflect no discredit to the service. During the last general war Dublin contributed more than its quota to the ranks of the British army, and military records could attest that no better soldiers ever served than the 'jackeens' of the Irish capital.[21]

The effect of economic trends was noticed in Ulster where, due to the ready availability of employment, recruiting parties for the infantry, Royal Artillery and Royal Marines had an initial difficulty in raising recruits. *The Times*, publishing an excerpt from *The banner of Ulster*, commented on the difficulties of raising recruits:

> The thing may be easily accomplished in Connaught, but not so in this part of the country. The people here are able to earn tolerably good wages at present, and we never have any Northerners very anxious for mounting the cockade while they are honestly able to earn a comfortable subsistence.[22]

The official declaration of war on 28 March 1854 made men more keen to enlist and recruiting difficulties in Ulster eased. It is not surprising that Ulstermen were disinclined to leave employment and enlist in the army when, before 28 March 1854, war was not an absolute certainty. After the declaration of war, however, there was a rush to enlist in Ulster and it would appear that recruiting parties were still having no problem getting recruits well into 1854. *The Times* of 13 October 1854 reported:

> The demand for men has been cheerfully responded to in the capital of Ulster. There are now no less than eight recruiting parties from different regiments stationed in Belfast, and it is mentioned that each day the recruits sworn in average about six; consequently, as the enlistments for the past two months have been nearly at the same rate, it may be calculated that Belfast has already contributed upwards of 1,000 men to the ranks of Her Majesty's troops.[23]

20 E.H. Nolan, *Illustrated history of the war against Russia* (2 volumes, London, 1856–7), i, p. 99. **21** *The Times*, 11 Feb. 1854. **22** Ibid. **23** Ibid. 13 Oct. 1854.

Some Irish newspapers carried the news of the declaration of war on 28 March 1854 in their evening editions, as they received the news that afternoon by electric telegraph. The *Dublin Evening Post* of 28 March commented on the declaration of war in its editorial:

> Whatever may be the issue of the present contest, France and England enter upon it with clear hands and a clear conscience. Neither hesitated in spurning the tempting but disgraceful proposals that were made to them, and their combined naval and military forces are now in movement to teach the diademed free-booter that his code of practical morality has nothing in common with the rights of constitutional monarchs, and that his insulting proposals have been regarded in their proper light by those whom he sought to entrap. They commence the war under the most favourable auspices. Right and integrity, and the sympathy of all well-constituted minds are on their side, and though they cannot command success, they have done more already, they have deserved it.[24]

Other Irish newspapers, such as the *Cork Examiner*, did not receive the news of the declaration of war in time for their morning editions of 29 March 1854. On the morning of 29 March the editorial in the *Cork Examiner* stated:

> In the Commons it will be seen, a message from the Throne was delivered on Monday night by Lord John Russell, referring briefly to the efforts that had been made in order to preserve peace, and deploring that the dread alternative could no longer be averted. Of the war, of which we are thus on the threshold, no one can see the duration or consequences, and perhaps few now living may witness the termination.[25]

Many Irish newspapers, such as the *Belfast Newsletter*, carried the news on the morning of 29 March 1854 while several, including the *Cork Examiner*, could not include the news until their morning editions of 30 March. The *Cork Examiner's* editorial on 30 March read:

> No alternative is left us, the decision has been taken out of our hands and, unless we would submit, with our allies, to crouch under the insolent dictation of a barbaric power, and see the liberties of Europe disappear under the tramp of the Cossack, we had no other course than to do what has now been done in sad and solemn form.[26]

Illustrations in journals such as the *Illustrated London News* show how the declaration of war was met with scenes of enthusiasm in the towns and cities of the British Isles. Dublin was no exception and the city was gripped with war-hysteria. *The Times* Dublin correspondent reported:

24 *Dublin Evening Post*, 28 Mar. 1854.   **25** *Cork Examiner*, 29 Mar. 1854.   **26** Ibid., 30 Mar.

Dublin is just now the theatre of an 'excitement' of a wildly different character
from that which for over 20 years had divided the popular mind. The recruiting
sergeant is at present the hero of the day, and the 'Repeal Button', and all other
insignia of the old agitations, if again reproduced on the stage, would utterly fail
to attract the same amount of devotion which is freely paid to the fluttering
ribands of the Queen's forces.[27]

Yet there were dissenting voices who tried to discourage Irishmen from
joining the British army. *The Times* of 16 February 1854 reported that the
Catholic priests of Kilkenny, where the 46th Foot was recruiting successfully,
had delivered sermons denouncing the war and those who took 'the Saxon
Shilling'. In a subsequent session of the Commons the Hon. Colonel William
Stuart Knox, MP for Dungannon, asked the chief secretary for Ireland, Sir John
Young, Bart., if such reports were true.[28] Young reported that he had made
enquires of the local constabulary, who could provide no evidence that 'such a
denunciation from the altar had taken place'. He concluded by stating that 'if
there had been, it was to no purpose for no check whatever had been felt in
engaging men to enlist in Her Majesty's service'.[29]

There were men in Ireland, however, who looked upon the outbreak of the
war as an opportunity to promote disaffection and insurrection in Ireland.
Several men who had been involved in revolutionary efforts in 1848 and 1849,
such as Thomas Clarke Luby, editor of the *Tribune*, John Mitchel, Michael
Doheny and John O'Mahony, saw that the war represented an opportunity for
rebellion in Ireland. Yet, despite their best efforts they only attracted a small
number of followers. John Mitchel then concentrated on trying to organise support
in America and even approached the Russian ambassador in Washington to ask
for a supply of arms. Michael Doheny and John O'Mahony, the leading figures
in the Emmet Monument Association, decided to attempt an invasion of Ireland
in September 1855, using an army they hoped to recruit from the Irish-
American community. This planned invasion came to nothing and the proposals
were abandoned in 1856.[30]

British diplomats in America were aware of this activity and were also
convinced that President Franklin Pierce, James Buchanan, then the American
ambassador in London, and William L. Marcy, the American secretary of state,
knew of these activities and perhaps even encouraged them. In October 1855,
John Fiennes Twisleton Crampton, the British ambassador to Washington,
wrote a letter of complaint to Marcy which stated:

1854.   **27** *The Times*, 16 Feb. 1854.   **28** Knox was the Conservative MP for Dungannon, Co.
Tyrone (1851–74). He entered the army in 1844 and served in the 21st Foot and later the 51st
Foot. In 1867 he was appointed as colonel of the Tyrone Artillery Militia.   **29** *The Times*, 16 Feb.
1854. Sir John Young, of Baileborough, Co. Cavan, later served as chief commissioner of the
Ionian Islands (1855–9) and governor of New South Wales (1860–7) and as governor general of
Canada (1868–72).   **30** R.V. Comerford, 'Churchmen, tenants and independent opposition,

In the latter part of July last my attention was called by Mr Barclay, Her Majesty's Consul at New York, to the existence of Clubs composed of the Irish population in that City for the purpose of enlisting and drilling volunteers to effect an insurrection in Ireland; it being their intention to embark in small parties in almost every ship going to Liverpool, and on reaching Ireland to divide themselves among all the counties; and it is stated to Mr Barclay that many of those composing the Irish Militia Regiments as well as the Police Force in that country had been corrupted and that their aid was counted upon by the conspirators of New York in their projected rebellion.[31]

In May 1855, Henry Hertz, an employee of George B. Mathew, the British consul in Philadelphia, was arrested for trying to recruit men for the British army. Charles Rowcroft, the British consul in Cincinnati, later stated that one of the key witnesses at the Hertz trial was the doorman of the United Irish Party headquarters. Rowcroft later reported an outbreak of anti-British feeling among the Irish communities in New York, Boston and Philadelphia in the autumn of 1855. He was also convinced that a party of Irish men were involved in a plot to have him arrested for a violation of the neutrality laws. This Irish revolutionary activity greatly worried Crampton throughout 1855 and, while the American authorities denied all knowledge or involvement in these activities, it must be remembered that the American government had also denied that an armed steamer was being built in New York for the Russians; Crampton had received information that this armed steamer was to be used to attack Cunard steamers on the North Atlantic route and had complained to President Pierce. Despite American assurances that this was not the case, the Royal Navy later intercepted this armed steamer and diverted it to Rio de Janeiro.[32] These Irish-American revolutionaries attracted little support, however, and their plans to promote disaffection in Ireland came to nothing.

In February 1854 regiments began to leave England for the East to be in position before war was actually declared. On 14 February 1854 the 1st Battalion of the Coldstream Guards marched from St George's Barracks to Trafalgar Square and from there proceeded to Chichester. They were cheered all along their route. The mood in Ireland was no different. On 24 February 1854 the first regiment to leave an Irish barracks, the 50th Foot, formed up on the Palatine Square of the Royal Barracks in Dublin. After an inspection the regiment, staff and band proceeded through Dublin to Westland Row, and boarded a train to Kingstown (Dun Laoghaire). The following contemporary account is

1850–56' in Vaughan (ed.), *A new history of Ireland*, v, pp 413–14.   **31** Trevor Royle, *Crimea: the great Crimean war, 1854–1856* (London, 1999), pp 386–7. In early 1855, Anthony Barclay, the British consul in New York, had been involved in an effort to recruit volunteers for the British Army. One of those involved had even opened a recruiting office at 36 Pearl Street, New York. **32** Ibid.

worth quoting at length to illustrate the public euphoria that prevailed as the troops marched out.

> The bands of three other regiments of the garrison led them along the line of route, one of the finest in Europe; and vast crowds accompanied then, vociferously cheering, while from the windows handkerchiefs and scarves were waved, and every token of a 'God Speed' displayed. As the regiment took the north side of the long and splendid line of quays for which Dublin is so well celebrated, the bands struck up 'Old Lang Syne', which the citizens took as a compliment, as the 'Blind Half-Hundredth', as the regiment used to be called, had often shared their hospitality. As they came to the Queen's Bridge, they played 'A good time coming', the bands took up the concluding line of each verse, as the instrumental music died away, and sang it. This vocal repetition was quite in unison with the habits and tastes of the Dubliners, and old Eblana echoed with the shouts of the people. When the regiment arrived at Essex Bridge, it crossed, passing up Parliament Street, where the Exchange steps presented a splendid position for the sight, and from which the cheering and waving of handkerchiefs was most enlivening as the corps turned down Dame Street. When they arrived in College Green, instead of wheeling to the left between the Bank of Ireland and the statue of William III, they kept to the right of 'King William' and leaving the university to the left, proceeded up Nassau Street and Leinster Street to Westland Row, affording by the longer route the better opportunity to the people to display their feelings. It also gratified the gownsmen who, at the front of Trinity College, welcomed the soldiery by waving of caps and shillelaghs, and various original demonstrations of good will, retired through the grand entrance into College Park, and climbing the railings, continued their healthy plaudits along the line of Nassau Street, and then penetrating to the rear of the College grounds by the school of Anatomy, met the procession again in Westland Row.[33]

The *Dublin Evening Post* reported:

> As the regiment proceeded through the streets the cheering of the populace was again and again repeated, and it is scarcely necessary to add that the waving of numerous white handkerchiefs by the ladies who filled the windows and balconies along the entire line of streets, contributed in no small degree to heighten the enthusiasm of the multitude.[34]

The 50th Foot were similarly met by a large crowd in Kingstown (Dun Laoghaire) itself and when the regiment's colours were carried on board their ship, the *Cumbria*, the 'cliffs resounded with cheers'.[35] The *Dublin Evening Post* reported:

> The *Cumbria* lay in close to the wall, and a gangway was run out to the shore, through which each company passed in succession amid the hearty applause of

---

33 Nolan, *The war against Russia*, i, p. 98. See also *Illustrated London News*, 4 March 1854. The 50th Foot had served in the Egyptian campaign of 1801 and many of the men had suffered from ophthalmia, giving rise to the regimental nickname 'The Blind Half-Hundred'.   **34** *Dublin Evening Post*, 25 Feb. 1854.   **35** *The Times*, 16 Feb. 1854.

the spectators. At the appearance of the regimental colours the band struck up the National Anthem and, whilst they were being carried on board by the officers, the vast assemblage waved their hats and handkerchiefs and cheered in the most enthusiastic manner, the acclamations being again and again renewed with great vigour and unanimity.[36]

These scenes were repeated again and again as different regiments left Dublin for the Crimea. In early March 1854 the 33rd Foot marched through Dublin and were met by enthusiastic crowds.

The line of march was, as in the former instance, crowded by a numerous concourse of spectators, who seemed anxious at the same time to witness the interesting spectacle and, by their presence and encouraging cheers, to testify to the gallant defenders of the country the sympathy and approval which their courage and devotion had awakened.[37]

General Sir William Butler later wrote of the scenes he had witnessed in Dublin when the Crimean war began.

While I was at school in Dublin the Crimean war began, and as the regiments in garrison were all sent to the East, their departure for the seat of war was an event of great interest to the schoolboys. Daily we used to accompany some regiment of horse or foot, cheering them as they marched through the streets.[38]

Major Oliver Fry RA recorded a trip to Kingstown in May 1854 to watch troops depart for the Crimea:

I went per train to Kingstown to see the large transport ships come to convey the 4th Dragoons to the East, some troops are embarked, others putting forage & c. on board. To me it is a melancholy sight; it reminds me of bygone times when I was able and willing to accompany them, when there was a Wellington to lead the sons of Britain to glory; we have no Wellington now.[39]

Similar scenes witnessed the departure of troops from Victoria Barracks in Cork. Lieutenant Temple Goodman of the 5th Dragoon Guards wrote to his father of his departure from Cork:

We left Queenstown at 2 p.m. on Sunday (which however did not seem much to me like a Sunday) in a thunderstorm, in spite of the rain all the people turned out to cheer us as we sailed by.[40]

36 *Dublin Evening Post*, 25 Feb. 1854.   37 Ibid. 2 Mar. 1854.   38 General Sir William Butler, *Sir William Butler. An autobiography* (London, 1911), pp 12–13.   39 William H.P. Fry (ed.), *Annals of the late Major Oliver Fry, RA* (London, 1909), p. 77. Major Oliver Fry (1773–1868) was one of the Fry family of Frybrook, Boyle, Co. Roscommon.   40 Philip Warner, *The fields*

Margaret Kirwin, an Irishwoman who travelled to the Crimea with her husband, Private John Kirwin, 19th Foot, later described the regiment's departure from London:

> In April 1854, half the Regiment left the Tower of London under the command of Colonel Unett. It was beautiful sight as all the ladies and gentlemen of London waved their handkerchiefs and threw oranges and other things at the soldiers. Old women were crying at parting with their sons. Others blessed them, praying they might live to return. Fifteen of us women accompanied the Regiment from the Tower.[41]

Another troop of the 5th Dragoon Guards had been stationed at Clonmel and were cheered through the town on their departure. *The Times* of 24 March 1854 reported:

> Yesterday morning a troop of the 5th Dragoon Guards, which had for some time been stationed in Clonmel, marched out on their way to Cork, where they are to embark for active service in the East. They were greeted on passing the Infantry Barracks with three hearty cheers from their military brethren and were accompanied out of town by a large crowd of civilians of all classes who cheered them on their way in true Tipperary fashion.[42]

The departure of the 11th Hussars, commanded by Lord Cardigan, from Portobello Barracks in May 1854 received quite an amount of press attention. On receiving orders to prepare to depart on active service, Cardigan ordered the troopers to hand in their sabres so that they could be sent to be sharpened by a Dublin cutler. Typically the cutler that Cardigan employed, John Lamprey of 29 Westmoreland Street, was one of the most eminent in Dublin; cutler to the lord lieutenant and sword-maker to the East India Company.[43] Cardigan later announced that his officers were having pieces of leather sown into their cherry-coloured cavalry overalls in order that they might better withstand the rigours of active service. Such announcements were unique to the 11th Hussars and, as was usual, Cardigan's efforts to impress were criticized in the press. *The Times* of 22 April 1854 ridiculed the regiment's uniform:

> The splendour of these magnificent light horsemen, the shortness of their jackets, the tightness of their cherry-coloured pants are as utterly unfit for war service as the garb of the female hussars in the ballet of Gustavus, which they so nearly resemble.[44]

of war: a young cavalryman's Crimea campaign (London, 1977), p. 11. **41** Mark Marsay, 'One woman's story. With the 19th Foot by Margaret Kirwin' in *Newsletter of the Friends of the Green Howards Regimental Museum*, vol. 3 (September, 1997), p. 14. Margaret Kirwin married John Kirwin in 1852. She went to the Crimea, serving as the washerwoman for 5 Company. In 1895 she described her experiences to the editor of the *Green Howards Gazette*. **42** *The Times*, 24 Mar. 1854. **43** *Dublin directory*, 1854. **44** *The Times*, 22 Apr. 1854. The 'Ballet of Gustavus'

Cardigan gave such comments the dignity of a reply, stating in a letter to *The Times* that 'In the 11th the men's jackets are longer and their overalls looser than almost any other cavalry regiment in the service.'[45] When finally ready, the 11th Hussars travelled through Dublin, in full dress, to Kingstown, where they boarded the troopships *Tyrone* and *Asia*. The morale of the regiment would appear to have been good. The *Illustrated London News* of 27 May 1854 described their embarkation on the *Tyrone*:

> This fine vessel is up for 60 horses in the lower hold, 70 men between decks, and 6 officers in the poop cabin. She had on board 54 horses, 62 men and 5 officers. Of infantry she accommodates 600 troops and 25 officers. The men were in high spirits and fraternised with the sailors admirably; all joining in the evening twilight in singing, in very good style, 'Annie Laurie', 'Auld Lang Syne' and other favourite songs.

Troops who did not even sail to the East found themselves treated as heroes in Ireland as people became more excited at the prospect of war. When the majority of the 89th Foot sailed out of Cork in April 1854, a depot and service company was sent to Waterford barracks. A contemporary newspaper recorded the reaction in the town:

> In the Town-hall the Union Jack, the Tricolour and the Crescent were blended over the Mayor's seat, and the fine apartment was decorated with other flags and evergreens. Soon after the arrival of the soldiers, the Mayor and the High Sheriff, accompanied by the Bishop of Cashel, and the Roman Catholic Bishop who, we are informed, met this day for the first time, went down to the hall to receive the guests; and a procession was formed, with the Mayor bearing his wand of office at its head, the officers and troops following, amounting to about 250 men.[46]

Not everyone was quite so enthusiastic, however, at the departure of these regiments from their barracks. The troops sent to the East left behind their wives and children, each regiment being allowed only six married woman for every 100 soldiers to look after the welfare of the men. In 1854 only single men were enlisted as recruits. If a soldier then wished to marry, he had to get permission from his commanding officer and only six men in every hundred were allowed to marry. This was termed being married 'on the strength'. These soldiers' wives could then earn some money by washing and cooking for the other men living in their husbands' barrackrooms. In 1856, only twenty of the 251 barracks in the British Isles had separate rooms for married couples. In the

was a comic light opera running in London in 1854 in which some of the female dancers wore hussar-style uniform.   **45** Cecil Woodham-Smith, *The reason why*, pp 137–8. A satirical verse later appeared in *Punch* ridiculing the overalls of the 11th Hussars; 'Oh, pantaloons of cherry! Oh, redder than raspberry! For men to fight in things so tight, it must be trying, very!'   **46** Marcus

other barracks married couples had to live in the common barrackroom and, in most cases, only a hanging blanket separated them from the other soldiers.

While married couples' quarters were cramped and lacked any privacy, at least provision was made to move these 'official' wives and children when regiments moved station. Many recruits were married when they enlisted and simply concealed the fact. Also many soldiers married without their commanding officer's permission. No provision was made to look after these 'unofficial' wives and children when a regiment moved station.[47] As a result of this policy, thousands of woman and children found themselves stranded in the barrack towns of Ireland without any means of support when regiments began to leave for the East. In late April 1854 throngs of woman began to petition their local paymaster's office for funds. The *Illustrated London News* of 22 April 1854 described the scene in Dublin:

> Those who, a few days since, beheld the Dublin district pay office thronged with deserted beings craving their miserable pittance to enable them reach their parishes cannot readily forget the scene. Many were in rags, emaciated and care-worn, presenting most deplorable aspects. There were others more respectable in appearance, striving to maintain a decent exterior in the presence of spectators. Nearly all were accompanied by one or more children. Anxiety and sorrow were stamped on the features of these supplicants for the public bounty; but the generality shrunk from the exposure to which their pressing necessities urged them.[48]

Such scenes were familiar in barrack towns all across the British Isles as every time regiments went on campaign, or even when they merely changed stations in the British Isles, these 'unofficial' dependants found themselves stranded. Officers of most regiments endeavoured to raise and distribute a certain amount of money themselves. Proposals, such as employing these woman in military clothing factories to earn their keep, were usually expounded when the problem became serious. Also philanthropic efforts such as the Seaton Needlework Fund were organized after the war by private citizens in an effort to help Crimean widows.[49] In May 1854 a benefit concert was held in the Great Exhibition building in Kildare Street and the proceeds were divided among the families of soldiers who had departed for the war. The situation of officers' wives was also far from secure and officers had to pay for moving their families.

The above newspaper accounts show that the Irish public were quite enthusiastic as the major powers of Europe moved towards war. The scenes of public gaiety and the apparent rush to enlist mirrored the situation in the major

Cunliffe, *The Royal Irish Fusiliers, 1793–1968* (London, 1970), pp 210–11.   **47** Paget, *History of the British cavalry*, ii, pp 319–20.   **48** *Illustrated London News*, 22 Apr. 1854.   **49** The Seaton Needlework Fund was organized after the war and operated under the patronage of General Lord

towns in England and France. It was an interesting, and ironic, aspect of this war that the very newspapers who had whipped up public support for the war, were soon publishing graphic accounts of the sufferings of the soldiers in the Crimea. In the towns of Ireland, however, the initial mood was enthusiastic. Yet the plight of the stranded army wives and children, so many of whom would soon be widows and orphans, amply illustrated the harsh realities of war.

The Irish in the British army in the nineteenth century

The interest of the Irish public in the war is perhaps not surprising when one considers the large numbers of Irishmen in the British army during the Crimean war. At the outbreak of the war the British army was, as was nearly always the case, badly-prepared. The army was not large by European standards and was stretched to its limit providing troops for garrisons in all over the Empire. It was decided that a force of just 27,000 could be raised for service in the East, though this number would be increased during the campaign.

Throughout the nineteenth century Irishmen formed a significant part of the British army. Ireland had traditionally been used by the British army as a source of recruits and, at the beginning of the Crimean war, there were eight Irish regiments in the British army. Three were cavalry regiments, all of which served in the Crimea, and five were infantry regiments, only two of which were in the Crimea. The Irish regiments were as follows (those marked with an * served in the Crimea):

    4th (Royal Irish) Regiment of Dragoon Guards.*
    6th (Inniskilling) Regiment of Dragoons.*
    8th (The King's Royal Irish) Regiment of Light Dragoons (Hussars).*
    18th (Royal Irish) Regiment of Foot.*
    27th (Inniskilling) Regiment of Foot.
    86th (The Royal County Down) Regiment of Foot.
    87th Regiment of Foot (Royal Irish Fusiliers).
    88th Regiment of Foot (Connaught Rangers).*[50]

Statistics are available for the early part of the nineteenth century which show that a large number of Irishmen served in the army of the post-Napoleonic period. It is difficult today to assess why British army recruiting parties were so successful here. An English cavalry recruit, George Loy Smith, later admitted that he had enlisted as the recruiting party were very impressive in their colourful uniforms.[51] It is certain that many Irish recruits enlisted as they thought that a

Seaton, commander-in-chief in Ireland (1855–60).   **50** Henry George Hart, *Army List* (1854).
51 George Loy Smith, *A Victorian RSM* (Tunbridge Wells, 1987), p.7.

military life would be an adventurous one, with the added possibility of travelling abroad. As Ireland lacked any heavy industry, economic considerations must also have caused many Irishmen to join the colours. Daniel Bourke from Cork answered 'the call made for volunteers' made early in the war, and joined the 1st Battalion of the 18th (Royal Irish) Regiment of Foot. He later emigrated to New South Wales and, writing about his Crimean experiences at the end of his life, he confessed that he had joined purely for monetary reasons. The attractions of the meagre pay soon wore off, however. By the time his battalion reached Malta on their journey to the East he wrote 'from Malta our lot was getting no better. We were beginning to miss the comforts of our homes in dear old Ireland.'[52] Another Irish soldier, Philip O'Flaherty, a native of Co. Mayo, joined the 7th Foot in Manchester at the beginning of the war due to the economic demands being put on him by his father and brother.[53]

The usual assumption that the majority of Irish recruits enlisted due to their dire poverty does not hold true, however. Recent research by Cormac Ó Gráda has shown that Irish recruits in the early nineteenth century were better developed physically than their English counterparts, suggesting that, while they may well have been poor, 'their poverty did not deny then adequate and more nutritious food when growing up'.[54] Ó Gráda also found that the Irish serving in the Royal Navy in the 1850s were taller than their English counterparts. His research into the stature of Irish recruits serving with the East India Company's army at the beginning of the century showed that they too were taller than English recruits. Ó Gráda's findings would seem to suggest that, while Irish recruits were often from poor backgrounds, their diet was superior to that of English recruits.[55]

On the basis of a sample of the muster rolls of several of the regiments that went to the Crimea, it would appear that the Irish soldiers who served in the war had enlisted in the 1830s, 1840s and also when war was declared in 1854. The number of Irish who had enlisted in the early 1850s was quite small and this could well have been due to the relative economic prosperity that Ireland enjoyed before war was declared. The outbreak of the Crimean war had major economic effects in Ireland but the prices of grain, cattle and all types of food had been rising since July 1853 when the Russian army invaded Turkey's Danubian Principalities. In the months preceding the war, corn and grain merchants had deliberately held grain in storage in the hope that the outbreak of war would push up prices. Throughout the early months of 1854 there was

52 NAM, MS 6807/152: 'The experiences of Private Daniel Bourke, 18th Foot', an unpublished memoir written in 1910.   53 Philip O'Flaherty, *Philip O'Flaherty. The young soldier: containing interesting particulars of the war in the Crimea* (Edinburgh, 1855), p. 7.   54 Cormac Ó Gráda, *Ireland before and after the Famine: explorations in economic history, 1800–1925* (Manchester, 1988), p.27.   55 Ibid. pp 25–7.

little movement in the grain market as stocks were held back. During the first months of 1854, newspapers reported the near stagnation of the grain and cattle markets and, not only did prices not improve, but they actually began to fall. The decision to hold back grain stocks resulted in the prices of other foodstuffs rising considerably. The price of bread also rose and in January 1854 there were bread riots in Exeter and Taunton in England.[56] When war was declared at the end of March 1854, grain prices rose and remained high for the rest of the war. Cattle prices also increased considerably and by April 1854, cattle-dealers were reporting an advance of 10s. to 15s. per head. In May the distillers of Cork announced that they were going to increase the price of whiskey by 6d. per gallon; raising the price to 8s. 2d. The declaration of war marked the beginning of a period of agricultural prosperity for Ireland and this period of growth was maintained until the early 1860s.[57]

While Irish merchants were quite pleased with this state of affairs, the rise in food prices had a major effect on the lives of the labouring classes and the effects of these price rises were noted by the Poor Law Commissioners. The rise in food prices created much hardship in the early months of 1854 but the position of the labouring classes improved as the wages paid to casual labourers soon began to increase. This came about due to a shortage of farm labourers caused by the increased numbers of young healthy men either emigrating or enlisting in the army and militia. During the period January 1853 to January 1854, a total of 173,148 emigrated. During the period 1855 to 1856, a total of 78,854 emigrated.[58] The success of army and navy recruiting parties also reduced the number of able-bodied young men in the labour market. William Hamilton, a poor law commissioner in the Leinster and Munster districts, commented on the rise in wages in his report of April 1855:

> The number of the class of labourers without constant employment, and who I have referred to as getting high wages in times of pressure, is happily diminishing, owing to the emigration of former years, and demand for recruits for the army and militia.[59]

The eagerness to enlist displayed by those at the bottom end of the economic scale is striking and, when the generally poor pay and conditions in the British army are considered, reflects the dire situation that many of the labouring class found themselves in. In early February 1854 over 100 boys left the Limerick workhouse in order to enlist in the regiments recruiting in the town.[60] Farmers also increased the area of land under cultivation, in an effort in make the most

---

56 *Illustrated London News*, 21 and 28 Jan. 1854.   57 W.E. Vaughan, 'Ireland *c*.1870' in W.E. Vaughan (ed.), *A new history of Ireland*, v (Oxford, 1989), p. 781.   58 *The Times*, 18 Apr. 1854. 59 *Annual report of the commissioners for administering the laws for the relief of the poor in Ireland* [1945], HC 1855, xxiv, 523.   60 *The Times*, 11 Feb. 1854.

of the rise in prices and thus created a further demand for labourers. William P. O'Brien, a poor law commissioner in the Connaught and Munster districts, noted an increase in the demand for labourers and an increase in the wages paid in his 1855 report and gave the following as the reasons for same:

> Owing to the unavoidable lateness of the Spring operations generally, together with the great increase in the extent of cultivation which has been induced by the irresistible attraction that 'war prices' never fail to represent to the farming classes.[61]

It was also noticed that many small farmers, who had previously hired themselves out during harvest season, had increased the area of land that they cultivated and now actually hired labour. The most obvious benefit for farm labourers was the increase in wages. In the poor law commissioners' report of April 1855, James Crawford of the Dublin unions reported that the shortage of labourers in the County Dublin area had caused a rise in wages to an average rate of 6s. per week. The previous average in his area had been 5s.[62] In his report for April 1856, William Hamilton noted that labourers wages in his area (Tipperary, Waterford, Wexford and Kilkenny) had averaged between 5s. and 7s. and 6d. per week in 1855. In 1856 labourers wages averaged between 6s. and 7s. 6d. per week and, in some places, labourers were paid even higher rates.[63]

It can only be concluded that the demand created by the outbreak of the war for agricultural produce was a good thing for both small farmers and labourers. The decision of grain merchants to hold back produce, however, caused great hardship during the first months of 1854. Yet the economic situation improved and remained buoyant for the remainder of the war. Prices of livestock increased and army remount officers, travelling the country and buying horses to replace the thousands lost in the Crimea, noted that prices increased at Irish horse fairs during the war. The declaration of war in March 1854, therefore, caused a minor economic boom in Ireland that had an impact on all aspects of the economy.

It would appear, therefore, that the Irish economy was experiencing a period of growth in 1853 and 1854. Due to the increased demand for labour this would also suggest that Irish recruits did not enlist in the army for purely economic reasons. Indeed the newspaper coverage of the enthusiasm displayed in the towns in cities of Ireland in March 1854, would seem to suggest that recruits of 1854 were at least in part inspired by ideas of patriotism and adventure. Some recruits also joined due to family tradition and influences. Edward Montgomery, born in Clitheroe,

61 *Annual report of the commissioners for administering the laws for the relief of the poor in Ireland* [1945], HC 1855, xxiv, 523.   **62** Ibid.   **63** *Annual report of the commissioners for administering the laws for the relief of the poor in Ireland* [2105], HC 1856, xxviii, 415.

Lancashire of Irish parents, joined the Corps of Sappers and Miners as a boy soldier in March 1854.[64] His father was also serving in this corps at the time.[65] Born in July 1841, he was only twelve years and eight months old when he joined the army and went to the Crimea.[66] It is quite common to find the names of men of the same family serving in regiments in the Crimea and several cases of fathers and sons serving in the same regiment have been found. James O'Malley, from Galway, later wrote of what motivated him to enlist in the 17th Foot:

> When I was young, I had a notion that I would like to join the army and be a soldier to fight for the honour and glory of my Queen and country. I had frequently seen splendid, well-proportioned, brave-looking soldiers, gaily-dressed, marching in Galway, with the band in front of the regiment, discoursing sweet music, which thrilled my soul with a feeling of enchantment. I used to march after them, keeping time to the music, until they reached the Castle Barracks, and I made up my mind to enlist as a soldier.[67]

Irishmen joined the British army throughout the nineteenth-century, and in large numbers. A report of May 1841 gave details of the numbers of each nationality serving in the years 1830 and 1840. The report's findings show that Irish soldiers formed 42.2% (42,897 men) of the army in 1830 and 37.2% (41,218 men) in 1840.[68] This pattern was maintained later in the century and the Irish were especially numerous in the infantry. There seems to be every indication to suggest that this was the case throughout the nineteenth century and the British army of the Crimean war must also have had large numbers of Irishmen. Indeed, David Fitzpatrick has argued that, considering the size of the Irish population, the Irish were over-represented in the British Army throughout the century.[69]

The lack of official statistics for the Crimean period remains a problem as the *Grand annual return of the British Army* was not instituted until 1868. Between 1830 and 1840 there was a drop of 5% in the number of Irishmen in the British Army. Between 1840 and 1868 (the next year in which we have official figures) there was a further drop of 7.2%. One could argue that a reduction of 3–4% in the numbers of Irish serving by 1854 was a reasonable figure, exactly half-way through this twenty-eight year gap in the published

---

64 Montgomery's father was from Thomastown, Co. Kilkenny, while his mother was from Killarney, Co. Kerry. **65** Edward Montgomery, 'A memoir', unpublished manuscript in a private collection. **66** In 1912 it was announced in *The Sapper*, the journal of the Royal Engineers, that Montgomery had been the youngest soldier to serve in the Crimea. **67** James O'Malley, *The life of James O'Malley, late corporal of the 17th Leicestershire Regiment, 'Royal Bengal Tigers'* (Montreal, 1893), p. 5. **68** *Return of the number of English, Scotch and Irish non-commissioned officers and privates in the British Army, in each of the years on the 1st day of January 1830 and 1840*, HC 1841 (307), xiv, 93. See also H.J. Hanham, 'Religion and nationality in the mid-Victorian army' in M.R.D. Foot (ed.), *War and society* (London, 1973), pp 159–183, notes 318–20. David Murphy, 'The Irish in the Crimean war, 1854–6': unpublished PhD thesis, Trinity College, Dublin, 2000, pp 25–39, Appendix 2, 298–9. **69** David Fitzpatrick, 'A peculiar

figures. It would be reasonable to assume, therefore, that in 1854 that 33% of the army was Irish. By the end of 1856, 4,273 officers and 107,040 men of the British army had served in the Crimea, 111,313 men in total.[70] If we assume that at least 33% of the British contingent in the Crimea was Irish, this would mean that over 37,000 Irishmen served with the army in the Crimea.

This supposition is supported by research currently being carried out by members of the CWRS, who are writing the histories of certain regiments which served in the Crimea. Indeed, it has been found that, in some Crimean regiments, 40–45% of the soldiers were Irish. Henry G. Farmer of the Irish Military History Society estimated that there were 35,416 Irishmen in the British Army in 1854 and that a further 11,997 joined in 1855. He also stated that another 12,222 Irishmen enlisted in 1856, producing a total of 59,635 by the end of the Crimean war. Farmer did not indicate the source of these very precise figures, however.[71]

At the outbreak of war there were many regiments stationed in Ireland such as the 5th Dragoon Guards (Dundalk), the 11th Hussars (Dublin), the 14th Foot (Cork), the 17th Foot (Cork), the 39th Foot (Fermoy) and the 50th Foot (Dublin). All of these regiments took part in the Crimean war and had been based here for a number of years, recruiting locally. At the beginning of 1854, eight cavalry regiments and twenty-eight infantry regiments were stationed in Ireland or had their headquarters or depot company in an Irish barracks. All of these regiments must have recruited in the districts in which they were stationed. Statistics are available for the number of recruits admitted into the British Army from 1844 to 1847. The following table illustrates the numbers which enlisted in each country:

Table 1. Recruits joining the British Army, 1844–7

	England	Scotland	Ireland	At HQ's or depots	Total
1844	5,586	966	2,294	1,690	10,536
1845	3,410	919	2,550	2,320	11,199
1846	10,056	1,745	5,532	6,545	23,878
1847	5,645	1,685	8,188	3,114	18,632

Source: *Report showing total number of recruits for the British Army admitted from 1844 to 1847*, HC 1848 (228), xli, 23.

The increasing number of Irish enlisting towards the end of this period is an interesting feature. This could well be due to the economic hardship associated

tramping people' in W.E. Vaughan (ed.) *A new history of Ireland*, v. pp 623–61. **70** John Sweetman, *The Crimean war* (Essential Histories Series, London, 2001), p. 89. **71** J.J.W. Murphy, 'An Irish Sister of Mercy in the Crimean war' in *Irish Sword*, v, no. 21 (Winter 1962),

with the Famine. It would also be reasonable to assume that, considering the large number of regiments with HQ or depot companies in Ireland, that a large percentage of those who enlisted at HQs and depots were Irish.[72]

The statistics that remain for the rest of the nineteenth century would seem to prove that there was a large number of Irishmen in the army at this time. David Fitzpatrick has estimated that there were around 50,000 Irishmen in the British Army in the early 1850s.[73] It is perhaps time to assess the contribution that these men made to the war effort. Also, by examining the remaining documentary sources, we can get some idea of their varied experiences.

It must be pointed out that there were also Irishmen serving in other armies during the war. There was a General Coleman, known as 'Fehti Bey', who had apparently fled from Ireland following the 1848 rising and who served with the Turkish army in the Crimea. Richard Debaufre Guyon also served in the Turkish army under the *nom de guerre* of 'Kurschid Pasha' or 'Guyon Pasha'. He had served with the Austrian army but supported Louis Kossuth during the failed Hungarian revolution of 1848 and later fled to Turkey. Guyon's entry in the *DNB* described him as being the son of an English naval officer and stated that he was born in Bath. Yet the *Irish American* of 29 August 1849 stated that he was Irish, of Huguenot descent, and a native of Cratloe, Co. Clare. Also, E.H. Nolan in his *History of the war with Russia* was quite specific and described both Guyon and Coleman as Irishmen in Turkish service. It is also interesting to note an Irish Militia Company, raised in New York in 1849, was named after Guyon. At the outbreak of the American Civil war, the Guyon Cadets, became Company I of the 69th Regiment of the New York State Militia.[74] 'Guyon Pasha' fell into disfavour after the Turkish defeat at Kurekdere but, in 1855, served on the staff of General Sir William Fenwick Williams and was prominent in the defence of Kars. There were also Irish officers serving in the British army who were attached to the Turkish contingent in the Crimea. One such officer was Major John Henry Scroope Bernard of Castle Bernard in King's County. An officer in the 18th (Royal Irish) Regiment of Foot, he was attached to the Turkish army for the duration of the war.[75]

There were also Irish soldiers serving in the French army in the Crimea and Charles Richard Sutton, Comte de Clonard, who was perhaps the last Irish-born general in the French army, served in the campaign. Born in Co. Wexford in 1807, he was educated at the Ecole Speciale Militaire and served with the

p. 251.   **72** *Report showing total number of recruits for the British army admitted from 1844 to 1847*, HC 1848 (228), xli, 23.   **73** David Fitzpatrick, 'A peculiar tramping people' in Vaughan (ed.), *A new history of Ireland*, v, pp 623–61.   **74** F. von Allendorfer, 'Irish Officers in the Turkish Service' in *Irish Sword*, ii, no. 9, (Winter 1956), p. 377. See also J.L. Garland, 'Irish Officers in the Turkish Service' in *Irish Sword*, iii, no. 11 (Winter 1957), p. 132.   **75** Burke, *Landed gentry of Ireland* (1912), 41. John Henry Scroope Bernard's younger brother, Richard Wellesley Bernard, had formerly been in the Austrian service and also served in the Crimea and was present at the

Foreign Legion in Algeria between 1840 and 1848. A lieutenant-colonel during the Crimean war, he was mentioned in dispatches and in the official French report on the fall of Sevastapol. Promoted to brigadier-general in 1857, he subsequently commanded the Paris and Lyons garrisons.[76]

While the disbandment of Napoleon's Irish Legion in September 1815 had ended the long tradition of Irishmen serving France in specifically Irish regiments, there were still officers of Irish extraction in the French army in the 1850s.[77] The most notable of these was General (later Maréchal de France) Marie Edmé Patrice Maurice de MacMahon. MacMahon commanded an infantry division in the Crimea and led his division during the successful attack on the Malakov Bastion on 8 September 1855. He later served as governor of Algeria, commanded the Army of Alsace during the Franco-Prussian war and was president of France (1873–9).[78] Another French officer of Irish descent was Austin O'Malley, son of Colonel Patrick O'Malley who had served under General Humbert in 1798 and fled to France after the rebellion. Austin O'Malley attended St Cyr and served in North Africa and the Crimea. He later served with MacMahon at the battle of Magenta and ended his military career as a brigadier-general in command of the military district of Marseilles.[79]

Elliot O'Donnell's *The Irish abroad* (London, 1915) also states that there were full companies of Irishmen in the French army during the Crimean war but he unfortunately gives no source for this statement. Yet there may well have been Irish troops or even full companies in the French army in the Crimea. During the Franco-Prussian War an Irish field ambulance corps of 300 men was formed and served in the French army while there was also an Irish company in the French Foreign Legion.[80] The 1st and 2nd Regiments d'Infantrie of the French Foreign Legion also served in the Crimea, numbering around 4,500 men. It is possible that there were Irishmen in these regiments. Further research in the records of the French army's Service historique de l'armée de terre at Château de Vincennes might provide more information on this subject.

The Sardinian army list, the *Annuerio Militare Ufficale dello Stato Sardo*, mentions several officers who were not Italian and who may have been Irish.[81]

battles of Alma, Balaclava and Inkerman. He was later chamberlain at the court of Dublin during the vice-royalties of the dukes of Abercorn and Marlborough.   **76** Bernard Browne, *County Wexford connections* (1986), 24. See also John H. McGuckin, Jr., '18th and 19th century Irish émigrés in France' in *Familia*, ii, no. 6, 1990, 26–32. Charles Richard Sutton retired from the French army in 1869 and died at Lille, 21 February 1870.   **77** J.G. Simms, 'The Irish on the Continent, 1691–1800' in T.W. Moody and W.E. Vaughan (eds), *A New History of Ireland*, iv (Oxford, 1986), pp 629–54. **78** Martin Windrow and Francis K. Mason, *The Wordsworth dictionary of military biography* (London, 1990), pp 177–9.   **79** Richard Hayes, *The last invasion of Ireland* (Dublin, 1937), 267–8. Austin O'Malley died in 1869. He was buried with full military honours at Montparnasse cemetery in Paris.   **80** John Fleetwood, 'An Irish field-ambulance in the Franco-Prussian war' in *Irish Sword*, vi, no. 24 (Summer, 1964), pp 137–48. See also G.A. Hayes-McCoy, 'The Irish company in the Franco-Prussian war' in *Irish Sword*, i, no. 4 (1952–3), pp 275–83.   **81** Corpo Reale Di Stato

There are references in both the 1854 and 1855 lists to a Francis Maffey, who served in the ministry of war, and a Luogotenente Joseph Boyer who served in the 2nd Reggimento Granatieri Di Sardegna.[82] There is also a reference to an naval officer named Alexander (Alessandro) Wright and it is believed that he was from Ulster.[83]

There had also been Irishmen in the Russian army during the eighteenth and nineteenth centuries. The most notable of these was Count John O'Rourke whose son, Count Joseph O'Rourke (1772–1849), finished his career as a general of cavalry. There were still descendants of the O'Rourke family serving in the Russian army at the outbreak of the Crimean war. The Russian army list of 1854 mentions a Jacob Quinlan who was serving as an army surgeon at a Moscow hospital. It is possible that he was the son of James Quinlan from Kilsheelan in Co. Tipperary who had served as a surgeon in Napoleon's army and been wounded, and left behind, during the campaign of 1812. James Quinlan (d.1826) had later entered the Russian service and it is quite possible that Jacob Quinlan was his son.[84] There is a possibility that Irish deserters from the British army and the Royal Navy later served in the Russian army during the war. During the siege of Sevastapol several truces were arranged to bury the dead and fraternisation was common among Russian, French and British soldiers. A British soldier later wrote that, during one of these truces, he met an Irish sailor who had deserted from the Royal Navy in order to marry a Russian woman. The Irish deserter had then joined the Russian army and informed his listener that there were other Irish deserters serving in his regiment.[85] It is quite possible, therefore, that there were Irishmen serving, not only in the British army, but also in the Turkish, French, Sardinian and Russian armies during the Crimean war.

Irish generals in the Crimea

The quality of the military leadership in the Crimean war has been commented on in the numerous histories of that war. It is sufficient to point out here that the majority of the British generals were quite old and had not seen any campaigning since 1815. Lord Raglan, the 64-year-old master-general of the ordnance, was given command of the army. He had served under Wellington in Spain and France, and had last seen action at Waterloo. Raglan was undoubt-

Maggiore, *Annuerio Militare Ufficale dello Stato Sardo per l'Anno 1854* (Turin, 1854). See also Corpo Reale Di Stato Maggiore, *Annuerio Militare Ufficale dello Stato Sardo per l'Anno 1855* (Turin, 1855).   **82** Ibid.   **83** Information kindly supplied by Warrant Officer Luigi Diana, Biblioteca Militare Centrale, Rome.   **84** J. McAuliffe Curtain, 'James Quinlan, formerly surgeon-general to the Tsar of Russia' in *Irish Journal of Medical Science*, 6th series, no. 493 (1967), 7–15.   **85** Edward Small (ed.), *Told from the ranks* (London, 1898), p. 39.

edly brave. He had been first into the breach of the defences at the storming of
Badajoz and had lost an arm at Waterloo. Yet he had never commanded an army
in the field. Raglan had spent the previous forty years in administrative posts
and was simply not up to the task. He had also spent much of his career as
Wellington's understudy and was psychologically unsuited for the job as he had
spent a lifetime carrying out Wellington's instructions rather than coming up
with ideas of his own.

The divisional commanders that he appointed for this campaign also had
very little practical experience between them. Only one was under sixty (the 35-
year-old duke of Cambridge), while only two of them had ever led a division in
the field. There had been opportunities for officers to gain battlefield experience
during the first half of the century, most notably during the Sikh wars of 1845–6
and 1848–9. Due to the fact that service in India was unpopular, the majority of
the divisional commanders had not served in the Sikh wars and were thus very
inexperienced.

There were a number of senior officers of Irish birth among the divisional
and brigade commanders. Two in particular were to have a significant impact
on the outcome of the war. The first, and most notable, of these Irish generals
was Lieutenant-General Sir George De Lacy Evans, who was appointed to
command the Second Division. De Lacy Evans was born in 1787 at Moig in
Co. Limerick and was perhaps the most experienced divisional commander of
the war. Educated at the Woolwich Military Academy, he was commissioned
into the 22nd Foot in February 1807 and went with this regiment to India. He
served in the campaign against the Pindarees before joining Major-General
John Abercromby in the campaign in Mauritius. Exchanging into the 3rd Light
Dragoons in March 1812, he served throughout the Peninsula Campaign with
Wellington and was present at the battles of Hormaza, Vittoria and Toulouse. A
posting to America meant that De Lacy Evans fought in British-American War
of 1812–14. He fought at the battles of Bladensburg and Baltimore and seized
the Capitol during the storming of Washington. He was severely wounded at
the battle of New Orleans in January 1815 but had recovered enough to return
to Europe and obtain a staff posting under Wellington. He was present at the
battles of Quatre Bras and Waterloo in June 1815. His distinguished services in
Spain, America and at Waterloo earned him three successive promotions and
he finished 1815 as a lieutenant-colonel, remaining with the occupying armies
in France until 1818.

In 1830 De Lacy Evans went into parliament, contesting the Rye by-election
of that year as a Radical. While he lost this seat in the next general election, he
later served as MP for Westminster (1833–41 and 1846–65). He also fought in the
first Carlist war (1833–40) in Spain, commanding the British Legion, a force of
10,000 men raised in England, with the permission of the British government, to

fight in support of Queen Cristina. 2,800 of the this force, initially around 7,800 men, were Irish.[86] De Lacy Evans was appointed to command the British Legion with the rank of lieutenant-general in the Spanish army and, choosing his own officers, managed to mould the British Legion into an effective force. He led the British Legion at numerous actions including Hernani, Fuenterrabia and Arlaban. While the involvement of the British Legion was criticized in the Tory press, De Lacy Evans' services were rewarded with promotion to full colonel (June 1837) and he was later made a KCB (1838). In 1846 he was promoted to major-general.[87]

Sir George De Lacy Evans was therefore, one of the more experienced British commanders, having seen service in India, Spain, America and Europe. He was seen as something of a surprise choice, however, given his Radical leanings. Also he had openly criticized the appointment of some of the other divisional commanders, such as the duke of Cambridge. He was to be one of the few generals to emerge from the Crimea with his reputation intact and was to play a significant role in the battles of the Alma and Inkerman.[88]

The second Irish general to play a major part in the Crimean war was Brigadier-General (later Sir) John Lysaght Pennefather, who was given command of the 1st Brigade of the 2nd (De Lacy Evan's) Division. Pennefather was born in 1800 in Co. Tipperary, the son of a Church of Ireland clergyman, the Revd John Pennefather. Entering the army as a cornet in the 7th Dragoon Guards in January 1818, he remained with this regiment until April 1826 when, as a captain, he transferred to the 22nd Foot. In October 1839 he was made lieutenant-colonel of this regiment and four years later took the 22nd Foot to India, campaigning in the Scinde with Sir Charles Napier. This regiment, it was noted, was made up mostly of Irishmen, and bore the brunt of the action at the battle of Meeanee on 17 February 1843. Pennefather was shot through the body and it was originally thought that he would die of this wound. He recovered, however, and was promoted to full colonel in June 1846, giving up command of the 22nd in 1848. In the following year was appointed as assistant quartermaster-general in the Cork district.

Pennefather was also an officer of some experience, therefore. He was very popular with his men, who enjoyed the fact that he was extremely foul-mouthed when angry. This propensity for using foul language became even more pronounced in action and had been a source of great amusement to his men in India, who were amazed to find that Pennefather's language was as bad

86 Edgar Holt, *The Carlist wars in Spain* (1967), p. 86. The breakdown of the original British Legion was 3,200 English, 2,800 Irish, 1,800 Scottish.   87 Hart, *Army List* (1860), p. 8, p. 220. See also Holt, *Carlist wars in Spain*, Tim Pickles, *New Orleans 1815* (London, 1993) and *DNB*. 88 Edward M. Spiers, *Radical general: Sir George De Lacy Evans, 1787–1870* (Manchester, 1983).

as their own. Pennefather was to play a major part in the coming war, especially at the battles of the Alma and Inkerman and in the siege of Sevastapol.[89]

There were also many other senior officers with Irish backgrounds and connections, far too numerous to be dealt with here. One such officer was Colonel Sir Charles Hastings Doyle who, it was hoped, would follow family tradition and gain martial glory in the East. One of the Doyles of Bramblestown, Co. Kilkenny, his family had supplied men for the officer corps of the British army for generations. His father was Lieutenant-General Sir Charles William Doyle, a distinguished Peninsula veteran. His great-uncle, General Sir John Doyle had raised the 87th (Prince of Wales Irish) Foot in 1793, redesignated the 87th Regiment of Foot (The Royal Irish Fusiliers) in 1811.[90] Charles Hastings Doyle was born in 1805 and had attended Sandhurst, before joining the 87th Foot in 1819. He served in the West Indies and Canada before being appointed as assistant adjutant-general in Limerick, with the rank of lieutenant-colonel. In June 1854 he was made a full colonel and appointed as assistant adjutant-general to the army's 3rd Division. He took seriously ill at Varna, however, and returned home. It was ironic indeed that this soldier, with such a distinguished ancestry, should play such a small a part in the campaign.[91]

There was also a significant number of Irishmen who served as battalion commanders in the Crimea and, again, they were far too numerous to give a full list here. Examples of these would be Lieutenant-Colonel Richard Waddy from Wexford, who commanded the 50th Foot, and Lieutenant-Colonel Richard Denis Kelly from Co. Galway, who commanded the 34th Foot.[92] Indeed, when one considers the large number of Irish officers who commanded battalions or held senior staff posts, one can see that the Irish were over-represented in these areas also.

These officers also tended to send letters home on a frequent basis and also keep journals describing their experiences. This is, of course, an absolute boon for anyone researching the subject of the Crimean war. One of the reasons why the Crimean war enjoyed such public interest at the time was due to the fact that higher literacy rates in the army ensured that both officers and men frequently sent letters to their families. Many of these letters were published in contemporary newspapers or as collections of letters after the war. One of these collections was published by Sir Anthony Coningham Sterling, who was born in Dundalk in 1805. Sterling's account, *The Highland Brigade in the Crimea*

89 Hart, *Army List* (1860), p. 11, p. 261. See also *Annual Register* (1854), *DNB* and Patrick Mercer, *Inkerman 1854* (London, 1998).   **90** Anthony Makepeace-Warne, *Brassey's companion to the British army* (1998), p. 301.   **91** Arthur H. Doyle, *A hundred years of conflict, being some records of six generals of the Doyle family, 1756–1856* (1911).   **92** Richard Waddy was the son of Cadwallader Waddy, MP, of Kilmacow, Co. Wexford. He was made a CB in 1855 and a KCB in 1877, finishing his career as a brigadier-general. Richard Denis Kelly was from Mucklon, Co.

(1895) was one of the most popular accounts of an officer's experiences in the war. There were also collections of letters and journals that were never published and some of these, such as Captain John Charles William Fortescue's letters and journals, are held in Irish libraries.[93] Fortescue's journals represent an invaluable source and will be referred to later in this study.[94] The large number of Irish officers and men ultimately created a large amount of sources pertaining to the Irish involvement in the Crimean war and many of these have never been studied by Irish historians.

It can be seen, therefore, that Irish soldiers formed a large part of the British army at the outbreak of the war. The success of recruiting parties in Ireland during the war ensured that the number of Irish soldiers remained high. The army's officer corps also had many Irish officers, some of whom would play a major part in the coming campaign. Public reaction to the announcement of the war, and support for departing troops, was expressed in scenes of wild enthusiasm. The eventual declaration of war also had a major effect on Ireland's economy. It will be shown in this book that Irish involvement was significant in all aspects of the campaign and that the Irish public remained keenly interested in the events of the war.

Galway. He was made a CB in 1858 and a KCB in 1860 and finished his career as a general. **93** John Charles William Fortescue, then a captain in the Royal Regiment of Artillery. Born in April 1822 at the family home in Stephenstown, Co. Louth, he had been commissioned into the Royal Regiment of Artillery as an ensign in June 1841, and served throughout the Crimean war. He kept a journal of his experiences and also copies of the orders he received.   **94** Burke, *Landed gentry of Ireland* (1912), p. 239. See also Hart, *Army List* (1860), pp. 54, 70. NLI MS 19,459. 'The journal of Captain John Charles William Fortescue, RA, September 1854 to June 1855'.

2

The experiences of Irish men and women in the Crimea

The army departs for the east

While some regiments of British infantry had been ordered to the east in February 1854, it was not until after the declaration of war in March 1854, that major troop movements began. Many of the regiments which had left England and Ireland in February had travelled only as far as Gibraltar and Malta. On 22 April 1854, at a conference in Paris, the allied commanders decided that they should initially move their armies to Varna. It was also decided that from Varna they should move to Silistria in order to help the Turkish army under Omar Pasha raise the siege of that city. The infantry regiments at Gibraltar and Malta were ordered to proceed to Varna and further regiments, that were still in England and Ireland were ordered to the East. Squadrons of cavalry and batteries of artillery were also ordered to embark for the East. Towards the end of April 1854, the service squadrons of the cavalry division embarked. Table 2 gives details of their departure:

Table 2. Cavalry regiments ordered to the East

Regiment	Station	Embarked at	Sailed
17th Lancers	Brighton	Portsmouth	25 April
8th Royal Irish Hussars	Exeter	Plymouth	27 April
11th Hussars	Dublin	Kingstown	10 May
13th Light Dragoons	Brighton	Portsmouth	12 May
5th Dragoon Guards	Cork	Queenstown	27 May
1st Royal Dragoons	Manchester	Liverpool	30 May
6th Inniskilling Dragoon Guards	York	Davenport	30 May
4th Royal Irish Dragoon Guards	Dundalk	Kingstown	3 June
4th Light Dragoons	Brighton	Plymouth	19 July

Source: John and Boris Mollo, *Into the valley of death* (London, 1991), p. 11.

As has been shown in Chapter I, large crowds turned out to cheer these regiments through the towns and cities of Ireland. The troops may have been elated at such a send-off but they found conditions on board ship extremely uncomfortable. While the infantry had to endure cramped conditions, the conditions for the cavalry and artillery were even more uncomfortable as their horses took up space and also had to be cared for constantly. Despite this, many of the soldiers travelling to Varna seemed to have enjoyed the trip, perhaps even getting to see Gibraltar or Malta when their transport ships berthed to take on provisions. Private Francis Crotty of the 31st Foot described his journey in a letter to his friend, James Barry of Fermoy, Co. Cork. The letter was written on 22 July 1854, following his arrival at Varna.

> We arrived safe in Cork and embarked upon the *Kangaroo* screw steamer, a very fine vessel but wretched accommodation. We were in fact huddled together on deck like pigs in a Bristol steamer, with scarcely room to move, many had not room to lie down from the time we started to the present day (22nd). The voyage in every other respect was a pleasing one. We were seven days reaching Malta, and every day had something of interest in which served to break the tediousness of the voyage. The scenery in and about Malta was indeed splendid, and the bay, covered with gaudily painted gondolas filled with sedate-looking Maltese gentlemen come out for pleasure and rowing around the vessel, made it one of the most picturesque sights I ever witnessed. Málta itself seemed to be a very beautiful place; there were some very handsome looking buildings and strong fortifications. The artillery and soldiers cheered us loudly as we came in, some men-of-war lying in the harbour manned their yards and gave us three hearty cheers, which we returned with a hearty goodwill, yelling as Irishmen only can.[1]

While Crotty may have felt that conditions on board his ship were cramped, the cavalry faced a much more uncomfortable trip to Varna. Cornet Henry Timson of the Inniskilling Dragoons wrote home on the conditions aboard ship:

> My horses are well and, I hope, will get out safe. We are all very comfortable and have a very nice ship ... much better than they generally are.[2]

This optimism was to be short-lived. The journey to Varna was to become notorious for the hardships endured by both men and horses, due to the ill-conceived way supplies and horses were loaded aboard ship. Official regimental histories endeavour to convey the idea of a well-organized transfer. The history of the 8th Royal Irish Hussars described the journey thus:

1 Lt-Commander D. Niall Brunicardi, 'A letter from Varna' in *Irish Sword*, xiv, no. 57 (Winter, 1981), pp 316–20. Francis Crotty was born at Brigown, Mitchelstown, Co. Cork. He had originally enlisted in the 31st Foot at Cork in November 1843, but transferred to the 33rd Foot in June 1854. The harbour he describes in Malta appears to be the Grand Harbour at Valetta. The 'gondolas' are local boats called *luzzu* and *dghajsa* which are traditionally painted in bright colours.   2 NAM, MS 6807/244, letters of Henry Timson, 21 March 1854.

All told, five large transports were provided for the exclusive use of the regiment, giving most ample accommodation. The horses were all carried below in the holds, in which were first stowed iron and wooden tanks. These were covered with shingle over which strong stalls and a flooring of planks were fitted, with battens to provide firm hold for the horses. The mangers were strongly fixed, and there were also about six spare stalls in each ship, so that in case a horse fell or required grooming, he could be shifted to clean stall.[3]

This description is contradicted by the remaining accounts of the officers and men who travelled with the fleet and wrote home telling of cramped conditions, poor footing for the horses and the stupidity of sealing water supplies beneath the floor. Many horses died during the voyage. George Loy Smith of the 11th Hussars later wrote of the cramped conditions of the horses and the shipboard routine:

The trumpeter sounded 'Stables' three times a day, and every man attended his horse as far as possible the same as in barracks. Several barrels of vinegar were shipped for the purpose of refreshing the horses, by sponging their heads well over with it, especially the nostrils. Slings were provided too for the horses to rest on. These I soon began to suspect must be made on a wrong principle, for, if a horse slipped, they rather tended to throw him down than support him, and there was more difficulty to get a horse up, and more danger of him being killed with one on, than if he had fallen without one.[4]

One of the first equine casualties of the 8th Royal Irish Hussars was a fine grey belonging to Mrs Fanny Duberly.[5] She complained from the outset of the poor conditions for the horses. As the journey progressed her grey deteriorated despite the best efforts of her husband, Paymaster Henry Duberly, and their Irish groom, Private Timothy Connell, and eventually it had to be shot. The care of the horses became a full-time occupation for both the soldiers and the sailors on the transports. On the ships that had water tanks beneath the horse stalls, the animals had to be moved constantly to get at fresh water. In rough weather conditions in the horse decks became even worse. Troop Sergeant-Major Cruse of the 1st Royal Dragoons described such a scene:

Four or five of the horses (were) in a terrible plight, loose, down under the other horses, who were all plunging dreadfully at every lurch of the ship. It took me the whole night and up to 10 o'clock the next morning before I could get them all secured, some of them dreadfully bruised.[6]

3 The Revd Richard H. Murray, *The history of the VIII King's Royal Irish Hussars* (London, 1928), ii, p. 408.   4 George Loy Smith, *A Victorian RSM. From India to the Crimea* (Tunbridge Wells, 1987), p. 80.   5 Fanny Duberly, wife of Captain Henry Duberly, Paymaster of the 8th Royal Irish Hussars. Mrs Duberly wrote *Journal kept during the Russian war* (London, 1855). 6 Paget, *A history of the British cavalry* (London, 1975), ii, p. 33.

While conditions on the sailing transports were bad, regiments who travelled on steam ships had an additional problem. Captain Portal of the 4th Light Dragoons travelled on the steamship *Simla* and later described how two troop horses:

> On the main deck got perfectly mad from the heat and at last became so dangerous to all the horses near them that they had to be destroyed. I am afraid that we shall loose many more from the intense heat. The poor beasts who stand below close to the engines are in perfect steam all day and night too. We ought not to have any horses here at all.[7]

All regiments were to lose horses during the voyage to Bulgaria, then part of the Ottoman Empire. Despite the predictions of Captain Portal, the 4th Light Dragoons only lost four horses. The Inniskillings lost more horses than any other regiment. They faced the same problems of heat and cramped conditions, but disaster struck 200 miles out of Plymouth when one of their transport ships, the *Europa*, caught fire. Cornet Timson later wrote of their desperate plight:

> We went on very well until Wednesday night, about 10 o'clock, when I was in bed and was awoke by the cry of 'fire'. I jumped up as quick as I could and put on a pair of trousers and shirt and went out on deck. The men of the ship ran to the boats, notwithstanding the captain of the ship ordering them not to go away. The mate went away with four sailors in a boat which would have held 8 or 10 men more. In less than an hour the whole ship as far as the poop was in flames and there were only two boats left, one was the horse boat which was too large to get off, but some of the men tried to get off but could not. I got away in the last boat with the Adjutant and the doctor and about 22 more men, nearly all soldiers. It was a very rough night and rained a great deal and we had no oars, so we could not do any thing but sit still.[8]

Cornet Timson had an uncomfortable night until picked up by a Prussian schooner. Transferred to the frigate HMS *Tribune*, he found that all he now possessed was 'drawers, socks, shirt and trousers'. The Inniskillings had lost nineteen men, including the commanding officer, the veterinary surgeon and some of the women accompanying their husbands. Fifty-seven horses had also been lost. This was the most serious loss incurred by the force sailing to the East. Over 130 horses were lost in total during the voyage.

The initial objective of the army was to reach Constantinople. The first cavalry regiments to land there were the 17th Lancers and the 8th Royal Irish Hussars on 20 May 1854. Both regiments were stationed at Kulalie barracks overlooking the city, a most impressive-looking building, but squalid in the extreme on the inside. The troops arrived at Constantinople with great expec-

---

7 Captain Robert Portal, *Letters from the Crimea* (London, 1900), 25 July 1854.   8 NAM, MS 6807/244, letters of Henry Timson, 7 June 1854.

tations and from the sea the city looked impressive indeed. Those who went ashore were gravely disappointed however. Captain Portal wrote that he could 'compare it to no Irish village for filth'. Francis Crotty was somewhat more charitable:

> Constantinople has been so often described that I need say no more than that it looked from the water a perfect paradise. Scutari lay on our left, Constantinople on the right as we came in. The troops are in the habit of confounding the two places together, and seem to make them both out as one city. The harbour was full of men-of-war, English, French and Turkish. The English men-of-war cheered as usual. Plenty of every description of fruit was brought alongside in boats; wine and brandy were also plenty and cheap; the only difficulty was to get at it, as the officers kept a watchful eye on the Turks who were selling it. I managed to do them, however, and smuggled a few bottles, the last of which I finished this morning in drinking a health to all my dear friends in Fermoy.[9]

The camp at Varna and the outbreak of cholera

The army did not remain long in Constantinople. Indeed the 8th Royal Irish Hussars had only completed the process of disembarking when orders were received to proceed to Varna. This journey was a further 160 miles by sea and was decided upon as the allied commanders wanted to make an immediate show of support for Turkey. Just fifty-five miles north of Varna the Russians were besieging Silistria and it was feared that the city would fall. The process of disembarking at Varna was fraught with difficulties. Mrs Duberly, travelling with the 8th Royal Irish Hussars wrote that it was 'a difficult and dangerous operation as the horses had to be lowered into boats and rowed ashore, and many were restive and frightened'. George Loy Smith of the 11th Hussars described how the last of his regiment went ashore, in a more orderly fashion, on 24 June 1854:

> About 8 a.m., commenced disembarking, which took us three hours. One horse managed to disengage itself from the slings, so fell into the sea and swam ashore. Tents, picket posts, ropes and camp kettles we brought with us, so that in half an hour the disembarkation was completed, the horses were all picketed and the tents up.[10]

On arrival a decision was made to set up the cavalry camp at Devna, about fifteen miles outside Varna. The local authorities guaranteed the allied commanders that this was 'a very healthy spot'. This was totally untrue, the area having a long history of outbreaks of cholera, and was known to inhabitants as

---

9 Brunicardi, 'A letter from Varna', pp 316–20. Crotty had been stationed in Fermoy before volunteering to join the 33rd Foot.   **10** Loy Smith, *Victorian RSM*, pp 88–9.

'the valley of death'. This fact soon became known to army surgeons. Humphrey Sandwith wrote that the area around Varna was 'a notoriously unhealthy spot, and it is pretty certain that our full-blooded troops will soon sicken under malarious fever'.[11] With 50,000 allied troops in the vicinity of the port, sanitation was an immediate problem. Local food supplies were also soon exhausted. On 11 July 1854 cholera broke out in the French camp and, due to the proximity of the British camp, the disease spread rapidly through the army. Within a fortnight over 600 men died, many being buried in the camp area, ensuring that the disease remained rampant. Margaret Kirwin, the wife of Private John Kirwin of the 19th Foot, later described her experiences after landing at Varna. Her account is worth quoting at length as it is a vivid description of the conditions endured by an army wife while on campaign.

> The 19th landed at Scutari and remained for about three weeks, then went on to Varna. Here there was a report that the Russians were coming down on us. At once all the women were moved to the rear. We marched on up to Devna and remained for a fortnight. There I bought a little wash tub, and carried my cooking things in it. This was the whole of my baggage which I carried on my head during the march. I also had a water bottle and a haversack to carry biscuits in. The priest and minister had to carry their own bottles and sacks, like the soldiers. On the march the men kept falling out from the heat and they kept me busy giving them drinks. When we got to Monastne the (washing) duty of No. 5 Company fell to me; there were 101 in it and the clothes were brought by its transport horse. I stood in the midst of the stream from 6 a.m. to 7 p.m. washing. The Colour Sergeant would not keep account and some men paid and some did not, so that I was left with very little for my trouble. The men were dying fast of the cholera and black fever and were buried in their blankets. No sooner had we moved up country than the Turks opened the graves and took the blankets. After this we buried them without covering, save for branches and brambles. One man, Sergeant Murphy, came in from a day's marching protecting the Colours and before his wife fried his beefsteak he was dead. From my hardships, standing in the river washing, I took two internal complaints and thought I was dying; the men made a shade for me with boughs. I left it, close to death, for the burial of Sergeant Murphy.[12]

On 10 August 1854 much of Varna was destroyed by fire, along with vital supplies. Shortly afterwards it was discovered that cholera had spread to the fleet offshore. Cornet Timson of the Inniskillings wrote of the army's plight:

> The cholera has been very bad here. The 4th Dragoon Guards have lost, I think, 20 men, the 5th Dragoon Guards 32 and the doctor, and ourselves 18 men. Varna was on fire the other night and nearly all of it burned down. The Greeks set the

11 Paget, *British cavalry*, ii, p. 35. 12 Mark Marsay, 'One woman's story. With the 19th Foot by Margaret Kirwin' in *The Newsletter of the Friends of the Green Howards Regimental Museum*, no. 3 (September 1997), pp 14–15.

town on fire; some of the French caught them putting more fuel on the fire and killed them. The Guards have lost a great many men and the French have lost something frightful, they buried 50 one night.[13]

By 28 August 1854 the 5th Dragoon Guards had lost three officers and thirty-four men to disease, while the 4th Royal Irish Dragoon Guards had lost twenty-three men. Their colonel remarked that it was 'difficult to find a spot here where burying has not been'. He also commented on the equipment of the ambulance detachment:

> Large Wagons with little harness, with heavy old Pensioners riding little Ponies of the Country, are expected to draw these machines. Anything so shameful as the way this Corps has been sent out cannot be conceived. It cannot be made serviceable as at present constituted, and has been sent out a mere clap-trap to please the newspapers and House of Commons.[14]

Poor conditions in the field hospitals led to further fatalities. One infantry officer wrote in a letter home that all those taken to the General Hospital at Varna had perished. The 8th Royal Irish Hussars was one of the worst affected regiments. By the end of July1854 about 25% of their number were in hospital. This put a great strain on those remaining. The adjutant, Major De Salis wrote: 'you may fancy what work the healthy ones have to go through, every man has to look after two horses, and it seems quite a shame to get them up in the morning, they look so tired and wretched.'[15] By the end of September the 8th Royal Irish Hussars had lost 30–35% of its entire strength.[16] The regimental history stated tersely: 'In the three and a half months since their arrival in the East, ninety-five men were non-effective or dead at the time of disembarkation in the Crimea.'[17]

Despite the efforts of medical staff to put an end to the epidemic, cholera remained a problem to some extent for the remainder of the campaign. The practice of moving sick men onto the ships ensured that the disease travelled with the allied army at all times. No system of quarantine was ever established and cholera became part of the daily lot of many army surgeons. Surgeon Pine of the 4th Royal Irish Dragoon Guards recorded in his journal in September 1854 that there were 'some cases of cholera with diarrhoea and jaundice appearing in camp'. On 10 October 1854 his journal records:

> A cold night with high northerly wind. I am better today. Morning very cold, afternoon and evening warmer. At work all day. After Brigade duty lost Captain

---

13 NAM, MS 6807/244, letters of Henry Timson, 18 August 1854.   14 Paget, *British cavalry*, ii, p. 40.   15 Ibid. p. 40. Major Rudolph Leslie De Salis, second son of Jerome, 4th Count De Salis, DL and JP of counties Armagh and Middlesex. The De Salis family also had an estate at Loughgur, Co. Limerick.   16 Murray, *History of the VIII Hussars*, ii, p. 411.   17 Ibid.

John Lowe with cholera. Diarrhoea increasing. Visited Morgan on shipboard. He is better.[18]

Continuing his letter to his friend James Barry of Fermoy, Francis Crotty described his experiences in Varna:

It is now more than month since I wrote the beginning of this letter, and since then I have seen more of Turkey that I would wish. It is an awful country, the sun often 120° in the shade, almost hot enough to roast one's dinner. After disembarking at Varna we remained there in camp 3 days then marched to a place called Alladyn, stayed there a few days and joined the Light Division under General Brown, at a place called Devna.

We have since advanced towards Shumla, from which place we are distant twenty miles. The country looks very beautiful, being covered with fruit trees and a low, scrubby kind of bush. The only trees are walnuts, which are very plentiful. Grapes abound but are not ripe, we are strictly forbidden to eat them. Cholera is very prevalent; we have lost 46 men and 6 women since we came to Bulgaria, and some regiments, especially the 5th Green Horse, are nearly annihilated.[19]

The men who arrived as replacements later in the campaign were more susceptible to disease. Medical officers noted that new recruits seemed to succumb to cholera more frequently and assumed that soldiers who had been in the army for several years had been hardened by years of service. A typical example of a new recruit who succumbed to disease in the Crimea was Private Henry Boulton from Cork. He joined the 17th Lancers in late July 1855 and, in August 1855, died of cholera in the hospital at Scutari. Also Captain the Hon. John William Hely-Hutchinson arrived with the 13th Light Dragoons in May 1855, only to die at Scutari the following July. Seventeen of the Irishmen who appear on the Light Brigade muster rolls are recorded as having died of cholera.

There were also some cases of men who died in unusual circumstances. Pat Brennan, who had enlisted in the 17th Lancers in 1849, was drowned while swimming in the reservoir at Yenibazaar in August 1854. Michael Mahoney from Newbridge was robbed and murdered by locals shortly after arriving at Devna with the 8th Royal Irish Hussars.[20]

Alongside the danger of disease the troops had to contend with poor supplies. Captain Wombwell of the 17th Lancers wrote of the conditions in camp:

18 NAM, MS 6807/262, journal of Surgeon C. Pine, 10 October 1854.   19 Brunicardi, 'A letter from Varna'. Crotty began this second instalment of his letter on 24 August 1854. The '5th Green Horse' was the nickname of the 5th Dragoon Guards, so-called due to their green uniform facings. 20 Muster Rolls for the Light Brigade regiments, 1854–57. PRO WO 12/659–661 (4th Light Dragoons); PRO WO 12/844–848 (8th Royal Irish Hussars); PRO WO12/1012–1017 (11th Hussars); PRO WO 12/1118–1120 (13th Light Dragoons); PRO WO 12/1339–1341 (17th Lancers).

> This camp life is most wretched, nothing to be obtained to eat for any money. All we get is our ration of course brown bread, and $^3/4$ of a lb. of mutton, miserably thin and hardly fit to eat, the same that is served out to the men.[21]

Trooper Lucas of the Inniskillings was equally unimpressed. He described his troop's daily meat ration:

> What they called mutton was something between a dog and a goat. They scarcely weighed more than about 10 pounds each. It took about 6 of them for a Troop's ration.[22]

Some men noticed barrels of peas, pork and beef 'with the date 1828 plainly marked on them'. The men usually slept twelve to a tent and James O'Malley of the 17th Foot later recalled sleeping sixteen to a tent on some occasions.[23]

The horses suffered incredibly. Their food was poor and they remained in the open for twenty-four hours a day, enduring temperatures of over one hundred degrees in June, and the cold of the night. Not surprisingly outbreaks of glanders and farcy resulted in the death of many more horses. The 1st Royal Dragoons had to shoot thirty horses due to various diseases. Re-supply of any materials was difficult. The Commissariat Department, as will be shown later, was notoriously inefficient and supplies of boots and clothing were impossible to obtain. By the end of September 1854 morale was at an all-time low. Drunkenness, court-martials and floggings became commonplace.

The 'Sore Back Reconnaissance'

The first effort at any kind of a military expedition was also not over-inspiring. Around 23 June 1854, rumours began to circulate in the British camp that the Russians had raised the siege of Silistria. By 25 June 1854 this story was confirmed, the news exceeding original hopes. The Russians under Prince Gorchakov had not only left Silistria but had been routed by the Turkish army. The Russians were now in full retreat across the Danube. Lord Raglan immediately sent orders to Lord Cardigan, commanding the light cavalry, to make a reconnaissance and ascertain 'if the Russian army was still on this side of the Danube'.[24] What followed was the first cavalry expedition and reconnaissance in force of the campaign. By the end of this reconnaissance on 11 July 1854 the total lack of preparation of the army for field conditions had become obvious.

---

21 Paget, op. cit., p. 38.   22 Ibid.   23 James O'Malley, *Life of James O'Malley* (Montreal, 1893), p. 63.   24 Cecil Woodham-Smith, *The reason why: the story of the fatal charge of the Light Brigade* (London, 1953), p. 154.

In fact the 'Sore Back Reconnaissance', as it became known, showed up all the problems that were to plague the allied forces for the remainder of the campaign.

The reconnaissance force was made up of 121 men of the 8th Royal Irish Hussars and seventy-five men of the 13th Light Dragoons. There was also a troop of Turkish lancers attached to the force. The initial and most serious problem lay in the choice of Lord Cardigan as commander of the expedition. He was a most unpopular officer and had shown himself to be an absolute stickler for military regulations. The daily routine of his troops was organized as though the regiments were still on station in England or Ireland. All dress regulations were enforced and stable duties and inspections were carried at their set hours, even in the blazing sun. Major De Salis of the 8th Royal Irish Hussars noted how the Turkish troopers and horses coped much better than the British, as they had adapted their routine to suit the climate. He later wrote of the prime mistake made by British cavalry officers as ignoring the benefit of the Turks' local knowledge; 'there was plenty of grass and we always had a Turkish Regiment brigaded with us, we had no experience and we omitted to take advantage of theirs'.[25] Cardigan himself was renowned for treating the Turks under his command very badly, ignoring their experience of both the climate and terrain. Captain Crewell of the 11th Hussars described Cardigan's treatment of Turkish soldiers while on a field day:

> Just returned from a Brigade field day, we had a quantity of Turks out with us whom the Earl treats very badly, he gives them no orders and then swears at them for not being in their proper places. Had we been fighting Russians, we would have lost Maule and his troop of RHA. He was ordered to pound away at the 17th, and then was left on the ground, at the mercy of the enemy.[26]

Despite the fact that no tents or spare clothes was carried, each horse carried in excess of twenty stone on the expedition. Cardigan pushed the column hard, a serious problem due to the total lack of local water. He himself later wrote that along the line of march 'no fountains were to be found at any intermediate places'. On 29 June 1854 the allied cavalry reached the Danube and found that the Russians had indeed retreated across the river. Cardigan now decided to patrol along the banks of the river and return through Russova, Silistria and Shumla. It is often suggested that the patrol ultimately gained no useful intelligence. Woodham-Smith has commented:

> No close observation was kept on the enemy and no information of military usefulness was gained, though he (Cardigan) observed with great interest many

25 Murray, *History of the VIII Hussars*, pp 410–11. **26** Captain Godfrey T. Williams, *The historical records of the Eleventh Hussars, 'Prince Albert's Own'* (London, 1908), p. 183. The '17th' in this case refers to the 17th Lancers.

decaying monuments of antiquity. From the further bank of the Danube the Russian General Luders through his glass watched with interest the English horsemen galloping about and, though they were within range of his guns, forbore to fire.[27]

This negative opinion does not entirely hold true. Cossack outposts were reconnoitred at Russova on the far bank of the Danube. On 3 July 1854 at Silistria a Russian force of 40–50,000 men was closely observed. These facts were forgotten due to the hardships suffered by both men and horses. Cardigan had decided to take the longest possible route back to camp. The expedition to the Danube and back could have been undertaken in eight to ten days. The journey actually lasted seventeen days, at least a full week more than was necessary, travelling in incredible heat with little water available. Cardigan himself became ill with dysentery and sent for the surgeon of the 8th Royal Irish Hussars, Dublin-born Henry Somers. Somers complained bitterly to Cardigan about the conditions endured by the men. He later told Mrs Duberly that Cardigan responded, 'Yes, Mr Somers, I am a Brigadier, I may say a Major-General; for I conclude that the brevet is out by this time, and yet, sir, I can feel for the men.'[28] It is certain that this was not the reaction that Somers was hoping for. Mrs Duberly also commented on how the conditions of the march affected the horses:

> During the march, when twenty horses were being led with frightful sores on their backs, the men staggering under saddles and kit, he met a party of French officers, and immediately ordered them to mount. Lockwood (of the 8th Royal Irish Hussars) said, 'He had the greatest difficulty to induce the men to put saddles on the backs.'[29]

When the column finally returned to Devna camp, some men were so exhausted that they could no longer walk or ride. Somers had to hire ox-drawn carts to carry the sick men back to camp. Eighty horses were put on the sick list and were still classed as being non-effective the following August. Five of these eventually died, the remaining seventy-five were re-classified as being fit only for light work. Yet Lord Raglan was pleased with the result and later wrote to Cardigan:

> You have ascertained for me that the Russians have withdrawn from this end of the Dobrudsha and that the country between this and Trajan's Wall is not only clear of the enemy, but is wholly deserted by the inhabitants. These are important facts.[30]

Cardigan was also pleased with his own personal performance and recorded later that he had 'borne it well' and eaten 'almost the same food as the men'.

27 Woodham-Smith, *The reason why*, p. 155.   28 Paget, op. cit., ii, p. 37.   29 E.E.P. Tisdall, *Mrs Duberly's campaigns: an Englishwoman's experiences in the Crimean war and Indian Mutiny* (London, 1963), p. 155.   30 Paget, op. cit., p. 37.

Those that had accompanied him on the escapade were less forgiving. Captain Shakespear of the Royal Horse Artillery felt that Cardigan was:

> The most impractical and most inefficient cavalry officer in the service. He may do all very well when turned out by his valet in the Phoenix Park, but there his knowledge ceases. We are all greatly disgusted with him. He is every grade of rank between a Major-General and a Private. We have field days every other day now. Cardigan kills the horses with pace. We wish we were with Scarlett and his Heavy Cavalry.[31]

The 'Sore Back Reconnaissance' illustrated the problems inherent in the organisation of the British army. This combination of poor planning, inade-quate supply and bad leadership was to become a feature of the campaign. There is a suggestion that a small party of Royal Horse Artillery, one officer and twelve gunners, travelled over the same ground shortly after Cardigan's expedition, in order to carry out a proper reconnaissance.

The army departs for the Crimea

The news that the Russians had retreated from Silistria made the allied leaders decide on a new course of action. As early as June 1854, Lord Raglan had been informed that the British cabinet and the French government had decided that the great Russian naval base at Sevastapol should be taken. Public opinion also favoured such a course of action. On 16 July 1854, Raglan received a dispatch informing him that:

> The fortress [Sevastapol] must be reduced and the fleet taken or destroyed: nothing but insuperable impediments should be allowed to prevent the early decision to undertake these operations.[32]

In light of the poor information available regarding the strength of the enemy, Lord Raglan and the French commander, Maréchal St Arnaud, reluctantly agreed to embark for the Crimean peninsula. The fleet reassembled in Varna Bay and towards the end of August 1854 the army began to embark. Despite the misgivings of the commanders, the decision to move was a godsend for the troops. Harriet Martineau was later to write that 'the migration to the Crimea saved our force; and only just in time. In another month not a man would have remained alive'.[33] This was by no means an exaggeration. Disease, poor conditions and deteriorating morale threatened to destroy the allied forces in Bulgaria. Francis Crotty later described the conditions in the camp at Varna:

31 Ibid.   **32** John Sweetman, *Balaclava 1854* (London,1993), p. 15.   **33** Harriet Martineau, *England and her soldiers* (London, 1859), p. 71.

We know no more about how the world wags than the dead. The men are all nearly sick of this inactive life. Our strength is ebbing away fast from the enervating effects of the climate; the slightest exertion throws us into a most profuse perspiration. I have seen water running off the men's faces just as if it came off a spout in one continuous stream. In fact, if I had not seen it and experienced it myself, I would not believe it.

He went on to describe Commissariat practices and the rations the men were issued:

There are scarcely any roads through this country that I have seen, what they call roads being mere tracks, caused by buffalo carts and arabas employed by our Commissary, which said Commissary is not quite so efficient as we were led to believe at home it was. For instance, since I came here I have neither seen nor tasted this porter which they said was provided for the troops at 3d per quart, (all moonshine!). Our rations here consist of one and a half pounds of meat (versus carrion), and one pound of bread, with something less (sometimes a great deal) than a small glass of rum each day. The remainder we get by paying for it, such as coffee, sugar and rice. Sometimes we can get salt and often none. Everything was cheap in this country when the army came here first, but simple as the natives are in their habits and appearance, they soon found out that they could charge any price for an article of food and they would be sure to find purchasers. Consequently, a goose bought when we first came here for 2 piastres (4d) costs 6 now; eggs which we bought for 1 piastre (2d) a dozen costs 6 piastres, everything else the same. The only drink we are allowed is rum mixed with water, wretched bad and dearer than at home. So much for the meat and drink; now for the washing and lodgings. We wash all our own linen, as the women who were sent out with the regiment are too lazy to wash themselves, and dear knows I for one cannot blame them. We pay 6d for as much soap as you would buy at home for a penny, and 3d for a cake of blacking. We are all of course under canvas and sleep on bare ground, and I often laugh when I hear a fellow shout to another to stand off his bed. I'll describe mine; my greatcoat doubled under me, my smock frocks answer all the purposes of a pair of sheets and a blanket over all. We are not allowed have hay or straw of any description, the Doctors say the bare ground is the healthiest, so that we need not expect the luxury of a bed until we return home again, or go to our last bed, the grave.[34]

It is perhaps not surprising that the men were glad to hear that the army was leaving Varna. The effect of this news was instantaneous and the morale of the men immediately improved. Incidents of drunkenness and indiscipline declined. Lieutenant Walker, ADC to Lord Lucan, summed up the feelings of most when he wrote, 'I am so glad to leave Bulgaria. I was never so glad to leave a place in all my life, not even the West Indies'.[35] One Irish officer, Captain Edwin Richards of the 41st Foot, displayed his displeasure at being ordered to remain at Varna in a letter of 2 September 1854:

---

34 Brunicardi, 'A letter from Varna'.

The 41st embarked yesterday with the rest of the Division, and here I am, miserable, unfortunate wretch, left with the sick men of the Brigade. I feel as if I would go mad. They are no doubt for the Crimea, and will have hard fighting. The junior captain of each Brigade throughout the Army has been left behind; and unfortunately I am the youngest in mine. I went to Generals Adams and Pennefather, and neither could do anything for me: they were both very civil; but said it fell to my lot, and they could not with justice try to keep anyone else. General Adams wrote me a very kind letter about it. My brother officers are as much disgruntled as I am about it, but that does not make me less miserable. There is, however, a captain of the —— sick at Constantinople and the General said if I could effect an exchange with him I could go on, so there is some chance.[36]

The allied army arrived at Calamita Bay on 14 September 1854, and proceeded to disembark. The regimental historian of the 8th Royal Irish Hussars, the Revd Richard Murray, again wrote that the operation was well organised. Accounts of those who were there paint a rather different picture. No such disembarkation had taken place since 1801 when the Royal Navy landed General Abercromby's force at Aboukir. At Calamita Bay a certain amount of confusion reigned. The boats for both men and horses proved to be inadequate. The first two days were taken up in getting the infantry ashore. During the afternoon of 14 September 1854, the weather suddenly worsened and the landings had to be postponed. At sunset rain began to fall heavily, drenching those ashore who now faced the night without tents or extra clothing. Many infantrymen took ill and several died during their first night in the Crimea.

On 16 September 1854 the cavalry began to disembark. The arrangements made for getting the horses ashore were basic to say the least. Some of the horses were lowered by slings into flat bottomed boats and taken to the shoreline. Because of a lack of suitable boats, many horses were taken close inshore and then pushed overboard and had to swim the rest of the way. Lord George Paget of the 4th Light Dragoons described the scene:

> It is distressing to see the poor horses, as they are upset out of the boats, swimming about in all directions among the ships. They swim so peacefully, but look rather unhappy with their heads in the air and the surf driving into their poor mouths. Only one has been drowned as yet, to our knowledge. We get on but slowly with our disembarkation.[37]

The fact that the landings were completed with so few casualties was due to the welcome inactivity of the Russians. Had the Russians moved up artillery the

35 Paget, op. cit., p. 43.   **36** *Illustrated London News*, 20 Jan. 1855, p. 67. Captain Richards was the son of Captain Edwin Richard RN, of Rawindon House, Co. Carlow and the grandson of Solomon Richards of Solsborough, Co. Wexford. The regiment of the sick officer in Constantinople was deleted from the reproduced letters in the *Illustrated London News*. **37** Paget, op. cit., p. 44.

whole process could quickly have become a disaster. A Russian officer did appear on 14 September with a troop of horse, but contented himself with taking a copious amount of notes. For the troops themselves the greatest problem was the loss of their valises and spare clothing. These were left on ship and not returned to them until early December, by which time the Russian winter had set in. George Loy Smith of the 11th Hussars wrote of his first night on Russian soil:

> Shortly afterwards we marched inland, about three miles, then took up a position in front of the infantry, threw out pickets, then picketed our horses and bivouacked. My man Sampson brought me some boards from an adjacent village; these, spread over with hay, made a tolerably comfortable bed. With the aid of a waterproof sheet, with which I had provided myself before leaving Dublin, and with a few sticks I formed over it a covering.[38]

Colonel Shewell of the 8th Royal Irish Hussars noted the loss of the tools required for entrenching, building shelter, digging camp drains and cutting wood. He immediately pointed this out to the Commissariat but later wrote that 'repeated requisitions were made for them without success until 14th December'. The next few days were spent collecting baggage wagons and animals. The 8th Royal Irish Hussars carried out some patrolling, sighting a Cossack camp on 17 September 1854. Lieutenant Seager described the peregrinations of the Irish Hussars in a letter to a friend:

> We landed in the Crimea, on the 16th September in Calamita Bay, without any opposition and immediately had to march 24 miles into the country on a foolish expedition after some supposed Cossacks we never caught sight of, the whole of our regiment and part of the 13th went under Lord Cardigan, who is always doing something to render the Light Cavalry inefficient. He brought us back to the beach at 11 o'clock, the night very dark, having passed through a salt lake and lost our way, besides putting us through a field day, and a great many other unnecessary movements, we had to link our horses together, and passed the night on the beach in our cloaks. We marched the next day, Sunday, almost 5 miles distant along the Sevastapol road and remained there two nights, during which the Cossacks were hovering around us in thousands, burning all the villages and forage on our route but took care to keep a respectable distance from us, although our strength is not more than 800.[39]

The skirmish on the Bulganek and the battle of the Alma

Despite the calm of the general officers the allied army was in a most precarious position. The army was spread along the coast, with no central base.

---

38 Loy Smith, op. cit., p. 97.   **39** NAM, MS 8311–9, letters of Captain Edward Seager, 28 September 1854.

It was entirely dependant on the fleet lying offshore which, as no ports had yet been captured on the Crimean peninsula, would be unable to assist in the event of an attack. A concentrated attack by the Russians at this point could have pushed the combined French and British army into the sea. Yet the Russian field armies were not prepared for an advance at this time and, on 19 September 1854, the allied army had gathered together and began to march southwards towards Sevastapol. As they travelled south, the army kept the coast on its right flank, the fleet providing support on that side. Cavalry was in such short supply (the French had virtually none) that the Light Brigade was fully employed in guarding the front, rear and left flank of the column. The shortage of cavalry was pointed out to Lord Raglan who then stated that he intended to keep them 'in a band box'. This protective policy led to the inactivity of the British cavalry during its first encounters with the Russians. While the allied generals did not realise it at the time, the practice of keeping the cavalry safe in the rear was to cause great disharmony. The men of the infantry divisions rightly felt that the burden of the dangerous work fell on them. The troopers themselves chafed at the imposed inactivity and unjustly blamed the Cavalry Division's commander, Lord Lucan.

On the afternoon of 19 September 1854, the army reached the Bulganek river, the first major physical obstacle on the route to Sevastapol. The river was at this time of year 'a small sluggish stream, which had at that time a greater depth of mud than water'. Lord Cardigan was sent forward with the 11th Hussars and the 13th Light Dragoons to reconnoitre. The ground across the river rose and fell in a series of gentle undulations and, after travelling about one and a half miles, the British cavalry came upon a formation of Russian cavalry, about 1,500 strong. Cardigan had sent out skirmishers, the Russians responding in kind, before Lord Lucan arrived and took command. The skirmishers of both sides then exchanged the first fire of the campaign, the British later claiming to have hit twenty-five Russians. An Irish artillery officer, Captain John Charles William Fortescue, later described the action in his diary:

> Lord Raglan instantly ordered three squadrons of our cavalry out, who were halted in the hollow as the Russian cavalry grew very strong. Our Horse Artillery and a battery were ordered up. The Russians in the meantime opened upon our cavalry from a 6-pounder battery, the balls ricocheting through and over us and it was all their own way until our guns came up, who soon turned the tables in our favour and after about half an hour's firing, they retired.[40]

40 NLI, MS 19,359: The diary of Captain John Charles William Fortescue RA, 19 September 1854. Captain Fortescue was one of the Fortescues of Stephenstown, Co. Louth. He later served as a JP, was appointed high sheriff (1861) and was also deputy-lieutenant of Co. Louth (1868–79).

At this point a mass of Russian infantry, accompanied by cavalry and artillery, could be seen advancing up the reverse side of the slope. Lord Raglan decided that he did not want to engage in a major battle at this point due the almost total exhaustion of his men, and sent a galloper with a request that Lord Lucan retire. The messenger, realizing the seriousness of the situation, relayed the request as an order. The 8th Royal Irish Hussars and the 17th Lancers were brought up to cover the withdrawal, and the cavalry retreated by alternate squadrons. The whole manoeuvre was carried out in drill-book fashion, something that was to be characteristic of the whole campaign. The first casualties of the campaign occurred at this point also. The Russian horse artillery galloped forward and opened fire on the retreating squadrons. A trooper of the 11th Hussars later wrote of the disconcerting experience of waiting under fire for the order to withdraw:

> I shall never forget the sensation of sitting perfectly inert on my horse, as long as I remember anything. There is nothing more trying. I recall how when some of us more nervous fellows, bowing our heads down to our horses' manes, how angry and indignant was the tone of Major Peel's remonstrance: 'What the hell are you bobbing your heads at?'[41]

This firing continued until 'C' and 'I' troops of the Royal Horse Artillery arrived and drove the Russian guns off. Five men were wounded in the 'Affair at the Bulganek', as it became known. Several horses were also killed and injured. After the action both Paymaster Sergeant Priestly of the 13th Light Dragoons and Trooper Williamson of the 11th Hussars claimed the dubious honour of being the very first British casualty. Trooper Williamson's troop commander was an Irish officer, Cornet Roger Palmer. Many years later he recalled how Williamson 'rode out of the ranks, his leg shot off and hanging by his overall. Coming up to me he said, quite calmly, "I am hit, may I fall out?"'[42]

This skirmish at the Bulganek was unsettling for the British cavalry in several ways. The troopers of the Light Brigade did not understand why they had been withdrawn so hastily. During their withdrawal they were jeered at by both the Russians and the British infantry. Lord Lucan increasingly became the focus of their resentment.

On the following day, 20 September 1854, the allied army fought its first major battle with the Russians at the Alma river. The Russian commander, Prince Menshikov had arrived on the heights above the Alma on the 14th September with around 40,000 troops under his command and, recognizing a natural defensive position, had ordered two redoubts to be built: the 'Greater' and 'Lesser' redoubts. Yet part from this, he had not entrenched his position and

41 Paget, op. cit., p. 46.   42 Ibid., p. 47.

had not extended his left flank to the cliff edge, realising that Royal Navy ships could bombard that end of his line. Menshikov also felt sure that the causeway at that end of his line was impassable to troops but he would soon discover that it was not. Lord Raglan later described the formidable geographical obstacle that faced the allied army:

> The bold and almost precipitous range of heights, of 350 to 400 feet, that from the sea closely borders the left bank of the river, here ceases and formed their [the Russians] left, and turning thence round a great amphitheatre or wide valley, terminated at a salient where the right rested, and whence the descent to the plain was more gradual. The front was about two miles in extent. Across the mouth of this great opening is a lower ridge at different heights, varying from 60 to 150 feet, parallel to the river, and at distances from it of 600 to 800 yards. The river itself is generally fordable for troops, but its banks are extremely rugged and in most parts steep; the willows along it had been cut down, in order to prevent them from affording cover to the attacking party, and in fact everything had been done to deprive an assailant of any species of shelter.[43]

Lord Raglan continued:

> On the right, and a little retired, was a powerful covered battery, armed with heavy guns, which flanked the whole of the right of the position. Artillery at the same time was posted at the points that best command the passage of the river and its approaches generally. On the slopes of these hills, forming a sort of tableland, were placed dense masses of the enemy's infantry, while on the heights above was his great reserve; the whole amounting it is supposed to between 40,000 to 50,000 men.[44]

The allied commanders held a hasty meeting. Maréchal St Arnaud suggested a pincer movement but Lord Raglan preferred the concept of a frontal assault. He was also worried at not knowing more about the strength of the Russian positions but confirmed that he would endeavour to support the French attack. The allied army consisted of 30,000 French, 27,000 British and 7,000 Turkish troops. The British were on the left flank, the French in the centre, while the Turks were aligned on the extreme right of the allied line. The Irish general, Sir George De Lacy Evans was to play a major role in the attack and his 2nd Division straddled the Sevastapol road, referred to as the 'Great Causeway'. To his left was General Sir George Brown's Light Division and, to his right, there was a French division, under the command of Prince Napoleon.

At around midday the allied troops began their advance. The French divisions made rapid progress, reaching the top of the cliffs where they threatened the Russian left. They found it difficult to get artillery up the cliff, however, and, after

---

43 Philip Warner, *The Crimean war: a reappraisal* (2nd edn, 2001), 27–8.   **44** Ibid., p. 28.

their initial success, their attack faltered as Russian resistance stiffened. At around 1 p.m., Captain Louis Edward Nolan came to De Lacy Evans with orders to advance in support of the French and Turkish attack on his right. His advance was made difficult as Russian skirmishers had set fire to the villages of Bourliouk and Almatamak as they retreated and the battlefield was soon covered in a cloud of dense smoke. Captain Fortescue described the beginning of the battle:

> The battle began on the French side about 1.15 p.m. and for some time we were exposed to a tremendous cannonade from the Heights. Shot and shell flew thickly around us. Captain Sandby on Divisional Headquarters staff had his horse killed under him by a cannon shot.[45]

De Lacy Evans divided his force to either side of the burning village of Bourliouk and, sending Brigadier-General Adams to the right with his brigade, he took Brigadier-General Pennefather's brigade, and the 47th Foot, and moved along the unsheltered line of the Great Causeway. Menshikov had, however, moved a battery to cover this section of the road and, as De Lacy Evans and his men scrambled forward, they were fired upon by the sixteen guns in the causeway battery, an eight-gun battery to their right and the guns of the Great Redoubt on their left. Fighting through the burning village and across the river, the British troops eventually took cover under a steep bank on the Russian side.

De Lacy Evans then continued to lead his troops up the causeway, despite the fact that he had been wounded in the left shoulder by this time. He ordered the batteries of the Light and 1st Divisions to come up in support of his own and this left him with thirty guns at his disposal. He used them to support the Light Division's unsuccessful attack on the Great Redoubt. At this point, De Lacy Evans noticed that the 1st Division, consisting of the Highland and Guards Brigades, had stopped advancing. Realizing that there was no time to discuss the situation with Lord Raglan, he sent one of his ADCs to the 1st Division's commander, the duke of Cambridge, with instructions to tell him that he carried orders from Lord Raglan and that the 1st Division was to resume its advance immediately. In effect he told his ADC to lie to the duke in order to get the 1st Division advancing again in his support. The renewed advance of these three divisions drove the Russians out of the Great Redoubt but the matter of De Lacy Evans sending the duke of Cambridge what were effectively false orders, remained a matter of contention between the two men in years to come.

With the Russian left flank under pressure and the redoubts taken, Menshikov ordered a retreat and, while some Russian units retreated in good order, the majority of the army fled in panic. The British had lost 362 men dead and 1,640

45 NLI, MS 19,359: Fortescue diary, 20 September 1854.

wounded. De Lacy Evans reported that 540 men of his division had been killed or wounded, testimony to the crucial role they played in the attack. Russian casualties stood at around 6,000. A large quantity of Russian equipment was captured, including the carriage of the Russian commander, Prince Menshikov. Captain Fortescue wrote in his diary:

> His carriage and papers (Menshikov's) were taken and in it were papers which stated his opinion that he had taken up such a position that we should be unable to take it in less than three weeks, even if we did it then.[46]

It is easy to trace the movements of the Cavalry Division at the battle of the Alma. They were positioned well to the left of the main body of French and British troops, facing a large body of Russian cavalry and horse artillery, where they remained largely inactive. The Russians were equally inactive and sat facing their British counterparts and eventually withdrew. The Light Brigade then advanced and when they reached the high ground opposite they were faced with a mass of retreating Russians. A number of prisoners were taken when orders came for the cavalry to withdraw. This officially sanctioned inactivity was hard to justify. While the cavalry could not be used in the main engagement, it was one of their main functions to harass a retreating enemy. Yet Lord Raglan's concern for the welfare of his cavalry continued and Lords Lucan and Cardigan were forced to sit inactive, frustrated because they were not ordered to advance.

This was early in the campaign, however, and the character of the Russian cavalry had not yet been gauged. The curious feature of the Russian cavalry throughout the Crimean war was its own inactivity. When faced with opposition the Russian cavalry was inclined to do one of three things: run away, sit impassively looking on, or, advance aggressively and at the last moment come to a total halt. Such behaviour was the norm for Russian cavalry, most notable at the battle of Balaclava in October 1854. At the Alma sixteen squadrons of Russian regular cavalry and eleven of Cossacks remained inactive throughout the battle. The only orders that these men received from Menshikov told them to withdraw. It is not surprising, therefore, that Lord Raglan declined to send the 900 men of the Light Brigade and two troops of the Royal Horse Artillery against this mass of Russian cavalry, about 5,000 in number.

What was harder to explain was Lord Raglan's refusal to order a cavalry attack when the Russians broke and ran. Sir Colin Campbell, on his own initiative, advised Lord Lucan to move a troop of Royal Horse Artillery forward. This was done and 'I' troop pounded the retreating Russians, eventually capturing two howitzers. When orders arrived for the cavalry they were to escort field guns

46 Ibid.

forward, but not to attack. Lucan moved the Light Brigade across the river and
closed on the Russian rear. The 17th Lancers, Lucan's old regiment, got ahead
and Lieutenant Wombwell later wrote in his diary of the Russian disorder.

> We went forward at a gallop, cheering and hallooing as load as we could. We
> could see the enemy running as hard as they could go, throwing away their
> knapsacks, arms and even their coats to assist them in their flight. Morgan's
> Troop of my regiment were sent out to pursue and bring in prisoners, in which
> they succeeded very well, bringing in a good many. On coming up with the poor
> fellows they dropped on their knees and begged for mercy.[47]

Lieutenant Seager of the 8th Royal Irish Hussars described his regiment's part
in the action in a letter home:

> It is one of the most gallant affairs recorded in British History and we shall get a
> medal we think. The cavalry, although under fire, did not act until the retreat as
> we were protecting the flank from a large body of the enemy's cavalry. We
> galloped up the hill after the enemy taking a lot of prisoners, but they would not
> let us go far on account of our small numbers.[48]

An order from Lord Raglan told Lord Lucan to desist in his pursuit of the
enemy. Lucan was forced to call a halt and the prisoners were actually released.
Ultimately Raglan may well have been correct in his decision. Lieutenant
Wombwell of the 17th Lancers had come across 'an immense force of cavalry'
advancing aggressively towards the pursuers. The Alma was a confusing stop-
start affair for the men of the Cavalry Division. The troopers themselves could
not understand why the pursuit had not been followed through. The infantry
resented the fact that they had to do the majority of the fighting. Again Lord
Lucan became the focus of this resentment and he later sent an ill-tempered
note to Lord Raglan:

> Lord Lucan trusts that Lord Raglan has that confidence in him, as commanding
> the cavalry, that he would allow him to act on his own responsibility, as occasion
> would offer and render advisable, for otherwise opportunities of acting will
> frequently be lost to the cavalry.[49]

No reply from Lord Raglan was recorded to this communication.

Both of the Irish generals, De Lacy Evans and Pennefather, had been prominent in the attack but there was no real occasion for any of the commanders to
display great tactical ability. The battle was won due to the courage the infantry
showed in advancing under heavy fire. Two Irishmen were awarded the Victoria

---

47 Ibid. p. 49.   **48** NAM, MS 8311–9, the Seager letters, 28 September 1854.   **49** Woodham-
Smith, *The reason why*, p. 195.

Cross for the bravery they showed during the battle.[50] Sergeant (later Major-General Sir) Luke O'Connor, from Elphin, Co. Roscommon, was serving with the 23rd Foot in General Sir George Brown's Light Division. When the attack began he advanced beside the officers carrying the colours.[51] When the officer carrying the Queen's Colour was shot, O'Connor picked it from the ground. During the storming of the Great Redoubt, he was wounded but remained with the Queen's Colour until the battle was over. He was recommended for a decoration and also commissioned for his bravery at the Alma. O'Connor was first member of the British army to be awarded the Victoria Cross.[52] His VC action was later the subject of a painting by Chevalier W. Desanges. Sergeant John Park from Londonderry was serving with the 77th Foot and was also awarded the VC for 'conspicuous bravery' at the battle of the Alma.[53] Twenty-eight Irishmen were to win the Victoria Cross during the war and another two men, born in England but of Irish parents, were also awarded the Victoria Cross for their actions in the Crimea. (See Appendix A.)

The 'Affair at McKenzie's Farm' and the march on Sevastapol

On 25 September 1854 there occurred a potentially disastrous action which came to be known as the 'Affair at McKenzie's Farm'. As a contrast to the battle of the Alma, this was entirely a cavalry skirmish. While the troopers were no doubt glad to put an end to their inactivity, the end result was not very encouraging. This minor action only occurred at all due to the fact that both the allied and Russian armies began a flanking march at the same time, but heading in different directions and as a result were heading towards each other. After the battle of the Alma, the allied army had begun marching south to Sevastapol again, coming within sight of the town on 24 September 1854. The French commander, Maréchal St Arnaud, refused to attack the city immediately, which was at this stage almost defenceless. This inaction allowed the Russians the time to sink blockships in the harbour and strengthen the landward defences. Menshikov also decided to move the majority of his field army out of Sevastapol and withdrew northwards towards Bakhchisarai. Coincidentally, on

---

50 The Victoria Cross was instituted by a royal warrant dated 29 January 1856, towards the end of the Crimean war. The actual crosses were cast from the metal of Russian guns captured at Sevastapol. The first VCs were awarded for bravery in the Crimean war. **51** Each British regiment carried two colours: the Queen's (or King's) Colour and the Regimental Colour. The Queen's Colour was a Union Jack while the Regimental Colour was in the colour of the regiment's uniform facings. **52** W.A. Williams, *The VCs of Wales and the Welsh regiments* (Clwyd, 1984), pp 15–16. See also *Ireland's VCs*. O'Connor was presented with the VC by Queen Victoria at the first investiture in Hyde Park, 26 June 1857. He later served in the Indian mutiny and the Ashanti war of 1873–4. **53** *Ireland's VCs* p. 13.

25 September 1854, Lord Raglan decided that the allied army should move southwards and take the port of Balaclava in order to have a base for the forthcoming siege. Due to the route that both armies took it was now likely that their paths would cross at some point on the Bakhchisarai to Balaclava Road. Essentially both the allied army and a Russian army of some 10,000 men were now using the same road, one army moving northwards, the other southwards. The place of the inevitable encounter was McKenzie's Farm, named after a Scottish naval engineer who had supervised the building of Sevastapol's defences at the turn of the century.

The main body of the army was led southwards by Lord Lucan. An advance guard made up of the entire cavalry division, two troops of Royal Horse Artillery and a battalion of the Rifle Brigade travelled along the road, the country thereabouts being thick with scrub and oak forest. Lord Raglan followed this vanguard with his personal staff and an escort of forty men of the 8th Royal Irish Hussars under Captain Chetwode. Due to bad map-reading Lord Lucan took a wrong turn off the main road with the cavalry and riflemen. When Lord Raglan arrived at the turnoff he found the Royal Horse Artillery officers debating the error and they eventually began back along the correct route, minus Lucan and the advance guard. After travelling a short distance they breasted a hill and found McKenzie's Farm before them, the Russian rear guard still in possession. Captain Walker, an ADC to Lord Lucan, later wrote of how the small party 'came in sight of the farm and, to our great astonishment, found a Russian rearguard, and an immense train of baggage and ammunition, directly in our front'.[54]

Despite the small size of the force with him at this point, Lord Raglan decided to attack immediately. The Russians were visibly disconcerted at his sudden arrival and he used their surprise to his advantage. Captain Walker was sent to the rear to find Lord Lucan, while the Royal Horse Artillery was ordered forward to engage the enemy. Captain Chetwode took his forty men of the 8th Royal Irish Hussars forward where they dismounted and began skirmish towards the farm. Captain Shakespear of the Royal Horse Artillery described the initial clash:

> Suddenly the road turned to the right and to our astonishment a regiment of infantry was formed across the road, front ranks kneeling within 30 yards of us. They fired a volley, but were so bewildered nothing touched us. They then bolted into the bush. We came into action to the left and poured in common case.[55]

Captain Fortescue described the action in his diary:

> At about two o'clock we came to a cross-roads near McKenzie's Farm along which, to our surprise, we found the Russians marching with baggage and

54 Paget, op. cit., p. 52.   55 Ibid. p. 53.

ammunition wagons. The cavalry and Maude's troop advanced and the guns opened upon them, after a chase of about one and a half miles, the Russians running like sheep. Apparently an army of about 20,000 was on the march from Sevastapol in the direction of Bakhchisarai and we took them by surprise.[56]

Captain Walker had meanwhile found the 17th Lancers and the Scots Greys and he brought them up to support the vastly outnumbered Irish Hussars. A troop of dismounted Greys skirmished through the wood. Faced with this determined opposition the last of the Russians fled, leaving the wagon train. Some prisoners were also taken. About seventy wagons fell into the hands of the British troopers. Six held small arms ammunition, of a calibre totally dissimilar to that British weapons, and this was destroyed. The other wagons contained the personal baggage of Prince Menshikov and the officers of the Russian 12th Hussars. Lord Raglan allowed the men to take what they wished from these. An officer of the 8th Royal Irish Hussars described how his men went through the baggage train:

> The troops were allowed to pillage. In a few moments the ground was strewed with every kind of thing … handsome Hussar uniforms, rich fur cloaks, every kind of undergarment, male and female. Several wigs I saw being offered for sale, amidst the laughter of the men. French books and novels of an improper kind were not infrequently met with in the baggage of the Russian officers. All these were offered for sale and disposed of to the highest bidder. A gold Hussar pelisse would sell for about 30s. or £2.[57]

A potential disaster had been averted. Lord Raglan had risked death or capture and the main body of the army could have been surprised. The determination of the British troops present and the confusion among the Russians had resulted in a favourable outcome. When Lord Lucan finally arrived he was greeted abruptly with the statement 'Lord Lucan, you are late.' Lucan made no reply. Lord Cardigan arrived as the wagon train was being looted. Raglan remarked to him, 'The cavalry were out of their proper place. You took them too low down'. Cardigan calmly replied that he 'did not command the cavalry'.[58] This kind of exchange was to become a feature of the war. Lord Lucan was to bear the blame for all mistakes committed by the Cavalry Division.

It could not be denied that the cavalry commanders had performed badly. Apart from the fundamental mistake in map-reading, no outriders had been posted and the ancillary roads were not scouted. The cavalry had failed in one of its primary duties, that of reconnaissance. If the Cavalry Division was 'the

56 NLI, MS 19,359. Fortescue diary, 25 September 1854. The 'Maude's troop' mentioned is a reference to Captain Maude's 'I' Troop, Royal Horse Artillery.   **57** J. Gough Calthorpe, *Letters from headquarters* (London, 1857), i, pp 217–18.   **58** Woodham-Smith, op. cit., p. 200.

eyes and ears' of the army, then the allied army was indeed blind and deaf. This became manifestly apparent later in the same day when a troop of the 4th Light Dragoons came across the main Russian army, 10,000 strong, within three miles of McKenzie's Farm where Lord Raglan and his staff had settled down for the evening. Despite the previous scare, no orders were given to reconnoitre the area until late in the day. It was not uncommon during the campaign for large bodies of troops to pass close to each other totally undetected.

By 27 September 1854, British and French troops were gathered on the heights above Sevastapol. The flank march had been carried out successfully, due more to good fortune than planning. The allied army was now spread out over a wide area and, after the contact at McKenzie's Farm, the Russians were aware of the army's position. Lord Raglan greatly feared an attack while the troops were in this disorganised state and later wrote that 'we were in a dangerous situation'. The voice of caution won out in allied councils, and a decision was made not to attack Sevastapol immediately. A siege operation was decided on with Balaclava chosen as headquarters. The general who was particularly influential in deciding this course of action was General Sir John Fox Burgoyne, the officer commanding the army's engineers. Burgoyne, who was a Peninsular war veteran, served as chairman of the Irish Board of Public Works from 1831 to 1845, and was appointed as a relief commissioner in 1847.[59] He suggested that the allied army should move to the south of Sevastapol and begin constructing siege lines. While the allied commanders discussed this course of action, the Russians took the opportunity to strengthen the town's defences. The soundness of Lord Raglan's decisions at this point and his reliance on Burgoyne's advice have often been questioned.

By marching south from Calamita Bay to Balaclava it had become necessary to cross a series of rivers, the Bulganek, the Alma, the Katcha, the Belbeck and lastly the Tchernaya. This choice of route caused delays and unnecessary hardships. Each river posed practical problems and also the possibility of an attack by the Russians. A more direct route would have been to simply sail into Balaclava, as it was virtually undefended, and then march on Sevastapol. This was what the last of the heavy cavalry actually did, leaving Varna between 24 and 27 September 1854 and sailing into Balaclava with a Royal Navy escort. The Inniskillings were the last to arrive on 7 October 1854, delayed by the *Europa* fire.

French and British troops spent twenty-eight days, from 27 September to 25 of October 1854, in the area around Sevastapol without any contact with the Russians. It was not until 9 October 1854 that they began digging siege

---

59 General's Burgoyne's son, Lieutenant (later Captain) Hugh Talbot Burgoyne RN was born in Kingstown and won the VC during the war.

trenches. On 17 October 1854 the actual bombardment of Sevastapol began. The cavalry spent most of this time patrolling as Lord Raglan had realized that, with his troops concentrated around Sevastapol in siege positions, he was in danger of being attacked from the rear. The task of guarding the rear of the allied siege lines fell to the cavalry and they were kept constantly on the alert. Major Phillips of the 8th Royal Irish Hussars wrote of 'alarms night and day; horses kept saddled for three days at a time, and ever ready'.[60]

Both Raglan and Menshikov realized the precarious nature of the allied position. If Balaclava was attacked and retaken the French and British troops would be in an impossible position. All chances of supply and re-enforcement would be lost while Lord Raglan would be caught between two Russian armies. The resources available for the defence of Balaclava were small, the majority of the allied army being committed to the siege operations. Lord Raglan had a detachment of marines, the Cavalry Division, 500 men of the 93rd Highlanders and about 2,500 Turkish infantry to defend Balaclava. In terms of artillery he had 'I' Troop Royal Horse Artillery, a battery of Royal Field Artillery and naval guns placed in Balaclava and in a series of redoubts along the Woronzow Road. The whole allied campaign relied on this road as the sole means of re-supplying the armies at Sevastapol. Due to his lack of confidence in the Turks, Lord Raglan had stationed them in the redoubts along either side of the road. The Russian attempt to take the port and control the Woronzow road resulted in the famous battle of Balaclava on 25 October 1854. Indeed the later battles of Little Inkerman (26 October 1854), Inkerman (5 November 1854) and Tchernaya (16 August 1855) represented further attempts by the Russians to capture Balaclava in order to cut the allied armies lines of supply.

Irishmen in the Cavalry Division

The Crimean war is still viewed by many as a 'cavalry war', due to the fame that the charge of the Light Brigade during the battle of Balaclava later achieved. In reality it was the courage and determination of the infantry which won the crucial battles of the Alma, Little Inkerman and Inkerman. The infantry, artillery and engineers also had to prosecute the siege of Sevastapol. In reality the Cavalry Division did not play a major part in the war. Despite this, the charge of the Light Brigade became the stuff of poetry and has had numerous histories written about it.[61] Due to this fact, and also due to the fact that many Irishmen served with the brigade, it is worth examining the role of the cavalry in the war.

60 Paget, op. cit., p. 59.   61 In December 1854, Tennyson wrote his famous poem 'The charge

It is often stated that the Cavalry Division that served in the Crimean war was the finest body of mounted troops ever to leave the shores of the Britain. This is true up to a point. They were well-equipped, well-mounted and their morale was high. The troops were, however, inexperienced and badly led. The Chobham Camp exercises of 1853 had also shown that the men were seemingly unable to care for themselves in the field. While there had been spectacular cavalry successes in recent wars in India, such as at the battle of Aliwal in 1846, the British army had not fought a European army since Waterloo. Officers tended to dislike serving in India and would often go on half-pay if their regiment was ordered there. Because of this attitude, the majority of the Cavalry Division's officers in the Crimea had not experienced active service in India. Indeed officers who had served in India were often viewed as social inferiors and were discriminated against. Colonel William Ferguson Beatson had served in India and in the First Carlist war and was eminently qualified to command a cavalry brigade. In the Crimea, however, he was given command of Turkish irregulars before serving as an ADC to Brigadier-General the Hon. James Yorke Scarlett. Beatson was typical of the many officers whose experience of active service was ignored.

The Cavalry Division was to be made up of squadrons of both heavy and light cavalry, formed into separate brigades. The Heavy Brigade, commanded by Brigadier-General the Hon. James Yorke Scarlett numbered around 1,300 men. Squadrons of the following regiments made up the Heavy Brigade:

> 1st (Royal) Regiment of Dragoons.
> 2nd (Royal North British) Regiment of Dragoons (Scots Greys).
> 4th (Royal Irish) Regiment of Dragoon Guards.
> 5th (Princess Charlotte of Wales) Regiment of Dragoon Guards.
> 6th (Inniskilling) Regiment of Dragoons.[62]

These regiments had all been stationed in Ireland during the previous ten years and there were many Irishmen serving in their ranks. The Scots Greys sent two service squadrons to the Crimea during the war and three of the regiment's twenty-four officers were Irish. Just over 580 of the regiment's troopers served in the Crimea. Forty of these were Irish.[63] In fact, the regiment's youngest trooper in the Crimea was Edward Farrell, who had enlisted in February 1852, aged 15.[64]

---

of the Light Brigade' after reading W.H. Russell's account of the charge in *The Times*. In March 1881, he began writing his little-known poem 'The charge of the Heavy Brigade'. This first appeared in *Macmillan's Magazine* in March 1882. The last two lines read 'Glory to each and to all, and the charge they made! Glory to all the three hundred, and all the Brigade!'. Christopher Ricks (ed.), *The poems of Tennyson* (London, 1969).   **62** All regimental titles from H.G. Hart, *New Annual Army List* (1854).   **63** The Royal Scots Dragoon Guards Museum, Edinburgh, MS GB46 G176–9, 'Nominal Roll of the officers and men who sailed with the Scots Greys for the Crimea'.   **64** The Royal Scots Dragoon Guards Museum, Edinburgh, 'D' Troop Roll Book, 1857.

The Light Brigade, commanded by Major-General the earl of Cardigan, was made up of service squadrons of the following regiments:

    4th (The Queen's Own) Regiment of Light Dragoons.
    8th (The King's Royal Irish) Regiment of Light Dragoons (Hussars).
    11th (Prince Albert's Own) Regiment of Hussars.
    13th Regiment of Light Dragoons.
    17th Regiment of Light Dragoons(Lancers).

In addition, six guns of the Royal Horse Artillery were brigaded with the Cavalry Division to provide support. Command of the Cavalry Division was held by Lieutenant-General the earl of Lucan.

Recruiting officers and NCOs had, over the previous decade, had tried to retain the character of the Irish regiments. Also, both the 5th Dragoon Guards and the 11th Hussars, while not classed as Irish regiments, had been stationed in Ireland before the outbreak of the Crimean war. The 5th Dragoon Guards had been based in Dublin at Islandbridge Barracks since 1850. It can be assumed that a certain number of Irishmen joined the regiment during the years stationed there. Indeed the regiment was known as 'The Green Horse' due to the colour of regiment's uniform facings. It was said that by the 1850s this could also be taken to refer to the large number of Irish in its ranks. The 11th Hussars, under the command of Lord Cardigan, was stationed at Portobello Barracks at the outbreak of the war. They had been in Ireland since 1852, and had been stationed in Dundalk and Newbridge before to coming to Dublin.

From a study of the muster rolls for the regiments of the Light Brigade for the years from 1854 to 1857, information regarding the number of Irish in each regiment can be discerned (see Table 3).

Table 3. Irishmen in the Light Brigade, 1854–7

Regiment	Service Sqd.	Replacements	Total	Irish
4th Light Dragoons	300	54	354	27 (7.6%)
8th RI Hussars	313	91	404	91 (22.75%)
11th Hussars	315	163	478	27 (5.6%)
13th Light Dragoons	312	29	318	30 (9.3%)
17th Lancers	314	177	491	53 (10.6%)

Sources: Muster Rolls for the Light Brigade regiments, 1854–57. PRO WO 12/659–661 (4th Light Dragoons); PRO WO 12/844–848 (8th Royal Irish Hussars); PRO WO12/1012–1017 (11th Hussars); PRO WO 12/1118–1120 (13th Light Dragoons); PRO WO 12/1339–1341 (17th Lancers).

Two Hundred and tweny-eight of the men who served with the regiments of the Light Brigade between 1854 and 1857 were Irish, around 11% of the total force. The 228 described here as Irish were those who were definitely born in Ireland. Information regarding place of birth on muster rolls of this period is not complete and entries for many of the enlisted men do not provide this information. It is possible, therefore, that there were more Irishmen present but that their origin was not noted on their enlistment details. For instance, there is no reference to the birthplace of Edward Grennan on the muster rolls of the 4th Light Dragoons. In 1896, Fr Patrick Duffy SJ, who had served in the Crimea as a chaplain, met Grennan in Australia.[65] Grennan told him that he was from Mountrath in Queen's County, yet the muster rolls do not record this. It is also unwise to assume that men with typically Irish names such as 'O'Reilly' or 'Kelly' were in fact Irish-born. While such men undoubtedly had Irish parents or ancestors, it is common to find details of English birth in such cases. Sergeant Joseph Malone, who won the Victoria Cross at Balaclava, was born in Eccles, Lancashire, and would be a typical example of one of these soldiers with an Irish name but who was born in England. Of these 228 Irishmen serving with the regiments of the Light Brigade in the Crimea, 15 were officers and 213 were enlisted men

The number of Irish varied from regiment to regiment and it would be incorrect to assume that Irish regiments were composed of Irishmen. At the outbreak of the Crimean war the 8th Royal Irish Hussars was stationed at Exeter. The regiment had headquarters at Canterbury and Bombay and had not been stationed in Ireland since 1850. The 17th Lancers had the next greatest number of Irishmen in the ranks of its service squadron. In 1854 the 17th Lancers were stationed at Brighton with the regimental headquarters at Canterbury and Bengal. Conversely the 11th Hussars had been stationed in Ireland for several years before the war but had a far smaller number of Irishmen in its ranks. It could be argued that the 17th Lancers had a high public profile. The money lavished on them while under Lord Lucan's command was common knowledge. Known as 'Bingham's Dandies' the opportunity of enlisting in such a unit could well have been more attractive for prospective recruits. Yet the reputation of Lord Cardigan's 11th Hussars, 'the Cherrybums', was equally well known and they also had the advantage of being stationed in Ireland. In this light the success of the 17th Lancers in attracting Irish recruits is less easy to explain.

When the above regiments were ordered to provide service squadrons for the war in the East, they also set up depot troops at Newbridge and Maidstone, to

---

65 Irish Jesuit Archives, Dublin, MS J 457. Letter of Fr Patrick Duffy to Sr Mary Agnes of the Carmelite Convent in Tallaght, 21 November 1896.

enlist and train new recruits. The muster rolls for the Light Brigade regiments usually include the date of enlistment of each man. With this information the success of the recruiting drive of 1854 can be assessed. The majority of the Irishmen in the Light Brigade in the Crimea were men who had served for many years. Most had enlisted in the 1840s while a few men had enlisted in the 1830s. None of the Irish troopers of the 4th Light Dragoons enlisted after March 1854. Only three men joined the 8th Royal Irish Hussars after the outbreak of war, while seven joined the 11th Hussars. The Irishmen of the 13th Light Dragoons were all men with long service records, none joining after March 1854. Most had joined the regiment in the early 1840s. One trooper, C. O'Neill had enlisted before 1835. The most recent Irishman to join was Thomas Moody, who had enlisted with the 13th Light Dragoons in July 1853. The 17th Lancers was more successful with fourteen new Irish recruits after March 1854. The majority of Irishmen in this regiment had joined during the 1840s, whereas one trooper, Patrick S. Fagan, had been serving since 1830.

There is something of a disparity here, for the 8th Royal Irish Hussars, the regiment with the largest number of Irishmen in its ranks, can be seen to have attracted very few new recruits in the 1850s. The 8th Royal Irish Hussars muster rolls provide information that leads to some form of explanation. From 1844 to 1850 the regiment was stationed in Ireland and was here during the Famine. The regimental official history makes no mention of the conditions in the country, but it can hardly be coincidental that the a large number of the 8th Royal Irish Hussars' Irish troopers enlisted at this time. Five Irishmen enlisted in 1845, nineteen in 1846, eleven in 1847 and four in 1848. It could be argued, therefore, that many of these men enlisted in the regiment due to economic necessity. This could explain the large number of Irishmen serving in 1854 with the regiment as the effects of the Famine could have caused an increase in the number of Irishmen coming forward to enlist. The high number of Irishmen in the 17th Lancers is less easy to explain, especially when the numbers joining the regiment in 1854 are considered.

Details as to the trades of thirty-three of these men before their enlistment in the Light Brigade regiments were recorded on the muster rolls. There were twelve labourers, five servants, three grooms, three shoemakers, two woollen drapers, a butler, a blacksmith, a brass polisher, an engraver, a tailor, a saddler, a linen dyer and a ship's chandler. Information regarding the exact places of origin of these men is too incomplete to form the basis of any conclusions. It was common for attesting officers to merely write 'born in Ireland' when giving the details of an enlisted man's origins. Where further details were recorded they show that the geographical spread in terms of recruitment was wide. Enlisted men came from Dublin, Kildare, Cork, Meath, Westmeath, Offaly, Limerick, Antrim, the Lagan valley, Wicklow and Waterford. In short, most counties were represented.

Yet the information was not recorded in a large number of cases and therefore no
conclusions can now be reached to illustrate how different areas were represented.

Fourteen of the officers of the Light Brigade were Irish, among them some
men from the wealthiest families in Ireland. Lord Killeen, who was serving
with the 8th Royal Irish Hussars, was heir to the earldom of Fingal and large
estates in Co. Meath. John, Viscount Fitzgibbon, also serving with the 8th
Royal Irish Hussars, was heir to the earldom of Clare and estates in Clare and
Limerick. William Henry Palmer of the 11th Hussars was heir to large estates
in Mayo and Sligo. There was an interesting mix in the composition of the
officer corps of these regiments. There were men from titled families, college
alumni and even two men who risen from the ranks. The list of Irish officers
and warrant officers is as follows:[66]

Arthur James Plunkett, Lord Killeen and later 10th earl of Fingal. Born May
    1819, commissioned 1839 and, in 1854, a captain in the 8th Royal Irish
    Hussars. Eldest son of Arthur James Plunkett, 9th earl of Fingal and Baron
    Killeen of Killeen Castle, Co. Meath.[67]

John Charles Henry, Viscount Fitzgibbon. Born May 1829, commissioned
    1850. In 1854, a lieutenant in the 8th Royal Irish Hussars. The only legiti-
    mate son of Richard Hobart Fitzgibbon, 3rd earl of Clare.[68]

Cornet John Reilly, 8th Royal Irish Hussars. Enlisted 1848 and was commis-
    sioned 1854. Later served with 4th Light Dragoons.

Assistant Surgeon Henry Somers, 8th Royal Irish Hussars. Born 1819 in Dublin
    he entered the army in 1845. Promoted to surgeon in August 1854, he later
    served in the hospital at Chatham.

Lieutenant George Powell Houghton, 11th Hussars. Commissioned in 1853. The
    only son of George Powell Houghton JP, of Kilmanock House, Wexford.

Lieutenant Roger William Henry Palmer, 11th Hussars. Born 1832, commissioned
    1853, he was promoted to captain in July 1859 and later served in the Life
    Guards. The only son of Sir William Palmer, 4th baronet, of Castle Lackin,
    Co Mayo.

Cornet Arthur Lyttleton-Annesley, 11th Hussars. Born 1837, commissioned 1854,
    the eldest son of Arthur Lyttleton-Annesley of Camolin Park, Wexford.

---

66 Muster Rolls for the Light Brigade regiments, 1854–57. PRO WO 12/659–661 (4th Light
Dragoons); PRO WO 12/844–848 (8th Royal Irish Hussars); PRO WO12/1012–1017 (11th
Hussars); PRO WO 12/1118–1120 (13th Light Dragoons); PRO WO 12/1339–1341 (17th
Lancers).   **67** Lodge, *Peerage and baronetage* (1859), p. 243. See also Burke, *Peerage* (1970),
p. 1010.   **68** Lodge, *Peerage and baronetage* (1859), p. 131. Burke, *Peerage* (1912), p. 434. See
also Viscount Dillon, 'Irishmen in the Light Brigade, Balaclava, 1854' in *Irish Sword*, xii, no. 48
(Summer 1976), 254–6. Richard Hobart Fitzgibbon, 3rd earl of Clare, had married the divorcee,

Cornet William Daniel Kelly, 11th Hussars. Originally an enlisted man, he was commissioned in 1853.

Lieutenant-Colonel Charles Edmund Doherty, officer commanding the13th Light Dragoons. Commissioned in 1835.

The Hon. John William Hely-Hutchinson. Born September 1830, the second son of John Hely-Hutchinson, 3rd earl of Donoughmore. Commissioned 1847 and, in 1854, a captain in the 13th Light Dragoons.[69]

Cornet Hugh Montgomery, 13th Light Dragoons. Born 1830, eldest son of Hugh Montgomery of Ballydrain, Co. Antrim. Commissioned 1851.

Captain Robert White, 17th Lancers. Born 1827 in Dublin, educated at Trinity College, commissioned 1847.

Captain John Pratt Winter, 17th Lancers. Born 1829, commissioned 1848, son of Samuel Pratt Winter of Agher, Co. Meath.

Cornet John Chadwick, 17th Lancers. Born in Dublin, commissioned 1852, later served with 15th Light Dragoons and was adjutant of the Royal Hospital, Kilmainham.[70]

The battle of Balaclava

On the morning of 25 October 1854, General Liprandi moved from Tchorgun and positioned his troops to attack the redoubts along the Causeway Heights. His intention was to attack and take the port of Balaclava and thus cut the allied armies' supply route to the siege works at Sevastapol. This plan was in reality very simple and Balaclava was to be the objective of later Russian attacks. Liprandi was in command of the Russian 12th Division: 25 battalions of infantry, 35 squadrons of cavalry and 78 guns, a division of over 25,000 men. At around 5 a.m. the first reports of this Russian advance reached the allied camp and the cavalry stood to. Lord Lucan went up the valley with his staff to reconnoitre. On approaching No. 1 Redoubt on Canrobert's Hill they noticed that two ensigns were flying from its flagstaff. This was the pre-arranged signal for a Russian advance. The attack developed quickly. Cavalry vedettes signalled approaching infantry and cavalry. Immediately after this the Turks in No. 1 Redoubt opened fire on the advancing Russians. The battle of Balaclava had begun. It was just 6 a.m.

Lucan sent an ADC back to headquarters asking for reinforcements. Due to the size of the attacking Russian force, he felt that it was unlikely that he could

Diana Brydges Woodcock, in 1825. They already had a son at the time of their marriage who was not a legitimate heir to the earldom. **69** Lodge, *Peerage* (1859), p. 191. **70** Hart, *Army List*

check their progress with just his own division. Lord Raglan ordered the 1st and 4th Divisions to leave the siege lines at Sevastapol and to come to his assistance. Both divisions faced at least a two hour march. Due to various delays it was 10.30 a.m. before these reinforcements arrived. Lord Raglan and Lord Lucan were forced to fight the initial stages of the battle with the forces at hand.

The performance of the Turkish troops on the day has often been denigrated. Most contemporary accounts state that the Turks broke and fled immediately on seeing the size of the Russian army. Captain Fortescue recorded in his diary that the Turks offered no resistance and similar observations were made by many officers in their diaries and letters.[71] The idea that the Turks fled has been included in most histories of the war but modern research has shown that this accusation was untrue.[72] The Turks in both No. 1 and No. 2 redoubt delayed the Russian advance for over an hour. They were supported by 'I' Troop Royal Horse Artillery under Captain Maude. Maude brought his guns into action around No.1 redoubt, causing havoc in the first wave of Russian troops, but was himself badly wounded twenty minutes into the battle. Eventually, having suffered around 170 casualties and seeing that no reinforcements were arriving, the Turks were driven out of the first two redoubts. On seeing this, the Turks in the next two redoubts also fled. A moment of panic followed, the Turks being pursued by Cossacks until Lord Lucan sent forward his division and checked the Russian advance. The Turkish and British troops then retreated into the south valley, covered by the remaining members of 'I' Troop and a battery of the Royal Field Artillery. Lord George Paget described the feeling of retreating 'by alternate regiments, one of the most painful ordeals it is possible to conceive … seeing all our defences in our front successively abandoned … and straining our eyes in vain all round the hills in our rear for indications of support'.[73]

Until this time the two brigades of the Cavalry Division had not engaged the enemy. Around 8.45 a.m. the Russian sent four squadrons of cavalry to attack the village of Kadikoi to the north of Balaclava. The action that immediately followed became known as the fight of the 'Thin Red Line'.[74] The 93rd Regiment (Sutherland Highlanders) under Sir Colin Campbell broke all the rules of nineteenth century warfare by successfully stopping a cavalry charge while still formed up in a line four-deep. It was unheard of to face advancing cavalry without forming square, yet Campbell correctly gauged the mood of his own men. After two volleys the Russians turned and fled. It was now around 9 a.m.

Throughout this fighting the cavalry had remained inactive. The Cavalry Division was drawn up to the north of No. 6 redoubt, below the Chersonese

---

(1854).   71 NLI, MS 19,359. Fortescue diary, 25 October 1854.   72 Mark Adkin, *The charge* (London,1996).   73 Lord George Paget, *The Light Cavalry Brigade in the Crimea* (London, 1861), pp 165–6.   74 The 'Thin Red Line' was a phrase used by the Irish correspondent William

Uplands. At 9.15 a.m. the main body of the Russian cavalry under General Rikov began to advance along the North Valley. The Heavy Brigade under General Scarlett had just been ordered to move towards Balaclava to support the wavering Turks and were now moving along the South Valley. Both Scarlett and Rikov were unaware that their forces were in such close proximity as the high ground of the Causeway Heights between the two valleys impeded their view. From his position on the Sapouné Heights Lord Raglan could see this 'black-looking mass' of Russian cavalry and when it wheeled to its left he felt sure that his heavy cavalry were about to be annihilated. Neither body of cavalry had thrown out flankers or scouts. Lieutenant Alexander Elliot, an ADC to General Scarlett, later told the historian, A.W. Kinglake, how he glanced to the ridge on his left and 'saw its top fretted with lances. Another moment and the sky-line was broken by evident squadrons of horse'.[75] To his credit Scarlett immediately decided to charge to meet this threat. He had six squadrons with him, marching in two columns, numbering around 300 men. Due to the rough terrain the right-hand column had fallen behind. Scarlett formed up the three squadrons he had to hand, one squadron of the Inniskillings and two of the Scots Greys.

The Russians for their part seemed totally taken aback to find this British cavalry to their front. Lord Paget recorded 'the Russians halt, look about, and appear bewildered, as if they were at a loss to know what to do next. The impression of which bewilderment is forcibly engraven on my mind.'[76] They advanced down the hill and then came to a halt throwing out columns to left and right like the pincers of a scorpion and awaited the British charge. This was breaking one of the fundamental rules of cavalry warfare as it was unheard of to stand and receive a charge at the halt. After taking time to dress the alignment of his three squadrons, Scarlett led his men up the hill at the gallop, eager to get at the Russians while they stood motionless. The Inniskillings and the Greys eagerly followed him, charging together for the first time since Waterloo. When the two sides met the Russians closed in around the British troopers and furious fighting followed.

The fact that Scarlett's second column was delayed was actually a blessing on this occasion. The squadron of the 5th Dragoon Guards charged into the centre of the Russians when they arrived. The second squadron of Inniskillings attacked the Russian left while the 4th Royal Irish Dragoon Guards attacked the right. The Royals, while supposedly in reserve, also arrived and took part in the action. The Russians were now faced with British cavalry fighting uncowed in

---

Howard Russell in one of his dispatches.   **75** A.W. Kinglake, *The invasion of the Crimea: its origin and progress down to the death of Lord Raglan* (London, 1868–87), v., p. 89.   **76** Lord George Paget, *Light Cavalry Brigade*, p. 175.

the centre of their formation. Also, as they had closed in around Scarlett and his men, the British squadrons that arrived later caught the Russians facing inwards. The Russian cavalrymen, never over-confident, began to surge back and forth looking for a way to disengage. One of the best accounts of the confused fighting was written by an unknown Inniskilling Dragoon who sent a letter home in November 1854. He described the initial contact thus:

> The way the Russians form line is … with their Regiment on the centre and on the right and left flank they place their Cossack Lancers. As soon as our own squadron charged them their flanks whip round and covered us for a moment … so as Lord Lucan thought we were annihilated, it was for a moment only. Then you could see the Bold Inniskillings cutting and slashing away … it was only us and the Scotch Greys that charged. General Scarlett was in the midst of the fight and he kept saying 'Go along Inniskillings! The Greys are on your left!'. We got great praise for the day's work … we drove the enemy back and retook the batteries and we didn't leave the field till near midnight. Our regiment only lost two killed and twelve wounded.[77]

He went on to tell of his own part in the fighting:

> Now I will tell you what happened to me in the midst of the action. I charged some Cossacks and one of them shot my horse in the shoulder and he fell, almost dead, when I mounted a horse belonging to the 5th Dragoon Guards and a hat belonging to the Scotch Greys which I kept there all day. Then I fought with a Russian officer some time. Then some Cossacks came to his release but I managed to get his Gold Lace cocked hat and took off the lace. I got great praise for my day's work.[78]

It is ironic indeed that this successful cavalry action was overshadowed by the disastrous charge of the Light Brigade that followed a little later in the day. The casualties of the 'heavies' were light while the Russians finally broke and fled in disorder along the North Valley. The opportunity to pursue and totally rout this Russian force was lost, Lord Cardigan refusing to commit the Light Brigade to a pursuit despite the entreaties of his officers. In reality the fate of the Light Brigade was now sealed. The Russian cavalry and accompanying artillery retreated to the end of the North Valley and deployed. This was the position that the Light Brigade would later charge, having lost the opportunity to engage these Russian forces while they were on the move. It was now around 9.30 a.m. and an hour of total inactivity passed while the Russians strengthened their positions in the North Valley, on the Fedioukine Hills and on the Causeway Heights. At 10.30 a.m. the 1st and 4th Divisions began to arrive

77 NAM, MS 7703–52, letter of an unidentified Inniskilling Dragoon, 8 November 1854. The end of this letter was later damaged and the name of the trooper who wrote it has been lost. 78 Ibid. 79 Mark Adkin, *The charge* (London, 1996), p. 121.

on the plain and Raglan at last had his infantry support. Yet at the same time he noticed that the Russians were bringing up gun-teams to remove the guns in the captured redoubts. Conscious that his mentor the duke of Wellington had never lost a gun on campaign, he sent an order to Lord Lucan, the third to the cavalry division that day. It read:

> Cavalry to advance and take advantage of any opportunity to recover the Heights. They will be supported by infantry, which have been ordered on two fronts.[79]

Lucan on reading this simply re-aligned his division and waited for the infantry to arrive. He totally misread the meaning of the order and thought that he was to support the infantry attack while the reverse was the case. While the cavalry sat inactive valuable time was lost. All the while Lord Raglan became more agitated as he watched the Russians prepare to tow away the guns. Eventually he hastily dictated his ambiguous 'Fourth Order' and handed it to Captain Louis Edward Nolan to deliver to Lucan. It is worth taking some time here to discuss the origins of Captain Nolan as it would be difficult to find an historical character about whom so much utter rubbish has been written. The *DNB* records that he was born in Milan in about 1818 and this statement was apparently based on earlier accounts of his Nolan's life which appeared in A.W. Kinglake's and E.H. Nolan's histories of the Crimean war and also George Ryan's *Our heroes of the Crimea* (London, 1855).

This statement has been repeated in almost every book on the Crimea that has been written since 1855. It is true that Nolan's father, Major John Babington Nolan, worked as a consular agent in Milan (he was not the British vice-consul, as is usually stated) and that he spent his childhood in Italy, but Nolan was not born there. Also his mother was not an Italian, as has sometimes been stated. She was a Scot, Elizabeth Harleston Ruddach, and Nolan was born in Perth, Scotland in 1818. There is some excuse for finding these errors in books written before 1971 but, in that year, a retired British Army colonel, H. Moyse-Bartlett, wrote a comprehensive biography of Nolan, *Louis Edward Nolan and his influence on the British cavalry* (Leo Cooper, London, 1971). Moyse-Bartlett had access to Nolan family papers and was able to write an accurate biography of this fascinating figure. Yet books still appear stating that Nolan was born in Milan.

From an Irish perspective the story became more confused in 1954 when someone placed a query in the *Sunday Independent* asking if anyone knew where Nolan was born. Three conflicting replies to this query were printed – that he had been born in Kyleballyhue House, Co. Carlow, Crumlin in Dublin, and Tulsk, Co. Roscommon. This information was printed in the *Irish Sword* in

1955 in that journal's 'Queries' section. While Nolan's father was born in Co. Carlow (as was his grandfather), there is no evidence to suggest that Nolan was born in Ireland, or that he even visited here.[80] Also it has often been stated that Nolan and Cardigan hated each other, yet they never served together. Indeed, when Cardigan was appointed to command the Light Brigade, he tried to get Nolan on his staff. The misconceptions that have built up around Nolan are a prime example of how the inaccuracies and assumptions published by nineteenth century authors can affect the modern historiography of the war.

Just before 11.00 a.m. Captain Nolan delivered the fourth order to Lord Lucan. It read:

> Lord Raglan wishes the cavalry to advance rapidly to the front-follow the enemy and try to prevent the enemy carrying away the guns-Troop Horse Artillery may accompany-French cavalry is on your left.
>
> R. Airey
> Immediate.[81]

This rather ambiguous order was intended to send the Light Brigade to recover the captured guns in the redoubts. Lucan dithered, unable to grasp the meaning of the communication, apparently not reading the third and fourth orders in conjunction. Feeling that he was ordered to attack the main Russian position at the end of the valley, he later stated that he 'urged the uselessness of such an attack, and the dangers attending it'. On questioning the matter further Nolan erupted in a fit of impatient temper at Lucan's indecision. Pointing down the valley he replied heatedly, 'There, my Lord, is your enemy, there are your guns'. This series of events and excited exchanges set the Light Brigade on its ill-fated charge towards the Russian guns.

The front line of the brigade was formed by the 17th Lancers (Lucan's old regiment) and the 13th Light Dragoons, 147 and 128 men respectively. The second line was formed by the 11th Hussars, 142 men. The third line was formed by the 4th Light Dragoons and the 8th Royal Irish Hussars, 126 and

80 Also the 1968 film, *The charge of the Light Brigade*, starring David Hemmings as Nolan, has caused further misconceptions to creep in. The character in the film was a composite of several actual people and some of the events in the film never happened to Nolan. Yet while talking with people about Nolan, several have discussed events that he was never involved in, such as the 'Black Bottle Affair' of 1840. In May 1840, Lord Cardigan had Captain John Reynolds put under arrest for having a black Moselle bottle on the table of the 11th Hussars mess during dinner. Cardigan had assumed that it contained porter. The case was covered in detail in the British and Irish press.   **81** Mark Adkin, *The charge* (London, 1996), p. 127. Also NAM, 'The 4th Order from Lord Raglan to the Cavalry Division, 25 October 1854'. The haste with which this order was written is obvious by the total lack of punctuation. Also witnesses remembered Lord Raglan dictating an addition to Airey when he read the order back. It is generally held that the addition was the word 'Immediate'. Airey's handwriting was also fairly atrocious … recently described as 'not perhaps the best handwriting to read in a hurry under pressure'.

115 men.[82] Of the 1,570 light cavalrymen who had embarked for the Crimea, there were now only 658 fit for duty, approximately 42% of the original strength. While some troops were absent on despatch and escort duties (a full troop of the 8th Royal Irish Hussars was escorting Lord Raglan), sickness had greatly reduced their number. Lord Cardigan and his staff were present, to the front of the brigade, another three men. This makes a total of 661 men, supported by the carefully compiled official returns after the charge.

There were, however, undoubtedly more men present. Some modern historians of the charge support the figure of 673 men, increasing the figure by taking into account the claims of some paymasters and medical staff who later claimed to have ridden in the charge. It is now certain that there were some 'extras'. There were two Sardinian officers, Maggiore Govone and Luogotenente Landrani, officially at the front as observers for Sardinia-Piedmont. Despite the fact that their country had not declared war on Russia at this point, they insisted on taking part in the charge.[83] The butcher of the 17th Lancers, Private John Veigh (sometimes referred to as Vahy or Fahy), joined his regiment with the horse and equipment of a dead 'heavy' while still wearing his butcher's apron. The most bizarre 'charger' of the day was perhaps the rough-haired Irish terrier 'Jemmy'. The mascot of the officers of the 8th Royal Irish Hussars, he was noticed sitting behind Troop Sergeant-Major Harrison and Cornet Clowes as the regiment formed up. Jemmy scampered up and down the valley with his masters, suffering only a small cut to his neck.[84]

One hundred and fourteen of the men who formed up with these five regiments were noted on muster rolls as being Irish. The breakdown of Irishmen in each regiment will be given in a table later, but the regiment with the highest number of Irishmen was the 8th Royal Irish Hussars with forty-one. If we take the lower figure for the total strength of the Light Brigade, 661, approximately 17% of the brigade was Irish on 25 October 1854.[85]

The story of the charge of the Light Brigade has been told and retold. Yet the experience of the Irish officers and troopers deserves some attention. The 8th Royal Irish Hussars were to play a significant part in the fighting. Private Anthony Sheridan from Cavan, was a member of 'E' Troop of the 8th Royal Irish Hussars. On the twenty-first anniversary of the battle of Balaclava he

82 Adkin, op. cit., pp 12–20. It is now generally felt that when Lucan re-aligned the Brigade he wanted a 2/2/1 formation, with the 8th Royal Irish Hussars forming the third line by themselves. This order was misunderstood, resulting in the peculiar formation above. 83 Mike Hinton, 'Sardinians who charged' in *The war correspondent*, xvii, no. 4 (January 2000), pp 42–4. Govone was a staff officer while Landrani was an officer of the Reggimento Piedmonte Reale Cavalleria. Both were wounded in the charge and Landrani was captured. 84 Adkin, *The charge*, pp 12–20. 85 Muster Rolls for the Light Brigade regiments, 1854–57. PRO WO 12/659–661 (4th Light Dragoons); PRO WO 12/844–848 (8th Royal Irish Hussars); PRO WO12/1012–1017 (11th Hussars); PRO WO 12/1118–1120 (13th Light Dragoons); PRO WO 12/1339–1341 (17th

described to a correspondent of the *Illustrated London News* how he spent his morning:

> On the morning of that memorable day we stood with our horses saddled and ready for any emergency. Lord Raglan and his staff were on the hills above us, surveying the Russians with their field glasses, when they saw, as I supposed, the Turks leave their guns in the redoubt and run for their lives. There were five guns left, and each was loaded and not spiked when the Russians got up to them. Presently Captain Nolan, riding a horse of the 13th Light Dragoons, came up with a paper from Lord Raglan, and we imagined at once that we were to move. The order was for the First Division to charge on the guns left by the Turks, in order, as I suppose, that we might recover them from the enemy. Captain Nolan's words were, so it was reported, 'My Lord, charge on those guns'. I know when I heard the order given at first I said, 'God forgive me, but every man must do his duty'![86]

The commanding officer of the 8th Royal Irish Hussars, Lieutenant-Colonel Shewell had begun his day in his sick-bed but, on hearing that an action was imminent, got up to lead his regiment. On galloping up to take command of his regiment he was horrified to find some of his men smoking. Private John Doyle described the scene:

> I saw as he passed in front of us, that all at once his face expressed the greatest surprise and astonishment and even anger, and, walking on he broke out with – 'What's this? What's this? – one, two, four, six, seven men smoking! – Why the thing is inconceivable! Sergeant! Sergeant Pickworth!' The truth is we were warming our noses each with a short black pipe, and thinking no harm of the matter. 'Sergeant, advance and take these men's names.'[87]

Shewell was also heard to remark that 'no regiment except an Irish regiment would be guilty of it'. It was a tense time for all concerned. Private Denis Connor, an Irishman serving with the 4th Light Dragoons later recalled how his regiment sat waiting to charge:

> I was in the 4th Light Dragoons, now the 4th Hussars, under Lord George Paget. We were drawn up ready on the morning of the charge. All were perfectly cool and collected. When the order was given I heard men chaffing each other. One would tell another that he 'would lose the number of his mess that day', meaning that he would be shot; others said 'Here goes for victory!', whilst others declared they would have Russian biscuits for dinner.[88]

Around 11.00 a.m. Lord Cardigan gave the order to advance and the brigade, gradually increasing speed, began their charge down the valley, receiving fire

Lancers). **86** *Illustrated London News*, 31 Oct. 1875. **87** Anon., *United Service Journal*, Apr. 1856, p. 550. Also John Doyle, *A descriptive account of the famous charge of the Light Brigade at Balaclava* (1877). **88** *Illustrated London News*, 31 Oct. 1875, p. 439. Lord George Paget was

from their front and from both flanks. Private Connor described his experience in the charge thus:

> Lord George led our line gallantly. There was no flinching; but he made us laugh as he kept drawling out in his own particular tone, 'Now then men, come on', and on he went certainly. I saw Gowen's horse shot. The animal staggered, turned round two or three times and fell. I was one of those who tried to cut the traces of the Russian guns. I used my pocket knife, but found that within the leather were chains of steel. Our officers did more service with their revolvers than we could with our carbines. They fired five shots to our one, and that seemed to alarm the Russians. I don't think that we were away from our first position on the hill more than twenty minutes, and that included charge and all.[89]

Lieutenant-Colonel Shewell kept the 8th Royal Irish Hussars in firm control during the ride down the valley, never letting the pace of the regiment speed up. Lord George Paget said later that he had ordered Shewell to direct his unit by the progress of the 4th Light Dragoons. Due to Shewell checking the progress of his regiment, it was considerably behind the 4th Light Dragoons when the first line entered the Russian battery. They had also veered to the right of their original alignment, to such an extent that they passed by the right end of the Russian battery. Shewell halted the 8th Royal Irish Hussars three or four hundred yards to the right rear of the Russian guns. Some have claimed that this was a major error. Yet the position of this regiment allowed it to cover the retreat of the remnants of the brigade. Private Sheridan described the confusion that reigned:

> It was almost dark, with smoke and fog, and you didn't know where you were until you ran against a Cossack. You know your blood soon gets warm when you are fighting, and it didn't take us long to find out that we had nothing to do but to give them a point as good as their cut. I got cut with a sword on the forehead at the guns. It was not much, but it has left this scar here (pointing to his forehead). I remember it now. It was fearful. We were cut and shot at from all directions and it was each man for himself. People ask me sometimes if I killed anyone, but I'm not going to tell them, though I gave the Cossacks a great deal more than I got. If those lancers had hemmed us in, it would have been all up with us. I was in the second line going out, but there were no lines going in.[90]

For those who had survived the ordeal so far, it was now a great advantage that the 8th Royal Irish Hussars had become separated from the main body. The Russian cavalry had moved out into the valley and blocked the only route of escape. Lord Cardigan, considering his job completed by leading the brigade

the sixth son (third son by the second marriage) of Henry William Paget, 1st marquess of Anglesey (1768–1854), who commanded the allied cavalry at Waterloo and lost a leg during the battle. **89** Ibid. **90** Ibid.

to the guns, was by now calmly walking his horse back up the valley, leaving his men quite leaderless. The men of the 8th Royal Irish Hussars joined with Lieutenant-Colonel Mayow and some men of the 17th Lancers and Shewell took these under his command. He then noticed the Russian lancers who had debouched from under the Causeway Heights. Shewell immediately decided to charge them. As Lieutenant Phillips later wrote that, before the Russians formed line, they 'charged bang through them, thus opening a way for the remnants of the first line'.[91] In a totally disordered state the survivors of the five regiments made their way back towards their starting point. The charge had taken only twenty to thirty minutes. Still under fire the troopers returned in groups and singly, mounted and dismounted. The Heavy Brigade advancing some way down the valley in support and suffered more casualties here than in their own charge. Lieutenant Seager of the 8th Royal Irish Hussars described his return:

> After I found myself through the Russians, I saw the Colonel and the Major (De Salis) a long distance ahead going as fast as their horses would carry them, the batteries and rifles peppering them in grand style. On looking to see what had become of my men, I found that they had got through and scattered to the left.[92]

The experience of returning back up the valley was fraught with incident. Some men were captured by Cossacks while others caught loose horses and rode back. Sergeant Loy Smith of the 11th Hussars ran and walked back, avoiding enemy cavalry. Private Mitchell of the 13th Light Dragoons was almost captured but was saved due to the timely arrival of the French Chasseurs d'Afrique. Lieutenant Phillips of the 8th Royal Irish Hussars fought his way back with his revolver. The most bizarre retreat was perhaps that of Lieutenant Chamberlayne of the 13th Light Dragoons. Having lost his horse he was determined to keep his saddle and walked with it over his head to his own positions. Apparently the Cossacks roaming in the valley took him for a Russian looter and did not attack him.[93]

During the confusion of the retreat three men went to the aid of a wounded officer of the 17th Lancers, Captain Webb. They remained with him under fire and eventually carried him back for medical attention. In the *London Gazette* of February 1857, it was announced that all three had been awarded the newly instituted Victoria Cross. One of these men was born in Ireland, Quartermaster Sergeant John Farrell of the 17th Lancers. Another of these men was Lance Sergeant Joseph Malone of the 13th Light Dragoons, who had been born in England but was of Irish parents. Farrell's medal citation read:

---

91 Paget, *British cavalry*, ii, p. 100.   **92** NAM, MS 8311–9, the Seager letters, 1 November 1854.
93 Adkin, *The charge*, p. 204.

For having remained amidst a shower of shot and shell with Captain Webb, who was severely wounded, and whom he and Sergeant-Major Berryman had carried as far as pain of his wounds would allow until a stretcher was procured, when he assisted the Sergeant-Major and a Private of the 13th Dragoons (Malone) to carry that officer off the field. This took place on 25 October 1854, after the charge at the Battle of Balaclava, in which Farrell's horse was killed under him.[94]

At the same time that Farrell, Berryman and Malone were helping Captain Webb, the surgeon of one of the Irish regiments, James Mouat of the Inniskillings, had gone out to assist Captain Morris of the 17th Lancers. Assistant Surgeon Cattell, serving with the 5th Dragoon Guards, later wrote of the incident:

Private George Smith informed Sergeant O'Hara of the spot where Morris lay and Scarlett sent the staff surgeon with Troop Sergeant-Major Wooden to bring him in. They found a trooper trying to arrest the bleeding from the scalp. Presently some Cossacks attacked the party and the doctor, Mouat, said he had to draw his sword, which he described as 'a novel experience'.[95]

The experiences of many of the Irishmen on the day tended to rank above the ordinary. Troop Sergeant-Major Denis O'Hara of the 17th Lancers had to rally and take command of the remnants of his troop on the far side of the Russian guns, in the absence of any officers. He was later commissioned. He was accompanied on the day by his brother, James O'Hara, who would later distinguish himself by rescuing a wounded officer at the battle of Inkerman. The most colourful Irishman in the 17th Lancers was Trooper John Smith from Dublin. He was seen in close combat with several Russian gunners and was thereafter known as 'Blood Smith' or 'Fighting Smith'. Cornet Hugh Montgomery of the 13th Light Dragoons from Co. Antrim was equally pugnacious. Attacked by six Russian hussars, the men of his troop watched in amazement as he drew his revolver and shot four dead and then chased the remaining two away. He was killed going to the assistance of two of his men as he returned on foot up the valley. Trooper Thomas Lucas from St Bride's parish, Dublin, was carried in wounded by comrades. On examination it was found that he had received two sabre cuts to the head and five lance wounds to the body. Lieutenant George Powell Houghton from Wexford was hit in the head with a shell fragment as he charged with the 11th Hussars. Mortally wounded, he turned back and, as he was similar in appearance to Lord Cardigan and wore the same uniform, accounts of his return gave rise to stories that Cardigan had turned back early in the charge. Captain John Pratt Winter of the 17th Lancers from Agher, Co. Meath, was seen fighting desperately among the Russian guns. His wounded horse returned but he was never seen again.[96]

94 Farset Youth Ltd, *Ireland's VCs* (Belfast, 1996), p. 10. Farrell was born in Dublin in March 1826.
95 NAM, Autobiography of Assistant-Surgeon William Cattell, 5th Dragoon Guards, p. 13.
96 Adkin, *The charge*.

One of the most intriguing stories of the charge was that of Lord Fitzgibbon, of the 8th Royal Irish Hussars. The heir-apparent of 3rd earl of Clare, born at Mountshannon House, Castleconnell, Co. Limerick in May 1829, he entered the army in March 1850. He charged in the front rank of his regiment at Balaclava and did not return. He was officially listed as missing until Trumpet-Major William Gray and Trumpeter James Heffernon stated that they had seen him hit by two bullets shortly after the charge began. Lieutenant Seager also confirmed that he had missed Fitzgibbon at some point, and later wrote home that 'Fitzgibbon had gone, shot through the body'.[97] It was then assumed that he had been killed. Great efforts were made to find the body among those that were recovered and when these efforts failed it was assumed that the Russians had recovered and buried the body. Yet stories circulated that he had not been killed but only wounded. Several troopers came forward and stated that they had seen him, still mounted, as they returned from the Russian battery. Anthony Sheridan remained adamant, twenty-one years after the event, that he had seen Fitzgibbon:

> I saw Lord Fitzgibbon, who was mortally wounded, pull out his purse and offer it to any one of us who would dismount and accept it, as his Lordship did not like it to get into the hands of the Russians, but Lord!, we did not think of money at such a moment as that.[98]

On the death of the earl of Clare in January 1864, the title became extinct and his eldest daughter, Lady Florence Fitzgibbon, inherited her father's property. Rumours persisted that Lord Fitzgibbon had in fact been captured and, in 1877, reports began to appear in English newspapers claiming that he had returned from captivity in Siberia. Fitzgibbon had some distinctive physical characteristics; he was quite tall, had a cast in his left eye and often wore a monocle. A man matching this description visited the mess of the 8th Royal Irish Hussars in 1877, when the regiment was stationed at Hounslow Barracks. Stating that he was an ex-officer of the regiment, he was invited to dine with the officers and over dinner claimed that he was Lord Fitzgibbon. The story was officially denied yet the family took it seriously enough to place notices in the national papers requesting further information. In November 1877, when none of these notices had been answered, the family had another notice placed in *The Times*, dismissing the story as a mischievous rumour. It is quite possible, considering both the title and property that stood to be inherited, that someone was trying to pull off some form of confidence trick. There was a curious epilogue to this story, however. In 1892, when the 8th Royal Irish Hussars was stationed on the North-

---

97 NAM, MS 8311–9, the Seager letters, 1 November 1854.   **98** *Illustrated London News*, 31 Oct. 1875.

West Frontier in India, an elderly gentleman visited the officers' mess. As in the previous case the gentleman in question knew the regimental traditions and history and also matched the description of Lord Fitzgibbon. Officers were once again discouraged from repeating this story. It is believed that these events inspired Rudyard Kipling's short-story 'The man who was'.[99]

Table 4 shows the Irish casualties of the charge of the Light Brigade. Again it must be stressed that the muster rolls are somewhat incomplete. If a soldier was killed or taken prisoner, this information was usually recorded. It was also usually noted if a soldier was thought to have been wounded when captured. Information regarding those wounded does not always appear on regimental returns. This may account for the seemingly small number of wounded Irishmen. Some of those who charged were given only the slightest of attention on muster returns. The entries for Privates William Moloney and Thomas McNally, both of the 13th Light Dragoons, merely state that they took part in the charge.

Table 4. Irish casualties in the charge of the Light Brigade

Regiment	No. that charged	Irish	Killed	Wounded	Prisoner	Missing
4th Light Dragoons	126	19	5	4	2	1
8th Royal Irish Hussars	115	41	7	3	2	
11th Hussars	142	13	3	3		1
13th Light Dragoons	128	20	2	2	2	
17th Lancers	147	21	4	4	1	

Sources: Muster Rolls for the Light Brigade regiments, 1854–57. PRO WO 12/659–661 (4th Light Dragoons); PRO WO 12/844–848 (8th Royal Irish Hussars); PRO WO12/1012–1017 (11th Hussars); PRO WO 12/1118–1120 (13th Light Dragoons); PRO WO 12/1339–1341 (17th Lancers).

The morning's action had taken a great toll of the Light Brigade. Modern research indicates a death toll of 118, 21 of whom were Irish. One hundred and twenty-seven were returned as wounded, 16 of whom were Irish. Forty-five men were taken prisoner by the Russians, seven of whom were Irish. The regiment with the highest numbers of Irish present was the 8th Royal Irish Hussars. It lost 21 men killed, 19 wounded and 8 captured. It can be seen from the table above that a high proportion of these were Irish. It is now estimated that 362 horses were also killed. This was a tremendous blow as these were virtually impossible to replace. On the morning of 26 October 1854, the 13th Light Dragoons could parade only 18 mounted men. The Heavy Brigade also

99 Dillon, 'Irishmen in the Light Brigade', pp 254–6. See also Kevin Hannon, 'Limerick: The garrison town' in *An Cosantóir* (November 1989), pp 33–4.

suffered casualties but their total losses for the day were 10 killed and 98 wounded. Over half of these occurred while supporting the Light Brigade's retreat and casualties from their own charge were comparatively light. It has been estimated that the Russians lost over 600.[100]

After the battle of Balaclava the strength of the Light Brigade was effectively broken. It was never a viable military formation again. The cavalry would play virtually no part in the battles of Little Inkerman (26 October 1854) or Inkerman (5 November 1854). The harsh effects of the Russian winter caused further casualties of both men and horses. William Howard Russell noted that a batch of 600 horses arrived in the cavalry camp in December 1855. Within three weeks nearly 300 were dead.[101] With such losses in horses it was impossible to maintain an effective cavalry force. Eventually the Cavalry Division was reduced to providing men and horses to carry supplies and wounded to the hospital. Apart from a minor skirmish near Kertch in September 1855 and a reconnaissance 'in force' of the Western Crimea in October 1855, the cavalry played no further part in the campaign.

It has often been suggested by historians of the war that the effect of the two charges on 25 October 1854 was to utterly destroy the confidence of the Russian cavalry. There is no doubt that the Russian troopers seemed to lack a certain *élan*. Yet this could also be attributed to poor Russian leadership. Kinglake has written that 'for a long time afterwards it would have been impracticable to make the Russian cavalry act with anything like confidence in the presence of a few English squadrons'. This statement does not entirely hold true. Many newspaper correspondents wrote of the aggressive patrolling of Russian cavalry and Cossacks. Taking prisoners was their favourite pastime and, in the absence of British cavalry, the infantry often had to mount pickets to deter this practice. Russell himself wrote of the behaviour of Cossack patrols in January, 1855:

> Towards Baidir pickets of the same active but cowardly gentry were moving along to keep themselves warm. We had no cavalry outposts advanced towards them. Why not? Because we could not send out any conveniently. Those rugged ruffians, in sheepskin coats and fur hats, mounted on ragged ponies, with deal lances and coarse iron tips, are able to hold ground in drifting snow and biting winds which our cavalry, such as they are, could not face.[102]

When the rail line from Balaclava to Sevastapol was completed in 1855, it was noted how groups of Cossacks would descend into the valley to race the trains. These were hardly the actions of men cowed by the presence of British cavalry. It would seem more probable that the near total absence of an effective allied cavalry force prevented any further mounted battles.

100 Paget, op. cit., pp 103–4.   **101** W.H. Russell, *The war: from the landing at Gallipoli to the death of Lord Raglan* (London, 1855), p. 312.   **102** Ibid. p. 313.

In April and July,1855, the Cavalry Division was reinforced. The 10th Hussars and 12th Lancers arrived from India. The 6th Dragoon Guards, and the King's Dragoon Guards arrived from England. The 10th Hussars and the 12th Lancers were both at full Indian strength, 600 men. Lord George Paget remarked that this was 'about double what our 10 regiments muster'.[103] The original Cavalry Division was a shadow of its former self. While the winter of 1855 was totally different from the previous winter, the men being well supplied and quartered, the damage had already been done. The fine body of cavalry that had left British ports in 1854 had been destroyed due to inexperience and gross mismanagement. The experience of the 8th Royal Irish Hussars was largely typical of what British troopers had to go through during the war and there was a high proportion of Irishmen in the regiment during the campaign. The regiment was stationed in Dundalk, with a squadron in Belfast, on returning from the Crimea in 1856. Two hundred and ninety-three men had set out with the regiment in 1854. The regiments muster rolls show that 42 of this initial contingent were invalided home, 68 died of disease and wounds, one deserted, while only 26 were killed in action.[104]

The battles of 'Little Inkerman' and Inkerman

On 26 October 1854 the Russians attacked the allied positions again and this battle came to be known as 'Little Inkerman'. Colonel Federov led 4,300 Russian troops out of Sevastapol and attacked the exposed right flank of the allied army on Mount Inkerman. The Russian attack was concentrated on the 2nd Division, commanded by the Irish general, Sir George De Lacy Evans. The battle began at around 1 p.m. when the Russians attacked the picket of Lieutenant John Augustus Conolly. Conolly, serving with the 49th Foot, was born in Cliff, Ballyshannon, Co. Donegal, and was the fifth son of Edward Michael Conolly of Castletown, Co. Kildare, lieutenant-colonel of the Donegal Militia and MP for Co. Donegal.[105] Conolly won the Victoria Cross for his bravery during the battle of Little Inkerman. His men engaged the Russians and Conolly defended himself with his sword until it eventually broke. He then took his brass telescope and, wielding it like a club, attacked the advancing Russians.[106]

The pickets refused to withdraw, preventing De Lacy Evans from engaging the enemy with his artillery. He responded to repeated request from the picket commanders for reinforcements with the words 'Not a man!' Eventually he did send forward more companies and the Russians were driven back to Sevastapol.

103 Lord George Paget, *Light Cavalry Brigade*, p. 91.   **104** Murray, *History of the VIII Hussars*, vol. II, p. 413.   **105** Burke, *LGI* (1912), p. 129. John Augustus Conolly's elder brother, Captain Arthur Wellesley Conolly, 30th Foot, was killed at the battle of Inkerman.   **106** Patrick Mercer,

The battle was characterized by the dogged refusal of the pickets to give up their ground and even new and inexperienced troops fought tenaciously. The British had lost only 12 killed and 72 wounded. The Russians had over 270 casualties but they had gained valuable intelligence. They now knew that the right flank of the allied army on Mount Inkerman was its weakest point. The allied commanders made no efforts to re-reinforce this position or improve its defences and Mount Inkerman would be the scene of another desperate battle in November. De Lacy Evans later described the battle of Little Inkerman in a despatch to Lord Raglan.

> Our eighteen guns in position, including those in the first position, were served with the utmost energy. In half an hour they forced the enemy artillery to leave the field. Our batteries were then directed with equal accuracy and vigour on the enemy's columns, which, exposed also to the close fire of our advanced infantry, soon fell into complete disorder and flight. They were literally then chased by the 30th and 95th regiments over the ridges and down towards the bay. So eager was the pursuit, that it was with difficulty Major-General Pennefather eventually effected the recall of the men.

An Irish officer, Captain Edwin Richards, later described the battle of Little Inkerman in a letter to his parents, written 27 October 1854. In it he greatly over-estimated the number of Russian casualties.

> We had a pretty hot affair yesterday for about an hour and a half, it ended by our driving the enemy back with a loss of 1,000 killed and wounded on their side and only 58 and five officers on ours. They did very well indeed, when opposed to our pickets, who always wear greatcoats, but when we came on in red, and our men yelling like savages, they could stand it no longer. I believe there is something in the colour that frightens them. I do believe that we are the kindest enemies in the world. It is wonderful to see the attention our soldiers pay to the wounded Russians, and our surgeons take as much pains with them as our own. The enemy are certainly not to be despised. Two of their battalions advancing yesterday like men, under a heavy fire of our artillery.[107]

On 5 November 1854, the Russians attacked again, on this occasion sallying out of Sevastapol while the land army under Prince Gorchakov advanced on Balaclava plain. Russian forces of over 40,000 attacked the allied right flank at Mount Inkerman and, once again, the brunt of the attack fell on the 2nd Division. There were 7,400 British and 8,200 French troops available to meet them. De Lacy Evans, commanding the 2nd Division, had been injured in a fall

Inkerman 1854 (London, 1998), pp 38–40.   **107** *Illustrated London News*, 20 Jan. 1855, p. 67. Captain Richards was killed at the battle of Inkerman, 5 November 1854. In his last letter home 3 November 1854, he cheerfully remarked 'I am still alive and well, and in possession of my usual number of arms and legs'.

from his horse on 30 October and had given command of the division his fellow-Irishman, Brigadier-General John Lysaght Pennefather. When De Lacy Evans heard the firing begin, however, he got up from his bed and went to his division but, to his great credit, left Pennefather in command and remained by his side to give moral support. Pennefather for his part could not really engage in any tactical manoeuvring. The attack had begun at around 6 a.m. in dense fog and he could only exhort his men to hold their ground on Home Ridge. He moved forward his division into a position where he hoped that the fog and scrub would conceal his lack of numbers and awaited the arrival of French reinforcements. The battle was characterized again by the refusal of the British troops to give up their ground and was christened 'the soldiers' battle'. Five Irish soldiers won the Victoria Cross at the battle of Inkerman.[108] One Irish officer, Captain John Charles William Fortescue, described the battle in his diary entries for 5 and 6 November 1854.

> The battle began at daylight. The French came up in support, the artillery fire from the enemy was awful (worse than Alma), shells bursting in every direction. Our troops were obliged in several instances to go back for ammunition, also the artillery. The battle lasted until about 3.30 p.m.. We finally succeeded in driving back the enemy. Their loss must have been immense. Ours is about 2,000 killed and wounded. The Guards, 88th and 2nd Division suffered very severely. It was an awful day.
> (6th. Morning After). Rode over the field of battle. The number of dead Russians was astonishing. We were hoping to entrench our position. This ought to have been done before. At four o'clock Sir George Cathcart and our poor general were buried. Lord Raglan was present. Our loss is 2,300 killed and wounded, including 143 officers. The French 300 killed by a sortie in their trenches. The Russian loss is estimated at twenty thousand.[109]

Throughout the rest of 1854 and 1855 the allies conducted a long siege, constructing a series of trenches and siegeworks around Sevastapol. Many officers commented that the siegeworks were almost medieval in nature and the trench warfare that took place around Sevastapol forshadowed similar operations that took place in the American Civil war and, indeed, World War I. (The details of the this long siege and the various bombardments, sorties and assaults, are outlined in the 'Chronology', pp. xxff, above).

Life in the trenches before Sevastapol was monotonous, uncomfortable and dangerous. As was the case in World War I, military technology had superseded

108 Sergeant William McWheeney, 44th Foot; Private John Byrne, 68th Foot; Sergeant Ambrose Madden, 41st Foot; Lieutenant Mark Walker, 30th Foot; Sergeant John Park, 77th Foot. Park's VC was awarded for actions at the battles of Alma and Inkerman and also for his bravery during the attack on the Russian rifle pits on 19 April 1855. **109** NLI, MS 19,359. Fortescue diary, 5 and 6 November 1854. The actual losses were British 2,357 (597 killed), French 143 killed, 786 wounded, Russian 10,729 killed and wounded.

tactics and the Russian defenders were in a strong position. An Irish officer, Captain Hedley Vicars of the 97th Foot, described life in the trenches in a letter of 16 December 1854.

> I have only returned about half an hour from the trenches of the advanced work, where we have been since half-past four o'clock this morning. The rain poured in torrents all night. We turned out in the midst of it (three officers and 200 men), and started for the rendezvous, where detachments from the several regiments assemble, previous to marching off together for the trenches. We had to ford two mountain torrents, which considerably damped our feet and legs, if not our ardour! When we reached the ground, the rest had gone on; so we followed as well as we could, tumbling in the mud at every step. We arrived at last opposite the 21-gun battery (Gordon's) and the rain having suddenly changed to snow, we presented a rather wintry appearance as we entered the covered way. This was, in parts, knee-deep in mud, through which we plodded, not without great exertion. As we cleared the way, we passed a poor fellow of the 77th Regiment, lying on the bank, wounded in the shoulder, and soon after we encountered a sharp fire of musketry and a spent bullet struck me in the left side, but without doing me the slightest harm, thank God.[110]

The Russians did not sit idle during the siege and made several sorties from Sevastapol, attacking the allied trenches and trying to lit the siege. One Irish soldier, James O'Malley of the 17th Foot, later wrote of a Russian attack on the trenches held by his regiment and described the brutal nature of trench warfare outside Sevastapol:

> They poured into our trenches but as they came on we gave them the bayonet after discharging the contents of the barrels in their faces. This was one of the bloodiest encounters ever since the earth was cursed by war and, as the enemy again and again charged us, we got so jammed up as to be quite unable to shorten arms and, as we pulled the bayonet out of one man, we dashed the brains out of another with the butt end and when we could not reach their heads we struck them on the shins. Some of the men got clinched with the Russians and fists were frequently in use. The Russians must have had frightful loss when we ultimately drove them back as seventy-eight lay dead right in the trenches to say nothing of those who dropped outside or crawled away to die of their wounds elsewhere.[111]

The siege also had some bizarre moments and James O'Malley later wrote of how one soldier tried to break the tension of trench warfare.

> Orders had been issued to keep close under cover and strict injunctions given us not to expose ourselves unnecessarily. But one of our men, in order to express his

110 *Memorials of Captain Hedley Vicars, 97th Regiment* (London and Edinburgh, 1863), pp 131–2. Hedley Vicars was born in Mauritius in 1826, where his father was serving with the Royal Engineers. His family home was in Levalley, Queen's County. He was killed during the Russian attack on the trenches on 22 March 1855.   111 James O'Malley, *The life of James O'Malley*

contempt for Russian gunnery, and carried away by the enthusiasm of the moment, deliberately jumped upon the front of one of the trenches and, pointing to his hinder-most part, literally defied the Russians to strike it. This act of insubordination, however, cost him twenty-five lashes on the spot.[112]

On 16 August 1855, a Russian army again attacked the besieging allied armies. This battle, the battle of the Tchernaya, resulted in the Russians being driven back with heavy loss. British troops took no part in the battle, and the Russians were driven back by Sardinian and French troops. Following a final assault on 8 September 1855, French troops captured the crucial Malakov bastion and the following night the Russians abandoned Sevastapol south of the bay and the allies took possession. This event was heralded as the 'fall of Sevastapol' and was celebrated in France, England and Ireland. In reality, the Russians still held positions on the north of the bay. While further operations followed in the shape of expeditions to Fort Kinburn and Kars and Erzerum, a military stalemate followed, an armistice not signed being until February 1856.

It can be seen, therefore, that Irish troops played a significant part in the military campaign. Two Irish generals, Lieutenant-General Sir George De Lacy Evans and Brigadier-General John Lysaght Pennefather, both played a crucial role at the battles of the Alma, Little Inkerman and Inkerman. The soldiers, and the women who accompanied them, faced harsh conditions and suffered greatly due to disease, severe weather and lack of supplies. Their accounts of the Crimea, both in published accounts and in private letters, show that they endured terrible conditions and also played a significant part in the campaign. The large number of Irishmen who were awarded the Victoria Cross for their actions in the Crimea, illustrates the bravery and fighting spirit displayed by the Irish troops but it must be remembered that many must have shown incredible bravery without their actions being recorded. Yet the military campaign represented only one aspect of Irish involvement in the war and it will be shown in the course of this book that the Irish were involved in other areas of the war effort.

(Montreal, 1893), pp 84–5. **112** Ibid., p. 91. O'Malley also recorded how, on St Patrick's Day 1855, many of the officers and men wore sprigs of green in their headgear. The bands of the Irish regiments played appropriate tunes and later in the day there were horse races.

3

Irishmen in the naval campaigns
of the Crimean war

Background to the naval campaign

Most of the histories of the Crimean war written to date have concentrated on the campaigns on land. There have been very few attempts during the past century to illustrate the extensive nature of the naval campaign. With the exception of some contemporary biographies of Admiral Sir Charles Napier and Admiral Sir Edmund Lyons, little attention has been paid to the naval campaigns in the Black Sea and the Baltic. The notable exception to this rule is *The British assault on Finland: a forgotten naval war* (1988), written by Basil Greenhill and Ann Giffard. This work outlines the large scale of Royal Naval operations in the Baltic and illustrates just how effective the naval campaign was. During the last ten years, however, interest in the naval campaigns has increased. A minority of Crimean historians have made this subject their special interest and they have been promoting the theory that the naval campaigns had a decisive effect on the outcome of the war, and that they ultimately forced the Russians to seek an honourable peace. Andrew Lambert and Stephen Badsey stated in their book, *The war correspondents*:

> The Crimea never held the central position in strategic decision-making that it has achieved in historical studies. The war did not begin or end on the Crimean peninsula, it was not decided there, and the end of the sanguinary siege of Sevastapol on 9 September 1855 had little bearing on the Russian decision to accept the allied terms in March 1856. Furthermore, the British and French did not occupy the city of Sevastapol. Contemporary observers were well aware that the Crimean campaign was only part of the wider Black Sea theatre, and of the vital linkage with the equally significant Baltic theatre. In so far as allied military pressure had any bearing on the Russian decision to accept peace terms, that pressure came from the Royal Navy in the Baltic.[1]

1 Lambert and Badsey, *The war correspondents*, p. 275.

It is too easy to let events on the Crimean peninsula overshadow events in the Baltic. It is often forgotten that the first engagements of the war were naval ones. The Russian naval attack on the Turkish fleet at Sinope on 30 November 1853 was one of the events that brought Britain and France closer to declaring war. The Sinope battle, resulting in the death of 4,000 Turkish seamen, was portrayed in the British press as a massacre. All across the country public meetings were called urging the government to act and there were several such meetings in Ireland. Typical of these meetings was the large rally at the Victoria Hall in Belfast on 3 January 1854, where the speakers demanded that the government take decisive action.[2] It is significant that both the press and the public felt that the situation could be resolved by sending a naval force to the Black Sea. On 4 January 1854 British and French ships entered the Black Sea, increasing international tension. When allied ships, flying flags of truce, were fired upon while evacuating their diplomatic staff from Odessa on 13 April 1854, the scene was set for decisive naval retaliation. As a result of this action a squadron of British and French ships returned to Odessa on 22 April 1854 and bombarded the city, causing extensive damage. The naval option was being employed as a specific threat, therefore, before the declaration of war on 28 March 1854, and the first shots fired in anger came from Royal Navy and French warships.

It should also be remembered that, when war was finally declared in late March 1854, the only British plan for a war against Russia envisaged a naval campaign in the Baltic. Sir James Graham, first lord of the admiralty, had drawn up a plan which entailed a flotilla of Royal Navy ships sailing to the Baltic and enforcing a blockade of Russian ports. The next major objective of Graham's plan was the destruction of the Russian naval base at Revel (modern-day Tallinn). It was hoped that this strategy would draw Sweden into an alliance with Britain and France. This alliance with Sweden was seen as being essential in light of Russian influence in Denmark, their occupation of Poland and their friendly relations with Prussia. So the only comprehensive plan for war with Russia in 1854 envisaged the Royal Navy concentrating in the Baltic and reducing Russian bases through bombardment and amphibious landings.

Due to the decision to mount an expedition to capture the Russian base at Sevastapol, the Royal Navy was forced to send ships to the Black Sea. The Royal Navy was to remain over-stretched for the remainder of the war, splitting its forces between the two theatres in an effort to follow pre-war planning and control the Baltic, while also transporting and supporting the military expedition to the Crimea. In the later stages of the war, further naval operations were mounted in the Sea of Azov. Finally it should also be pointed out that naval gun-teams manned batteries during the siege of Sevastapol, playing an

2 *Newry Examiner*, 4 Jan. 1854.

important role in the land campaign. It can be shown that Irishmen played a significant part in all aspects of the Royal Navy's campaigns, Irish seamen serving with the Baltic fleet, the Black Sea fleet and with the Royal Naval Brigade before Sevastapol.

Irishmen in the Royal Navy in the mid-nineteenth century

At the outbreak of the war there was a large number of Irishmen in the Royal Navy. Unfortunately, while there are some official statistics for the years both before and after the Crimean War, there were no surveys carried out during the 1850s. In 1842, the Rt Revd Thomas Griffiths, vicar-apostolic, in his campaign for the appointment of Roman Catholic chaplains to the forces, maintained that one fifth of the men in the Royal Navy and Royal Marines were Catholics.[3] H.J. Hanham, in his article 'Religion and nationality in the mid-Victorian army', has argued convincingly that the majority of Catholics who served in the forces during this period were Irish, or the sons of Irish workers in England.[4] If one follows the basic premise of Hanham's article, one could assume that the majority of sailors recorded as Catholics were Irish. An admiralty return of 1866 compiled details regarding the religious denominations of seamen and also their standard of education. Of the 26,128 seamen and marines examined, it was found that 4,188 gave their religious denomination as Roman Catholic, around 16% of the total. It should be noted that boy seamen were excluded from the religious section of the report as it was seen as being unfair to ask boys so young to comment on their religious persuasions. The actual breakdown was as follows:

Table 5. Religious denominations in the Royal Navy in 1866

	Total	Total Examined	Church of England	Presbyterian	Other Protestant	Roman Catholic
Petty Officers	4,563	4,465	3,542	154	298	471
Seamen	17,572	17,478	12,488	673	1,196	3,121
Marines	4,194	4,185	2,870	176	543	596
Boys	4,055					

Source: *Statistical abstract of education and religious denomination in the Royal Navy*, HC 1866 (45), xlvi, 57.

3 Johnstone and Hagerty, *The cross on the sword* (London, 1996), p. 5.   4 H.J. Hanham, 'Religion and nationality', pp 159–83.

In all categories examined Catholics made up the second largest proportion. It is interesting, however, to note the comparatively small number of Catholic petty officers. A small number of men in all categories were not available for the Admiralty examiners to include in the survey. By 1876 the number of Catholics in the Royal Navy had dropped to just 11%, but this should be seen in the context of a greatly expanded navy. Numerically there were actually more Catholics serving in 1876. The figures for 1876 were:

Table 6. Religious denominations in the Royal Navy in 1876

	Church of England	Presbyterian	Other Protestants	Roman Catholic
Seamen	22,816	1,150	2,675	3,866
Marines	9,545	462	1,295	986
Total	32,361	1,612	3,970	4,852

Sources: *Returns of the religious persuasions of the seamen of the Royal Navy, and also of the Royal Marines, and of the chaplains,* HC 1876 (132), xlv, 619.

There are also statistics on the nationality of surgeons, assistant surgeons and dressers employed at the outbreak of the war. The recruitment of surgeons had been a major problem for the Royal Navy for many years due to the poor pay and allowances that these men received. Many newly-qualified surgeons, if they decided on a service career, preferred to become army surgeons as they received more pay. Also, while many army surgeons found that they enjoyed a very low social standing, naval surgeons held even less status and messed in the gunroom with the junior officers and midshipmen.[5] Desperate for surgeons at the beginning of the war, rates of pay were improved and 444 young men joined the service on a temporary basis as surgeons, assistant surgeons and dressers. Seventy-seven of these men were Irish, 17.5% of the total.[6]

Despite the dearth of official statistics of seaman's nationality during the Crimean war it is possible that, in light of the 1866 and 1876 figures, around 15% of the Royal Navy and Royal Marines were Irish in 1854. Admiral Sir Charles Napier's Baltic Fleet had, in March 1854, ships' crews totalling 8,880 men. The Royal Navy as a whole had just under 25,000 men serving as ships'

5 The life of Stephen Maturin, the fictional surgeon in Patrick O'Brian's seafaring novels, seems quite different from the realities of the mid-nineteenth-century gunroom. The grim reality was that the naval surgeons of the 1850s faced a life of bad pay, bad food and the poor company of adolescent midshipmen. All a far cry from Maturin's life of urbane conversation, toasted cheese and Boccherini duets for violin and cello!   6 *A return of the number and names of the surgeons, assistant surgeons and dressers*, HC 1855 (293), xxxiv, 197.

crews. If only 15% of these men were Irish, a modest enough estimate, this would mean an Irish contingent of 3,750.

The enlistment of Irish recruits in the Royal Navy and coastguard service in 1854

As war became more of a certainty in the beginning of 1854 and public enthusiasm was whipped up in the press, young men flocked to join the Royal Navy and coastguard service. Newspapers reported that large numbers joined from all over Ireland but especially in the coastal counties of Cork, Waterford, Wexford, Limerick, Galway and Mayo. *The Times* of 14 February 1854 reported on the recruiting tour of Captain Kelly RN, who visited the ports on the west coast enrolling men from the coastguard services into the Royal Navy:

> Accounts form Galway announce that the *Amphitrite* cutter, under the command of Captain Kelly, had proceeded southwards from Galway, for the purpose of taking on board and landing at Queenstown such of the coastguard in the south of Ireland as are about to join the navy. No order had yet been received for draughting any of the men belonging to the Galway district into Her Majesty's vessels; but in the event of such an order arriving, which the next post may bring, the Collector of Customs there has received instructions to pay the men up to the day of their departure. In the city of Waterford an officer is fast enrolling able seamen, landsmen, and first class boys for service afloat.[7]

The Times of 20 February 1854 also reported on recruiting for the Royal Navy and HM Coastguard in Ireland:

> From Cork the accounts state that the enrolment of volunteers for the defence of the coast by Captain Jeringham, RN, is proceeding with unexpected rapidity. The number of eager applicants is quite prodigious, and the office of the Mercantile Marine Board is completely besieged by persons offering themselves. On Friday over 100 were enrolled, which, considering, that each individual has to undergo medical inspection and receive a certificate, may be considered rapid work. The persons who have been at present enrolled consist chiefly of fishermen; the next class that will be accepted will be such of the lumpers on the quays as can be furnished with a good character. There is little doubt that the coast volunteers of this port will soon amount to a very formidable body. On Tuesday evening Her Majesty's Cutter *Desmond* arrived at Tramore East, and embarked a number of men of the Coast Guard from the neighbouring stations for service in the Baltic fleet.[8]

Captain Jeringham would appear to have had great success as he travelled through the towns on the west coast. By early February he had already visited Tarbert, Kilrush, Carrigaholt and Galway, enlisting 252 men. *The Times* of 3

7 *The Times*, 14 Feb. 1854.   8 Ibid. 20 Feb. 1854.

February 1854 noted that he was 'heard with respect and even pleasure when addressing the hardy fishermen of the west coast'. Captain Jeringham was especially successful in the Claddagh district where he received support from an unexpected source.

> On his visit to the primitive colony located in the Claddagh district, the women with a courage and devotion worthy of patriotic heroines, exclaimed "Not only will our men enter with you, but our sons also, and if any of the tribe refuses, never fear, as we'll shame them into it, by offering ourselves as volunteers". Such was the noble sentiment of the Claddagh women, and the fishermen cheered in response to the appeal of Captain Jeringham, so happily wound up by the characteristic ardour of Irishwomen, when they learnt that their Island Queen requires the aid of her loyal Irish subjects.[9]

The Royal Navy ships initially assembled in small flotillas in various ports around the British Isles, before rendezvousing in Portsmouth and Plymouth. It was here that the two fleets for the Black sea and the Baltic were finally assembled. In Ireland the two main assembly points were at Kingstown (Dun Laoghaire) and Queenstown (Cobh). Other ports such as Limerick and Waterford were used as initial 'naval rendezvous'. While the ships waited to leave these Irish ports they received fresh drafts of sailors to bring there crews up to strength. As a result of this several of the Royal Navy ships that left Irish ports, such as HMS *Rodney*, were crewed almost entirely by Irish sailors.[10]

The Royal Navy shore establishment at Haulbowline, which had been neglected for years, experienced a new lease of life and became an important supply centre for the ships in both the Baltic and the Black Sea. In 1854 this base consisted of a 'victualing yard' with associated administration buildings. The wooden three-decker, HMS *Revenge*, served as depot ship. The victualing yard had been completed at the beginning of the century but, at the end of the Napoleonic wars, had been run down. From 1846 to 1851 the storage facilities had been used again to store corn imports used in relief efforts during the Famine. At the outbreak of the Crimean war the admiralty decided that the base would an ideal location for the collection and despatch of stores for the Crimea. By the end of the war it was one of the most important naval stores in the British Isles. Kingstown, Dundalk and Queenstown became major centres for the embarkation of troops at the beginning of the campaign. Indeed, in his book on the history of Kingstown, Peter Pearson estimated that as many as 20,000 troops passed through the harbour on their way to the Crimea.[11] These harbours also became centres where supplies were stored and then dispatched to the Crimea and the Baltic.

9 Ibid. 3 Feb. 1854.   10 John Winton, *The Victoria Cross at sea* (London, 1978), p. 35.   11 Peter Pearson, *Dun Laoghaire–Kingstown* (Urban Heritage Series, Dublin, 1981), p. 45.

Many merchant vessels with Irish home ports and crews worked as transport ships during the war. The British & Irish Steam Packet Company, established in 1836, chartered two of their most modern ships to work as troopships during the war. The first was the iron steamship *Foyle*, built in 1850, which had achieved a reputation for speed and reliability. The second British & Irish Steam Packet Company ship to serve as a troopship was *Lady Elington*, bought by the company in 1852.[12] The Cork Steam Ship Company, established in 1843, also chartered out their most modern ship, the screw-driven *Cormorant*. Built in 1853 she had very graceful lines and had been nick-named locally as 'the Cork Yacht'. The *Cormorant* had very unusual iron masts, seen at the time as an innovative feature. During a royal inspection of transport ships, Queen Victoria apparently remarked on these iron masts and ordered that measurements should be taken so that the introduction of such masts into the Royal Navy could be considered.[13] Numerous other Irish ships, less stylish and well known, were to serve as troopships and transports during the war.

There were also Royal Navy ships, serving as guardships in Irish ports, that were sent to the Baltic and Black Sea when the navy became overstretched. HMS *Ajax*, the guardship at Kingstown, was a typical example of such a ship. Built in 1809, this third-rate 74-gun ship had served in the British-American war of 1812–14 and had been fitted with new armament and steam machinery between 1845 and 1846. Commanded by Captain Michael Quin, she had previously been posted as the guardship in Cork, before serving as guardship at Kingstown. During the Crimean war, HMS *Ajax* served in the Baltic and took part in the bombardment of Russian coastal forts. In 1858 she returned to Cork and served as the guardship there.[14]

The Baltic campaign

As has been stated previously, the only plan for a war with Russia that the Royal Navy had in 1854 was the one formulated by Sir James Graham. To a certain extent Graham's plan was simplicity itself. He felt that attacking Russian bases in the Baltic and enforcing a blockade would force the Russians to sue for peace. In pursuit of this aim, Admiral Sir Charles Napier was sent to the Baltic with a squadron of ships in March 1854. His initial intention was to attack the Russian base at Revel and destroy enemy ships but, on his arrival, Napier found that the Russians had withdrawn their ships. It was also hoped that such a show of force in the Baltic would encourage Sweden to join the allied side. Napier was relying on this and needed Swedish troops if he was to

12 Hazel P. Smyth, *The B+I Line* (Dublin, 1984), p.105, p. 107.   **13** Ibid. p. 189.   **14** John De

carry out the planned amphibious attacks on Russian bases. Sweden's decision to remain neutral forced him to revise his plans totally. When the landings eventually did take place, French troops were used. As the best regiments of the French army were in the Crimea by that time, the French regiments sent to the Baltic were made up of reservists who did not display the same *élan* as their countrymen in the Crimea.

Napier's final problem was a lack of gunboats capable of moving inshore to attack the Russian bases. While his orders specifically stated that he should send ships close inshore to bombard Russian bases, he had no vessels with a shallow enough draft which could actually do so. As early as July 1854 Napier wrote to the admiralty requesting gunboats, but his request was ignored. The Royal Navy did pursue an aggressive policy, however, and ships often came close inshore to bombard Russian positions. Due to the great range over which these bombardments took place, key Russian positions, such as the Bomarsund and Kronstadt fortresses, rarely suffered severe damage

In an effort to overcome this lack of offensive potential, Napier advised his officers to enter Baltic ports and attack Russian shipping moored in the harbours of the Gulf of Finland. In May 1854 a raid was organised against the port of Ekenäs (modern-day Tammisaari), a small port to the north east of Hangö Point where Russian ships were landing supplies. Ekenäs was extremely difficult to reach as it was situated on an island, sheltered behind the mass of islands of the Åland Archipelago. The raid was led by an Irish officer, Captain (later Admiral Sir) Hastings Reginald Yelverton, who commanded HMS *Arrogant*, a screw-driven frigate of forty-seven guns. Yelverton was born in Straffan, Co. Kildare, in March 1808, entering the Royal Navy in August 1823.[15] In September 1843 he was promoted captain and had taken command of HMS *Arrogant* in October 1853.[16] Attached to Admiral Napier's Baltic fleet, HMS *Arrogant* had initially worked as a blockade ship, patrolling the entrance to the Gulf of Finland. On 16 May 1854 Yelverton took his ship, in company with HMS *Hecla*, into the series of channels that led to Ekenäs. Yelverton had to negotiate twelve miles of channels and his ships were fired on by Russian infantry and artillery during the whole journey. The two ships fought a running battle with three companies of infantry and a field battery of four cannons which followed them along the banks of the channel as they approached Ekenäs.

Despite this opposition Captain Hall of HMS *Hecla* managed to board and capture the barque *Augusta* which was carrying a cargo of salt. The two ships, towing their prize, faced stiff opposition on the return journey as the troops on

Courcy Ireland, *A history of Dun Laoghaire harbour* (Dublin, 2001), p. 96.   **15** Yelverton had been born Hastings Reginald Henry, the third son of John Joseph Henry. In 1849, he married Lady Gray and assumed her family name of Yelverton. Frederic Boase, *Modern English biography* (London, 1892–1901), vol. 3, p. 1582.   **16** Ibid.

shore had been reinforced by three companies of the Finnish Grenadier Sharpshooter Battalion and a battalion of the Prince Frederick Grenadier Regiment. In the narrow channels of Vitsand, Yelverton's force came under heavy fire but nevertheless managed to make the open sea. Casualties on the two ships were surprisingly light, HMS *Arrogant* had two men killed and four wounded while HMS *Hecla* had one man killed and four wounded. The Russian forces had one officer and three men killed and six wounded. Giving the short ranges over which the action was fought, such a light casualty figure seems surprising. Yelverton's force was spared serious casualties as the Russian field guns were apparently of a very small calibre and could not inflict major damage on the ships.[17] In his report of 20 May 1854, Captain Yelverton described some of the difficulties that they had faced:

> I did not expect to find the enemy so well prepared to receive me. Owing to the *Hecla's* light draft of water, she led the way ... a task not easy to perform in a narrow and intricate passage, exposed as she was to the first of the enemy's fire.[18]

Sir James Graham described the action in the House of Commons as:

> A feat which, though not on a large scale, was a gallant one, and, as an exploit, worthy of the best days of the Royal Navy.[19]

The captured barque *Augusta* was taken to Sheerness with a prize crew under Arthur L. Galbraith, mate of HMS *Arrogant. The Times* of 26 June 1854 estimated ship and its cargo of salt to be worth £70,000.[20] This raid brought the total of merchant vessels captured in the Baltic to forty-nine.

Yelverton took part in another unusual expedition in August 1854. He was informed by Admiral Napier on 7 August 1854 that important despatches from Tsar Nicholas to Russian commanders were being landed at Wårdö Island and from there were being taken to Bomarsund. This was happening on a regular basis and Napier said to Yelverton that he was surprised that no-one had attempted to 'stop this kind of thing'. Yelverton discussed the matter with his officers on board HMS *Arrogant*. Lieutenant John Bythesea volunteered to try

---

17 Basil Greenhill and Ann Giffard, *The British assault on Finland* (London, 1988), pp 8–10. 18 Ibid. p. 209.   19 Ibid.   20 The amount realized for any ship and cargo condemned by the prize court of the Admiralty was divided into eight shares. The captain of the ship that captured the prize was awarded three shares. The senior lieutenants, masters and marine captains were awarded a share between them. Junior lieutenants and lieutenants of marines received a share between them. Midshipmen and warrant officers also received a share to divide between themselves. The remaining two shares were divided among the rest of the ship's crew. If the ship was operating under the orders of an admiral or commodore, then this officer would receive one of the captain's shares. Dean King, John B. Hattendorf and J. Worth Estes (eds), *A sea of words: A lexicon and companion for Patrick O'Brian's seafaring tales* (New York, 1995), pp 296–7.

and intercept the dispatches and he was accompanied by Leading Stoker William Johnstone.[21] On the night of 9 August 1854 the two men rowed ashore and, after a three-day wait, intercepted the Russian couriers near Wårdö. Both men were later awarded the Victoria Cross.[22]

The lack of gunboats made it impossible to move close inshore to attack the major Russian fortresses, one of the original objectives of the expedition. In an effort to pursue some form of aggressive action, Royal Navy ships often came as close inshore as was possible and bombarded the Russian forts. This often resulted in spectacular, if somewhat ineffective, artillery duels. It was in such an attack in June 1854 on the Bomarsund fortress in the Gulf of Finland that an Irishman, Charles Davis Lucas, won the first Victoria Cross ever awarded. Lucas was born at Druminargale House, near Poyntzpass, Co. Armagh, in February 1834. His father, Davis Lucas, had previously lived in Clontibret and was a member of the Lucas family of Castleshane, Co. Monaghan. Charles Davis Lucas joined the Royal Navy in 1848 and initially served in HMS *Vanguard*. He then served as a mate in HMS *Fox* during the Burma War of 1852–3 and was present at the captures of Rangoon, Pegu, Dalla and Prome.[23] At the beginning of the Baltic campaign Lucas was serving on HMS *Hecla*, the six-gun steam paddle-sloop, commanded by Captain William H. Hall, which had accompanied Captain Yelverton of HMS *Arrogant* in the expedition to Ekenäs in May.

On 21 June 1854 Captain Hall led his ship and also HMS *Odin* and HMS *Valorous*, through the narrow Bomarsund channel towards the Åland Islands. There was a large Russian fort there guarding the entrance to the Gulf of Bothnia and, at around 9 p.m., the three ships began a spirited bombardment which lasted until 1 a.m. in the following morning. Hall and his ships used up all their ammunition during the engagement without causing any serious damage. Admiral Napier was highly critical of this fact, commenting in his report, 'If every captain when detached chose to throw away all his shot and shell against stone walls, the fleet would soon be inefficient.'[24]

During the bombardment the three Royal Navy ships were fired upon by the main fortress batteries and also by artillery and riflemen. At the height of the fighting a live shell landed on the deck of HMS *Hecla* and lay there with its fuse hissing. The sailors on deck immediately took cover but Lucas ran forward, picked up the smoking shell and threw it overboard. It exploded before it hit the water but caused only minor damage. Only two sailors were slightly hurt. There was no doubt that, but for Lucas' quick action, many of the sailors

21 Greenhill and Giffard, op. cit., pp 253–5.   **22** Ibid. pp 20–2.   **23** Winton, *The Victoria Cross at sea*, pp 19–20. See also *Ireland's VCs*, p. 9.   **24** D. Bonner-Smith and Captain A.C. Dewar RN (eds), 'Russian War 1854. Baltic and Black Sea: official correspondence' in *Journal of the Navy Records Society*, lxxxiii (London, 1943), p. 81.

crowded on deck would have been killed or wounded. Captain Hall wrote of the incident in his report to Admiral Napier:

> And with regard to Mr Lucas I have the pleasure to report a remarkable instance of coolness and presence of mind in action, he having taken up and thrown overboard a live shell thrown on board the *Hecla* by the enemy, while the fuse was still burning.[25]

Admiral Napier, although highly critical of the action itself, praised Lucas in his report to the Admiralty, finishing his report:

> Their Lordships will observe in Captain Hall's letter, the great courage of Mr C.D. Lucas, Acting Mate, in taking up a live shell and throwing it overboard, and I trust their Lordships will mark their sense of it by promoting him.[26]

Lucas was immediately promoted to acting-lieutenant and his promotion was later confirmed by the Admiralty. Recommended for a decoration, he was awarded the first-ever Victoria Cross in February 1857 and attended the first VC investiture in Hyde Park in June of that year.[27]

Due to the lack of shallow-draft gunboats, several raids on Russian bases were carried out using ships' boats. As was to happen later in the Sea of Azov, small parties rowed inshore, cutting out Russian ships and setting fire to stores. In May and June 1854, a series of such raids were carried out on the coastal villages of Brahestad (modern-day Raahe), Uleaborg (Oulu) and Torneå. Two Irishmen played a prominent role in these raids. They were Mate John G. O'Connell, who commanded the second gig of HMS *Leopard* and Nicholas Murphy, also a warrant officer, of HMS *Vulture*.[28] These shore parties destroyed forty-six vessels and large quantities of stores in their raids.

The Blockade of Russian ports

The most successful feature of the Royal Navy's campaign in the Baltic was the effectiveness of their blockade of Russian ports. The Russian fleet was simply not in a position to oppose the Royal Navy's blockade squadrons. Their one significant

25 Ibid. pp 82–4.   26 Ibid. p. 81.   27 Lucas subsequently served on HMS *Dauntless*, HMS *Calcutta*, HMS *Cressy* and HMS *Liffey*. He was promoted to commander in February 1862 and captain in October 1867. Retiring from the Royal Navy in October 1873, he was promoted to rear-admiral, on the retired list, in June 1885. In 1879 he married Frances Russell Hall, the daughter of Admiral Sir William H. Hall, who had been his captain on HMS *Hecla*. He later served as a JP for Kent and Argyllshire. He died, 7 August 1914, at Great Culverden, Kent, and was buried at Mereworth, near Maidstone. *Who was who 3*. See also John Winton, *The Victoria Cross at sea*.
28 D. Bonner-Smith and Captain A.C. Dewar, RN, (eds), 'Russian War 1854. Baltic and Black Sea: official correspondence' in *Journal of the Navy Records Society*, lxxxiii (London, 1943), p. 64.

achievement was to develop naval mines and float them against British ships outside Kronstadt. Yet even this tactic achieved no long-term result and, although HMS *Merlin* suffered some damage from a mine, the Royal Navy soon developed a method for sweeping the Russian mines. There was nothing to prevent British ships stopping and searching all ships entering the Baltic and seizing cargoes bound for Russia. By the end of 1855 over 200 ships had been seized. This made it inevitable that Russia would eventually have to sue for peace. Just as Sevastapol would eventually fall when its supply lines were cut, Russia could not prosecute a war indefinitely without re-supply from outside.

Royal Navy and HM Coastguard ships were also patrolling the shipping lanes in the English Channel and the Atlantic in an effort to intercept ships bound for Russia. The blockade was not only confined to the Baltic and Russian ships were subject to the attentions of the Royal Navy while travelling in the Atlantic and the English Channel. Several ships were stopped and seized after leaving Spain and Portugal, bound for the Baltic. Captain Patrick O'Malley, of HM Coastguard, was based in Queenstown and he detained two ships bound for Russia in 1855. O'Malley was in command of HM Coastguard Cutter *Eliza* and the first ship that he detained was the *Argo* commanded by Captain Gustaf Stenman. He intercepted this vessel ten miles to the south-west of Cork harbour. The *Argo* was flying the Russian flag and carrying a cargo of molasses. O'Malley detained a second ship late in 1855, the *Maria* under Captain F.M. Petit. This ship was flying the Belgian flag but was bound for Russia with a cargo of salted hides, estimated to be worth just over £660. The *Maria* was also intercepted to the south of Cork harbour. It is interesting to note that the *Argo*, a Russian registered ship, was not condemned by the Admiralty court and that the ship and cargo were restored to the owners. The Belgian ship, *Maria*, was condemned by the Admiralty court as being a lawful prize.[29] The blockade was not confined to the Baltic Sea, therefore, and patrol ships sailed from Irish ports seeking ships bound for Russia.

The lack of inshore gunboats seriously restricted the course of the campaign in the Baltic and, while gunboats of the *Arrow* class were ordered in March 1854, it was not until the summer of 1855 that they were available for service, yet even these had too great a draught to move close inshore. Admiral Napier became the focus of public criticism due to the lack of success and was replaced by Admiral Dundas in 1855. A further class of gunboat, the *Gleaner* class, was to have more success and the class was ordered in large numbers. Powered by a small 60 hp engine, they drew only seven feet of water and mounted two 68-pounder Lancaster guns. There were also extremely cheap and easy to build. A further twenty boats

---

29 *Return of all vessels and goods taken at sea as prize during the late war, either by revenue cutters or vessels attached to the coast guard service*, HC 1856 (325), xli, 247–59.

of the *Dapper* class were ordered, the order later increased to ninety-eight. A large flotilla of these gunboats successfully bombarded the Russian naval dockyard at Sveaborg in August 1855.[30]

While public attention was focused on the siege of Sevastapol, the Royal Navy was enjoying real success in the Baltic. This programme of naval expansion was christened 'The Great Armament' in the press and, throughout late 1855 large numbers of gunboats and armoured floating batteries were built. The peace settlement of March 1856 robbed them of their purpose, but they were all gathered together for a royal naval review in Spithead in April 1856. This massive fleet consisted of 160 gunboats, divided into four squadrons. The Blue Squadron of forty-four ships, mostly *Gleaner* class, gunboats was commanded by Captain Yelverton, in the 81-gun ship, HMS *Brunswick*.[31] Many of these gunboats were later sent to different stations abroad and were used to support British foreign policy, giving rise to the term 'gunboat diplomacy'.[32]

The Black Sea campaign

While Admiral Napier was assembling his fleet for service in the Baltic, a second fleet was being formed for service in the Black Sea. This put Royal Navy resources under an extreme strain as it was found that there was a shortage of both ships and men to fight two naval campaigns at the same time. To a certain extent this problem was never rectified and both fleets were to remain short of both men and ships. Indeed many senior officers in shore establishments, who should have been heading towards a quiet retirement, found themselves faced with full work schedules. One venerable Irish officer, Rear-Admiral Sir Francis Beaufort (1774–1857), hydrographer of the Royal Navy, spent the last two years of his career supervising the drawing of charts of the Baltic and Black Seas. Beaufort, who had entered the Royal Navy in June 1787, had to call on all his cartographic skills to produce a series of charts for the ships maintaining the blockade in the Baltic and also for the ships in the Black Sea, before retiring in late 1855.[33]

Ship building programmes had also been organised too late and many ships laid down in 1854 were not in commission by the end of the war. The prime example of this were the gunboats of 'The Great Armament'. The shortage of

30 Anthony J. Watts, *The Royal Navy: an illustrated history* (London, 1994), pp 19–20.   **31** *The Times*, 23 April 1856. Created a CB in July 1855, Yelverton later served as naval ADC to Queen Victoria (1856–63) and was C-in-C of the Mediterranean station (1870–4). He was promoted to admiral in July 1875 and was appointed as a lord of the admiralty in 1876. He was also created KCB (1869) and GCB (1875).   **32** Watts, *The Royal Navy*, p. 20.   **33** Alfred Friendly, *Beaufort of the Admiralty; the life of Sir Francis Beaufort, 1774–1857* (London, 1977). Rear-Admiral Sir Francis Beaufort was born in Navan, Co. Meath, the son of the Revd Daniel Augustus Beaufort,

manpower was also never satisfactorily remedied and by the end of the war ships of the Baltic fleet were enlisting Swedish sailors.[34] Many ships and sailors served in both the Black Sea and the Baltic during the war. Irish-born Lieutenant James Vaughan served in both the Baltic and the Black Sea with HMS *Scout* at the beginning of the war, before transferring to HMS *Britannia*, engaged in the blockade of Sevastapol.[35]

In March and April 1854 a second expedition was organized to go to the Black Sea and capture the major Russian naval base at Sevastapol. A mixture of transport and warships assembled at Devonport, Portsmouth, Plymouth, Liverpool, Kingstown and Queenstown and began embarking troops and supplies. Most of the warships also carried troops while travelling to the Black Sea. In late April 1854 the ships began to sail in small groups and also singly. The Admiralty felt that there was little chance of a Russian attack on these ships and the implementation of an escort system was not considered necessary. During the voyage to the East ships stopped at Gibraltar and Malta to take on water and supplies, before travelling on to Constantinople and Varna and disembarking their cargoes. In Early September 1854, after a frustrating and cholera-ridden period spent in Varna, the troops were re-embarked and the fleet set sail again, this time for the Crimean peninsula. Landings at Calamita Bay followed, with little incident on 14–15 September 1854.

Due to the lack of a land base, however, the ships had to remain close inshore to provide support and supplies as Lord Raglan's column began its march southwards along the coast road. The fleet was also the only source of heavy artillery support and, when the allied and Russian armies finally met at the Alma on 20 September 1854, the Royal Navy ships bombarded the left of the Russian line. With the seizure of Balaclava harbour, Admiral Sir Edmund Lyons, commanding the Royal Navy in the Black Sea, had a base from which to operate. The Russians, realizing that their naval force based at Sevastapol was no match for the assembled French and British ships, sunk their ships in Sevastapol harbour.

There was now very little that the Royal Navy could do to assist in the taking of Sevastapol. A blockade was duly mounted but, as the harbour was effectively closed due to the Russian blockships, this was totally unnecessary. On the 17 October 1854, however, the fleet carried out a major bombardment of Sevastapol from the sea, the effects of which were not exploited by Lord Raglan. As the army preoccupied itself with its siege operations, Admiral

Rector of Navan. **34** Several of the sailors who served with the Royal Navy in the Sea of Azov were Italian, including Louigi Mordio who served on HMS *Miranda*. Also, a sailor named Spero Bonicci served on HMS *Medina*. Bonicci is a very common name in the Maltese Islands. PRO, ADM 171.25, Azoff [*sic*] Clasp Roll. **35** Dun Laoghaire Genealogical Society, *Memorial inscriptions of Deansgrange cemetery*, ii, part 1, p. 9.

Lyons sought ways in which the assembled ships and sailors could engage in some form of aggressive activity.

A Royal Naval Brigade was formed in October 1854, under the command of Captain Stephen Lushington of HMS *Albion*. The first contingent was made up of 1,020 seamen with 20 lieutenants and 15 midshipmen serving as the brigade's officers. These sailors were sent ashore to assist with the transport of supplies and the building of earthworks around Sevastapol. Naval guns, mostly of very large calibre, were also landed and placed in batteries overlooking Sevastapol, manned by men of the Royal Navy. Fifty 32-pounders, eight 68-pounders and two 95-cwt Lancaster guns were landed with the first contingent and installed in formidable naval batteries. The naval batteries were usually named after the ship from which the men and guns had landed. Hence the Diamond Battery was served by seamen from HMS *Diamond* under Captain Peel. The two Lancaster Batteries, crewed by seamen from HMS *Lancaster*, were armed with 68-pounders. These massive guns caused devastating damage when bombardment of Sevastapol began on 17 October 1854.[36]

One obvious result of this naval presence on land was that seamen frequently became involved in the battles of late 1854. In many cases this involved bringing up supplies of ammunition or helping to evacuate casualties. At the battle of Inkerman, 5 November 1854, over 1,200 seamen were ashore serving in the field and manning siege batteries. Over 600 of these seamen were present at the actual battle and many became involved in the fighting. Four seamen won the Victoria Cross at the Battle of Inkerman. One of the Victoria Cross recipients was Able Seaman James Gorman who was born in Essex in 1832, but whose his parents were from Waterford. He had joined HMS *Albion* as a boy seaman, first class, on 13 July 1850 and was rated ordinary seaman on 13 May 1852. He volunteered to join HMS *Albion*'s shore detachment and had come ashore with the rest of the Naval Brigade on 1 October 1854.[37] Gorman was sent to help serve the guns of the Right Lancaster Battery, which became the focus of a major attack when the Russians began to advance at 6 a.m. on the morning of 5 November 1854. When the battle began the main Lancaster Battery was shelled from the rear by a battery of Russian 13-pounders, while the Right Lancaster Battery was attacked by a mass of Russian infantry. The soldiers posted to protect this battery were nearly all killed or wounded in the first onslaught. Five seamen, including Gorman, picked up rifles and began to fire on the advancing Russians. Wounded soldiers reloaded the abandoned rifles that were lying around and passed them to Gorman and his comrades, allowing them to keep up a constant fire. In

---

36 John Winton, 'Was Able Seaman James Gorman, VC, an Aussie?' in *The war correspondent*, xvi, no. 2 (July 1998), pp 22–5.   37 Ibid. See also Winton, *The Victoria Cross at sea*, pp 32–4 and *Ireland's VCs*, p. 81.

this way they managed to drive the Russians off but two of the seamen were killed as they lay across the parapet to get a better aim. The three surviving seamen, James Gorman, Thomas Reeves and Mark Scholefield, were awarded the Victoria Cross in February 1857.[38] At the time this gazette appeared, Gorman was serving on the China Station and his medal and citation were sent out to him and presented by his commanding officer.

Gorman's later life has been the subject of some debate. Reference works on the Victoria Cross, including *The register of the Victoria Cross*, John Winton's *The Victoria Cross at sea* and *Ireland's VCs* record that he died in Southwark, London, 27 December 1889. This was due to the fact that one James Devereux claimed after the war to have changed his name to Gorman, joined the Royal Navy and won the Victoria Cross in the Crimea. Styling himself 'James Gorman Devereux', he lived out the rest of his life in St Saviour's parish, Southwark, and when he died in 1889, it was recorded on his death certificate that he was A 'holder of the Victoria Cross'. Indeed James Gorman Devereux had even succeeded in convincing his own family that he had won the Victoria Cross and his sons were later adamant that they had seen the medal.

John Winton noticed several discrepancies in this story while writing *The Victoria Cross at sea* but it was not until 1989 that he discovered the full details of James Gorman's later life. The real James Gorman actually went to Australia in 1863, on retiring from the Royal Navy, and was appointed as drill master and gunnery instructor of the Nautical School *Ship Vernon* in 1867. In April 1878 he was promoted to second mate of NNS *Vernon* and, in 1881, was appointed as foreman of magazines at Spectacle Island, an Ordnance Department establishment. He also married twice while in Australia, in 1864 and 1881. Gorman appears in the *Australian almanac* from 1875, listed as 'James Gorman, VC' and pension records in the Public Record Office in Kew confirmed that his pension was paid through the Royal Naval commandant's office in Sydney. Gorman died in October 1882 in New South Wales. The case of James Gorman Devereux is perhaps one of the most blatant cases of someone masquerading as a Victoria Cross holder. There have been numerous instances of this type of fraud but such men are usually found out at some point. This case is especially interesting as the impostor got away with his fraud for such a long time, creating a series of discrepancies in works such as *The register of the Victoria Cross*.[39]

Gorman was of course very lucky to have survived the day's action. Many seamen were killed at the battle of Inkerman and at later battles outside Sevastapol. One of the eight fatal Royal Navy officer casualties of the land campaign was Lieutenant Thomas Osborne Kidd RN, who was born in Dublin in

---

38 *Illustrated London News*, 20 June 1857. See also *London Gazette*, 24 February 1857.
39 Winton, 'Was Able Seaman James Gorman, VC, an Aussie?' pp 22–5.

1830. He was the eldest son of Joseph and Ann Kidd of Armagh and entered the
Royal Navy in May 1849, being promoted to lieutenant in July 1854. Thomas
Kidd had served on several ships including HMS *Wellesley*, HMS *Excellent* and
HMS *Royal Albert*. He was serving on HMS *Britannia* when the Naval Brigade
was being formed and volunteered for service ashore. It would seem that by the
end of September 1854 he had been chaffing at the imposed inactivity on HMS
Britannia. In a letter of 28 September to his parents he wrote:

> There is a report that they are going to sink their ships in the mouth of the
> Harbour, but still we hope that they will allow us to do that for them. We are in a
> great state of anxiety to have something to do besides looking after wounded. We
> go on shore sometimes with a couple of bottles and biscuits in a haversack on our
> backs, and are in some little use that way.[40]

By volunteering for service ashore, Lieutenant Kidd fulfilled his desire to
see action and served with the besieging batteries and in the trenches before
Sevastapol. In April 1855 he was transferred to HMS *Albion*, also James
Gorman's ship, and joined their detachment ashore. He was killed in the trenches
before Sevastapol during the assault of 18 June 1855. His commanding officer,
Captain Stephen Lushington, wrote to his parents that evening, describing the
circumstances of his death:

> The Electric telegraph will have told you the reverse the Army met with before the
> forts of Sevastapol, but I fear will have left you in doubt as to the fate of your gallant
> son. After passing through the terrific fire of the Redan and leaving more than half
> his party under its walls and receiving my orders to take the remainder of his party
> back into Camp, he again returned to the advanced trenches in an attempt to recover
> some wounded sailors, receiving a musket ball in the chest, which I grieve to say
> proved shortly fatal. He lived about three quarters of an hour after reaching Camp
> and was quite sensible to the last. Lieutenant Kidd was one of the finest fellows in
> the Brigade and had lately been appointed a Lieutenant in my ship the *Albion*. I will
> not attempt to offer consolation for so severe a bereavement, that I must leave to
> time and a higher power, but he always did his duty when living and died as a sailor
> wishes, in the faithful and gallant discharge of his duty.[41]

In a postscript, Captain Lushington added:

> The Revd Mr. Robson attended your son in his last moments and assures me that
> he died perfectly happy and in an excellent state of mind.[42]

William Howard Russell of *The Times* also noted the death of Lieutenant Kidd
in his dispatch of 20 June 1855.[43]

40 T.G.F. Patterson, 'A letter from the Crimea' in *Irish Sword*, vi, no. 25 (Winter 1964), p. 286.
41 Ibid. pp 286–7.   **42** Ibid. See also *The Times*, 20 June 1855.   **43** There is a memorial to

The naval crews who manned the siege batteries were often at the centre of fierce action. As well as being attacked during Russian sorties from Sevastapol, they were also the focus of Russian counter-battery fire. The attention that the naval batteries drew was not surprising, as the naval gun-crews achieved many successes and were responsible for several major breaches in the Russian walls. John Sullivan, born in Bantry, Co. Cork, in April 1830, played a significant role in siege of Sevastapol. He had joined the Royal Navy as a boy seaman, second class, in November 1846. In March 1852 he joined the predominantly Irish crew of HMS *Rodney*, with the rank of ordinary seaman. Rated able seaman that June, he was made leading seaman in November 1853 and 'captain of the mizzen-top' in February 1854. Sullivan had apparently decided on a long-term career in the Royal Navy, signing on for another seven years service in July 1853.[44]

In October 1854 he volunteered to serve ashore and was put in charge of one of the 68-pounder guns which had been landed from HMS *Terrible*. Sullivan and his gun-crew soon distinguished themselves in action and were credited with making the first serious breach in the walls of the Malakov Bastion. They were also credited with destroying a Russian magazine inside Sevastapol and helping to beat off the Russian attack during the battle of Inkerman. Sullivan and his crew were then transferred to No. 5 Greenhill Battery, a position under constant fire from a nearby Russian battery. On 10 April 1855 their commanding officer, Commander Kennedy, called for a volunteer to go out towards the Russian lines and place a flagstaff on a mound of earth to act as an aiming point for No. 5 Greenhill Battery. As the Russian battery was concealed behind this mound, it was thought that the flagpole would improve the sailors' gunnery. As the senior rating in the gun-crew, Sullivan felt that it was his duty to volunteer for this dangerous task. Although under constant rifle fire, he calmly carried the pole out of the British lines and planted it on the mound in front of the Russian battery, even gathering stones to pile at its base to secure it. He returned unhurt to his own battery. Commander Kennedy commended him for his bravery and remarked that his 'gallantry was always conspicuous'. Mentioned by Admiral Lyons in his dispatches, Sullivan was awarded the Victoria Cross in the first VC list of February 1857. During the course of the war he was also awarded the Crimean Medal with Inkerman and Sevastapol Clasps, the Turkish Crimean Medal, the Sardinian *Al Valore*, the French Legion d'Honneur, the Royal Humane Society's silver medal and the Conspicuous Gallantry Medal. This last decoration, the CGM, was instituted in August 1855 and only ten were awarded in 1855.[45] Sullivan's experiences in the Crimea illustrate the way in

Lieutenant Kidd in St Patrick's Cathedral (Church of Ireland), Armagh.   **44** Winton, *The Victoria Cross at sea*, pp 35–6.   **45** Ibid. See *Ireland's VCs*, p. 13. Also *London Gazette*, 24 February 1857.

which members of the Naval Brigade often found themselves in the very thick of the action. (Sullivan's later career will be referred to in Chapter 7.)

The Azov campaign

In May 1855 it was decided to detach some of the ships of the Black Sea fleet to form a flotilla to operate in the Sea of Azov. Admiral Lyons had pointed out months previously that the Russians were using supply ships operating in the sea of Azov to ferry supplies to Kertch. These supplies were then carried overland to re-supply Sevastapol and the Russian land army that was operating outside the city. Kertch was, therefore, the main base for Russian logistical operations. It had extensive flour mills and was also used to store the fish caught by the fishing fleets of the numerous villages along that coast. Foraging parties were also active in the area, gathering fodder for the Russian army's horses. Admiral Lyons rightly concluded that, if Kertch was taken, Sevastapol would be without hope of re-supply and must eventually fall. Early in May 1855, therefore, an allied expedition set sail for the Sea of Azov with the intention of capturing Kertch. The French commander, General Canrobert recalled the expedition, following telegraphed instructions from Paris where the emperor was hoping to negotiate a peace settlement. His action put him in an embarrassing position among the allied commanders and he later resigned. General (later Maréchal) Pélissier took command of the French forces and, an experienced and tough soldier, he refused to respond to the constant stream of telegrams being sent from Paris by the emperor. In order to re-establish good relations with his allies, Pélissier agreed to repeat the Kertch expedition at the end of May. On 23 May 1855 Captain Edmund Lyons, the son of Admiral Lyons, set sail for the Sea of Azov with a formidable force. Fifty-six allied ships, including frigates, gun-boats and transports, sailed north eastwards across the Black Sea to the Straits of Kertch, carrying 15,000 infantry. The flotilla was later augmented by twenty-four launches armed with rockets and 24-pounder howitzers.[46]

When the allied flotilla arrived in the straits, the Russians actually blew up their own forts and retreated. The expedition encountered no serious opposition on land or sea and the Sea of Azov was soon in allied control. On the 25 May 1855 both Kertch and the nearby town of Yenikale were occupied. Within a week Captain Lyons' flotilla had sunk four steamers and 246 other merchant

---

46 Lambert and Badsey, *The war correspondents*, pp 196–219. HMS *Somerset*, a Duke Class (Type 23) Frigate, was sent to the Adriatic in May 1999 during the NATO operations against Serbia to serve as an escort ship with a squadron of American missile frigates. This was the first time that a Royal Navy ship came under foreign command since the Crimean war. Information

vessels. They had also seized large quantities of corn, flour and gunpowder, all valued to be worth over £15,000. The small force also seized over 17,000 tons of coal.[47]

An interesting feature of the Kertch expedition was the series of raids carried out by parties of sailors who rowed ashore to destroy Russian supply dumps. These raids were usually carried out by very small parties and are often compared by naval historians to the commando raids of World War II. On 29 May 1855 Lieutenant William Buckley (HMS *Miranda*), Lieutenant Hugh Talbot Burgoyne (HMS Swallow) and Gunner John Roberts (HMS *Ardent*), volunteered to land on the beach near the town of Genitchi in an attempt to destroy a large Russian storehouse. To do this they had to use a small ship's boat to get close inshore and were totally out of range of any covering fire from the fleet. It was also known that there were a large number of Russians in the area. Lieutenant Hugh Talbot Burgoyne had been born in Dublin in July 1833, the only son of Lieutenant-General Sir John Fox Burgoyne, colonel-commandant of Royal Engineers and previously chairman of the Irish Board of Works (1831–45). Hugh Talbot Burgoyne had entered the Royal Navy as a cadet in 1847 and had been promoted to lieutenant in January 1854. At the time of the Kertch expedition he was senior lieutenant in the eight-gun sloop, HMS *Swallow*.[48]

The raid that the three men carried out on 29 May 1855 was highly successful. After landing on the beach near Genitchi, they were fired on by Russian infantry but had time to set fire to a corn store and ammunition dump. In the confusion that followed the resulting fire and explosion, they managed to avoid a troop of Cossacks sent to cut off their retreat and recovered their boat on the beach. They returned to the flotilla and were met with the praise of their comrades. All three were later awarded the Victoria Cross. Admiral Lyon's later described the raid as 'a service of imminent risk'. Burgoyne was later mentioned in dispatches for further actions in the Sea of Azov. In June 1855 he was given command of the four-gun sloop HMS *Wrangler* and was promoted to commander in the following month. In a report of 8 August 1855, written to Commander Sherard Osborn, he described one of the actions that were typical of the Azov campaign:

> I have the honour to acquaint you, that in pursuance of your instructions, I proceeded in Her Majesty's steam gun vessel *Wrangler* under my command, to the anchorage off Petrushena; and having anchored in 13 feet of water, at a distance of about 5,000 yards, I proceeded in the gig of this vessel, accompanied by the paddle-box boat of Her Majesty's ship *Vesuvius*, towards the town; and when about 800 yards distant, commenced throwing rockets, but (although they

provided by Nigel Andrews, Assistant Defence Attaché, British Embassy, Dublin.   **47** Winton, *The Victoria Cross at sea*, pp 37–41.   **48** Ibid.

were well directed and some of them lodged in enormous stacks of hay in the vicinity of the town) failed in setting fire to it. As no troops had appeared, I deemed it prudent to land and destroy some stores and small stacks of hay. On nearing, a rocket was fired in the direction of our intended landing place and several rifles were also fired, still no troops appeared and no resistance was offered; but on getting within ten yards of the shore, a number of troops emerged from their ambush and commenced a sharp fire and well directed, on the boats, which was returned by us; fortunately no accident occurred, although the enemy's fire was well kept up.

Burgoyne's report continued:

I considered it advisable to move the *Wrangler* nearer the shore and accordingly sent Mr Perks, second master of this ship, to sound, and commenced trimming ship to get her on an even keel; having succeeded in reducing the draught to 10 feet 10 inches and Mr Perks having discovered a passage which led to within 2,000 yards with 11 feet of water, proceeded; and on arriving at an anchorage about 1,900 yards off, commenced firing shot, shell and carcasses and on hauling off at sunset, the town was on fire in two places near the hay.[49]

While such actions were made in an attempt to reduce the amount of supplies available to the Russian army, they also inflicted hardships on the civilian population. Yet Royal Naval officers were, on other occasions, quite chivalrous. An Irish naval officer, Captain John Moore of HMS *Highflyer*, described an incidence of chivalry in a report to Admiral Lyons in April 1855:

I have the honour to inform you that I arrived off Kertch on the 24th inst. In rounding Cape Takli I observed a small coasting craft moored under the rocks, and on my boats bringing her off, I found on board of her a travelling carriage. I availed myself of this circumstance to send in a flag of truce by the *Viper,* offering to return the carriage to the owner, which was accepted by Baron C. Wrangell, commanding the army in the south of the Crimea.

Yet Moore's excessive good manners belied his real intention. His report continued:

Major Gordon and Commandant de Sain went in the *Viper* and by this means were able to make a tolerably close reconnaissance without exciting suspicion and on the following day the carriage was landed in their presence on the beach near Kamiesch Point which enabled them to observe the favourable nature of the beach for disembarkation. A demi-battery of field artillery was observed to be stationed in the village of Kamiesch.

49 Peter Duckers and Neil Mitchell, *The Azoff campaign* (Shrewsbury, 1996), p. 84.

Indeed Moore would appear to have been very clever indeed and used the return of this 'gentleman's carriage' to gather a good deal of information. A report of 26 April 1855 concluded:

> We were able to make our reconnaissance without attracting suspicion under the flag of truce and also to prove that the beach was a good one. I also hoped to have proved to them that the road across the marsh was a practicable one for artillery by observing the carriage drive away; but it still remains opposite the Cossack guard-house, where it was landed. I hope the owner will send me a haunch of venison.[50]

The success of the Azov campaign was crucial to the outcome of the Crimean war and Irish seamen, such as Moore and Burgoyne, played a significant role. Burgoyne was present at the first Victoria Cross investiture in Hyde Park in June 1857.[51] In March 1858 he was commended for the assistance he gave in extinguishing a fire in Valparasio, while serving aboard HMS *Ganges*. Promoted to captain in May 1861, he served as second-in-command of the Anglo-Chinese Flotilla before taking command of HMS *Wyvern* in 1865. Burgoyne then served on the North American and West Indies stations aboard HMS *Constance*. In 1870 he took command of HMS *Captain*, an ironclad turret-ship built to a controversial design. There had been a long and bitter argument about the ship's design between Edward Reed, Chief Constructor of the Royal Navy, and Captain Cowper Cowles, RN, HMS *Captain*'s designer. Reed maintained that HMS *Captain*'s draught was too deep, that she had too little freeboard and that she carried too much top hamper. He was convinced that in a heavy sea HMS *Captain* would be swamped and would sink. Burgoyne sided with Captain Cowles, however, and wrote that he felt that the ship was seaworthy stating that she had 'proved herself a most efficient vessel both under sail and steam, as well as easy and comfortable'. Shortly after midnight on 7 September 1870, HMS *Captain*, sailing in company with other ships, was caught in a squall off Cape Finisterre and overturned and sank. Burgoyne was last seen clinging to an overturned boat, urging survivors to swim towards one of the ship's boats, and he remarked to Gunner James May, one of the eighteen survivors, 'My God May, I never thought we were coming to this.' Burgoyne apparently made no attempt to swim to the one remaining boat and was drowned, along with 471 other men, including Captain Cowles. The victims of this disaster are commemorated on a plaque in St Paul's Cathedral.[52]

50 Ibid. pp 22–3. **51** Ibid. See *Ireland's VCs* p. 14. Also *London Gazette*, 24 February 1857.
52 Winton, *The Victoria Cross at sea*, pp 38–9. See *DNB*. See also Lieutenant-Colonel the Hon. George Wrottesley RE, *The life and correspondence of Field Marshal Sir John Fox Burgoyne, Bart.* (2 volumes, London, 1873).

Thirty-one Royal Navy ships took part in the Azov campaign and the roll for the Azov Clasp in the Public Record Office in Kew records that 2,307 sailors and marines were entitled to this clasp, which would have been worn on the ribbon of the British Crimean Medal. There were cases, however, of men who served on two or three different ships during the campaign and their names are repeated on the roll. Also sixty-six men deserted before they actually received the award.[53] Around 2,200 men were actually awarded the Azov Clasp and the roll records that 193 of these were Irish, 8.7% of the total. There are also other men on the roll who have Irish names but their place of birth is not recorded.[54]

The campaign in the Azov, which continued throughout the summer and autumn of 1855, was a resounding success and the sea literally became an allied lake. The final blow for the Russians came when their pontoon bridge across the Genitchi Strait was seized and destroyed in July 1855. This action cut Russia's main supply route to the south and Sevastapol. Supplies now had to travel an extra 120 miles overland, using bad roads. The re-supply of Sevastapol became a logistical nightmare and Admiral Lyons' prediction eventually came true. The Russians were forced to accept that Sevastapol would eventually fall. Also the Russian field army, which had always been a threat to the besieging allied armies, was forced to move away from the city due to the lack of supplies.

The eventual success of the army before Sevastapol created yet another problem. When French troops captured the crucial Malakov defence works, the Russians merely evacuated the area of the city south of the bay. While the allies took possession of that part of the city, the Russians remained in position north of the bay. This was an immensely unsatisfactory situation and total military stalemate ensued, relations between the allies gradually worsening. The French wished to preserve the *status quo* and await the outcome of peace negotiations. The British, having failed in their assault on the Redan on 8 September 1855, felt that honour demanded further military action. Eventually French co-operation was secured for an operation against Fort Kinburn, a defensive position which commanded the confluence of the Dnieper and Bug rivers. In essence the operation was merely an effort to boost British morale. Fort Kinburn was in a commanding position but was poorly built and armed with obsolete 24-pounders. Yet ten miles upriver was the shipbuilding yard of the Black Sea fleet, Nicolaiev, and also two battleships.

Ten thousand troops were landed near the fort on 17 October 1855, the first anniversary of the opening bombardment on Sevastapol. Yet the troops were

---

53 There are several Irish sailors who are recorded as having deserted, marked as 'Run' on the Azov Clasp Roll. One Irish sailor, Ordinary Seaman John Cassidy of HMS *Medina* deserted in Constantinople in July 1855. It would be interesting to discover how these men managed to return home, if they ever did.   54 PRO, ADM 171.25, Azoff Clasp Roll.

not used, as Admiral Lyons sent in his flotilla of gunboats and mortar vessels and pounded Fort Kinburn until it was in ruins. Despite this success the French refused to attack Nicolaiev and Odessa, again in the hope of a peace settlement. The emperor also wished to preserve Odessa as a possible base in the event of further operations in 1856.[55]

Irish casualties in the naval campaigns

The various actions in which the Royal Navy was engaged, both at sea and on land, inevitably resulted in casualties and there were many Irish among these. Frank and Andrea Cook researched published lists of casualties and compiled *The casualty roll for the Crimea* (London, 1976). This casualty roll contains details of the losses of the Royal Naval Brigade in the siege of Sevastapol and also Royal Navy casualties during the naval bombardment of the city on 17 October 1854. The casualties of the Royal Naval Brigade, which numbered around 1,200 all ranks, are summarized in Table 7:

Table 7. Royal Naval Brigade casualties

	Killed	*Died of disease*	*Wounded*
Officers	8	3	30
Men	116	41	431

Source: Frank and Andrea Cook, *Casualty roll for the Crimea* (London, 1976).

One of the fatal officer casualties was Lieutenant Thomas Osborne Kidd. There also many Irish names among those on the Royal Naval Brigade's casualty roll. There are sixty-five men included in this list who have Irish names.

The naval bombardment of Sevastapol on 17 October 1854 was also a costly business. As the Royal Navy's ships moved close inshore to bombard the Russian positions, they were engaged by the Russian batteries and most of the ships involved suffered damage and casualties. The casualty roll for this action reflects the ferocity of this action, fought over very short ranges. Forty-three men were killed, including Ordinary Seaman James Tracey of HMS *Sphinx*, who fell overboard and was drowned during the action; 261 men were wounded. Again a number of Irish names appear in this casualty roll. There are 29 men on this casualty roll with Irish names.[56] No one has, as yet, compiled a list of casualties from the Baltic campaign.

55 Lambert and Badsey, *The war correspondents*, pp 262–74.   56 Ibid. pp 221–5.

The National Archives of Ireland has a document that gives the names of men who were definitely Irish and who were killed or died of disease during the Crimean war while serving with the Royal Navy. In July 1863 funds were collected in the parishes of Whitegate, Upper and Lower Aghada and Farsid in Co. Cork, and distributed to the families of local men who had been killed in the war. These parishes are located to the south east of Cork harbour and were very near the Royal Navy depot at Haulbowline. They were apparently prime recruiting areas for the Royal Navy and a large number of men from these parishes were killed during the war. The clerk who compiled this list in 1863 also noted details of the 1841 census in the margin and, when these figures are viewed in conjunction with Crimean deaths, the impact that these losses had on the locality becomes apparent. The following table illustrates the number of Crimean war losses alongside the figure recorded for 1841 male population.

Table 8. Crimean war casualties in the parishes of Whitegate, Aghada and Farsid, Co. Cork

	Crimean war dead	1841 male population
Whitegate	110	513
Upper Aghada	54	97
Lower Aghada	16	50
Farsid	44	98

Source: NA, MS 6077, 'Lists of men from Aghada and Whitegate Parishes Co. Cork serving in the Royal Navy, and lists of those killed or died in the war'.

Just over £260 was given to the families of these men. This list of casualties contains a separate list of local men who had died while serving with the Royal Navy after the war. Included in this list were Thomas Murray of HMS *Cleveland*, who fell overboard near Gibraltar in December 1859, and Thomas Halloran of HMS *Orion*, who was killed in China in May 1857. Also included in this list was Mary Leary who was raising her brother's children after he had been killed in a fall aboard ship. John Sullivan, who had lost an arm in the Crimea, was noted for being in receipt of a pension of one shilling a day from one J.P. Lyons.[57]

This document is a most interesting and valuable record of the collection and distribution of funds on a local level for the use of families of Crimean dead. Also when the list of dead is compared with the 1841 census figures one can only assume that such massive losses had a devastating effect on the lives

[57] NA, MS 6077, 'Lists of men from Aghada and Whitegate Parishes Co. Cork serving in the Royal Navy, and lists of those killed or died in the war'.

of these small parishes. If such losses were repeated in other sea-going communities around the country, the effect would have been to cause a massive social dislocation. Many demographic historians tend to blame such sudden reductions in the male population on emigration. It would be interesting to carry out further studies to discover if the numerous wars of the nineteenth century resulted in similar dramatic reductions in the male populations in specific areas in Ireland.

The extensive nature of the Royal Navy's campaigns during the Crimean war is a subject that deserves both further study and comment and it can also be argued that the naval campaigns had a decisive effect on the outcome of the war. Irishmen played a significant role in these campaigns in the Baltic, the Black Sea and the Sea of Azov. Irish seamen were also responsible for some incredible acts of bravery, resulting in four Victoria Crosses as well as other decorations. There were Irish merchant ships and coastguard sailors involved in the war. The enthusiasm with which Irishmen joined the Royal Navy at the beginning of the war seems quite remarkable. Yet one can only guess at the devastating effect that Crimean war losses had on the maritime towns and small fishing villages of Ireland.

4

The experiences of Irish surgeons, nurses and chaplains in the Crimea

Irish surgeons in the British Army

The conditions in the hospitals in the Crimea, and the sufferings of the sick and wounded, have been the focus of many histories of the Crimean war. It would be true to say that the army's surgeons, many Irishmen among them, had to treat terrible wounds and also work in dreadful conditions. One Irish surgeon, Robert McDonnell, briefly described his Crimean experiences in a letter of 20 October 1855:

> I have been to the front, spent about two months in camp, was on the ground when Sevastapol was blazing, had fever which nearly did for me, and have now returned to Smyrna, after diverse peregrinations, to finish my recovery and refatten my calves.[1]

While this brief description of McDonnell's was quite light-hearted, some of his letters home, as will be shown later in this chapter, described the horrors of working in a field hospital. Yet these Irish surgeons, many having received their medical education in Trinity College, Dublin, also had to learn to deal with the disorganized conditions that existed in the British Army's medical services.

The records of the British Army's medical services are very comprehensive and, now deposited in the Royal Army Medical Corps Museum at Keogh Barracks, Aldershot, have been the subject of intense study. The Wellcome Historical Medical Library sponsored a study of the list of commissioned medical officers in the 1960s. This was published in two volumes as *Commissioned officers in the medical services of the British army, 1660–1960* in 1968, under the editorship of Robert Drew. Study of this list has revealed a large number of Irish surgeons who served in the Army Medical Service during the Crimean war. Just over 100 of the 400 or so army surgeons and purveyors who served of the Crimean war were Irish. (See Appendix B.)

1 NLI, MS 18,491, Robert McDonnell Letters, 20 October 1855.

An interesting feature of this list of commissioned surgeons is the long length of service that some of them completed. The surgeon with the longest service, who served in the Crimea, was George Hume Reade. Born in England in 1793, he actually joined the Army Medical Service in September 1813 as an apothecary.[2] Such instances of extremely long service were not uncommon. The longest serving Irish surgeon in the Crimea was James Piers Moore, born in Dublin in 1811. He entered Trinity College, Dublin, in 1829, graduating BA in 1834.[3] Joining the Army Medical Service in March 1837, he was appointed as an assistant surgeon to the 94th Foot. He served in the Crimea as a surgeon-major and was awarded the Turkish Order of the Medjidie, 5th Class. James Piers Moore finally retired on half-pay in September 1865, with the honorary rank of deputy inspector-general of hospitals.[4]

It is impossible in the space of this study to give full details of the 106 Irish surgeons who served with the Army Medical Service in the Crimea. It is useful, however, to outline the career of just some of these men to show the experience that some of these Irish surgeons had. An Irish surgeon who was to achieve some renown for his work in the Crimea was Thomas Connor O'Leary, who was born in Tralee, Co. Kerry, in May 1821. He was educated at Trinity College, Dublin, graduating BA in 1844 and MB in the following year. Joining the Army Medical Service in July 1847 as an assistant surgeon, O'Leary served as a full surgeon with the 68th Foot in the Crimea, and was also awarded the Order of the Medjidie, 5th Class.[5] During the war he achieved a reputation as a surgeon of some skill. One of his most notable successes was in the treatment of a young soldier of the 68th Foot, who was severely wounded in the right hip. Determined not to amputate the leg, O'Leary removed around five inches of the patient's thigh bone in a tricky operation, and formed a false hip joint. While the soldier's leg was shortened by a number of inches, the difference was made up by the use of a boot with a raised sole. In an inspection of Crimean invalids at Brompton Barracks, Queen Victoria met O'Leary's patient and described his work as a 'triumph of surgery'.[6] O'Leary continued in the service after the war, retiring with the rank of surgeon-general in May 1881. He died at Bath in February 1885. There is no doubt that O'Leary was just one of the many fine surgeons who worked in the Crimea,

2 George Hume Reade served in the Peninsula (1813–4) and also the British-American war (1812–14). Serving in Canada (1818–29), he also acted as colonel commanding the 3rd Regiment of Canadian Militia. In the Crimea, Hume Reade was employed as principal apothecary, but died in Scutari in November 1854. Two of his sons, Surgeon-General Sir John Cole Reade KCB, and Surgeon-General Herbert Taylor Reade VC, also later served in the Army Medical Service. 3 *Alumni Dublinenses*.   4 Robert Drew (ed.), *Commissioned officers in the medical services of the British army, 1660–1898* (London, 1968), i, p. 301.   5 *Alumni Dublinenses*. Also Drew, *Commissioned officers in the medical services*, p. 340.   6 Captain Peter Starling, RAMC., 'Queen Victoria's visits to the hospitals at Fort Pitt and Chatham, 1855–6' in *The war*

but whose successes were overshadowed by the incompetent manner in which the medical services were run.

John Gibbons, born in Westmeath in May 1826, and who joined as an assistant surgeon in June 1850, also had a long career in the Army Medical Service. Surgeon Gibbons served in the Crimean war, the Indian Mutiny and the Afghan war of 1878–9. He was awarded the Legion of Honour and a CB (military) in 1879. Retiring with the honorary rank of surgeon-general in June 1882, he died in Dublin in December of the same year.[7] Examples of Irish surgeons who served in several campaigns were not uncommon. Joshua Henry Porter was born in Dublin in May 1831 and joined the Army Medical Service in June 1853. He saw service in the Crimea with the 97th Foot, later served in the Indian Mutiny and was present at the siege and final capture of Lucknow. Porter also served with the British Ambulance in France during the Franco-Prussian War of 1870–1 and was assistant professor of surgery at the Army Medical School at Netley (1874–9). During the course of his career he received numerous honours including the Order of the Medjidie and the Alexander Memorial Prize and Gold Medal (1876). He also published *The surgeon's pocket book: an essay on the best treatment of wounded in war* (1880). Surgeon-Major Porter died at Cabul in January 1880.[8]

Army surgeons also had to work under dangerous conditions in the Crimea. It was quite common for the Russians to fire on surgeons and stretcher parties as they tried to bring in the wounded after a battle or one of the numerous assaults on Sevastapol. Many Irish surgeons also later served during the Indian Mutiny. One Irish surgeon, William Bradshaw, served in the Crimea and then won the Victoria Cross during the Indian Mutiny. Bradshaw was born in Thurles, Co. Tipperary, in February 1830 and joined the Army Medical Service in August 1854. He was sent to the Crimea in November 1855 as an assistant surgeon with the 50th Foot and served throughout the siege of Sevastapol. For this he received the Crimean Medal with Sevastapol clasp, and the Turkish Crimean Medal. He served with the 90th Foot in the Indian Mutiny, and was present with Major-General Sir Henry Havelock's column at the first relief of Lucknow (in effect a reinforcement of the defenders) in September 1857, where he was wounded. Bradshaw found himself as one of the defenders of the besieged Residency until its evacuation in the second relief of November 1857. He later served with Lieutenant-General Sir James Outram in the defence of the Alambagh and had the eventual satisfaction of seeing Lucknow recaptured in March 1858.[9] Awarded the VC, as well as the Indian Medal with Lucknow clasp, for his actions at Lucknow in September 1857, Bradshaw's *London Gazette* citation read:

correspondent, xvi, no. 1 (April, 1998), p. 36.   **7** Drew, op. cit., pp 348–9.   **8** Ibid. p. 361. See also H.G. Hart, *Army List* (1860), p. 338–9.   **9** H.G. Hart, *Army List* (1860), p. 240.

For intrepidity and good conduct when ordered with Surgeon Home, 90th Regiment, to remove the wounded men left behind the column that forced its way to the residency of Lucknow, on the 26th September, 1857. The Dhooly bearers had left the Dhoolies, but by great exertions, and not withstanding the close proximity of the Sepoys, Surgeon Home, and Assistant Surgeon Bradshaw, got some of the bearers together, and Assistant Surgeon Bradshaw with about twenty Dhoolies, becoming separated from the rest of the party, succeeded in reaching the residency in safety by the river bank.[10]

Assistant Surgeon Bradshaw went on half-pay in October 1860 due to ill health. He died, 9 March 1861, at Thurles.[11]

Oliver Barnett, born in Clogher, Co. Tyrone, in November 1830, was also to have a distinguished career as a military surgeon. He joined the Army Medical Service in November 1854 and served in the Crimea, Egypt (1882) and the Sudan (1885). Between 1873 and 1880, he served on the staff of three viceroys of India, Lords Mayo, Northbrook and Lytton. He finished his career as a surgeon-general in June 1885, but died at Eastbourne the following month.[12] George Langford Hinde, born in Dublin in October 1832, had an equally impressive career. He was appointed as an assistant surgeon in May 1855 and sent to the Crimea. During the course of his long career he also served in South Africa (1881) and the Sudan (1884–5). He retired as a surgeon-major-general in January 1892 and was created a CB in 1899. Hinde died at Reading in February 1910.[13]

Not all the Irish surgeons had such impressive records, however. Henry Grange, of Portarlington, Co. Offaly, joined the Army Medical Service in September 1854, and was posted to the 47th Foot and served in the Crimea and the Indian Mutiny. His service in both these campaigns could not be faulted and he was present throughout the siege of Sevastapol, witnessing the final assault of 8 September 1855. In India he was detached from the 47th Foot, and was in medical charge of a squadron of the 2nd Dragoon Guards at the action at Azimghur on 7 April 1858, in which he had a horse shot.[14] Grange's career ended abruptly, however, when he was dismissed from the service by sentence of general court martial in April 1862.[15]

Equally ignominious was the case of Assistant Surgeon Henry Charles Boate, born in Dungarvan, Co. Wexford, in August 1828. Appointed as an assistant surgeon to the 6th (Inniskilling) Regiment of Dragoons in November 1852, he was posted with his regiment to the Crimea.[16] After the charge of the Heavy Brigade, at the battle of Balaclava on 26 October 1854, he was reprimanded for being absent from his post. Boate protested against this charge on the basis that he was not required to take part in military action. His commanding

10 *London Gazette*, 18 June 1858.   11 *Ireland's VCs* p. 25.   12 Drew, op. cit., p. 382.   13 Ibid. p. 392.   14 Hart, *Army List* (1860), p. 262.   15 Drew, op. cit., p. 378. Also Hart, *Army List* (1860), pp 262–3. Grange's dismissal was apparently for 'gross neglect of duty'.   16 Ibid. p. 358.

officer, Lieutenant-Colonel White, in turn pointed out that he had removed himself from the field and was, therefore, unable to carry out his medical duties. Boate ultimately resigned in disgrace in April 1855, but continued to protest his innocence to his brother officers.[17]

It should be noted that the men above merely represent a small sample of the one hundred and six Irish surgeons contained in the list of commissioned officers of the Army Medical Service. While the careers of a few of these men ended in disgrace, the majority had long and distinguished careers. The Crimea also proved to be a dangerous place for army surgeons. Several of the Irish surgeons died of disease while one, Assistant Surgeon John F. O'Leary, from Cork, was killed while attending wounded men in the trenches before Sevastapol.

The Army Medical Service

At the outbreak of the Crimean war the medical services of the British army were still organized in the same manner as they had been at Waterloo, nearly forty years before. No efforts had been made at reorganizing medical arrangements in the preceding years, despite the previous proposals of eminent army surgeons such as James Guthrie, Sir James McGrigor and Sir Charles Bell. All at some time had suggested that the British army's medical services be centralized in one regiment or corps but this proposal had not been followed up by the Horse Guards.[18] There was also no ambulance corps or even a company of medical orderlies in the army. As early as 1811, John Frederick Frank had suggested that an army hospital corps be established but his proposals were ignored for over forty years. For the first half of the nineteenth century, therefore, there were no improvements made to the status or administration of the army's medical services. The Crimean war was to prove that such change was drastically necessary.

Since the establishment of a standing army in 1660, British army practice was to appoint surgeons on a regimental basis. In 1854 surgeons were still appointed in this way. The director-general of Army Medical Service, Sir Andrew Smith, appointed suitably qualified candidates directly to a battalion. Apart from regimental surgeons, there was also a small number of surgeons which made up the Medical Staff. This body supplied the medical officers to the military hospitals in the British Isles. Additional surgeons were recruited from civilian practice in time of war to help staff hospitals at home and general hospitals in the field.

17 It is interesting to note that Surgeon James Mouat, also of the 6th (Inniskilling) Dragoons won a VC for his bravery at the battle of Balaclava. Mouat went to assist Captain Morris who was lying wounded following the charge of the Light Brigade. He dressed Morris' wounds while under fire and helped carry him to safety.   18 Redmond McLaughlin, *The Royal Army Medical Corps*

There were also a small number of purveyors attached to hospitals. These officers, usually surgeons who had been promoted, were responsible for the purchase and distribution of food, drink and medical comforts in the hospitals. They also handled all accounts. In 1853 there were only five deputy-purveyors distributed between hospitals in England, Ireland, Jamaica and Gibraltar. A royal warrant of April 1853 augmented the Purveyor's Branch and a second warrant of October 1855 increased the number of personnel in this branch still further.[19] Two Irishmen served as purveyors in the Crimea.[20]

In 1854, the Army Medical Service had no proper unit of medical orderlies or stretcher-bearers. Traditionally, regimental bandsmen acted as stretcher-bearers and medical orderlies, and laboured to provide some immediate comfort to casualties in the field. In virtually all cases these men were given no proper training, and often ran the risk of contracting serious diseases from sick soldiers in their care. In previous campaigns civilians had also been hired to do this. The involvement of Florence Nightingale and Mary Stanley brought the shortcomings of the Army Medical Service to public notice, resulting in a series of inquiries into medical matters after the war. Equally the manner in which *The Times* correspondent, William Howard Russell, reported the war, ensured that the way in which the British army cared for its wounded was front page news. Yet even when the service's problems were made public, change came only gradually. A Medical Staff Corps composed of medical orderlies (a corps of other ranks without officers) was established in June 1855.[21] This corps was subsequently redesigned as the Army Hospital Corps in August 1857. In 1873 the Army Medical Department composed of medical officers was established. These two units were not amalgamated until September 1884. Fourteen years later the Royal Army Medical Corps, a corps of both surgeon-officers and enlisted orderlies was formed.[22] It had taken virtually the whole of the nineteenth century for suggestions first put forward by surgeons serving under the duke of Wellington to be implemented.

Regimental surgeons were usually appointed with the rank of acting assistant surgeon for a probationary period. This was not a commissioned rank and acting assistant surgeons were classed as warrant officers. On completion of this probationary period, they were commissioned as assistant surgeons. In cavalry and infantry regiments, assistant surgeons ranked with second lieutenants while surgeons ranked as captains. In the Guards, assistant surgeons ranked as ensigns, battalion surgeons as captains and senior surgeons as lieutenant-colonels. Guards' surgeons took precedence over surgeons of line regiments when the

(London, 1972).   **19** Drew, op. cit., xxxiii–xxxiv.   **20** These were Purveyor-in-Chief James S. Roberts from Co. Wicklow and Purveyor David Fitzgerald, who was also from Ireland.   **21** Nine companies of 78 men each. There was only one officer at the depot to oversee administrative matters.   **22** Anthony Makepeace-Warne, *Brassey's companion to the British army* (London,

Guards acted with other units in the field.[23] Purveyors ranked as lieutenants for the first fifteen years of their service and after that time as captains.

Despite this apparent recognition of medical learning, students of medical colleges were often discouraged from entering military service due to the comparatively low pay and very real dangers. In some regiments the surgeon was not viewed as an officer in a real sense. It became known that, in certain regiments, surgeons and veterinary-surgeons were not viewed as 'proper officers', and had to sit at a separate side table in the mess. Even when such facts became known, newly qualified surgeons still joined as regimental surgeons, viewing the relative security of the position and the opportunity for travel, as some compensation for abandoning civilian practice.

It must also be pointed out that the Army Medical Service was conservative in terms of medical practice. Anaesthetics had been available since 1847 and the first operation carried out under anaesthesia in Ireland took place on 1 January 1847, performed by John McDonnell (John McDonnell's son, Robert, served as a civilian surgeon in the Crimea). John McDonnell had read about the experiments in the use of anaesthetics that had been carried out at the Massachusetts General Hospital in Boston in 1846. After carrying out tests on himself, he performed an operation under general anaesthesia at the Richmond Hospital in Dublin, amputating the arm of Mary Kane of Drogheda.[24] This operation by McDonnell predated Sir James Young Simpson's first successful operation using anaesthesia which did not take place until 4 November 1847. Army surgeons generally refused to use ether or chloroform, however. The main reason for this was the belief that the application of an anaesthetic would put a patient's system under an additional strain, no doubt leading to profound shock and death. Medicinal brandy and opium were usually administered only as post-operation sedatives.

Also, while Joseph Lister (later Baron Lister) had begun research into the use of antiseptics in 1852, it was not until the 1860s that his ideas became widely known. Indeed, while German army surgeons used antiseptic methods during the Franco-Prussian war, it was not until the mid-1870s that similar methods were first used by British army surgeons. In the Crimea, surgeons did not wash their hands, or their operating tables, between operations. As was also the case in the American Civil war, they would spend several hours after each battle performing operations, their hands, arms, operating tables and aprons covered in blood. It is not surprising, therefore, that so many soldiers died due to post-surgical infections that they contracted in the army's field hospitals.

The medical situation which prevailed in the Crimea has been outlined in several works. Most prominent amongst these would be John Shepherd's *The*

1995), pp 294–5.   **23** Drew, op. cit., xxvi.   **24** Davis Coakley, *Irish masters of medicine* (Dublin,

Crimean doctors (2 volumes, Liverpool, 1991), Cecil Woodham-Smith's *Florence Nightingale* (London, 1950) and Sue M. Goldie's *Florence Nightingale: letters from the Crimea* (London, 1997). It is sufficient to point out here that the total breakdown of administration services resulted in disaster. There were no provisions made for the transportation of the wounded and, when the army landed at Calamita Bay in September 1854, they had not even any ambulance wagons. The wounded from the battles of the Alma, Balaclava and Inkerman, after initial treatment in the Balaclava hospital, were transported in farm carts to the port for evacuation. The wounded were then loaded onto cramped transport ships and travelled to the army's hospitals and taken to the Barrack and General Hospitals at Scutari. There were two other hospitals in the vicinity of Scutari, one at Kulalie and the other, for officers only, at Kadikoi. Even further away were the hospitals at Varna, Gallipoli and Abydos. In early 1855 hospitals were established at Smyrna and Renkioi in an effort to relieve the Scutari hospitals. There was also a Royal Naval hospital at Therapia.

The journey to these hospitals was over 300 miles and resulted in the death of many of the sick and wounded en route. At the hospitals themselves administrative chaos reigned and, due to the total neglect of hygiene, the diseases of cholera, typhus and typhoid spread. On several occasions at Scutari there were so many sick and wounded that some had to accommodated in the hospital's stables. It was to the great credit of Florence Nightingale that she could rectify some of the problems of the army's hospitals, not only through her organizational skill, but also through her workmanlike relationship with the secretary at war, Sidney Herbert. Yet modern research has shown that between November 1854 and March 1855, 4077 soldiers died at Scutari. For every man that died of wounds, a further ten died of disease and often these diseases were contracted after arriving in the hospital. Such statistics have resulted in the gradual erosion of the myth of the 'Lady of the Lamp'. While an excellent administrator and concerned with the men's personal hygiene, Florence Nightingale was not concerned with the environmental improvements that would have reduced the amount of disease at Scutari.[25] It was in this administrative and medical nightmare that many Irish surgeons received their first experience of working as military surgeons.

Irish civilian surgeons in the Crimea

Not all of the Irish surgeons who worked in the Crimea were commissioned officers in the Army Medical Service. At the outbreak of the war a call was made for volunteers from those in civilian practice to work as surgeons on a

1992), p. 85.   **25** Nightingale's recent biographers, such as Hugh Small, author of *Avenging Angel*, have questioned the validity of the Nightingale myth. This was also the main theme of the

temporary basis. As previously stated it was in this way that the British army acquired the staff that were to work in the general hospitals. Such men were usually given the title of acting assistant surgeon, which was not a commissioned rank, and came with the rank of warrant officer. As a result the details of such men were not entered into the roll of commissioned officers and details on them are more difficult to obtain. Twenty-six civilian surgeons served in the Crimea, three of whom were definitely Irish. One of these Irish civilian surgeons who served in the Crimea in a temporary capacity was Robert McDonnell. McDonnell was significant in that he came from a distinguished medical family and was a man who had received a very intensive medical training. Also some of the letters that he sent home from the Crimea survive in the National Library of Ireland. They provide a useful insight into the life and experiences of an Irish doctor in the Crimea. The McDonnell letters are in fact one of the best accounts of the experiences of a Crimean surgeon that still exist.

Robert McDonnell was born in Dublin on 15 March 1828, the son of John McDonnell. The family also had a home at Kilsharvan in Co. Meath and it was here that Robert McDonnell spent much of his childhood. The McDonnell family had an impressive record in the annals of Irish medicine. Robert McDonnell's grandfather, James McDonnell (1763–1845), was born in Belfast and later founded the Belfast Fever and General Hospital.[26] His father, John McDonnell (1796–1892), had based himself in Dublin in 1813 and joined the House of Industry Hospitals in 1835 as a surgeon. He became a senior fellow of the Royal College of Surgeons in Ireland and later medical member of the Local Government Board.[27]

Robert McDonnell studied in Trinity College and graduated BA in 1849 and MB in 1851.[28] In the same year McDonnell obtained the licence of the Royal College of Surgeons in Ireland and was admitted as a fellow of the RCSI in August 1853. He then went abroad, spending some time in further study in Edinburgh, Paris and Vienna. At the outbreak of the Crimean war, McDonnell volunteered to serve as a surgeon with the army assembling for the campaign in the East. Originally attached to the British Hospital at Smyrna in early 1855, he later volunteered to work in the general hospital in the camp before Sevastapol.

Ten of his letters from the Crimea survive, the majority being sent to his mother, Charity McDonnell (née Dobbs), while others were sent to his uncle, the Rt. Hon. Sir Alexander McDonnell, Bart., and to his brothers, James and Alexander. His letters show that he was a keen observer of the events around him and, while some of his letters to his mother were obviously not very graphic, he

BBC's *Reputations* documentary on Florence Nightingale in July 2001.   **26** Eoin O'Brien, Lorna Browne and Kevin O'Malley (eds), *The House of Industry hospitals, 1772–1987* (Dublin, 1988), pp 54–5.   **27** Sir Charles Cameron, *History of the Royal College of Surgeons in Ireland* (Dublin, 1886), pp. 429–32. See also DNB.   **28** G.D. Burtchaell and T.U. Sadleir, *Alumni Dublinenses*

managed to convey the full horror of working in a military hospital. Included in
this collection of letters is a floorplan of the hospital at Scutari. It is probably the
only one in existence and it is, therefore, an especially valuable document itself.
In a letter of 14 July 1855 McDonnell briefly laid down his reasons for volunteering to go to Sevastapol in a letter to his elder brother James McDonnell:

> I have barely time to write by this post to say that I am under orders for the
> Crimea. I have been attached to the General Hospital of the Third Division and
> go next Thursday. My reasons for doing all this, which is in a great degree
> optional, I have not time to go into, but they are, believe me, such as would fully
> satisfy you, the Doctor and Uncle Alexander. My mother is the only thing against
> it, tell her I consider it really my duty and, as to the dangers, they are no greater
> than those to which a medical man must always be exposed.[29]

The 'Doctor' McDonnell refers to may have been his father or Robert Moore
Peile, the surgeon to whom he had been apprenticed. The two men had apparently
become firm friends during his years of training. Also, it should be pointed out
that when McDonnell writes of the Third Division's 'General Hospital' he is
referring to what would be called, in the modern sense, a field hospital.
'Marching', 'Flying' and 'Field' hospitals had existed since the army of William
III, but such terms had fallen out of use after the campaigns of Marlborough.
By the nineteenth century such hospitals were referred to as 'General Hospitals',
which were responsible for the immediate treatment of casualties.[30] In his first
letter, 3 August 1855, from his new post, 'The General Hospital, rear of the 3rd
Division, Camp Before Sevastapol', McDonnell wrote to his mother telling her
of his new quarters:

> Here I am right snugly settled and just as nicely circumstanced (surgically
> speaking) as my heart could desire. I have been attached by Dr Hall to the
> General Hospital. I have been assigned to 3 wards containing 14 beds, with every
> application and comfort for my patients which can be reasonably expected in
> camp. I live along with Dr McLeod in a wooden hut. Five of us mess together
> and live very well I can tell you.[31]

Yet McDonnell was no doubt casting his new quarters in a good light. In a later
letter to his sister and brother, Rosie and 'Bucks', on 29 August 1855, he con-
trasted his previous quarters in Smyrna with those he had in camp. The letter is
worth quoting at length:

> You remember I dare say the grand description I wrote you of the splendid house
> I lived in at Smyrna, with its gallery and corridors and magnificent pillars and the

(2nd edn, Dublin, 1935).   **29** NLI, MS. 18,491, Robert McDonnell Letters, 14 July 1855.
30 Drew, op. cit., xxiv.   **31** McDonnell Letters, 3 August 1855.

fountain and the gold fish and the orange trees and the lemon trees and sesame and roses and vines, and my own room with the Turkey carpets and splendid beds and mosquito curtains.[32]

Referring to himself as a 'prince who has been driven from a palace to live in a cottage or small house', McDonnell then described his present accommodation:

Imagine to yourself a hut made together of thin boards, the size of a small mud cabin, having no chimney and a door in each end of it. Each officer's hut is divided into two rooms by a wooden partition. In one of these little rooms then, which forms half a hut, I and my friend, Mr Complin, live, and here we keep everything we have except our horses. Opposite to the door, one on each side, are our iron bedsteads, hard enough I can tell you. My pillow is my great coat stuffed into a bag. I have no mattress, under our beds are our port manteaus and such things as can be stored there. In each side of the hut a piece of board has been cut out to make a window but there is no glass in them. At each window there is an old barrel turned upside down. These are our dressing tables, on them our basins and on a little ledge under the roof is soap, sponge writing case etc. On each side of the door are shelves and big boxes on their sides and raised up on stones so as to make cupboards. Here are, in a strange sort of arrangement, packed tea, sugar, coffee, pots, pans, kettles, coffee pots, blacking and blacking brushes, pots of preserved meat, pickles, bread, rice, sacks of barely for the horses, candles and candlesticks and empty bottles, pepper, salt etc. etc. Across a beam that crosses the roof hang the saddles and bridles. Between the beds, two boards supported on each end on barrels, form our table and two stools complete the furniture. The floor is covered with boards which are not nailed down, but spring up and down as you walk on them.[33]

While such conditions were no doubt not what McDonnell was used to, at least he was not living in a cramped tent in the field. The enlisted men were sleeping twelve to a tent, while officers slept two to a tent. But to give McDonnell his due he had previously been quartered in a tent on his arrival in the Crimea. A Commissariat Department chit remains amongst his letters for a tent he occupied before obtaining quarters in a hut.

The period that McDonnell spent in the Crimea was one of hard fighting, culminating with the final assault on Sevastapol on 8 September 1855. In his letters to his mother, however, he tended not to write of his work as an army surgeon in an explicit way. In one letter to his mother, 3 August 1855, he wrote of the fate of one casualty:

The bombardment went on actively last night and is still, but with what object nobody knows, for no assault is contemplated. We have had some wounded today but not many. One poor boy, an officer in the 3rd, has just come up, having compound fractures of both thighs, also of the left leg and a fracture of both bones of the right forearm. He is sinking fast.[34]

32 McDonnell Letters, 29 August 1855.   33 Ibid.   34 Ibid. 3 August 1855.

In his letters to his uncle and brothers he was inclined to be more descriptive. In a letter written on his return to Smyrna, McDonnell wrote frankly of his work in the general hospital:

> I went to the camp in July while the hospitals were still pretty well filled with the wounded of the unfortunate 18th June. I was at times exceedingly hard worked and that too over cases which, from a variety of causes, become soon to be horrible and disgusting to such a degree that, I assure you, I have often been sickened. Aye, so that I had to leave the hut hurriedly and, having got rid of my last meal in a quiet corner, come back again to my work, and that when I was in the poorest health, spirit and conditions. Yet you see for such work as this our profession gets but few KCB's.[35]

While wounds sustained in combat were always horrific, the surgeons in the Crimea were also experiencing for the first time the effect of the minié bullet. In his quest for a tighter fitting, high velocity rifle bullet, Captain Minié of the French army had created a bullet with a hollowed base. This design, he found, ensured a tighter fitting round and therefore higher velocity and greater accuracy. Captain Minié had unwittingly created a hollowed bullet that had devastating effects on the human body. While the Russian army did not have enough minié rifles for all its regiments, there were still enough in use to cause severe wounds during the various battles of the war. The effect of minié bullets on arms and legs in particular, resulted in the amputation of damaged limbs. This practice of routine amputation was a feature of the war and the subject of several satirical cartoons on the subject of the military surgeon's skill. Yet in fairness there was no surgical method which could successfully treat wounds caused by minié bullets, a fact amply illustrated by the difficulties of surgeons in the American Civil war, where minié rifles were used extensively by both sides. It is not surprising, perhaps, that Robert McDonnell appears to have often felt despair at the inability of military surgeons to treat many wounds. In a letter of 15 August 1855 to his mother, McDonnell gave his opinion of military surgery in general:

> The year of the East, however, will be quite enough for me. The truth is that I find what is called Military Surgery is after so very limited compartment of the surgical art that I shall by that time have had enough of it. Military Surgery, on the whole, requires little more than steadiness in operating; the cases requiring nice discriminating diagnostic power are rare.[36]

---

35 Ibid. 20 October 1855. The Rt. Hon. Sir Alexander McDonnell, Bart., was resident commissioner of national education. He was made a privy councillor in 1846 and was created a baronet in 1872. The 'unfortunate 18th June' referred to here was the unsuccessful British assault on the Redan, June 1855.   36 McDonnell Letters, 15 August 1855.

McDonnell also witnessed military actions and described them in his letters. In the same letter of 15 August, he described the most recent Russian attempt to capture Balaclava, in an effort to deny the allied armies their main supply base. The attack was repulsed by French and Sardinian forces, British troops playing virtually no part. The Russians advanced from the interior across the Tchernaya river, and the resulting battle was named after this river. As this action took place on 16 August 1855, one can only assume that McDonnell's letter had been started on 15 August and then continued in instalments over a number of days. He described the action thus:

> James will remember how many a time we have visited in the churchyard at Donore looking down at the Boyne and wishing we could see a battle there. Well I have seen such a sight, only from a much greater height and in a much more extended plain. It will, I suppose, be called the Battle of the Tchernaya. Our accounts are (but you will know long before this all particulars) that the Russians wished to try an attack on Balaclava to cut off our communications with it. In order to make this attempt they came down the ravines which leak into the broad plain which joins the valley of Balaclava. Here are the Sardinian troops. Their (the Sardinians) outposts were driven in last night so that the troops were all ready and under arms at daylight, the French reserves all ready and our cavalry (which is now in splendid order) and a large supply of French cavalry also were kept just concealed behind the rising ground in the plain where the Sardinians are encamped. The Sardinians advanced to meet the enemy, but soon made a feigned retreat so as to draw them up the hill. Having thus retired on the French introduced to support them, and having succeeded in then drawing the Russians on the hillside, the whole cavalry and all advanced. The battle was short and decisive, it was all over by 7 o'clock: so that it was only the time of the retreat that I saw when I rode over the hill looking across this magnificent plain. They say there are 3,000 Russians killed. I saw an immense number of prisoners, at least 400, on their way to Karneish.[37]

McDonnell was also a witness to other events such as the explosion in the French Mamelon battery in late August 1855. In a letter of 29 August he wrote of the accident:

> I go to bed, however, and sleep soundly for the firing never disturbs me now. Sometimes an explosion wakes us all. There was a terrible one last night, a French powder magazine in the Mamelon battery. It was about 1 o'clock and we were all asleep when it occurred. The roar was dreadful at this distance of more than four miles. Some bullets that I had as trophies lying on a shelf near my bed were shaken off and tumbled on the floor. I surely thought for a moment there was a shell in my hut, but on rushing to the door I saw the smoke, the great column of smoke, in which many a poor fellow had been transferred to another world. Such things, however, don't happen often and I usually sleep uninterruptedly.[38]

37 Ibid.   38 McDonnell Letters, 29 August 1855.

During the months of August and early September 1855 there were incessant alarms and the troops were woken and prepared for battle almost every night. Keeping the troops in this constant state of readiness was very bad for morale and no word was passed to the troops as to the reason for these constant alarms. Indeed many were later to state that they felt relieved when orders finally came for the assault on 8 September 1855. McDonnell witnessed these numerous alarms and vividly described such an event in his letter of 29 August 1855:

> The bugle sounds for the men to get ready, an assault has been now so long extended that the men believe every turn out that they are really in for it. They are all more or less under the influence of drink. The row begins about two, the sergeants and corporals rooting out the men, cursing, swearing, damming their eyes and souls and the turning out and falling in is very unlike what you would expect from men who stand so near death. But I must tell you that the 'Pomp and Circumstance of Glorious War' loses much of its grandeur on close inspection. As you will see by looking at the screen in the library, 'playing at soldiers' is very different from fighting, and a review in the Phoenix shows soldering off very differently from a turnout at midnight in the camp before Sevastapol.[39]

At the beginning of September McDonnell took ill with 'Crimean fever' and, although he played down his illness in his letters to his mother, he was in reality very ill. In a letter written to his uncle Alexander from Smyrna, 20 October 1855, he described his condition during the final assault on Sevastapol:

> At last I began to get ill. It was a sort intermittent at first and I shivered every 3rd day. I was ordered on board ship but I thought I could fight it out and tried hard for I knew the assault was at hand and I was always as brisk as a bee, except on a shivering day, so that I was very well and still in attending on my patients on the 5th when the bombardment commenced.[40]

McDonnell's condition deteriorated and, by the time of the final assault on 8 September, he was confined to bed in his hut. His letter continued:

> I had the 'reception hut' on one side of mine, the 'operating hut' on the other. The howling of the wind, the battering of the rain, the groans of the wounded and the cries of those that were being operated on, were close in my ears.[41]

Yet even in his weakened condition he realized that a major attack had been launched. In the same letter he wrote of what he had witnessed of the final assault on Sevastapol:

> In the distance the firing had not ceased and the explosions of the magazines in the town were beginning. The excitement was terrible, so I could not resist

39 Ibid.   40 McDonnell Letters, 20 October 1855.   41 Ibid.

staggering over to the door (where I had a temporary betterness after a violent fit of vomiting), and looking over the top of it … and there was a sight! There were men going about with lanterns to show the way to those who carried up the wounded. There were stretchers arriving fast with wounded men and those that bore them could hardly walk but reeled to and fro and staggered like drunken men by reason of the storm. I could not see Sevastapol, but the sky over it. The sky caught the glare from the blazing town and ships. It was as if hell's gulph [sic] was opened where the harbour was. The blowing up of a magazine every now and then lightened the whole scene and made the earth shake for miles and miles around.[42]

Despite his illness McDonnell later got up and travelled into Sevastapol after the Russian evacuation to see the town. He wrote to his uncle:

It was madness, perfect madness, I think now in me to have attempted it. But I did and I was in the Malakov and the Redan, through the town and all round the docks while the ships in them had the flames creeping over their last remains. Joe Wright accompanied me on my first expedition; he carried a flask of wine for me. I carried another and beef too, and thus supported managed it. There were places where the odour was horrible from the shallow buried dead. In some places they were still unburied, from which I escaped in all haste.[43]

In a later letter to his mother, he added:

How I should have liked to have James along with me, visiting the batteries and fortifications. It would have excited his military ardour immensely to see how the French sapped up round the Malakov, but still more to see the bomb-proof chamber the Russians had made inside these wonderful defences.[44]

McDonnell's next letter to his mother was written on the 23 September 1855 from a steamer in the Black Sea. Due to the seriousness of his own illness, which he again played down in this letter to his mother, he was ordered to return to the hospital at Smyrna. He described conditions on board ship in this letter:

This is one of the finest ships in the whole transport service. There are on board 48 sick, or wounded officers, 70 soldiers and about 40 Russian prisoners.[45]

His letter went on to describe a prayer service held on board ship:

We had service on board, today being Sunday. It was the first time I ever had service on board ship, under the awning or quarter-deck. Almost all the sailors were present, and many pale faced officers with arms in slings and legs stretched on stools, or even on beds on the deck. Having the capstan as a reading desk, the Captain read the service to a singularly attentive crowd.[46]

42 Ibid.   43 Ibid.   44 McDonnell Letters, 23 September 1855.   45 Ibid.   46 Ibid.

Later McDonnell admitted that his illness was more serious than he had let on, concluding his letter:

> My hair which is closely cropped, is all falling out, so that I shall be obliged to have my head shaved when I get to Smyrna. I hope also, after recuperating there for a while, to get leave for a fortnight or so, when I shall take a trip, probably to Athens, unless the quarantine prevents it.[47]

Ultimately a quarantine requirement of five days did prevent McDonnell from travelling to Athens and he was forced to spend his leave in and around Smyrna. In the last letter which McDonnell sent from the East to his uncle, 20 October 1855, he was highly critical of the army leadership.

> The failure of the British attack on the Great Redan was a great disappointment. As far as I can see the fault lay with the generals. The men, in spite of their youth, showed great courage. I travelled down here with a French officer of rank who told me that it was contrary to the military rule to advance to assault so wide a space as the English did. The French had sapped up to within 10 metres of the Malakov, while our men had more than 200 metres to cross. It was, he said, 'Trop loin, trop loin!'.[48]

McDonnell continued by stating:

> But as far as I can see the Generals, Doctors, Engineers and all in the British Army, are a very second rate lot.[49]

He supported this statement with the following example of military incompetence:

> The Captain of Engineers now at Scutari could not survey a line of rail from the sea to the hospital. We had to send out a Civil Engineer to do it, and the same fellow, a Mr Brunton, had to go to Salonika to show the Military Engineers how to put up the hay reaping machines. None of them in fact know anything out of a certain limited routine. Take them out of that and they are at their wits end.[50]

McDonnell's last letter from the East was sent just before Christmas 1855 to his mother and he described some of the preparations for the festival:

> There is to be a magnificent ball here this evening, given by the admiral in command on board the *Princess Royal*. I here expect to meet all the youth and beauty of Smyrna, all of whom have no gathered here from the Dardanelles and the villages around here, and are looking forward to the gaieties of the carnival which commences very early.[51]

---

47 Ibid. **48** McDonnell Letters, 20 October 1855. **49** Ibid. **50** Ibid. **51** McDonnell Letters, 14 December 1855.

Robert McDonnell returned to Ireland in January 1856 as his health was not improving. He was awarded the Crimean medal with the Sevastapol clasp and the Turkish Crimean Medal, and was also highly praised by his superiors. As he prepared to leave Smyrna, John Meyer MD, the medical superintendent of the hospital wrote:

> My Dear Sir, I cannot permit you to leave Smyrna without offering you my best thanks for the manner in which you have invariably performed your duties throughout your connection with the Smyrna Hospital Staff, and I would at the same time express to you the high sense I entertain of your talents and ability as a professional man. For your voluntary services in the Crimea I consider you entitled to special thanks. You only left the field when compelled by severe illness.[52]

Sir Henry Storks, medical commandant at Smyrna wrote:

> Dr McDonnell discharged his responsible duties with great zeal and intelligence, and I am glad to have the opportunity afforded me of expressing the sense I entertain of his humanity and kindness to the sick and wounded soldiers of the army, and of the devotion he at all times displayed for the public service. Dr McDonnell volunteered his services wherever the Government might consider them useful.[53]

He was also later praised by Sir John Hall, principal medical officer of the army in Turkey. Robert McDonnell went on to have a distinguished career. He proceeded to the degree of MD in Trinity in 1857 and in the same year was appointed by Lord Carlisle as medical superintendent of Mountjoy prison. In this capacity he oversaw many improvements in the hygienic conditions in the prison. He resigned from this post in 1867 due to a clash with the prison authorities, who continually denied him the freedom he desired to manage all medical arrangements in the prison. He became a surgeon in Jervis Street Hospital in 1863 and, three years later, was elected as a surgeon and professor of descriptive anatomy in Steevens' Hospital.

McDonnell, like his father, was also responsible for an Irish medical 'first'. In 1865 he carried out the first blood transfusion in Ireland. He co-operated with Francis Cruise in the development of Cruise's endoscope, the forerunner of the modern cystoscope.[54] Twice elected by the Senate of the Dublin University as a member of the University Council, McDonnell also served as an examiner at the Royal College of Surgeons in Ireland. He was elected president

---

52 Cameron, *History of the Royal College of Surgeons in Ireland*, pp. 431–2. 53 Ibid., p. 432.
54 Davis Coakley, *Irish masters of medicine* (Dublin, 1992), p. 197, p. 200. On one occasion Cruse stated that if McDonnell put some objects in a corpse, he would be able to identify them using his endoscope. One of the objects that McDonnell placed in the corpse during this test was a spent minié bullet that he had found in the Crimea.

of the RCSI in 1877, and in 1885, became the first president of the Academy of Medicine in Ireland. McDonnell was also active in many learned societies, writing numerous articles for surgical and scientific journals, and was elected a fellow of the Royal Society in June 1865. He was a member of the Royal Irish Academy and was president of the Pathological Society. McDonnell served as a member of a number of government commissions including the Royal Commission of inquiry into the Medical Acts (1881–2), the Royal Commission on Prisons in Ireland (1882–3) and the Royal Commission on the Education and Employment of the Blind (1885–6).[55]

In 1865 McDonnell married Mary Macaulay Molloy who died four years later.[56] He later married Susan Isabella McCausland, the daughter of Sir Richard Bolton McCausland, and they had one son.[57] McDonnell died suddenly at his Dublin home, 89 Merrion Square, on 6 May 1889, aged only 61. To say his death was unexpected would be an understatement. He had dined the previous evening with his father, John McDonnell, then aged 93. Also on the day of his death McDonnell had carried out a normal day's work.[58] The cause of death was believed to have been the rupture of an aneurysm. The burial took place in the family's burial plot in Kilsharvan, Co. Meath.[59]

Robert McDonnell was a typical example of the kind of highly trained surgeons who volunteered to leave civilian practice and assist at the army's hospitals for the duration of the war. His letters from the Crimea serve to illustrate the life that these men led while on campaign. Robert McDonnell's writings constitute one of the best Irish accounts of the war. Indeed his letters are perhaps one of the best sources on the life of a Crimean surgeon which remain in any public collection.

Robert Spencer Dyer Lyons was another Irish civilian surgeon who served in the Crimea. Born in Cork, he had been educated at Trinity College and had become a licentiate of the RCSI in 1849. He established a reputation as a pathologist and pioneered the use of the microscope in pathological examinations. In May 1855 he was appointed as pathologist to the British army in the Crimea and was given the specific task of investigating the diseases that were breaking

---

55 Cameron, *History of the Royal College of Surgeons in Ireland*, pp. 429–32. It is interesting that one of the recommendations of the Royal Commission of Inquiry into the Medical Acts was that the Merchant Shipping Act of 1854 be amended. This act prevented surgeons with qualifications from 'colonial' colleges from serving as ship's surgeons in the Mercantile Marine. The commissioners also pointed out that the Medical Act of 1858 excluded such surgeons from serving in the army or navy. *Report of the Royal Commissioners appointed to inquire into the granting of medical degrees, with evidence, appendices and index* [C 3259], HC 1882, xxix, 489. 56 Mary Macaulay Molloy was the daughter of Daniel Molloy JP, of Clonbela, King's County. 57 Sir Richard Bolton McCausland of Ballinrobe, Co. Mayo and 61 Fitzwilliam Square, Dublin. 58 *The Times*, 7 May 1889. 59 *Irish Times*, 7 May 1889. See also David Murphy, "'As if hell's gulph was opened". The letters of Robert McDonnell, a volunteer surgeon in the Crimean war' in *Soldiers of the Queen*, no. 96, March 1999, pp. 6–10.

out in the British and French camps. Following the battle of the Tchernaya, he worked as a surgeon in the French field hospital. In 1856 he was appointed as professor of medicine and pathology at the medical school of the Catholic University of Ireland in Cecilia Street. He travelled to Lisbon in November 1857 to assist the medical authorities during the yellow fever outbreak there and later served on the staff of St George's Hospital in Dublin, where had special responsibility for training military surgeons. Interested in prison reform and forestry projects, he was a Liberal MP for Dublin City from 1880 to 1885. He died in Dublin in December 1886.[60]

The third Irish civilian surgeon who served in the Crimea was Anthony Brabazon (1821–96), the son of the Revd George Brabazon of Co. Meath. He entered Trinity College, Dublin, in January 1838 and graduated in 1846. He later studied at Aberdeen and served in the hospital at Scutari during the Crimean war. After the war he settled at Bath where he was appointed as physician to the Royal Mineral Water Hospital.[61] It should also be pointed out that some surgeons who were serving with the armies of the East India Company, took leave and went to serve in the Crimea. These surgeons have never been the subject of sustained research and there may well have been several Irish surgeons among them. One of these surgeons, Surgeon-Major William Eddowes of the Bengal Army, died in Dublin in January 1880 and is buried in Deansgrange Cemetery. His headstone records that he served in the Crimean war, the Indian Mutiny and the Second Afghan war (1878–80).[62]

Irish nursing sisters in the Crimea

The involvement of the Irish Sisters of Mercy in the Crimean war was also significant and there is now a considerable literature on these Irish nuns. Evelyn Bolster has written an excellent history, *The Irish Sisters of Mercy in the Crimean war* (Cork, 1964). Sr Aloysius Doyle published an account of her Crimean experiences in 1897, *Memories of the Crimea*, while excerpts from Sr M. Francis Bridgeman's Crimean journal were published in the *Irish Catholic* in 1950. Selections from the letters of Sr Joseph Croke were also published in *Irish Sword* in 1962. Indeed one could well argue that the involvement of these Irish nuns in the Crimea is the only subject, with a Crimean war connection, that has been given any attention by Irish authors. Ken Horton of the CWRS is also engaged in major research on the subject of nursing in the war. As a result

60 *The Times*, 21 December 1886. See also Sir Charles Cameron, *History of the Royal College of Surgeons in Ireland* (Dublin, 1886), 619–21.   **61** John Shepherd, *The Crimean doctors* (Liverpool, 1991), i, Appendix I. See also *Alumni Dublinenses*.   **62** Information kindly supplied by Phil Lecane of the Royal Dublin Fusiliers Assocaition.

it is not intended to examine the subject here in detail and the role of the Sisters of Mercy is only touched on where relevant. Their involvement in the war was seen as a major event, firstly because of the fact that women were being allowed to journey with the army as nurses, and, secondly, due to the fact that among these nurses were members of a Roman Catholic religious order. It should be remembered that it was originally intended that they should carry out medical, rather than spiritual, work. Florence Nightingale remarked that the motivation behind this decision was primarily one of economy. In a letter of 11 January 1856 to Lieutenant-Colonel Lefroy, she outlined the attitude of Sir John Hall, principal medical officer, to the nuns:

> Relying on the 'Purveyors Statement', Dr Hall reminds the Government that the Nuns, whom he calls 'Sisters of Charity', but who are really nuns, are the least expensive Nurses who can be employed-& on this, & on other grounds, he seems to intimate that they ought to be exclusively employed in Military Hospitals.[63]

The first contingent of religious sisters sent to the Crimea consisted of twenty-five nuns, twenty Sisters of Mercy and five Sisters of Charity. Eleven nuns were recruited from the different houses of the Sisters of Mercy in Ireland. They initially travelled to London where they were joined by three nuns from the order's house in Liverpool and one from Chelsea. They formed a temporary community under the control of their superior, Sr M. Francis Bridgeman.[64] Another group of ten nuns was formed in London, five Sisters of Mercy, from the convent at Bermondsey, and five Sisters of Charity from Norwood. This second group was put under the control of Sr M. Clare Moore, an Irishwoman who had been superior of the Mercy Convent in Cork before moving to Bermondsey in 1839.[65] The party under Sr M. Clare Moore travelled to the East first, arriving at the base hospitals at Scutari on 4 November 1854, the day before the battle of Inkerman.[66] This party also had to help treat some of the casualties from the battle of Balaclava, who were still in the hospital at this time. Apart from the experience these nuns gained in treating the wounded they also formed good relations with Florence Nightingale. It must be stated, however, that the direction and spiritual welfare of these nuns was to be a major problem for the Irish chaplains during the war. It can be shown that there was

---

63 Sue M. Goldie, *Florence Nightingale: letters from the Crimea* (London, 1997), p. 192.   **64** Sr M. Francis Bridgeman had been superior at the Mercy Convent in Kinsale during the Famine and had played a leading role in the relief efforts there. She was an able administrator and competent nurse and was seen by Florence Nightingale as a threat to her authority at Scutari.   **65** Sr M. Clare Moore is depicted standing to the left of Florence Nightingale in Jerry Barrett's painting *The mission of Mercy* (1857). Matthew Paul Lalumia, *Realism and politics in Victorian art of the Crimean war* (Epping, 1984), p. 108.   **66** Sr M. Clare Moore and Sr M. Francis Bridgeman are usually referred to as 'Mrs Moore' and 'Mrs Bridgeman' in contemporary texts, due to the nineteenth century custom of using the title 'Mrs' for heads of religious houses.

competition amongst the Irish chaplains to work with the nuns. Also the tense relations between the superior of the Cork nuns, Sr M. Francis Bridgeman and Florence Nightingale was to cause further problems. Finally, the refusal of the hospital authorities to allow the nuns to engage in spiritual instruction was to be a major issue, not only for the Catholic chaplains, but also their respective bishops in England and Ireland.

The problems that Florence Nightingale had with the nursing nuns focused on the second party under Sr M. Francis Bridgeman, which did not arrive until 17 December 1854. Three other Sisters of Mercy came out to Scutari as replacements, bringing the total of nuns who served in the Crimea to twenty-eight. Florence Nightingale's relationship with Sr M. Clare Moore and her nuns remained, in general, cordial. The second party of nuns, it should also be pointed out, arrived with the nurses of Mary Stanley, Florence Nightingale's one-time friend, and now nursing rival. The ill-feeling Nightingale felt for Sr M. Francis Bridgeman and her nuns was, perhaps, motivated by this association. Sr M. Francis Bridgeman was also a woman of some experience and was used to being in a position of authority. Nightingale, a comparative novice in the field of nursing, saw Bridgeman as a threat. The second party of fifteen Irish nuns also refused to be split up and be distributed among the various hospitals. In a letter to Sidney Herbert, secretary at war, written from Scutari on Christmas Day 1854, Florence Nightingale wrote of the various proposals put forward for the use of these nuns:

> The second proposition which the Superior of the new Nuns (who has obviously come out with a religious view-not to serve the sick, but to found a convent, completely mistaking the purpose of our mission) makes it that the whole of the 15 nuns should come in or none – they cannot separate and they cannot separate from her – Why? Because it would be 'uncanonical'.[67]

In a later letter to Sidney Herbert, Florence Nightingale further remarked that 'The fifteen new Nuns (in conjunction with Mary Stanley) are leading me the devil of a life'.[68] There was also perhaps a deeper motivation for this animosity between Florence Nightingale and the Irish Sisters of Mercy. In the summer of 1852 she had travelled to Dublin to investigate the possibility of entering the order herself. This was the result of the brief flirtation that she had with Rome. During her time in Dublin, Florence Nightingale apparently witnessed some incident in a hospital which left her permanently disenchanted with the Roman Catholic Church. She later referred to a 'terrible lesson learned in Dublin', and her interest in the Sisters of Mercy disappeared.[69]

---

67 Goldie, op. cit., pp 55–6.   **68** Ibid. p. 61.   **69** Woodham-Smith, *Florence Nightingale*, p. 103.

Ultimately the relationship between Florence Nightingale and Sr M. Francis Bridgeman never improved. Problems regarding the employment of the Irish nuns, their accommodation and spiritual welfare were a constant feature of their time in the Crimea. The opening of the hospital at Kulalie in January 1855 relieved much of the tension. Sr M. Francis Bridgeman took ten of her nuns to this new hospital, leaving five with Florence Nightingale at Scutari. She insisted, however, that the five left behind at Scutari remained under her control. During the succeeding months the Irish nuns carried out heavy nursing work. The majority of their cases were not wounded, but were men who had fallen ill or were suffering from the effects of the severe winter. Sr Aloysius Doyle later described the cases of frostbite that they had to treat:

> The men who came from the Front had only thin linen suits-no other clothing to keep out the Crimean frost of 1854/55. When they were carried in on stretchers, their clothes had to be cut off. In most cases the flesh and the clothes were frozen together, and as for the feet, the boots had to be cut off bit by bit, the flesh coming off with them. Many pieces of flesh I have seen remaining in the boots.[70]

The Irish Sisters of Mercy travelled in late October 1855 to the hospital at Balaclava. This move allowed the nuns to give immediate aid to those who were wounded in the siege operations around Sevastapol. It also put them out of the control of Florence Nightingale and it should be noted that, while Nightingale did not want these nuns at the Scutari hospital, they soon established a reputation for nursing efficiency at the hospital at Balaclava. Modern research has shown that a soldier was more likely to die at Scutari than at the Balaclava hospital and it is perhaps a pity that Florence Nightingale could bring herself to form an alliance with Sr M. Bridgeman in order to make use of the nursing experience of her party of nuns.

Ultimately two of the Sisters of Mercy number were to die in the Crimea.[71] On 12 April 1856 the Irish nuns left Balaclava and began the journey home. A peace treaty, the Peace of Paris, had been signed on 30 March 1856, yet there had been no fighting since the end of September of the previous year. The Irish nuns were able, therefore to begin preparations immediately for their departure as the hospital was virtually empty. There is no doubt that the Sisters of Mercy inspired a certain fondness in the soldiers. One of their party, Sr Joseph Croke, described their departure from the Crimea:

> Every heart beat light-going home after such scenes and going home alive! We looked at each other when we went on board and the look told much and each one read it correctly. We had our favourite 89th down 'on pass to see us off', and

---

70 Revd J.J.W. Murphy, 'An Irish Sister of Mercy in the Crimean war' in *Irish Sword*, v, no. 21 (Winter, 1962), p. 255.   71 Sr Winifred Spry and Sr Mary Butler.

our three orderlies who worked with us from the commencement, they were breaking their hearts, God bless them! Poor fellows, we owed them much of the little personal comfort we had. We left the curious harbour of Balaclava amid the blessings and prayers of all and the tears of many.[72]

There were also lay nurses who worked in the army's hospitals under the direction of Florence Nightingale and Mary Stanley and there were Irish nurses among them. Alicia Blackwood (*née* Lambert) was the sister of the 8th earl of Cavan and she worked with Florence Nightingale at Scutari.[73] Another of these nurses was Maria Theresa Longworth and she later became involved in a celebrated legal case. Born in Cheetwood, near Manchester in 1832, she met William Charles Yelverton, later 4th Viscount Avonmore, in 1852 and the couple began to correspond.[74] In 1855 she volunteered to serve as a nurse with the French Sisters of Charity in the Crimean war and met Yelverton again at Galata Hospital and they became engaged. Yelverton's family objected to this engagement and, in April 1857, Yelverton performed a form of marriage ceremony, reading aloud the Church of England marriage service, in their lodgings in Edinburgh. They were later married in the Catholic chapel in Rostrevor in Co. Down. In June 1858, Yelverton married Emily Marianne Ashworth, youngest daughter of Major-General Sir Charles Ashworth and widow of Professor Edward Forbes, the noted naturalist. Maria Theresa Longworth subsequently sued for restitution of conjugal rights and a series of legal cases followed in the English, Irish and Scottish courts, all of which she ultimately lost. She died at Pietermaritzburg, Natal, in 1881. Yelverton succeeded his father in October 1870. He died at Biarritz in April 1883. The case of the Yelverton/Longworth marriage was given much coverage in the press. It inspired James Roderick O'Flanagan's novel *Gentle blood, or The secret marriage* (Edinburgh, 1861) and Cyrus Redding's *A wife and not a wife* (London, 1867).[75]

The reports in the newspapers of hospital conditions in the Crimea also became a cause of concern in Dublin. In February 1855 the lord mayor of Dublin, Joseph Boyce, sent a letter to all the hospitals in the Dublin area asking if they could accommodate any of the sick and wounded that were returning from the Crimea. The response from all the hospitals was very positive. The governors of the Meath Hospital wrote back to say that they could accommodate forty to fifty wounded soldiers while the governors at Jervis Street Hospital said they could take

72 Murphy, 'An Irish Sister of Mercy in the Crimean war', p. 261.   73 Lady Alicia Blackwood, *A narrative of personal experiences and impressions during a residence on the Bosphorus throughout the Crimean war* (London, 1881).   74 Yelverton was a major in the Royal Artillery and served in the Crimea. In March 1861 he was suspended from military duties and was placed on half-pay in the following month.   75 Maria Theresa Longworth, *The Yelverton correspondence, with introduction and connecting narrative* (Edinburgh, 1863). Joseph McArdle, *Irish legal anecdotes* (Dublin, 1995), pp 51–2. See also *DNB*.

thirty. By the end of February all the hospitals had responded to the lord mayor's query and he wrote to Colonel Thomas Larcom, the military secretary at Dublin Castle, to say that a total of 265 beds had been made available by the Dublin hospitals for Crimean sick and wounded.[76] Larcom wrote back to say that the matter was being considered and a further letter followed on 9 May 1855 in which he informed the lord mayor:

> Should the extensive arrangements which the Government have made prove insufficient for the demands of the service, Lord Panmure will gladly avail himself of this liberal and philanthropic offer.[77]

When one considers that the government's 'extensive arrangements' were proving to be inadequate in most areas, the refusal of this offer of help seems ungracious in the extreme.

The Crimean war still remains the blackest period in the history of the British army's medical services. The final casualty list taught a harsh lesson: 2,755 men had been killed in action, while a further 2,019 died of wounds. 2,874 were discharged due to wounds or being incapacitated by disease. 16,323 had died of disease.[78] These stark figures, along with the accounts of administrative incompetence published in the newspapers, resulted in a series of inquiries. Due to the public interest in the whole affair, the Horse Guards took the unusual step of publishing the final reports of these committees which included the Report upon the state of the hospitals of the British army in the Crimea and Scutari (1855) and *Report of the commission of inquiry into the supplies of the British Army in the Crimea* (1856).

It can be seen that Irish surgeons played a significant part in the medical history of this war, both as commissioned medical officers and civilian volunteers. The involvement of the Sisters of Mercy added yet another Irish dimension to this campaign. The letters of Robert McDonnell also provide a vivid insight into the experiences and difficulties of surgeons in the Crimea.

Roman Catholic chaplains in the British Army

Another group of men who were concerned with the soldier's spiritual and physical welfare were the army chaplains. The Crimean war was a significant period in the history of the Army Chaplains' Department in that Roman Catholic chaplains were granted official status for the first time since the 1790s.

76 National Archives, C.S.R.P. (1855), file 4590.   **77** Ibid., Larcom to Boyce, 9 May 1855. During Lord Palmerston's administration the offices of secretary for war and secretary at war were combined and Lord Panmure held this new position.   **78** John Sweetman, *The Crimean war* (London, 2001), p. 89.

In 1794 a Catholic priest, Alexander MacDonnell of Glengarry in Scotland, had received a commission from King George III to serve as a chaplain to the Glengarry Fencibles. Yet MacDonnell was an exceptional case and was the first Catholic priest to serve as a military chaplain since the end of James II's reign. Despite the fact that they were not commissioned or paid, many Catholic priests ministered to troops in barracks all over the British Isles. While most officers tolerated their men attending non-Anglican religious services, there were no regulations covering Catholic worship and the reactions of different officers betrayed the lack of any real policy. In January 1795 Trooper John Hyland of the 14th Light Dragoons, stationed in the Royal Barracks in Dublin, was tried by court martial and sentenced to receive 200 lashes for complaining about not being allowed to attend mass. In 1798, however, an officer of the Royal South Down Militia was court-martialed and reprimanded for not allowing men under his command to attend mass.[79] There was, therefore, no universal policy regarding the treatment of Catholic soldiers and the position of Catholic chaplains.

Apart from spiritual work, other uses had been found for Catholic priests in the past. During the Peninsular war, Wellington used priests from Coimbra University in Portugal, including James Warren Doyle, later bishop of Kildare and Leighlin, as interpreters, couriers and also spies. Patrick Curtis, later archbishop of Armagh, was at Salamanca when the French invaded Spain and also assisted Wellington. He was arrested by the French as a spy in 1811 but was later released.[80] Yet, despite carrying out such services during the Peninsular war, Catholic priests were not employed as official army chaplains. In 1827 the War Office recognized officiating chaplains for Presbyterians. The same recognition was given to Catholic chaplains in 1836. (Wesleyans applied for such status in 1856 and it was finally granted in 1881.) Yet no provisions were made to provide funds for Presbyterian or Catholic worship and no chaplains were appointed for either group.

The lack of provision for Catholic chaplains in early 1854 in no way indicated any discrimination on the part of the Adjutant General's Department, who were responsible for the appointment of chaplains. The Anglican chaplain-general, first appointed to command army chaplains in 1796, never had enough money or men. Before 1796, the selection of regimental chaplains was in the gift of colonels of regiments, a system that was open to abuse. Many chaplains appointed a deputy to carry out their regimental duties on being appointed and it was also difficult to find clergymen who were willing to serve abroad. In

79 Tom Johnstone and James Hagerty, *The cross on the sword: Catholic chaplains in the forces* (London, 1996), pp 1–2. See also Colin Johnston Robb, 'The story of the Royal South Down Militia', an unpublished history in the Linen Hall Library, Belfast.   **80** *DNB* on James Warren Doyle and Patrick Curtis. See also W.J. Fitzpatrick, *Secret service under Pitt* (1892), pp 378–9.

1796, this system was abolished and one chaplain was appointed to each brigade by the chaplain-general.

In 1846 the Revd George R. Gleig was appointed as chaplain-general, a post he was to hold for thirty years. Gleig had a military career, serving as a lieutenant in the 85th Foot at the battle of New Orleans in 1815, before studying theology and being ordained.[81] An energetic man, he did much to improve his department and promote the need for more chaplains yet in 1848 there were only four Anglican chaplains in the army. The maintenance of a proper Chaplains' Department, however, was very low on the list of the priorities of the adjutant-general, Sir James Escourt, and despite the best efforts of Gleig, there were only seven chaplains in his department at the outbreak of the Crimean war. Only one, the Revd H.P. Wright, was not committed to a post and thus able to depart immediately with the army for the East. Four new Anglican chaplains were gazetted in May 1854, two of whom died in the Crimea by the end of the year.[82] Crimean chaplains was paid an annual salary of £200.

In 1842 the Rt Revd Thomas Griffiths, vicar-apostolic, issued a circular instructing Catholics on how to petition their MPs regarding the appointment of chaplains. He stated in his circular:

> That you petitioners further show that with respect to Her Majesty's army your petitioners are confident that full one third of that army consists of Catholics. Yet, although a sum of £12,000 is allocated by the army estimates for purposes of religion and divine service, yet not above £800 thereof, that is less than one fifteenth of the whole, is applied to Catholic purposes, so that great destitution of religious instruction and divine service pervades in the British army.[83]

The large number of Irish troops made the need for Catholic chaplains obvious, and the subject of spiritual care for these men became the subject of much debate. William Howard Russell of *The Times* wrote on the subject and accused the government of not providing for the spiritual welfare of men who were expected to fight, and perhaps die, in the war. Faced with such criticism the government was forced to act and Cardinal Wiseman of Westminster, Bishop Grant of Southwark and Bishop Brown of Chepstow, were contacted by officials from the Horse Guards and asked to provide chaplains.[84] Bishop Grant was in Rome for much of the war and, as a result, the Horse Guards dealt with Dr Henry Manning, previously Anglican archdeacon of Chichester and, since 1851, a Roman Catholic priest in the diocese of Southwark. (In 1861 he succeeded Cardinal Wiseman as archbishop of Westminster.) After being contacted by the Horse Guards, Bishop Brown in turn wrote to Archbishop Cullen of Dublin:

81 Tim Pickles, *New Orleans, 1815* (London, 1993), p. 53.   **82** Sir John Smyth, *In this sign conquer: the story of the army chaplains* (London, 1968), p. 70.   **83** Johnstone and Hagerty, *The cross on the sword*, p. 5.   **84** Ibid. p. 6.

One of my priests is willing to go to the Crimea if the necessities of the poor
soldiers be not adequately provided for by others. To me his loss will be severe,
as I have none to replace him at his mission which I shall be compelled to close.
Yet I cannot in my conscience be an obstruction to his zeal, considering the
thousands who are left without the sacraments, and the hundreds who die without
them in the Crimea. Will anybody of the Irish clergy be liable to go to the Crimea
early so as to spare me so great a sacrifice? The English missions have sent
nearly twenty, while the vast proportion of Catholic soldiers are Irishmen.[85]

Archbishop Cullen was very much in favour of such a move and, although
short of priests in his own diocese, dispatched several, including Fr Michael
Cuffe, Fr William Moloney, and two Jesuits, Fr William Ronan and Fr Patrick
Duffy. Indeed, Cullen spoke openly in support of the war. In a sermon in April
1854, he stated:

During the course of this momentous struggle it will be our duty to beg sincerely
of God, to bring the war to a speedy and successful issue, and to restore the
blessings of peace, nor should we forget to offer up a special petition for our own
brave Catholic countrymen who have gone forth to fight the battles of the
Empire. Placed in the midst of danger and exposed to great spiritual destitution,
they stand in need of all the charitable assistance of the faithful.

He continued by stating that 'It is a war against a most powerful monarch, who
has always been a most dangerous enemy to our holy religion.'[86] The *Dublin
Evening Post* of 4 November 1854 noted that the Irish hierarchy were active in
encouraging donations to the Patriotic Fund and quoted a Galway priest who
had described the war as 'a war between tyranny and liberty'.[87]

Other Irish priests who were to serve in the Crimea were Fr Augustine Maguire
from Cork, the Irish Redemptorist Fr Denis Sheahan (working in the diocese of
Southwark in London in 1854), Fr Patrick Meany and Fr John Shiel. A total of
twenty-one Catholic chaplains served in the Crimea, eight of whom were Irish.

The official position regarding Catholic chaplains was that they were to
report directly to the commanding officer of the regiment or division to which
they were attached. This officer would then forward reports to the secretary of
state for war, Sidney Herbert. This procedure was confirmed in 1858 and meant
that Catholic chaplains were not directly under the control of the chaplain
general, ecclesiastical control being vested in the Roman Catholic bishop of
Southwark. There were occasions, however, when the senior Anglican chaplain,
the Revd H.P. Wright and, after his return home in early 1856, the Revd J.
Sabin, felt obliged to approach their Catholic colleagues in an effort to sort out
problems. Yet the Catholic and Anglican chaplains in general got on well

85 Dublin Diocesan Archive, Cullen Papers, 332/5/II, folio 12.   86 E.H. Nolan, *Illustrated history
of the war against Russia* (London, 1857), i, pp 160–1.   87 *Dublin Evening Post*, 4 Nov. 1854.

together. Responding to an article describing denominational differences published in *The Times*, the Revd Wright wrote:

> The critics will find that the thermometer at 7 degrees below zero is an effectual cooler of all wretched theological disputes and a dripping bell-tent particularly calculated to put a damper upon all unkind feeling.[88]

Irish Jesuits in the Crimea

Among the Irish Crimean chaplains there were, as has been already mentioned, two Irish Jesuits and it is useful to focus on them as the record for both men, held in the Jesuit Archives in Leeson Street, Dublin, is comparatively complete. Also a letter sent by one of them, Fr William Ronan, remains in the Dublin Diocesan Archive and is perhaps one of the best surviving accounts of the experiences of a Crimean chaplain. The first of the Jesuit chaplains, Fr Patrick Duffy, was born in Dublin in May 1814 and joined the Society of Jesus at Stonyhurst in August 1834. Having studied in France and Rome, he was ordained in March 1848. When war broke out he was based at St Francis Xavier's Church in Gardiner Street, Dublin. The second Jesuit chaplain, Fr Ronan, was born in July 1825 in Newry, Co. Down, and was educated in St Patrick's College, Maynooth, and in France. Ordained in 1848, he entered the Society of Jesus in November 1850 was also based at St Francis Xavier's Church at the outbreak of the war.[89] When the two Jesuits embarked for the Crimea in late 1854, Fr Ronan had been specifically instructed to look to the welfare of the Irish nuns at Scutari. Fr Duffy's brief was to join one of the divisions in the field. Fr Ronan's initial impressions were outlined in a letter to his superior in Dublin, Fr Robert Curtis, in January 1855, and it is worth quoting at length:

> When I arrived here on Monday last, I found the nuns placed in a disagreeable position. Their situation and the steps I have taken to better it should, I feel, be made known to you for your approval. To understand the matter more fully it is necessary to remark, that besides other places of less importance, there are three great hospitals here. The first and most important is the barracks. It contains 3,000 sick. The second is the general hospital which is half a mile distant from the barracks. The third is near a little village called Kulalie, about seven miles from Constantinople. The two last hospitals have about 1,000 invalids. On my arrival here I found five of the nuns lately arrived in the barrack hospital, with the five who came out first. Mrs Moore, their Reverend Mother, acted as Superior of all. The remaining ten religious were left at Therapia, where they still remain

88 Smyth, *In this sign conquer*, p. 76.   **89** Irish Jesuit Archives, Leeson Street, Dublin. 'Menologies', ii, pp 63–7; 'Memorials of the Irish Province, SJ', 1, viii, pp 395–6; 'Menologies', ii, pp 18–24.

living in a private house without any employment. I further learned that these ten cannot have accommodation either in the barracks or in the general hospital because their number far exceeded Miss Nightingale's demands and expectations. This is the substance of my interview with Mrs Moore. I was informed by Mrs Bridgeman, the Superior of the lately arrived religious, of Miss Nightingale's desire to have five of our Irish nuns under the direction of Mrs Moore. This request was made to, and refused by, Mrs Bridgeman on the grounds that she had been appointed their Superior and could not transfer her authority to anyone. She has another reason for her refusal, namely that the convents from which the Irish nuns were taken have no confidence in Mrs Moore, and refuse to allow their subjects to pass to her authority. I must say that my impressions of Mrs Moore are not favourable for reasons which I will presently explain. This then was the first difficulty that I had to encounter.

The second was that the Sisters in the barrack hospital, to hear mass, were obliged to pass along an immense corridor filled with men, some of whom were dressing, others were mostly undressed. Mass is celebrated in a room where two or three priests sleep and it was not unusual for some of the clergy to get up at the same time that the nuns were assembled at the Holy Sacrifice. This abuse, I felt, could not be tolerated. I was informed by the chaplains that the nuns gave no instructions to the poor sick. I applied for information in very credible quarters, and I found this to be the real state of things. I then called on Miss Nightingale to know what were her intentions with respect to the nuns at Therapia. She could give no security for their employment. I told her that by my position as chaplain and guardian of the nuns, I had full powers to direct their movements, or to take them home if not required, or if they could not observe here the essentials of the religious state. I then, after consulting with the best authorities within my reach, proposed the following conditions as necessary if she wished them to remain.[90]

Fr Ronan then drew up and presented a proposal laying out how the nuns were to be employed, housed and how they were to attend religious services. He finished by demanding that the Sisters of Mercy have:

full liberty throughout their respective hospitals to instruct Roman Catholics particularly when requested to do so by the patients themselves. The Sisters of Mercy on their part pledge themselves not to interfere in the religious conscience of Protestants. They also engage to give undistinguishing relief according to their ability, to the corporeal sufferings of all.[91]

Fr Ronan put this to the other chaplains and they signed their agreement. And he finishes his letter: 'Miss Nightingale too agreed to them but refused to sign them. Things then began to look better.'[92]

This report was acted upon by the bishops in Ireland and England. The major problem for them was the refusal of Brigadier-General Lord William Paulet, commandant at Scutari, to allow the Sisters of Mercy to provide religious instruc-

90 Cullen Papers, 332/7/2, Ronan to Curtis, 3 February 1855. Note that the superiors of the two groups of Sisters of Mercy are referred to as 'Mrs Moore' and 'Mrs Bridgeman'.   **91** Ibid. **92** Ibid.

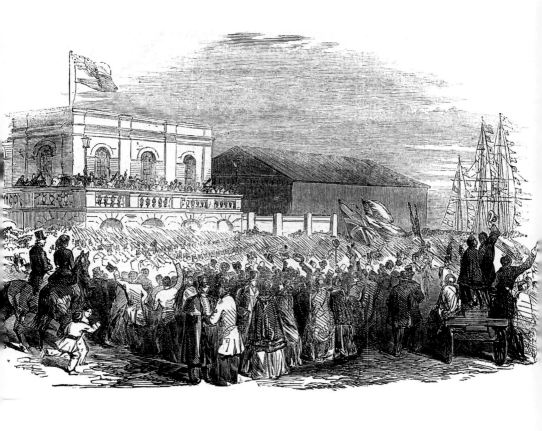

1 The 50th Foot marching through Kingstown (Dun Laoghaire) on their way to board the troopship *Cumbria* on 24 February 1854. The 50th Foot was the first regiment to leave Dublin for the Crimea. The regiment was commanded by Lieutenant-Colonel Richard Waddy, from Wexford (*Illustrated London News*, 4 March 1854).

2 The 11th Hussars boarding the troopship *Tyrone* in Kingstown (Dun Laoghaire). The regiment had been stationed at Portobello Barracks (now Cathal Brugha Barracks) and was commanded by the earl of Cardigan (*Illustrated London News*, 27 May 1854).

3 Lieutenant-General Sir George De Lacy Evans. Born in Moig, Co. Limerick in 1787, De Lacy Evans was an officer of vast experience and had served in the Peninsular war, the American war of 1812–14 and in the Waterloo campaign. He commanded the 2nd Division in the Crimea and was prominent in the battles of the Alma and Inkerman.

4 (*above*) Brigadier-General John Lysaght Pennefather. Born in Co. Tipperary in 1800, Pennefather served in the Peninsular war and in India. He commanded the 1st Brigade of the 2nd Division in the Crimea and was prominent at the battle of Inkerman.

5 (*opposite, top right*) A group of the 8th Royal Irish Hussars in the Crimea. This Roger Fenton photograph is somewhat unusual as one of the enlisted men's wives, who had accompanied the regiment to the Crimea, is pictured in the background.

6 (*opposite, bottom right*) A group of officers and NCOs of the 8th Royal Irish Hussars in the Crimea. The officer on horseback is Captain Lord Killeen, eldest son of Arthur James Plunkett, 9th earl of Fingal and Baron Killeen of Killeen Castle, Co. Meath. The third officer from left, in the dark jacket and smoking a pipe, is Paymaster Henry Duberly, husband of Fanny Duberly who later published *Journal kept during the Russian war* (London, 1855).

7 Rear-Admiral Charles Davis Lucas, born in Druminargale House, near Poyntzpass, Co. Armagh. In June 1854, he was serving aboard HMS *Hecla* in the Baltic and was awarded the first-ever Victoria Cross for his bravery during the attack on the Bomarsund fortress.

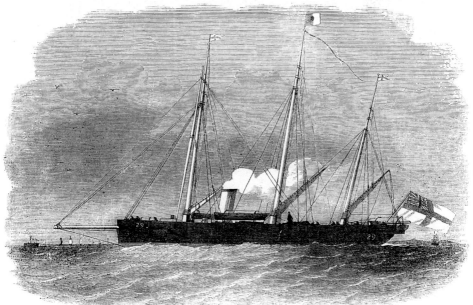

8 (*top*) A contemporary illustration showing Charles Davis Lucas throwing a live shell off the deck of HMS *Hecla*. He was subsequently awarded the first-ever VC for this action.

9 (*bottom*) HMS *Seagull*, commanded by an Irish officer, Commander Montagu O'Reilly (*Illustrated London News*, 12 July 1856).

10 Robert McDonnell FRCSI, who served as a civilian surgeon in the Crimea. This portrait, by Sarah Purser, hangs in the college hall (courtesy of the Royal College of Surgeons in Ireland).

11 William Howard Russell, the Dublin-born *Times* correspondent, photographed in the Crimea by Roger Fenton.

12 (*opposite, top left*) A dancing competition in the Café du Noveau Monde in Kadikoi following the armistice in 1856. A navvy, described as 'a wild young Irishman' outdanced three Russians and 'some ambitious Englishmen' in a good-natured dancing competition (*Illustrated London News*, 23 August 1856).

13 (*opposite, bottom left*) A Roger Fenton photograph of the railway yard in the Balaclava. The navvies' huts can be seen on the hill in the background.

14 (*above*) The Dublin Crimean Banquet, 22 October 1856; 5000 soldiers, seamen and guests gathered in the Bonded Warehouse (Stack A) to celebrate the end of the war (*Illustrated London News*, 8 Nov. 1856).

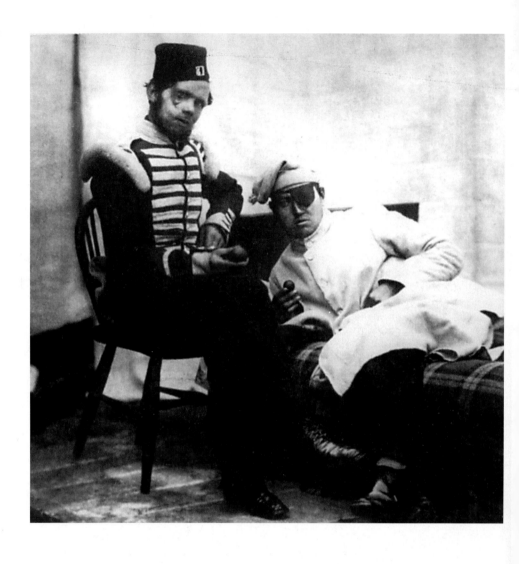

15 Crimean invalids holding the musket and cannon balls that wounded them. On the right, Thomas O'Brien of the 1st Royals.

16 *(opposite)* Soldiers returned from the war. On the left, Corporal Murphy of the Royal Artillery. They are posed in front of a Russian gun captured at Sevastopol.

17 (*above*) An Irish veteran of the war. Clemence Brophy of the 34th Foot, photographed here at Chatham Hospital.

18 (*opposite, above*) Two Irish veterans at the Royal Hospital, Chelsea, in 1875. Dennis Connor and Anthony Sheridan (mistakently named as 'J. Sheridan' in the illustration) had both taken part in the charge of the Light Brigade (*Illustrated London News*, October 1875).

19 (*opposite, below left*) John Lyons of the 19th Foot. Born in Carlow in 1823, he won the VC in the Crimean war. This photograph was allegedly taken after his death in Naas in April 1867.

20 (*opposite, below right*) Trooper Robert Moneypenny, of the 8th Royal Irish Hussars, and bulldog. Moneypenny survived the charge of the Light Brigade and was later an in-pensioner in the Royal Hospital, Kilmainham. He died in the RHK in 1906.

DENNIS CONNOR, 4TH HUSSARS.

J. SHERIDAN, 8TH HUSSARS.

18

19

20

21 (*top*) A 36-pounder Russian cannon on the Armaghdown Bridge in Newry, Co. Down (private collection).

22 (*bottom*) A 9-pounder Naval Brigade howitzer, of Crimean war vintage, in Clancy Barracks, Dublin (private collection).

tion to the men in their care. In March 1855, Bishop Grant wrote to Archbishop Cullen, stating that 'Lord William Paulet will forbid the nuns to speak of religion at all. If this be a fact we must have the order revoked or we must recall the nuns at once.'[93] Despite the efforts of the bishops, this situation was to remain a problem until the end of the war.

Perhaps one of Fr Ronan's worst problems was the attitude of one of his fellow chaplains, Fr Michael Cuffe. Cuffe, a secular priest, displayed animosity towards both the Irish and English Jesuits who served in the Crimea. His behaviour worsened when he was informed that Ronan was to replace him as chaplain to the Irish nuns in January 1855. By this time Cuffe had clashed with Lord William Paulet, Florence Nightingale and most of his colleagues. A letter of 4 January 1855 from Dr Manning in London to Archbishop Cullen stated:

> I regret to say that I have received today from the War Office a request that the Reverend Michael Cuffe may be recalled from the hospital at Scutari on the ground of variances with the authorities of the hospital and indiscretions no doubt arising from good intentions.[94]

A letter from Bishop Thomas Grant of 20 March 1855 confirmed that there were problems with Cuffe's behaviour:

> As to Mr Cuffe the request for his recall was made to Dr Manning by the War Office in consequence of a statement of Miss Nightingale of the harsh way in which he had spoken to her.[95]

Bishop Grant concluded that the request for Cuffe's removal was 'fully justified'.[96] Cuffe defended himself to Archbishop Cullen in a letter of 12 February 1855 in which he suggested that he was the victim of a malicious attack from his fellow chaplains:

> A few imprudent priests and a plotting woman far from under the eye of their superior can create much confusion and effect much evil. Such are some of my English colleagues, such is Mrs Moore, the superior of the English sisters of Mercy. To their imprudence and intrigue have I fallen a victim … victim I recall the expression … for to be invited by your Grace to discharge henceforth my ministry among and for my faithful, simple-minded, generous Irish, I shall never hold to be a grievance but a pleasure the most consoling.[97]

Despite this acrimony Cuffe managed to stay on in the Crimea due to the shortage of chaplains. Also, as Archbishop Cullen was absent in Rome for much of this period, it is doubtful that he had the time or inclination to give this

93 Cullen Papers, 332/5/II, Grant to Cullen, March 1855.   94 Ibid. Manning to Cullen, 4 January 1855.   95 Ibid. Grant to Cullen, 20 March 1855.   96 Ibid.   97 Ibid. Cuffe to Cullen, 12

matter much attention. No copies of letters from Archbishop Cullen to Cuffe
remain in the Dublin Diocesan Archive. During the next months, Cuffe con-
tinuously referred harshly to the other chaplains. Talking of one of the English
Catholic chaplains, Fr Bagshawe, he wrote: 'I have always looked upon this
Reverend gentleman as more than half mad'. Florence Nightingale was referred
to as being 'all-powerful and imperious' while Fr Clarke was 'always sick' and
therefore a burden.[98] Indeed Fr Cuffe had in general not a good word to say about
any of those priests and religious working in the Crimea. The notable exception
to this rule was Fr William Moloney who, it can be seen from the surviving
letters, supplied Cuffe with much information that he had not come across
himself. When Cuffe finally left the Crimea in December 1855, he was serving
as chaplain with the Light Division, which was ironic as he had tried to pass on
this job to other chaplains including Fr Ronan. Cuffe sent a copious amount of
ingratiating letters to Archbishop Cullen and his letter of 15 September 1855,
sent from '88th Regiment, the Camp before Sevastapol' would be typical:

> My Lord, I am grateful for the receipt of your two letters. I shall, please God,
> make it my study to profit by the instructions which they impart. I am still much
> pleased with camp life, if there be any change in my health it is an improvement.
> I do what I can to encourage the men to come to confession, with very many I
> succeed. With many I find it impossible. My division formed the chief storming
> party on the 8th instant. It is dreadfully cut up. So much so that it is generally
> supposed that if there will not be peace, it will spend the winter within
> Sevastapol. Your Grace never expects any war news from me. If indeed you did
> I fear you would be disappointed for very little such do I attend to. Father Ronan
> I understand has gone home on leave of absence from Kulalie. Father Woollett
> has succeeded him for the time being. Father Woollett I understand, but not
> officially, is appointed Superior of the Mission. Father Pauline has lately come
> out as chaplain. He is stupid, deaf and toothless for old age. He is stationed, poor
> man, in Balaclava.[99]

When the relationship between Cuffe and Ronan was particularly bad in 1855,
the senior Anglican chaplain, made efforts to secure some form of recon-
ciliation. This was one of the few occasions when he interfered in the affairs of
the Catholic chaplains. Cuffe, characteristically, made little of Wright's efforts
in his letters to Dublin, dismissing Wright's statement that he was the senior
chaplain.[100]

This incessant squabbling between secular and regular priests must have
seemed somewhat bizarre to the authorities at the different hospitals. In a letter
to Sidney Herbert, secretary at war, written in April 1856, Florence Nightingale

February 1855. **98** Ibid. Cuffe to Cullen, 15 March 1855. **99** Ibid. Cuffe to Cullen, 15
September 1855. The attack 'on the 8th instant' that Fr Cuffe referred to were the assaults on the
Redan and Malakov, 8 September 1855. It was typical of him to barley mention major military
events in his letters. **100** Ibid. 332/7/1, Cuffe to Cullen, 27 August 1855.

described the hostility between the different groups and her attitude to them. While she obviously viewed the various factions with some ill-feeling, the letter gives a good indication of the atmosphere which prevailed. She wrote:

> The Revd Mr Duffy, Jesuit, has been instructed to refuse Confession & therefore Holy Communion to, or even to visit those Bermondsey Nuns, whom I brought up with me from Scutari to one of the Land Transport Hospitals, & he calls them, among other epithets, in a note to themselves, a 'disgrace to their church'. For none can be so coarse as a RC priest. This note we have sent to Dr Grant, Bp. of Southwark, for approval. Cardinal Wiseman has recalled the Revd. Mr Unsworth, Senior RC Chaplain here, who always took part against the Jesuits & Irish Nuns 'under these circumstances'. On the other hand, the secular priests repudiate the Irish Nuns, & do the civil by the Govt. & me & the Bermondsey Nuns with principle [sic] and interest-& even Father Cuffe, who used to call me 'Herod', now licks my hand, as the Provost Marshal says, 'like a good 'un'. Irish 'Regulars' are little else than 'Rebels' as has truly been said here.[101]

An Irish Redemptorist and casualties among the Irish chaplains

The Irish Redemptorist priest, Fr Denis Sheahan, was one of the first Irish chaplains to join the British army in the East. He was working in London when troops began to leave for the east and volunteered to work as a chaplain. Sheahan arrived in Constantinople on 17 April 1854 and a letter he wrote to a friend in Ireland was passed on with his permission to the *Newry Examiner* for publication. He described his initial impressions thus:

> I arrived here on Monday last, and have for ten days been leading a soldier's life, residing in the barracks and faring on a soldier's rations. The barracks is an enormous building, capable of holding about 10,000 men. But the accommodation is very bad. Nothing, however, must be said on that score, as a general consent must have existed between all who have come out here to forego even ordinary comforts.[102]

On the moral and spiritual state of his charges, Sheahan wrote:

> Many of the soldiers give great consolation; but I regret to say that amongst others drunkenness is largely prevalent. One cannot help noticing the very remarkable difference in point of morality and attention to religious duties between the regiments quartered for any time at Malta, and those that have come from other stations. There are some priests at Malta who interest themselves very much in our poor Irish soldiers, and they have done their work well. The English

---

101 Sue M. Goldie, *Florence Nightingale* (London, 1997), pp 246–7. The provost marshal mentioned here, Lieutenant-General Sir George Scovell, who was a Peninsular War veteran.
102 *Newry Examiner*, 10 June 1854.

Jesuits, headed by Father Segrave, in helping the soldier, are doing notable work, in which they merit greatly. And there are other priests at Malta who richly claim the gratitude of all countrymen of the soldier.[103]

Fr Sheahan was not impressed with Constantinople, however, stating 'It is dusty, dirty and unsightly, like everything else Turkish that I have seen'. Interestingly he signed off giving his address as 'attached to the British Expeditionary Force, Scutari, Constantinople'.[104] Fr Sheahan worked as chaplain to the 88th Regiment of Foot (Connaught Rangers) but took ill and died on 10 March 1855. A plaque was later placed in the Redemptorist Church in Clapham, the inscription reading:

> To the Reverend Denis Sheahan, Missioner Apostolic, as a record of gratitude for leaving this mission, where he was beloved and respected, to labour and die amongst their comrades in the Crimea, the soldiers of Her Majesty's 88th Regiment (Connaught Rangers) erected this tablet. Rest in peace.[105]

Irish priests continued to volunteer to serve in the Crimea until late in the war. In September 1855, Cork-born Fr Augustine Maguire left to serve with the army in the Crimea. He was then a curate at St Peter and St Paul's Church in Cork but had previously been a chaplain to the Cork Workhouse. Maguire was unsure of whether he was being sent to serve in a hospital or as a divisional chaplain. It is also interesting to note that his departure was announced in the *Cork Examiner* on 14 September 1855, four days after it had been reported that Sevastapol had fallen, indicating that further fighting was expected in the Crimea. Maguire must have been a popular priest as he was presented with 110 gold sovereigns before he left. This money had been raised by public subscription.[106]

Both Duffy and Ronan returned to Ireland toward the end of the war, Ronan in September 1855 due to bad health. Most of the chaplains suffered ill-health at some stage during the campaign and seven priests and two nuns died in the Crimea. Among those who died were Fr Denis Sheahan, Fr Patrick Meaney and Fr John Shiel, all of whom were Irish. All the chaplains who died in the Crimea had their names inscribed in the oak choir stalls in the garrison church of Domus Dei in Portsmouth.[107] The two Sisters of Mercy who died were Sisters Winifred Spry and Mary Elizabeth Butler. Both were buried in the graveyard

103 Ibid.   104 The use of 'British Expeditionary Force' as a name for the army now assembling is interesting. This is a term usually associated with the British army in France and Belgium during the First and Second World Wars, yet it was occasionally used in personal letters, newspaper articles and official correspondence during the Crimean war.   105 *Irish Sword*, iii, no. 13 (Winter, 1958), p. 233.   106 Evelyn Bolster, *A history of the Diocese of Cork. The Episcopate of William Delany: 1847–86* (Cork, 1993), p. 10. See also the *Cork Examiner*, 14 Sept. 1855.   107 Smyth, op. cit., p. 85.

on the hill above the general hospital at Balaclava. The marble headstone of Sr
Butler read:

> Sacred to the memory of Sister Mary Elizabeth Butler, Sister of Mercy, who died
> of fever at Balaclava, February 23rd 1856. May she rest in peace. Amen. This
> cross was erected by the M.S. Corps in the hospital at the time of her death.[108]

The missionary work of Philip O'Flaherty

Perhaps the most unusual man to engage in religious work during the Crimean
campaign was the Mayo-born, Presbyterian-educated, Philip O'Flaherty. While
officially a soldier in the 7th Foot (Royal Fusiliers), he had demonstrated a
particular ability for learning different languages and was employed as an
interpreter in August 1854. O'Flaherty used this knowledge of languages to try
and spread some idea of Christianity to the local people wherever he was
stationed. He wrote to his mentor, the Revd Michael Brannigan, Presbyterian
minister of Ballinglen, Co. Mayo, in August 1854 telling him of his work
around Varna.

> I am making great progress in the Turkish language, and am learning the Russian
> and Spanish. Whenever I get the chance of meeting a respectable Turk in the field, I
> begin to reprove him for the abominable habit in the country in having many wives.
> I bring England as an example, where each man has only one wife, however rich he
> may be. I tell him in England is Christianity, while they are led astray by the wicked
> suggestions of a false prophet. I tell them of His life and death, and how He rose in
> the world by warfare, and by persuading His followers, if they fell in His service,
> they would go to heaven. I tell them of God and his Christ. I bring simple truths out
> of my Bible, in translating which into Turkish I spend my leisure hours, and say
> many things that I hope may be of use to them.[109]

As time passed, O'Flaherty became more enthusiastic to continue this mission
of spreading the Gospel. In a letter of September 1854 he wrote of another
encounter with some locals:

> I also spoke to them about England's religion; and about several of their
> abominations ... of their false Prophet and his doctrines ... of the truth of
> Christianity, and of Jesus Christ being the only saviour. The women even took off
> their own veils to speak and listen to me, which, I assure you, is a great honour
> to a Christian.[110]

---

108 The Hon. John Colborne (60th Royal Rifles) and Frederic Brine (RE), *Memorials of the
brave; or resting places of our fallen heroes in the Crimea and at Scutari* (London 1858), p. 39.
109 Philip O'Flaherty, *Philip O'Flaherty* (Edinburgh, 1855), p. 21.   110 Ibid. p. 22.

Such actions were indeed courageous and it can only be assumed that O'Flaherty's passion for his subject overcame the obvious risks he ran of seriously offending his listeners. In another letter he expressed the desire to return to Constantinople after the war to undertake missionary work. O'Flaherty must have been unique in engaging in such missionary work amongst the locals.

The later careers of the Irish Jesuits

The events which the Jesuit priests, Fr Ronan and Fr Duffy, had witnessed profoundly affected the rest of their lives. Each of the men had clear recollections of their time in the Crimea and were keen to share them. On his return to Ireland, Fr Ronan worked in various parishes and was appointed as superior of the Galway Jesuit Community in 1880. In 1882, he became rector of the Jesuit house at Limerick and founded the Irish Apostolic School. Two years later, he embarked on a fund-raising tour of the United States and raised over £10,000. Fr Ronan finished his career as rector of Mungret College, Co. Limerick. On December 9, 1907, he was visited by General Sir William Butler, who later wrote of the meeting thus:

> He said to me some memorable things in that first and last interview I had with him on December 9th. Amongst other things he said, 'In the hospital near Scutari I suppose more than 1,000 poor soldiers from the Crimea were prepared for death by me. Some of them were able to utter only a ejaculatory prayer, some of them had little knowledge of their faith before that time, but I have never for one moment doubted that every one of these poor souls went straight to heaven and when I go I think they will elect me their Colonel and I shall stand at their head there. I pray hard that He may take me at any moment. I am quite willing to go but I say that I am ready to stay too, if He has any more work for me to do here'.

Butler added: 'It is an immense satisfaction to me that it was given to me to see this grand veteran on the last full day of his long and eventful life, all his faculties perfect.' It was somewhat strange that on the day after this interview Fr Ronan suffered a stroke and died. He was buried in the college cemetery.[111]

Fr Duffy returned to St Francis Xavier's Church, Gardiner Street, after the war and it was noticed over the following years that he had become 'entirely military in his ideas', which was an interesting comment to make as the Society of Jesus had been founded on military lines. In 1887, he published a spiritual work entitled *The eleven gun battery for the defence of the castle of the soul.*

---

111 General the Rt. Hon. Sir William Butler (1838–1910), born at Suirville, Co. Tipperary, entered the army in September 1858. In the course of his long career he served in Burma, Canada, Africa and was present at the Battle of Tel-el-Kebir in 1882. His artist wife, Lady Butler, painted several paintings with Crimean war themes including *After the charge* and *Calling the roll after*

The following year, he volunteered to go on missionary work to Australia at the age of 74! He spent the next ten years there and, in a letter to his sister, he told her of an encounter with a survivor of the charge of the Light Brigade:

> I asked the veteran what he thought of the action. He replied: 'Father, we did as we were bid, we obeyed at once, and without discussing the nature of the order, whether it was wise or foolish. That was no business of ours. That belonged to the commander, execution was our part, and that we did.' 'You are a soldier,' I said, 'every inch of you. You could not give me a better answer. Would that all we religious would do as you did, obey simply, promptly and cheerfully.'[112]

The veteran Duffy spoke to was Edward Grennan, of Mountrath in Queen's County, who had served with the 4th Light Dragoons in the Crimea. Duffy also sent a newspaper cutting from *The Argus* which detailed Grennan's experiences and wrote:

> The lesson taught is grand! I would advise the Mistress of Novices to read both (the letter and the newspaper cutting) to her novices and give them a lecture on obedience. The analogy the two warfares, the warfare of this world and the warfare of the soul, is very close.[113]

Duffy also made an interesting comment in a letter of 1889. In it he stated that he had recently met Sir Robert G. Hamilton KCB, the governor of Tasmania, at a levee. Duffy stated that Hamilton had thanked him warmly for carrying him wounded from the field and saving his life in the Crimea.[114] This would seem to suggest that the Crimean chaplains had helped evacuate the wounded from the battlefields in the Crimea. While this was part of chaplains' duties in the First and Second World Wars, there are, with the exception of Duffy's statement, no references to Crimean chaplains helping to evacuate wounded.

Duffy returned to England in 1899 and died, 27 September 1901, the result of a bad fall. He was buried in the St Ignatius Churchyard, Richmond, Surrey. The inscription on the tombstone reading: 'Here lies one that did a soldier's part.'[115]

It can be seen that the Irish chaplains working in the Crimea suffered due to the harsh living conditions, confused lines of command, internal bickerings and the hostility of some of the secular chaplains towards the Jesuit chaplains. Fr Ronan and Fr Duffy were the first of a long line of Irish Jesuit priests who were to act as British army chaplains. Perhaps the most notable of these Jesuit chaplains was Father William Doyle SJ, who was killed at the third battle of Ypres in August 1917 while going to the aid of a wounded man. The experiences of Fr Duffy and

an engagement. **112** Irish Jesuit Archives, MS J457, letter of Fr Patrick Duffy SJ, to Sr Mary Agnes of the Carmelite Convent, Tallaght, 21 November 1896. Edward Grennan died in an immigrants home in Melbourne in December 1896. **113** Ibid. **114** Ibid. letter of March 1889. **115** David Murphy, 'Irish Jesuit Chaplains in the Crimea' in *The war correspondent*, xvii, no. 1

Fr Ronan in the Crimea had affected each of the men greatly, physically and psychologically. They each returned in bad health, yet, at the same time, seemed to have viewed this period in the Crimea as a formative period in their careers as priests.

It should also be noted that there were Irishmen among the Anglican chaplains in the Crimea. The Revd Robert Crawford Halpin had begun his career in the army, being commissioned as an ensign in the 14th Foot in 1840. He then entered Trinity College, Dublin, graduating BA in 1843, and became an army chaplain in 1849. Sent to the Crimea, he was awarded the Crimean Medal with all four clasps.[116] He later served in the China war of 1860 and as chaplain to the Household Brigade.[117]

Following the outbreak of the Indian Mutiny in May 1857, thousands of troops were sent to India and once again there was a shortage of chaplains to minister to them. There would also appear to have been a shortage of chaplains during the previous year as, in February 1856, Bishop Grant again wrote to Archbishop Cullen seeking two priests for military service in India and finished his letter thus:

> Do try to help us. Government offers to send two more priests at 300 rupees per month (150 rupees pay, 5 rupees per day for field allowance), and I cannot find any to send. Make an effort and be generous for the sake of the poor Irish soldiers.[118]

The East India Company's armies had no Catholic chaplains in 1857. Catholic troops in the East India Company's armies had to depend on Catholic missionaries who also acted as unofficial chaplains to the troops. Fr Nicholas Barry, an Irish priest who had trained at All Hallows College in Dublin, went to India to work as a missionary in 1847. He was appointed as rector of Agra College, in Oudh Province, in 1853. Later in 1853 he went to Mussaorie in Gwalior and also served as chaplain to the Catholic troops in the area. The majority of priests who served as chaplains during the Indian Mutiny were men such as Fr Barry who had gone to India to work as missionaries and who found that they also had to minister to East India Company soldiers.[119] There is no record available of how many missionary priests served in this capacity during the Mutiny, but several priests were killed by the rebels. The Adjutant-General's Department only sent seven priests to India during the Mutiny, two of whom died.[120]

(April 1999), pp 42–7.   **116** The four clasps were Alma, Balaclava, Inkerman, Sevastapol. The Balaclva clasp is the rarest and it is unusual to find a chaplain who was awarded it.   **117** Boase. See also H.G. Hart, *New Annual Army List* (1860), p. 455.   **118** Cullen Papers, 339/1/II, Grant to Cullen, 18 February1856.   **119** Johnstone and Hagerty, *The cross on the sword*, p. 7.   **120** Fr Patrick Fairhurst died of sunstroke while Fr Charles Morgan died due to disease.

The usefulness of the Roman Catholic chaplains in both the Crimean war and the Indian Mutiny convinced the War Office that they should be retained in both peace and war. Despite quite an amount of bickering between regular and secular priests, they had, by attending to the spiritual needs of Roman Catholic soldiers, improved the morale in the army. Also, in February 1858, a minority Conservative government was formed under Lord Derby and, throughout 1858 and 1859, they implemented several measures which were designed to gain the support of the Irish Catholic community.[121] Derby's administration recognized that the issue of Catholic chaplains had to be resolved and, in 1858, Catholic chaplains were commissioned on a permanent basis, reporting directly to the Horse Guards. The major role played by Irish chaplains during the Crimean war contributed to this innovation. One must also not forget the attempts at missionary work carried out by Philip O'Flaherty. His off-duty activities, if not unique, were at least highly unusual, and stand as one of the more unorthodox aspects of the Crimean war.

It can be seen, therefore, that in both the medical and chaplaincy services there was a strong Irish contingent. While there was a high proportion of Irish surgeons in the Army Medical Service, the involvement of Irish civilian surgeons, nursing sisters and nurses was perhaps more interesting as all these people travelled to the Crimea voluntarily. The same can be said of the Irish chaplains who left their parishes in Ireland to go to the Crimea. They all worked in dreadful conditions and witnessed horrific sights as they carried out their work. In the case of the Irish Sisters of Mercy, the lay nurses and also the Irish Catholic chaplains, their involvement in the Crimea marked a development in the medical and chaplaincy services. Their involvement also acknowledged that modern warfare had the potential to effect those who were not even in the military.

---

121 R.V. Comerford, 'Conspiring brotherhoods and contending elites, 1857–63' in W.E. Vaughan (ed.), *A new history of Ireland*, v (Oxford, 1989), p. 416.

5

Irishmen in the support services
in the Crimea

An interesting feature of the Crimean war was the numerous ad hoc forces organised to carry out certain tasks when the army found that it lacked the personnel for many of the support services. The British army which left for the Crimea in 1854 found that it lacked the personnel for several of the support services that were an established part of the French and Sardinian armies. There were not enough surgeons nor medical staff and, as has been shown in a previous chapter, the army had to recruit surgeons from civilian practice. The Commissariat Department, responsible for supplying the army, was short of staff, and the army was constantly short of engineers. The army also had no provost troops whatever and, as the troops in the field were not being adequately supplied, the pilfering of supply ships and depots soon became a serious problem. Members of the British and Irish constabularies were recruited to serve as Commissariat Department staff and military police as a result of this problem.

The Mounted Staff Corps

The office of provost marshal is an interesting one and the first mention of a provost marshal being appointed to maintain discipline in the British army was in 1511. Provost staff were raised on a temporary basis only and were used to police the army, and to punish offenders, in wartime. During the Peninsular war, Wellington found that the efforts of the provost marshal and his assistant provosts were not sufficient to enforce discipline in the army. The need for a permanent provost corps became increasingly obvious as the war progressed and, after the success of the siege operations at Ciudad Rodrigo and Badajoz, Wellington's men gave themselves over to looting, rape and drunkenness. Wellington constantly requested that a permanent provost corps be established along the lines of the French Gendarmerie Nationale or the Spanish Policia Militar.

Finally, in early 1813, it was decided that a special corps should be formed to police the army. This was the Cavalry Staff Corps and it was made up of eleven officers and 180 men; the men were all volunteers from cavalry regiments. Command of this corps was given to Lieutenant-Colonel George Scovell of the 57th Foot. The Cavalry Staff Corps patrolled the line of march, protected supply depots and prevented troops from entering occupied towns and cities on looting expeditions. Despite their success and usefulness, the Cavalry Staff Corps was disbanded at the end of the campaign in 1814. Lieutenant-Colonel Scovell was asked to reform the corps in 1815 for the Waterloo campaign and it remained in France as part of the occupying forces until 1818. In the post-war reductions the Cavalry Staff Corps was disbanded and the responsibility for maintaining army discipline fell totally on the provost marshal and his assistant provosts once again.[1]

At the outbreak of the Crimean war there was still no permanent corps of military police and, when the British army arrived finally in the Crimea in September 1854, a local provost marshal was appointed: Captain W.D. MacDonald of the 93rd Sutherland Highlanders. He duly appointed deputy provost marshals, all of whom held the rank of sergeant. As early as July 1854 Sir George Scovell, now a lieutenant-general, had drawn up a memorandum on the formation of a staff corps to assist the provost marshal in the Crimea. Sir George Cathcart, adjutant-general, responded positively to Scovell's proposal and recommended that a staff corps be established following Wellington's example. It was also suggested that the invidious word 'police' be avoided in the unit's title and Cathcart suggested that the unit be titled the 'Mounted Staff Corps'. Lord Hardinge, the commander-in-chief, and the duke of Newcastle, secretary of state for war, approved of this idea as it followed a precedent of Wellington's, and they authorised the formation of the Mounted Staff Corps. In light of the proposed provost duties of the Mounted Staff Corps, it was decided to recruit fifty men of 'high character' and 'intelligence' from the Irish Constabulary and the London Metropolitan Police.[2] They were paid just over £100 a year as it was felt that they had greater individual responsibilities and thus deserved higher pay.[3]

Twenty-seven of the fifty members of the Mounted Staff Corps were recruited from the ranks of the Irish Constabulary. (See Appendix C.)[4] As this unit was officially a 'mounted' unit, its members were usually referred to as 'troopers' in the newspapers of the period and this remains the case in modern

---

1 Mike Chappell, *Redcaps: Britain's military police* (London, 1997), pp 7–11. See also G.D. Sheffield, *The Redcaps* (London, 1994). **2** It is interesting to note that the Sardinian army in the Crimea also included a troop of fifty Carabinieri Reali who served as military police during the war. **3** Mike Chappell, *Redcaps: Britain's military police*, pp 13–14. G.D. Sheffield, *The Redcaps*, pp 31–4. **4** *Constabulary List and Directory*, no. 27 (Dublin, 1855), pp 148–51.

studies of the Crimean war. The unit was raised in July 1854 and was stationed in London for training. The corps' uniform was quite elaborate, consisting of a plumed police-style helmet, a red tunic, braided in hussar-fashion, and black cavalry overalls with a double red stripe. They were armed with 1829 pattern light cavalry swords and also with Colt revolvers. The issue of this modern revolver was seen as being very progressive and the members of the corps were sent to the Colt factory in Pimlico to be trained in its use.[5] The Mounted Staff Corps also used the Nolan saddle, a saddle developed by Captain Louis Edward Nolan for the light cavalry. While this type of saddle was often used in India, it was not an 'issue' saddle and was only used when officers bought them privately for their men. Due to the shortage of horses they were mounted on Spanish ponies which were bought at Gibraltar when the corps stopped there on their way to the Crimea. A final unusual feature of their uniform was their adoption of a grey poncho that could also serve as a blanket or greatcoat by the adjustment of its numerous flaps and buttons.[6]

The men of the Mounted Staff Corps arrived in the Crimea on 24 November 1854 and historians of the Crimean war generally agree that, for a number of reasons, the corps was never used to its full potential. Firstly there was some confusion as to what their duties actually were. Cathcart and Scovell had envisaged that they be assigned to the local provost marshal, Captain W.D. MacDonald, for military police duties. The duke of Newcastle had also felt that they could be used to ensure that military camps were run correctly and properly cleaned. Others felt that the Mounted Staff Corps was a staff unit in a very narrow sense; to be used for carrying dispatches and mounting escorts. Cathcart, who had been ordered to the Crimea as the commander of the 4th Division, had assured Newcastle that he would brief Lord Raglan on how the corps was to be employed. It would seem unlikely that this briefing ever took place and Newcastle had to admit in December 1854 that Raglan had not even written to inform him of the arrival of the corps. Perhaps the greatest problem faced by the men of the Mounted Staff Corps was the indifference of Lord Raglan. Lord Raglan had never asked for such a unit to be raised and had very little interest in how they were employed. As a result the men of the corps were used for various duties and, to their great credit, they performed all the tasks that were assigned to them well.[7]

On their arrival in the Crimea, the Mounted Staff Corps was ordered to police the port of Balaclava. Troopers of the corps patrolled the port while other troopers stood sentry at the entrances to the town. These duties were carried out in an

Constabulary List and Directory, no. 28 (Dublin, 1855), pp 150–2.   **5** Samuel Colt opened a London factory in Pimlico in 1851. His Army and Navy model revolvers were two of the most popular revolvers among officers in the Crimea.   **6** R.J.K. Sinclair and F.J.M. Scully, *Arresting memories* (Belfast, 1982). Also Chappell, op. cit., p. 61.   **7** Sheffield, op. cit., pp 31–4.

effort to preserve discipline in the town and to protect the large quantities of supplies on board the ships in the harbour. Troopers of the corps patrolled the dockside, enforcing the order that forbade any soldier from boarding a ship unless he was a member of a supply party under an officer with written authority.

By 14 December 1854 this routine had been changed and an NCO and five men paraded daily at 8.45 a.m. and then proceeded to the house of the provost marshal. There they received their orders for the day or accompanied the provost marshal to assist him in his duties. The harsh winter conditions had a great effect on the Mounted Staff Corps. By the middle of February 1855 only twenty-eight troopers out of fifty were well enough to report for duty. Shortly afterwards a party of the corps, two NCOs and eight troopers, was stationed at Kamiesch Bay for the purpose of carrying dispatches between the French headquarters there and the British headquarters on the Col of Balaclava.[8] By September of 1855 their numbers were further reduced and William Howard Russell of *The Times* noted that the Mounted Staff Corps was used primarily for carrying dispatches as 'their diminished numbers did not render them available for any further service'.[9]

For a number of reasons, both the officers and men of the regular army did not like the men of the Mounted Staff Corps when they arrived in the Crimea. Officers tended to look at them as social inferiors; a letter of Lieutenant Temple Goodman, 5th Dragoon Guards, gives some indication of the attitudes that prevailed. This is an extract from a letter written 17 December 1854 and it describes a visit made to the scene of the charge of the Heavy Brigade in the company of some French cavalry and two Mounted Staff Corps officers:

> The ground where we charged is still covered with jackets, belts, pouches, horses etc., tho' visited by so many people from the ships who have carried away most of the relics. There are several graves here, where the less fortunate actors of the 25th lie, while here and there a white skull looks out partly uncovered by the birds and rain. While looking at these things I had got some way from the French who were going home, and I found several Cossacks coming after us, so thought it wise to make off. The rascals evidently thought they were going to catch me, as they came quite close to our outposts. There were two other officers of the mounted police who have just come out. They are great swells in their own estimation, and nothing would do but they must have a shot at the Cossacks, which however they did not get and were very near being caught for their trouble. I wish they had been quite for they are my great aversion, two horrid snobs, and think themselves regular cavalry men.[10]

---

8 The Col of Balaclava was the open plain to the north-west of Balaclava town, beyond the Sapouné Heights.   **9** Sheffield, Op. cit., p. 33.   **10** Philip Warner, *The fields of war: a young cavalrymen's Crimea campaign* (London, 1977), p. 111. In the 19th century the word 'snob' was used to describe 'one who meanly or vulgarly admires and seeks to imitate those of superior rank or wealth; one who wishes to be regarded as a person of social importance'. J.A. Simpson and

The two officers of the Mounted Staff Corps that Lieutenant Goodman referred to were undoubtedly officers of the London Metropolitan Police as there were no Irish Constabulary officers attached to the Mounted Staff Corps. There were officers of the Irish Constabulary in the Crimea but they served with the Commissariat Department. The rank-and-file were definitely hostile towards the troopers of the Mounted Staff Corps but, as G.D. Sheffield pointed out in his book *The Redcaps*, this probably indicates that they were doing their job properly. They were often accused of being heavy-handed in their policing but this must be viewed in the light of the slack discipline of the troops and civilians in the port area. There were numerous robberies and several murders in the allied camps during the war, all of which were investigated. The civilians were often more of a problem than the soldiers. The railway navvies, who arrived in 1855, were difficult to control. Many of these navvies were Irish and one navvy was flogged for robbery, despite numerous protests that the provost marshal and Mounted Staff Corps had no right to flog civilians. Yet this incident made the navvies modify their behaviour to a large degree. As William Howard Russell commented on their change of behaviour:

> The navvies, notwithstanding the temptations of the bottle, worked honestly and well, with few exceptions, and the dread of the Provost Marshal had produced a wholesome influence on the dispositions of the refractory.[11]

William Howard Russell had initially not been very charitable towards the Mounted Staff Corps, however. On the arrival of the corps in the Crimea, he had commented on their uniform thus:

> In fanciful helmet, red tunic braided in black cord, looking very much as if they were the advanced guard of some equestrian troop coming to open a circus in a village.[12]

Russell later modified his view and admitted that provost marshal and the men of the Mounted Staff Corps had their hands full dealing with 'navvies, Greeks and scoundrels of all sorts'. He ultimately concluded that they had 'performed a good deal of severe work during the winter'.[13]

The men of the Mounted Staff Corps did not leave many accounts of their experiences in the Crimea. Some letters and order books remain in the Corps of Royal Military Police Museum in Colchester. In January 1855 a letter appeared in *The Times*, written by a member of the Irish Constabulary serving

E.S.C. Weiner, *The Oxford English dictionary* (2nd edn, Oxford, 1989), xv, p. 860.   **11** Nicholas Bentley (ed.), *Russell's despatches from the Crimea* (London, 1966), p. 175.   **12** William Howard Russell, *The war: from the death of Lord Raglan to the evacuation of the Crimea* (London, 1856), ii, p. 221.   **13** Sheffield, op. cit., p. 34.

in the Crimea. The letter had been written by a sub-constable from the Maudlin Street Station in Kilkenny to a friend who was also serving as a constable in Ireland. Although *The Times* did not publish his name, this must have been written by Sub-Constable Richard Bradshaw who was the only member of the Irish Constabulary from Kilkenny to serve with the Mounted Staff Corps.[14] His letter provides a fascinating insight into the life of an Irish constable in the corps and is worth quoting at length. The *John Shepard* referred to was the transport ship used to take the Mounted Staff Corps to the Crimea. The letter was dated 7 December 1854 and was written in the Mounted Staff Corps camp near Balaclava:

'There are two sides to every picture.' Up to the time we came to Balaclava we had good times, but indeed the discomforts we are going through now you would scarcely believe. We left the *John Shepard* on the 23rd and pitched our tents a mile above Balaclava, just close to where the engagement of the 5th took place, and where so many of our countrymen fell. You could not believe that the fine army of England is reduced to what it is out here. The few horses that are left are scarcely able to carry their hides, and the poor men, from the cold and hardship they are going through, are scarcely able to walk. It is admitted by old soldiers to be the severest campaign that the English have been engaged in for the last century. The Russian Army that engaged our troops on the 5th are encamped about three miles on our right rear; we can see quite plain, sitting in our tents, the Cossack sentries and of course they can see ours. We have batteries placed in good position, and it would require a great force to dislodge us. Our duty, at present, is keeping the passages clear about Balaclava, and where there is such great traffic taking forage and everything else that the army requires, from Balaclava to where the main body of the army is encamped near Sevastapol. The roads are knee deep with mud and to see our poor men and horses dragging and pulling along the road, it would strike pity into any person's heart. There is a good deal of men dying; they take cramps from the cold in their feet. The hospitals here are full and they are sending them in shiploads to Scutari every day. We have an almost constant cannonading up at Sevastapol and I believe the besieged burn the most powder. The French are admittedly before the English, both in being able to 'carry on the war' in a foreign country, and in their advance on Sevastapol. By what I can hear, the Russian Fleet is protecting the town and must be dislodged before the place can be taken. The allied forces are throwing up batteries to play on the fleet. The Russians sally out at night to take the batteries and are beaten back again, and, I believe, that is the way things are going on there. The weather, as yet, is not colder than in Ireland, but when a man gets wet to the skin, he has no place to go to but a cold tent; and when he gets up in the morning he must go about collecting wood to boil his breakfast; which consists of green coffee, which must be roasted on the stable shovel, pounded and thrown into the water; that, with some biscuit, is our breakfast; biscuit and salt beef for dinner; and supper same as breakfast. We get two glasses of rum every day, which is chiefly the thing that keeps life in us, but we hope it won't be always as bad as it is now. If Sevastapol was once taken our condition would be

14 *Constabulary List and Directory*, no. 27 (Dublin, 1855), p. 150.

better. Why, if it is not taken, and that the troops have to winter here, history will record another 1812. Some of the Mounted Staff Corps are in excellent health and spirits and we hope, with the Divine assistance, to rub out and return to our native country again. Only two of our men died, one a mounted man from Waterford named Maguire, the other one of the English Constabulary.[15]

Bradshaw's descriptions of the conditions in the Crimea are accurate although he was incorrect as to the status and potential of the Russian fleet. By the time the Mounted Staff Corps arrived in the Crimea the Russians had scuttled their ships in Sevastapol harbour. Also Sub-Constable Maguire from Waterford did not die in the Crimea but had to return to Ireland due to illness.

Members of the Irish Constabulary also served with the Commissariat Department and their involvement was not confined to the Mounted Staff Corps. At the outbreak of the Crimean war the Commissariat Department found itself short of both men and equipment. In an effort to solve the shortage of manpower a call for volunteers from the British and Irish constabularies was made in the summer of 1854. The reasoning behind requesting volunteers from the constabularies was that it was felt that these men would be both more trustworthy and efficient controlling supplies. Another reason for using police in the Commissariat was the hope that they would reduce the amount of pilferage.

Sixteen Irish Constabulary officers and twenty-six men volunteered and served as Commissariat officers and store-keepers in the Crimea.[16] (See Appendix C.) They volunteered to serve for twelve months and the majority were in the Crimea from December 1854 to December 1855, although some members had to return home due to illness before the full year had passed. Some of the officers, such as 1st Sub-Inspector Chartres Brew, volunteered soon after the outbreak of the war and therefore saw longer service. The officers and men of the Irish Constabulary were stationed in various supply depots in Balaclava and their primary task was to ensure that only valid requisitions were filled. The Commissariat Department performed abysmally in the Crimea and inefficiency and pilferage were rife. One can only assume that the members of the Irish Constabulary were only moderately successful in their work with the Commissariat Department.[17]

15 *The Times*, 4 Jan. 1855, p. 10. The 'engagement of the 5th' that Sub-Constable Bradshaw refers to was the battle of Inkerman, 5 November 1854.   16 *Constabulary List and Directory*, numbers 27 and 28.   17 Sub-Inspector Chartres Brew was one of the first constabulary officers to volunteer to serve in the Crimea with the Commissariat Department. He had been born at Corofin, Co. Clare, in December 1815, the eldest son of Tomkins Brew, stipendary magistrate of Tuam. In 1835 he volunteered to join the British Legion that had been formed to fight in the First Carlist War in Spain. He fought with the British Legion, commanded by General Sir George De Lacy Evans, and was wounded. In 1840 he joined the Irish Constabulary and at the outbreak of the Crimean war was serving in South Tipperary. He volunteered to serve with the Commissariat Department and in February 1856 was serving as an assistant commissary-general. He was

The dreadful winter conditions in the Crimea and the various illnesses took their toll of the Irish Constabulary serving in the Mounted Staff Corps and with the Commissariat Department. Two officers who were attached to the Commissariat Department died; 2nd Sub-Inspectors Thomas C. Anderson and George Du Bourdieu. Many others became very ill and some, including Sub-Constables Thomas Mullen and John Kelly of the Mounted Staff Corps, had to return to Ireland before their year's engagement was up. Two other constables, James Vickers and John McCarthy, were taken prisoner.[18] Both were serving with the Commissariat Department and details of how they came to be captured are not clear. While one would expect members of the Mounted Staff Corps to run the risk of capture while carrying dispatches, it seems unusual that Commissariat staff should be captured. One can only assume that these two Irishmen were captured while taking supplies to the siegeworks at Sevastapol. Russian infantry and cavalry were constantly evading allied pickets and were quite aggressive in their efforts to gain intelligence and capture prisoners. It is quite likely that these two men were captured in this way. It is also possible that they were captured while on a sight-seeing trip like the one described earlier by Lieutenant Temple Goodman.

The use of members of the Irish Constabulary in the Crimea led to suggestions that a further call for volunteers be made for members of the force to form an infantry regiment. This proposal was made by Lord Palmerston in November 1854 and the idea was given a great deal of newspaper coverage. Several names were proposed for this new regiment or corps, the three most prominent being the 'Irish Guards', the 'Irish Brigade' or the 'Irish Greens'. Palmerston also suggested that drafts of men from the Irish Constabulary could be used to send replacements to the Guards regiments. The *Wolverhampton Chronicle* of 25 November 1854 carried the following story entitled 'An Irish Brigade for the Crimea':

> It is in contemplation to send out an Irish Brigade to the Crimea, to be composed of 5,000 men, to be called not a brigade, but 'The Irish Greens' and placed under the command of an officer of tried and proved ability and valour. Its is said that this brigade is to be formed of 5,000 volunteers from the ranks of the Irish Constabulary, certainly one of the finest armed forces in the world; active, hardy, and unflinching in the hour of danger. This may be mere idle rumour, but it carries with it an idea that might be very practical, probable and valuable. Such an addition to our forces in the Crimea would prove of the most important value.

awarded the British Crimean Medal with three clasps, presumably the Alma, Inkerman and Sevastapol clasps. On his return to Ireland he was transferred to Cork City. In 1858 he was offered the position of chief-inspector of police in British Columbia and went on to have a significant career there, serving also as a gold commissioner and judge. It is also interesting that he tried to recruit men from the Irish Constabulary in 1858 when establishing the colony's police force. *Dictionary of Canadian biography.*   **18** *Constabulary list and directory*, numbers 27 and 28.

These men are inured to hard service, their accoutrements are light, convenient and effective; and in every point a division of Irish Greens would not be the least valuable element in the war now upon us. The Irish Constabulary force at present numbers somewhat over 12,000 men, picked from the ranks of the comfortable classes, and it only requires the word to go forth to ensure twice-told 5,000 volunteers; but, if such a step be decided upon, it would be very desirable that some small addition should be made to their pay allowances. The present tranquil state of the country, its improving prospects, and the Irish militia in prospective, all add to the feasibility of the project.[19]

This proposal was ill-timed. William Howard Russell's damning accounts of how badly the campaign was being managed were appearing in *The Times* by late 1854. His accounts told of poor leadership and organization and the lack of supplies as the Crimean winter approached. The men of the Irish Constabulary were well aware, therefore, of the dire conditions in the Crimea and, not surprisingly, refused to respond to this appeal to their patriotism. Despite the patriotic tone of the piece in the *Wolverhampton Chronicle*, it did not merely require 'the word to go forth' to make members of Irish Constabulary volunteer. Indeed the officers and men of the Irish Constabulary were in regular contact with soldiers of the British army in Ireland and were no doubt well aware of the rate of army pay, conditions in the army and the quality of the leadership. The suggestion was naïve in the extreme and deserved to get the lack of response that it did. While temporary posts with the Mounted Staff Corps or the Commissariat Department were acceptable to some, serving as infantry in the Crimea was another matter entirely.

Yet in September 1855, the *Cork Examiner* reported that Lieutenant-Colonel La Touche Hatton of the Grenadier Guards was in Ireland on a recruiting tour of Irish Constabulary barracks and was trying, unsuccessfully, to persuade Irish constables to enlist. The *Cork Examiner* stated that La Touche Hatton was the object of 'much local satire' and continued 'a member of the force has devoted his leisure hours to the composition of an ode to honour the event'.[20] This is an interesting statement as there is a ballad in the White Ballad Collection in Trinity College Dublin entitled 'The Irish Guards: A new Song'. Written by Acting Constable Henry Vousden of Shahernavoit Station in August 1855, the tone of the ballad no doubt reflects the views of many of the Irish Constabulary regarding this proposal and could possibly be the 'ode' referred to in the *Cork Examiner*. The ballad begins:

The most of us are six foot high, from that to six foot four, such guardsmen as 'the pick' would make were never seen before, but your pay is very shabby, and then as for rewards, an Irishman has little chance of such things in the guards.

19 Robert J. Williams, 'An Irish Brigade for the Crimea' in *Irish Sword*, xiv, no. 55 (Winter, 1980), p. 195. **20** *Cork Examiner*, 10 Sept. 1855.

It continues:

> You tried the Metropolitans, but didn't go a man to volunteer his services to
> capture the Redan. And yet they are not cowards, and their feathers are not white,
> if you ask them to come forward in a manner that is right. But it isn't thirteen
> pence a day, beside a penny towards a drink of beer, can coax us to 'list in the
> guards. Whoever struck that ration out had very little wit, to think a Pennyworth
> of beer a Peeler's mug would fit. And if he ever was in Ireland, oh dear, how he'd
> have laughed to see a Peeler drinking fourpence hap'ny in a draught.

The ballad concludes:

> Then return to Lord P–l–n, and may just let him know the plan of filling up the
> Guards with Peelers is no go. That if he wants a regiment of valour and renown,
> he must ask us to form it as a body of our own. Commanded by the officers who
> have our best regards. And then you'll have a regiment of Royal Irish Guards.[21]

By the summer of 1855 Mounted Staff Corps numbers had been greatly
reduced due to illness and they had ceased to be an effective unit. After the
death of Lord Raglan on 28 June 1855, they formed part of the procession that
escorted his remains to Balaclava harbour on 3 July. The remaining men of the
corps formed a small troop and brought up the rear of the procession that
travelled from Lord Raglan's headquarters to the quay at Balaclava, where the
coffin was loaded on to the *Caradoc* transport ship. They then served as
outriders as the procession returned to the camp at Sevastapol.[22] In September
1855 the Mounted Staff Corps was disbanded and its members returned to their
stations in England and Ireland.

The difficulties that they had faced in the Crimea and the problems of trying
to raise a provost corps after the outbreak of war had finally convinced the
commander-in-chief, Lord Hardinge, that a permanent provost corps should be
established. As a result in June 1855 the Corps of Military Mounted Police was
formed to patrol the camp at Aldershot, which had recently been the scene of
numerous clashes between soldiers from different regiments. In 1885 the Corps
of Military Foot Police was formed, both corps being amalgamated to form the
Corps of Military Police in 1926. In 1946 the corps was granted the 'Royal'
prefix, becoming the Corps of Royal Military Police.[23] It was in the Crimea,
therefore, that a temporary staff corps was used by the British army for the last
time to carry out provost duties. What made the Mounted Staff Corps more
unusual was the fact that it was made up of men from the constabulary rather
than soldiers, as had previously been the case.

---

21 White Ballad Collection, volume I, OLS–X–1–532, ballad no. 64. Henry Vousden even
included his service number, 14,996, on this publication.   **22** Sheffield, op. cit., p. 33.
23 Anthony makepeace-Warne, *Brassey's companion to the British army*, p. 86.

The Land Transport Corps

At the beginning of the war the Commissariat Department was also desperately short of men and, as has been previously stated, found that it had to recruit civilians to help in the transport of supplies in the Crimea. This department had suffered drastic reductions in terms of staff and resources during the previous twenty years. These reductions culminated in the disbandment of the Royal Wagon Train in 1833. The Commissariat establishment in England had been greatly reduced while the establishment in Ireland had been done away with entirely.[24] Commissary-General James Filder, who accompanied the army to the Crimea, had few staff and almost no transport wagons or animals. As a result of this he recruited clerks, store-keepers and interpreters in Malta and later in Bulgaria to assist in supply duties. Graeme Crew in his book *The Royal Army Service Corps* has described these individuals as 'a weird collection of untrained, totally inadequate civilians, whose value to the Commissariat in the Crimea was more than doubtful'.[25]

Transport animals were also bought while the army was in Bulgaria, then still part of the Turkish Empire. This practice delighted the local population who charged far more than the animals were worth. Around 4,000 horses and mules, 2,300 draught oxen and 2,500 assorted vehicles were bought but, due to the shortage of shipping, most of these were left at Varna. When the army arrived in the Crimea in September 1854, it took only 75 mules and a few carts. Somehow the Commissariat Department expected to supply an army of over 30,000 men with this tiny transport force.[26] More animals and carts were bought later in the year, some from as far away as the Turkish possessions of Syria and Tunisia. Also, more civilians were recruited and the Commissariat Department soon had an interesting mixture of waggoners, camel-drivers and muleteers. As late as June 1855 the Commissariat Department was recruiting muleteers from Spain in an effort to solve their manpower difficulties.[27]

Mere numbers of men did not solve the problem, however, and the supply situation was soon desperately disorganized. There have been numerous accounts of the Commissariat Department's problems in the Crimea and it is sufficient for the purposes of this study to merely point out that the situation was caused by a number of factors. Firstly there was a shortage of supply ships and this slowed down the process of re-supply. Secondly there were not enough dock workers in Balaclava to actually unload the supplies that did arrive. This problem was not dealt with until January 1855 when 900 porters were hired in Constantinople and a party of dockers was recruited from London's docklands.[28]

24 The Hon. Sir John Fortescue, *The early history of transport and supply* (London, 1928), pp 74–5. **25** Graeme Crew, *The Royal Army Service Corps* (London, 1970), p. 34. **26** Ibid. p. 34. **27** *Illustrated London News*, 16 June 1855. **28** Ibid. 20 Jan. 1855 and 27 Jan. 1855.

There was also not enough administrative staff. Men from the Irish Constabulary, and also civilian store-keepers and clerks, were used in an effort to solve this problem. Finally, when supplies had been unloaded and sorted, there was not enough wagons and drivers to carry the supplies to the camp at Sevastapol. The recruitment of locals never resolved this difficulty and as early as June 1854 Lord Raglan had requested that a transport corps be formed. No notice of his repeated requests regarding this matter was taken until late 1854, and in January 1855 the Land Transport Corps was established by royal warrant. The new corps was established as a part of the regular army and, because of the supply situation in the Crimea, recruiting officers made determined efforts to attract muleteers and waggoners to the Land Transport Corps.[29]

There have been no comprehensive studies of the Land Transport Corps in the Crimea and the corps is usually included as a footnote in histories of the Royal Army Service Corps. It is certain, however, that many Irish served in this corps. In January 1855 the *Sligo Journal* carried the following small item:

> Drivers for the Crimea. Several smart young fellows from the neighbourhood have joined this useful corps and left for Dublin, en route for the seat of war.[30]

Recruiting for the first draft was completed in April 1855 and the second draft was at full strength by June 1855. The Land Transport Corps was commanded by Colonel W. McMurdo who was succeeded, during a period of ill-health, by Colonel Edward R. Wetherall, later deputy quartermaster-general in Ireland. The Land Transport Corps numbered just under 9,000 men, initially formed with two troops of Land Transport Corps in each brigade. This was later changed and each division had two Land Transport Corps battalions.[31] While the corps had been formed very late, by the end of the war they had become highly efficient and in a twenty-four hour period could carry three days rations for 58,000 men and 30,000 horses and 200 rounds of ammunition for 36,000 men. They could also evacuate 2,500 casualties in one day.[32]

Their uniforms were quite colourful and drivers of the Land Transport Corps wore double-breasted blue tunics with facings in the colour of the division to which they were attached. Officers and NCOs wore a blue forage cap while the men wore a wide-brimmed felt hat, often worn with one side pinned up to give a more rakish slouch effect. As a result of their somewhat flamboyant appearance, men of the Land Transport Corps are often noticeable in the background of contemporary prints. One *Illustrated London News* correspondent also complained that, despite their logistic function, 'they go about armed to the teeth'.

---

29 Crew, *The RASC*, pp 38–9.   **30** *Sligo Journal*, 21 Jan. 1855.   **31** Michael Barthorp and Pierre Turner, *The British army on campaign 2: The Crimea 1854–6* (London, 1987), p. 42.   **32** Crew, *The RASC*, p. 41.

There was a good reason for this. As troops could not be spared to escort supply columns, it was felt that the men of the Land Transport Corps should be armed to defend themselves and their wagons and mule loads. Each man was armed with a carbine and bayonet while officers carried a light cavalry pattern sabre and a revolver.[33] These were tough men indeed but even so they suffered a high casualty rate mostly due to the severe weather and the hard work.[34]

It would also appear that some of the Irish members of the Land Transport Corps were 'colourful' in their own right and several achieved a dubious notoriety after the war. Thomas Cawley, who had served in an infantry regiment and then in the Land Transport Corps in the Crimea, was a ringleader in the North Tipperary Militia mutiny in Nenagh in July 1856. (This mutiny will be dealt with in detail in Chapter 7.) Cawley was eventually arrested by Constable Aubrey of Nenagh Station while hiding in a cornfield at Annebrook near the town. Court-martialled on 25 July 1856, he was sentenced to ten years transportation.[35] Another ex-member of the Land Transport Corps, William Deery, gave evidence to police investigating the murder of James Murray, the Scottish steward of John George Adair, in November 1860. Murray had been murdered after a dispute developed between Adair and the tenants on his estate at Derryveagh, Co. Donegal, regarding shooting rights and trespassing sheep. Deery claimed to know not only who had murdered Murray but also who the local Ribbon society members were. Fourteen men were arrested on evidence supplied by Deery but, following further police investigation, his testimony was found to be false and, at the assizes in March 1861, he was sentenced to seven years for perjury.[36]

The Land Transport Corps was a most interesting corps and the work it carried out in the Crimea deserves to be the focus of further study. They had given good such service in the Crimea that it was decided to reconstitute the Military Train and this was carried out under a royal warrant of August 1856. Many members of the Land Transport Corps transferred directly into the new unit. It is certain that a number of Irishmen served in the Land Transport Corps during the war and further study of the corps records at the Public Record Office at Kew could give further information regarding this Irish contribution.

The Civil Engineering Corps

One of the major problems that faced the British army in the Crimea was the lack of a proper road system to carry supplies from the port of Balaclava to the siege

33 The men were armed with the 1840 Constabulary Pattern Carbine while the officers bought their own revolvers, usually Colt or Deane Adams revolvers.   34 Crew, Op. cit., p. 41.   35 *Nenagh Guardian*, 11 July 1956. See also E.H. Sheehan, *Nenagh and its neighbourhood* (Tipperary, 1976), p. 93.   36 W.E. Vaughan, *Sin, sheep and Scotsmen. John George Adair and*

works at Sevastapol. There was a road that ran from the port northwards to the village of Kadikoi and from there it ran westward to the Sapouné Heights. This road passed through the Sapouné Heights to the Col of Balaclava, where the gradient was less steep. It then crossed the plateau where one branch led to Sevastapol and the other went to Kamiesch. The road appeared on maps of the period and it was felt that it would enable the allied forces to supply the men besieging Sevastapol. In fact this was not a road in the proper sense but merely a series of tracks that had been formed over the years by the traffic travelling from Balaclava to Kamiesch and Sevastapol. The local inhabitants used the road to carry goods from the port and the heaviest traffic that had ever passed on it were arabas – local ox-drawn carts of about 700lb in weight. While the road followed the most convenient route, avoiding steep gradients, no attempts had ever been made to reinforce or metal this series of tracks. On their arrival in Balaclava, army engineers quickly realised that the road would deteriorate in the winter. Local inhabitants confirmed this and indicated that, in the very depths of winter, the road was impassable. There was one metalled road in the district. This was the Woronzow Road which ran south-eastwards from Sevastapol, through the Sapouné Heights, to the gates of the estate of Count Woronzow. The nearest it passed to Balaclava was three miles north of the port and as a result it was of little use in the efforts to supply the army. It was obvious that these roads would not be able to carry the massive amount of supplies needed at the siegeworks. The allied commanders, however, hoped that Sevastapol would fall before the onset of winter and no efforts were made to improve the roads. With the onset of winter the roads soon became impassable and a report by William Howard Russell to this effect was published in *The Times* on 18 December 1854. There was a public outcry when this report reached the public describing how men and horses were struggling vainly to carry supplies to the hungry troops at Sevastapol . The railway contractor Sir Samuel Morton Peto, who was also an MP, felt that a railway was the answer and suggested this to Lord Palmerston. A further meeting followed with the duke of Newcastle and eventually Sir Samuel Morton Peto, and his partners Edward Ladd Betts and Thomas Brassey, offered to ship out their own engineers, navvies and equipment, to survey and build the line and then to run it. What was more, they were prepared to do all this at cost and only asked that the money they spent on materials be refunded. Not surprisingly, the government accepted. The man that Peto, Betts and Brassey picked as their chief engineer was an Irishman, James Beatty.[37]

James ('Jim') Beatty was born on 31 March 1820 in Enniskillen, Co. Fermanagh, the son of Dr James Beatty.[38] His father had educated him privately,

the Derryveagh evictions, 1861 (Belfast, 1983), p. 33, pp 37–8, p. 64.   **37** Brian Cooke, *The Grand Crimean Railway* (2nd edn, Cheshire, 1997), p. 25.   **38** Dr James Beatty (1788–1855) of

teaching him English and classics himself before engaging a tutor to teach him mathematics. From an early age he showed an interest in engineering, avidly reading accounts of the great railway projects of the era, and his father encouraged him to follow a career in civil engineering. He joined the firm of Peto & Betts in 1842 and was initially employed on the construction of the Norwich to Lowestoft line. In late 1853 he went to Nova Scotia to survey the European and North American Railway; a series of railways that were to connect Halifax, the nearest port to Europe, with the interior of Canada and the United States. Beatty was faced with difficult conditions while carrying out this project and had to survey in dense forest. When winter set in, the surveying party endured three feet of snow on some occasions, living in arctic conditions in tents and on occasion reduced to eating salt pork and biscuit. Despite these hardships, Beatty had completed the survey by Christmas 1853, a period of just over three months, and returned to England in February 1854. Peto knew that he would make an excellent chief engineer for the Crimean railway project. Apart from his obvious technical abilities, Beatty also got on well with his men and inspired them to work hard without engaging in any strong-arm tactics.[39]

Beatty's first task was to help Betts to recruit the labour force required and he immediately advised that the size of the force be increased from 200 men to 250 men. The force was to be known as the Civil Engineering Corps and it was intended that these men should work in a civilian capacity only and not be subject to military law. Advertisements were placed in national newspapers and on 2 December 1854 the contractor's office in Waterloo Road in London opened to sign men on. The offices were quickly crowded with men who competed for the vacancies for navvies, gangers, masons, carpenters and blacksmiths. Beatty and Betts were able to take their pick and had their force of 250 men by the end of the day.

Many seemed to think that they were going to fight rather than build a railway. One reporter wrote that he overheard a navvy remarking, 'We'll give it to them with the pick and the crowbar, them Roosians, instead of the rifle.' Indeed this aggressive tone was repeated in several newspaper articles and cartoons. Despite a 'No more men wanted' sign being posted on the office door on 3 December 1854, men still came in droves hoping to be taken on.[40] The initial force had been recruited and it is interesting to note that apart from engineers, surveyors, navvies and clerks, Beatty and Betts also recruited five surgeons, four female nurses, a barber and two missionaries to care for the men's spiritual welfare. Indeed the Crimean railway navvies were, in many

Daring Street, Enniskillen. Educated at Edinburgh University, he was appointed as assistant surgeon to the Enniskillen Militia in 1810 and superintendent of the Enniskillen cholera hospital in 1832.   **39** Ibid., pp 25–6.   **40** Terry Coleman, *The railway navvies* (2nd edn, London, 1981),

ways, better organised than the army. By June 1855 the Civil Engineer Corps numbered 530.[41]

It is certain that a large number of the railway navvies who joined the Civil Engineer Corps and who worked in the Crimea were Irish. Terry Coleman in his book *The railway navvies* estimated that one third of the railway navvies in Britain were Irish in the 1840s and that the numbers of Irishmen working on railway projects remained high in the 1850s. There had been some violent clashes between Scots and Irish navvies during the 1840s, one of the worst of these occurring at Penrith and Gorebridge, ten miles from Edinburgh, in February 1846.[42] It is difficult to say how many of the Crimean navvies were Irish. It is interesting to note, however, that the bazaar situated near Kadikoi was later referred to by many of the navvies as 'Donnybrook Fair'.[43] Also, in 1857, the government of Sardinia-Piedmont published a series of drawings and maps which gave details of their army's positions in the Crimea. The maps were drawn by engineering officers of the Sardinian army and are perhaps the most detailed maps of the allied positions in the Crimea. The camp used by the railway navvies, usually just referred to as the 'railway huts' or the 'railway camp' on British maps, is referred to on the Sardinian maps as the 'Campo dei Lavoranti Irlandesi'.[44] This would seem to suggest that the Sardinian officers who drew these maps thought that the majority of the railway navvies were Irish.

In early December 1854 a surveying party left for the Crimea under Donald Campbell, one of Beatty's assistant engineers. Beatty remained in England to organise preparations for the expedition. It was fortunate that Peto also owned a shipping company, the Peto Steam Navigation Company, and the men and materials were loaded on his ships and also on other ships chartered for the purpose. After his Christmas leave Beatty travelled overland to Marseilles before boarding a ship for the Crimea. Meeting with Campbell and the survey party on 19 January 1855, he concurred with him on the route he had surveyed and immediately set to work. At this time Beatty had no workforce and he estimated that his force of navvies would not arrive in the Crimea for another ten days. Empowered by a letter from the duke of Newcastle he was allocated an area in the port of Balaclava to build a railway yard and on 27 January 1855 was allowed 150 men (later 200) of the 39th Regiment to help him begin the project. Peto had promised Newcastle that the railway would be functioning three weeks after the arrival of the force of navvies and Beatty was determined to keep this promise.

Beatty's plan was to run a double line of rails to the encampment near Sevastapol. From a point near the British siege lines, single lines would then

pp 213–6.   **41** Cooke, *Grand Crimean Railway*, pp 26–28.   **42** Coleman, *Railway navvies*, pp 93–102.   **43** William Howard Russell, *The war* (London, 1855), i, p. 333.   **44** Corpo Reale di Stato Maggiore, *Riccordo Pittorico Militare della Spedizione Sarda in Oriente, 1855–56* (Turin, 1857).

branch off to the numerous batteries to facilitate the carrying of ammunition and supplies to the batteries. Initially the railway wagons were hauled uphill to the siegeworks by teams of horses and then let run freely back downhill to the railway yard in Balaclava. Stationary winding engines were to be introduced and, somewhat later, locomotives. In a report of April 1855 Beatty described the task that faced him:

> What strikes a newcomer most on his arrival here is the immense extent of country covered by the Allied forces. From Balaclava on the extreme right is about nine miles inside the intrenchments [sic], the length of the defence and attacking works is over sixteen miles; so that, instead of being a siege concentrated against a certain point, it is a series of detached batteries against batteries. I mention this to show that a few miles of rails are soon swallowed up in attempting to give railway accommodation to the Army.

Beatty continued:

> As regards the labour furnished by the Army, I mentioned that 150 men of the 39th Regiment (afterwards increased to 200) had been placed at my disposal for a short time (from 27th January to 6th February); they were of the greatest assistance, as far as they went, in forming the line, and were becoming very fair navvies but, unfortunately, they were removed before they had the time to be of much real benefit to us. I took great interest in these men; the officers seemed to take a pride in their work, and I was almost in despair when they were taken away. Two hundred Croatians were given to me on the 1st February; they were at first literally useless, except as beasts of burden, and were only employed in carrying stones for the road. The want of interpreters who could speak English was also a great loss to us at first; however, by dint of perseverance, we at last broke about thirty of them to handle the spade and shovel and wheel a barrow. The remainder have been and are still engaged unloading the ships, for which they are extremely well qualified. With the exception of these 200 Croats and 200 sailors lent by Captain Lushington for about ten days, we have had no assistance in labour from the army; indeed the Quartermaster-General told me from the first that he could not spare any soldiers, and I do not believe that he could. The amount of fatigue duty and work in the trenches had fully occupied every available man in the army; and I feel quite certain that General Airey, from whom I have lately received the greatest kindness, would have willingly afforded me military aid if he could; but the truth was, until we begin to convey goods by rail, and relieve the army of their daily trudge to Balaclava, the trenches are not half manned.[45]

On the arrival of his workforce, Beatty began organizing living quarters for his men. He acquired a site above the town and, after levelling the ground and surveying the camp area, the navvies built their own huts and administrative buildings. It was later remarked that Beatty had a full night's sleep after the completion of this work, the first proper rest he had since arriving in the Crimea

---

45 *Illustrated London News*, 12 May 1855.

on 19 January 1855.[46] On 8 February 1855, not even a week after their arrival, they began laying track from the railyard in Balaclava along the route to the railhead at Sevastapol. Beatty occupied himself in setting up the stationary engines that were to pull the wagons to the railhead at Sevastapol. On 22 February 1855, just under three weeks after the arrival of the navvies, the first load of supplies was carried to Kadikoi. This fulfilled the promise that Peto had made to the duke of Newcastle that the railway would be operational three weeks after the arrival of his men. Beatty wrote in his report to Peto:

> The railway was commenced on the 8th February by the navvies; it conveyed commissariat stores to the Kadikoi on the 23rd; and on the 26th March it conveyed shot and shell to the summit at headquarters, four and a half miles from Balaclava, which with the Diamond Wharf branch and the double line from Balaclava to Kadikoi, makes upwards of seven miles of rail laid down in seven weeks.[47]

In the beginning of March 1855 Beatty had begun building the various branch lines and also began improving the railyard at Balaclava. Some Eastern Counties Railway sheds had been sent out from England and Beatty had these reassembled, still in their ECR livery, in Balaclava and they appear in the background in some early photographs of the yard. Beatty's main problem was the shortage of horses to pull his wagons while the stationary engines were being completed but he managed to obtain twenty army mules while waiting for more horses from England.

On 10 March 1855 the railway project suffered a setback. It has already been mentioned that, until the stationary engines were in place, horses pulled the wagons to the depots at Kadikoi and at the siegeworks and, on being emptied, the horses were unhitched and the wagons allowed to run downhill with a brakesman in each wagon. Beatty had recognized that this practice was inherently dangerous and, on 10 March, while a number of wagons were running downhill, one of the brakesmen lost control and ran into wagons in front of him on the line. A number of wagons were derailed and a Spanish muleteer riding in one of the runaway wagons was killed. Beatty later wrote that the accident was the fault of the brakesman as he had 'whether from nervousness or any such cause, lost his presence of mind and his command of the brake at the same time'.[48]

Beatty also became a friend of the photographer Roger Fenton, who arrived in the Crimea in early March 1855. His passage to the Crimea had been arranged by Sir Samuel Morton Peto and he had sailed on HMS *Hecla*.[49] Fenton unloaded his photographic wagon and equipment near the railway yard

46 Arthur Helps, *The life and labours of Mr Brassey, 1805–70* (London, 1872). **47** *Illustrated London News*, 12 May 1855. **48** Cooke, op. cit., p. 55. **49** HMS *Hecla* was the ship in which master's-mate, later lieutenant, Charles Davis Lucas had served in the Baltic in June 1854. Lucas,

in Balaclava on 8 March 1855 and soon after met with Beatty. Beatty helped him find stabling for his horses and also stored some boxes of equipment for him. Fenton was fascinated with the whole railway operation and got to know Beatty, the other engineers and navvies well. It is not surprising, therefore, that his first photographs were taken in the railway yard, dated mid-March 1855, including one of Beatty himself.

Having completed the whole line by this stage, Beatty then set about double-tracking the line, initially in the section between Balaclava and Kadikoi, with plans to double-track to the wharfside in the port. By the end of March 1855 he had also laid another branch line to the newly constructed Diamond Wharf on the west side of the harbour. On 2 April 1855 the train was used for the first time to carry wounded to the harbour, the first-ever hospital train to run. In many ways this was the culmination of Beatty's plans. The railway could now not only carry supplies and troops but also evacuate the wounded.

A few days later, however, 5 April 1855, the dangers of letting railway wagons run downhill to the railway yard again manifested itself and on this occasion Beatty himself was nearly killed. The 71st Foot, who had been working on siege trenches, marched to headquarters at the Col of Balaclava to be inspected by Lord Raglan. They then boarded railway wagons to go down the line to the railway yard. The first two groups of wagons descended safely but the third, carrying Beatty and the regiment's officers, ran out of control. Beatty tried to apply the brake but it did not work as the brake had been affected by the falling dew. One wagon was derailed and several men were pitched out when the wagon crashed. One man was killed and several were injured. Beatty was among the injured and, although he did not appear to be seriously hurt, his health began to decline during the following months.

Apart from the actual engineering difficulties and personal dangers of the railway project, Beatty was continually fighting against army bureaucracy. By the end of April 1855 Beatty felt that the railway was running efficiently enough to carry all the army's daily requirements of food and ammunition to the siegeworks. A Commissariat Department officer on friendly terms with Beatty, supplied him with details of the daily supplies of provisions required at the front, which amounted to around 112 tons of food, forage and fuel.[50] Yet despite the carrying capacity of the railway, Commissary-General Filder would not use the railway to carry provisions to the siegeworks. Beatty noted in his report of April 1855:

> Up to last night the railway had taken up, as nearly as can be, a thousand tons of shot and shell, 300 tons of small arms, 3600 of Commissariat stores (fuel and

from Co. Armagh, was later awarded the first Victoria Cross for the act of bravery he carried out on 21 June 1854.   **50** The Commissariat officer was Deputy Assistant Commissary-General

forage), besides upwards of 1000 tons of miscellaneous–viz. guns, platforms, huts, Quartermaster-General's stores, etc.

The biscuit, salt meat, and groceries the Commissariat-General [*sic*] Filder has not made any arrangements about issuing at headquarters yet. I have volunteered, time after time, to take everything up for Commissariat, and at one time it was settled that everything should go by rail, but this was countermanded. The Commissariat now have at their disposal every day thirty wagons or more, and these might be filled on average twice a day, sufficient to take up everything in the shape of stores; but the Commissariat men will not work before eight in the morning nor after half-past five in the evening and the Commissariat-General does not seem disposed to take any steps, by inducing them to work later in the evening or earlier in the morning, to make any further use of the railway – in fact he will not put himself out of the way one step to forward the comfort of the army, as far as the railway is concerned. Lord Raglan is, I believe, quite aware of this, and has strongly urged him to the point, but he is quite immovable; so that, as regards the food of the men, unless the divisions send down men, and draw their own rations at Balaclava, and get them up by rail on their own account, the Commissariat-General will not assist them.[51]

This kind of inefficiency was totally alien to Beatty's nature and he continued to point out to Lord Raglan and Commissary-General Filder that the railway was not being used to its full potential. He was supported by Colonel McMurdo, the business-like Scot who was in command of the Land Transport Corps. The two men got on well and Beatty wrote of McMurdo:

Colonel McMurdo is organising the transport service into an efficient corps, and I find him a good and energetic man of business.[52]

The two men co-operated well and they were also united in their dislike of Filder. This was just as well as, in April 1855, it was decided that the Land Transport Corps should take over the running of the railway. While Beatty wished to keep his navvies to maintain and repair the railway, he realized that they were too specialised a workforce to be kept in the Crimea. By the end of April 1855, however, the efforts of Beatty and McMurdo to force the Commissariat Department to use the railway were successful and Filder was sent a order from headquarters telling him to use the railway to carry the daily provisions to the siegeworks.

In June 1855 Beatty went to Turkey to organise fresh supplies of forage for the railway's horses and also find sources of coal. Large supplies of coal were needed to fuel the steam-driven stationary engines not to mention the various cranes, pumps and pile drivers. It is also believed that Beatty was asked by McMurdo to find coal for the Land Transport Corps' blacksmiths' forges. His main concern was to secure enough men to begin refurbishing the railway

James Baily. **51** *Illustrated London News*, 12 May 1855. **52** Ibid.

before the onset of winter. He managed to secure the help of 200 men of the Army Works Corps, and quashed a proposal of late September 1855 to remove the Land Transport Corps men from the railway. He requested more equipment from home which was dispatched promptly but due to the lack of manpower new railway wagons lay around unassembled in Balaclava harbour for weeks. In late August 1855 three small locomotives were dispatched to the Crimea and these were subsequently named *Alliance*, *Swan* and *Victory*. After being assembled, the first locomotive ran on the line on 8 November 1855. By the end of January 1856, there were five locomotives working on the line.[53]

Beatty's health had continued to decline, however, and at the end of November 1855 he left for home. His departure was regretted by many and William Howard Russell of *The Times* wrote:

> I very much regret that he has been obliged to retire from a post in which he rendered services not only to the army collectively but to many individuals in it who will always retain a deep sense of his kindness and friendly assistance in times of domestic difficulty about huts and transport.[54]

By December 1855 Beatty was in his London home at Bloomfield Terrace, Paddington. He was by now in constant pain and doctors were at a loss as to what to do. There seemed to be no outward appearance of disease or injury yet his condition deteriorated steadily. By February 1856 he was suffering from swelling in his throat and left arm and had difficulty breathing. It was now felt that his accident in April 1855 had led to the development of an aneurysm of the aorta and that this would eventually kill him. His doctors informed him of this and he took the time that was left to him to arrange his affairs. He died on 11 March 1856. A post-mortem examination confirmed that he had indeed suffered from an aneurysm of the aorta. His obituary notice in *Minutes of the proceedings of the Institute of Civil Engineers* referred to his energy, confidence and constant cheerfulness, an inspiration to those that worked with him. He was buried in Kensal Green Cemetery, Sir Samuel Morton Peto, Thomas Brassey and Edward Ladd Betts subscribing to an impressive monument. Sir Samuel Morton Peto used his influence to secure a pension for his widow, equivalent to a colonel's.[55]

It would be difficult to find another man who individually did more work in aid of the war effort. Beatty's energy and efficiency had seen the construction

---

53 Cooke, op. cit., pp 83–5.   **54** *The Times*, 15 Dec. 1855.   **55** *Minutes of the proceedings of the Institute of Civil Engineers* (1857). See also Cooke, op. cit., pp 138–9. In November 1849 Beatty had married Miss Sarah Jane Burke at Ballinamallard, Co. Fermanagh. They had two sons and two daughters. His eldest son was Dr Wallace Beatty who was educated at TCD. An eminent physician, he was later honorary professor of dermatology at TCD. His younger son, Henry James ('Jim') Beatty, also studied at TCD and qualified as a civil engineer. He emigrated to Australia

of the railway carried out on schedule while also seeing to the welfare of his workforce of over 500 men. He had supervised the conversion of the railway from one dependent on horses and stationary engines to one which used locomotives. He had also provided invaluable assistance to the Land Transport Corps, the Commissariat Department and also individuals such as Roger Fenton. Many feel that the second winter in the Crimea was not as bad for the troops as there were ample supplies by that time. This is only partly true. There had been large stores of supplies previously but there had been no way to get them to the troops. The railway provided a means of transporting ammunition, food, forage, clothing and all manner of supplies to the siegeworks. Brian Cooke in his book on the Grand Crimean Railway has referred to the project as 'the railway that won the war'. This is by no means an exaggeration and James Beatty was the most important figure in the construction of the railway.

An English traveller, John Gadsby, visited the Crimea in 1857 recording his experiences in his book *A trip to Sebastapol in 1857* (London, 1884). He wrote that he could find no trace of the railway and it must be assumed that British engineers salvaged some of the rail at least, when the locomotives were being returned to England. Any line, or traces of the railway, that remained had been removed by the Russians by 1857 and the actual route it had followed could only be discerned with difficulty.[56]

The Army Works Corps

While Beatty and his navvies of the Civil Engineer Corps were busy constructing and maintaining the railway, another civilian organization was raised to carry out civil engineering works. As has been previously stated, it was the state of the roads during the winter of 1854–55 that had caused concern. The railway project itself was a result of the concern over the poor state of the roads on the Crimean Peninsula and, as has been illustrated, was initiated and completed in a short space of time. The problem with the roads remained and, in the summer of 1855, the Army Works Corps was organised by Sir Joseph Paxton MP, to carry out general engineering works for the army. Sir Joseph Paxton, the designer of Crystal Palace, had suggested that such a corps be formed as early as August 1854. The corps, despite its title, was entirely civilian and, as had been the case with the railway project, navvies were recruited from the civilian workforce. Eventually 720 strong, the Army Works Corps arrived in the Crimea in the third week of August 1855. The superintendent of the Army Works Corps was another Irish engineer, William Doyne.[57]

where he worked as a railway engineer.   **56** John Gadsby, *A trip to Sebastapol in 1857* (London, 1884).   **57** Ibid., pp 101–2.

William Doyne was born at Old Leighlin, Co. Carlow, in April 1823, the second son of the Revd Thomas Doyne, a Church of Ireland rector. Like Beatty he showed an interest in engineering from an early age and, at the age of 16, entered the University of Durham to study engineering.[58] In 1840 he was articled to Edward Dixon, the resident engineer of the London and South Western Railway before working with Robert Stephenson. In 1847 Doyne was appointed as the managing engineer of the Rugby to Leamington Line. Elected an associate of the Institute of Civil Engineers in 1849, he was made a full member in 1851 following his presentation of a paper on the stresses experienced by railway bridge beams.[59]

In 1855 he was appointed as superintendent of the Army Works Corps, arriving in the Crimea in the second week of August 1855, about one week before the arrival of the rest of his workforce. Just as Beatty had done, he first began to organise accommodation for his workforce. On 27 August 1855, following the battle of the Tchernaya, Beatty asked Doyne for 200 men to help him to improve the railway line. Doyne agreed, indicating that a level of understanding had been reached between these two engineers. This was in contrast to Doyne's flat refusal to a request from Royal Engineer officers for men to dig trenches and build battery positions near Sevastapol.

While the Army Works Corps was to carry out general engineering duties for the army, Doyne's primary task was to build an all-weather road from Balaclava to the plateau and, at the end of August 1855, he began surveying to find the optimum route. His main difficulty was along the route from Kadikoi to the Col of Balaclava which now had three supply routes on this incline; the original unmetalled cart-track, the French road and finally the railway. It would seem that his original intention was to repair the old road from Balaclava to Kadikoi, partially metalled by the Turks, and from there to repair the French road. He quickly realized that this route would not serve as there were a series of very steep gradients along it and he decided to survey a completely new route. Doyne decided to run his road from Balaclava to Kadikoi, round the

---

58 The University of Durham established a course to provide instruction in civil engineering in 1831 but did this without appointing a professor of the subject. In April 1841, Humphrey Lloyd, then Professor of Natural and Experimental Philosophy and later Provost of Trinity College, Dublin, James McCullagh, Professor of Mathematics, and Thomas Luby sent a memorandum to the Board of Trinity College, Dublin, advocating the establishment of a School of Engineering. The Board agreed to this suggestion at the end of Trinity term 1841 and the new chair was duly created. This placed Trinity College, Dublin, alongside Durham, London and Glasgow, among the first universities to offer courses in civil engineering. R.B. McDowell and D.A. Webb, *Trinity College Dublin, 1592–1952. An academic history* (Cambridge, 1982). It is also interesting to note that Samuel Haughton, Professor of Geology, and Joseph Allen Galbraith, Professor of Natural and Experimental Philosophy, set up an unofficial school at the outbreak of the Crimean war to provide instruction to Trinity College students who were trying to pass the entrance exams for the Royal Military Academy at Woolwich, the academy that trained engineer and artillery officers for the British Army. *Freeman's Journal*, 21 Oct. 1890.   **59** *Australian Dictionary of Biography*.

eastern base of Frenchman's Hill and then up the north-east valley. His road was to run parallel to the railway line.

Having chosen his route, Doyne went to work with a will. The road bed was twenty-eight feet wide with a macadamized surface twenty-one to twenty-five feet wide. The numerous springs and streams that the road had to cross were contained by a series of culverts and a drainage canal was also built. By 6 October 1855 Doyne had 1,000 Army Works Corps men, 8,600 troops and 1,000 Croats at his disposal and on 10 November 1855 the road opened between Balaclava and the British headquarters at the Col of Balaclava, seven weeks after construction had begun. It was six and a half miles long, across difficult terrain; some of the road being built on terraces, and 60,000 tons of road metal had been laid. Doyne later ran branch lines to the French and Sardinian camps. While he had a larger workforce, Doyne's achievement rivalled that of Beatty in terms of the size of the project undertaken and the speed with which it was completed. The two men got on well together and would seem to have shared a similar temperament. Both displayed a professional attitude towards their respective tasks and could also encourage their men to work. They did clash, however, when Doyne asked Beatty to release the men he had loaned him. Doyne also had a disagreement in October 1855 with one of Beatty's assistant engineers, Donald Campbell, when he discovered that the railway navvies were taking some of his materials.

While the road building project came late in the war and was not as seen as being as notable as the railway project, Doyne's achievement should not be underestimated. The road system that he built served the Land Transport Corps well during the second winter and did not deteriorate in the bad weather. William Howard Russell of The Times wrote in December 1855:

> Our roads have stood the ordeal of this bad weather so well. The objectors who said Mr Doyne's roads were too wide, his ditches too deep and his drains too large, now hold their tongues. The French roads are not good and they have been forced to place large working parties on them.[60]

The English traveller, John Gadsby, later wrote of a trip he took along Doyne's road in 1857, travelling from Sevastapol to Balaclava, and remarked that this was not only the best road on the Crimean Peninsula but probably the best road in Russia.[61]

Doyne spent the next two years working in Ceylon as chief engineer on a railway project before moving to New Zealand in 1858 where he was employed surveying railway routes. In 1862 he was appointed to supervise the construction of the Launceston to Deloraine Railway, the first railway to be built

60 *The Times*, 15 Dec. 1855.   61 John Gadsby, *A trip to Sebastapol in 1857* (London, 1884).

in Tasmania. He was responsible for some fine pieces of engineering on this project; the King's Bridge on the South Esk being a particular example. By 1869 it was realised that the project would run massively over-budget and Doyne was vilified in the press. He continued working on railway projects and, having opened an office in Melbourne in 1866, decided to concentrate his business in Australia. He was appointed as consulting engineer to the Government of Western Australia in 1869 and supervised the Hobson's Bay dredging scheme in 1871. He died at St Kilda, Melbourne, 29 September 1877. His obituary in *Minutes of the proceedings of the Institute of Civil Engineers* described him as 'a clever, painstaking engineer, good mathematician, geologist and analytical chemist'.[62]

It is interesting that the two most important civil engineers in the Crimea were Irishmen and that both completed their respective projects efficiently and on time. Both James Beatty and William Doyne were prime examples of a new type of professional engineer and the speed with which they completed the railway and road projects must have caused quite a stir among Royal Engineer officers who seemed to have difficulties with many engineering tasks. Their energy and level of organisation was good and in total contrast to the hide-bound inefficiency of the army.

It can be seen, therefore, that the British force in the Crimea relied heavily on civilians who were used to carry out the tasks for which the army had no personnel. The use of men from the Irish Constabulary to carry out provost and Commissariat duties was a prime example of this. Also it would seem that Irish muleteers and waggoners were seen as prime recruits for the Land Transport Corps. It seems certain that a large number of the navvies of the Civil Engineering Corps and the Army Works Corps were Irish while the chief engineers of both corps were definitely Irish. Here again the involvement of Irishmen is obvious and illustrates yet another contribution that they made to the war effort. The services rendered by Beatty and Doyne were of the utmost importance. In both cases one could argue that their involvement had a major impact on the supply situation in the Crimea and the outcome of the war.

62 *Minutes of the proceedings of the Institute of Civil Engineers* (1878), pp 270–3. See also *ADB*.

6

Irish war correspondents, newspaper accounts and Crimean ballads

Irish correspondents in the Crimean war

The Crimean war saw the beginnings of war reporting and war correspondents were used for the first time to report for the national newspapers. Before the Crimea, British editors used excerpts from official dispatches and foreign newspapers, or paid junior officers to write reports. The Crimean war made British editors change their methods totally. The public showed a keen interest in the progress of the war and were not satisfied with second-hand accounts taken from foreign newspapers. Letters from officers in Varna, and later the Crimea, described conditions in the army and these descriptions often contradicted the official dispatches. It became obvious that the accounts being released by Horse Guards could not be relied upon. Also the practice of employing junior officers often proved unsatisfactory as these men put their military duty first and only sent dispatches to their editors when they found the time. At the outbreak of the Crimean war *The Times* employed Lieutenant Charles Nasmyth, on leave from the East India Company's Bombay Artillery, but he sent dispatches to London on a very irregular basis. Indeed when he reached the Turkish army at Silistria he volunteered to serve with the Turkish artillery rather than writing about the siege.[1] Yet the practice of using junior officers continued during the remainder of the century, the most famous soldier-correspondent of the nineteenth century was perhaps Winston Churchill.

The editor of *The Times*, John T. Delane, decided that his paper must send its own man to the Crimea. This was not a totally new idea as *The Times* had sent a correspondent to cover the Peninsular War in 1808 while the *Morning Post* sent a correspondent to Spain to cover the first Carlist war in 1837. Neither correspondent had, however, stayed in the field long enough to form an impression of how their respective wars were progressing and neither could be viewed as pioneers in the field of war-reporting. Delane decided to send an

---

1 Alan Hankinson, *Man of wars: William Howard Russell of The Times* (London, 1982), p. 47.

Irishman, William Howard Russell, who had been working for the paper since 1841. Several other newspapers also sent their own special correspondents. The *Daily News* had acted before any of the other newspapers and had sent another Irishman, Edwin Lawrence Godkin, to Turkey in late 1853. The *Daily News* later sent a second Irish correspondent, James Carlile McCoan, to the Crimea.

William Howard Russell has been the subject of numerous biographies and there is no need to describe his life in great detail here. In 1911, John Black Atkins wrote his comprehensive two-volume biography *Life of Sir William Howard Russell*. Atkins made extensive use of a an autobiographical essay that Russell wrote while in his sixties and called 'Retrospect'. This 'Retrospect' has since disappeared, apart from a few typewritten pages, so all subsequent biographies of Russell have had to rely on Atkins' work. Alan Hankinson's *Man of wars: William Howard Russell of The Times* (London, 1982) is perhaps the best recent biography of Russell.

William Howard Russell was born in March 1820 at the home of his maternal grandparents; Lilyvale, Jobestown, Co. Dublin. His father John Russell was a businessman and a member of a prosperous Co. Limerick family which included several sea-captains and Church of Ireland clergymen. His mother was Mary Kelly whose family had once owned extensive properties around Jobestown. While Russell was still very young, his father's business failed and he went to Liverpool in the hope of regaining his fortune through another business venture. When a second son was born in 1823 Russell was put in the care of his maternal grandparents at Lilyvale. His grandfather, Captain Jack Kelly, was a Roman Catholic and was obsessed with foxhunting. Master of the Tallaght foxhounds, his estate was badly-run due to the time he spent hunting. It would appear from Russell's own account of his childhood at Lilyvale that he enjoyed these years, and the eccentricities of Captain Kelly, enormously. When he was six or seven he moved to the home of his paternal grandparents at 40 Upper Baggot Street, this time due to the financial difficulties of Captain Kelly. His paternal grandfather, William Russell, had been a member of the Moravian church in Dublin and displayed strong Puritan tendencies. The two homes in which Russell lived in his early years were total contrasts but it would appear that he enjoyed the eccentricities of both households.

It is interesting that in 1835, when General Sir George De Lacy Evans was raising the British Legion to fight in the first Carlist war in Spain, Russell expressed a desire to join but was stopped by William Russell. He later wrote that, had he not been a newspaper correspondent, he would have been soldier. After attending the school of Dr E.J. Geoghegan at Hume Street (1832–7), he entered Trinity College, Dublin, in 1838 but would seem to have had very little idea of what he wanted to do, considering both law and medicine. He failed to obtain a scholarship and does not appear to have applied himself in his studies and left, in 1841, without a degree.[2]

In the same year his cousin, Robert Russell, who worked for *The Times* asked him to help him write about the elections and he later covered the 'monster meetings' of 1843. In 1844 he covered Daniel O'Connell's trial and then worked as a parliamentary correspondent. In many ways Russell drifted into journalism and often considered other ways of earning a living. While working in London he had begun studying for the bar and was called to the bar in 1850. Although he occasionally accepted legal work, he was really earning his living through writing by this time. After some time with the *Morning Chronicle* (1845–8), he rejoined *The Times* and covered the war in Schleswig-Holstein in 1850. The outbreak of the Crimean war gave him the opportunity to prove himself as a correspondent and influenced the rest of his life.[3] In February 1854, Delane obtained from Lord Hardinge, commander-in-chief of the British army, permission for a correspondent to accompany the Guards Brigade to Malta. Russell was asked to go and was promised that he would be home by Easter. He later went with the army to Varna and the Crimea itself, not returning home for nearly two years.

The second Irish correspondent who covered the Crimean war, Edwin Lawrence Godkin, has never been given the same attention as Russell. He has never been regarded as being of equal importance as Russell and has been the subject of only one biography; Rollo Ogden, *The life and letters of Edwin Lawrence Godkin* (New York, 1907). This book is in reality edited excerpts from his memoirs and letters. The lack of attention given to Godkin is unfair as his dispatches from the Crimea were well written and displayed a level of social awareness that is absent in Russell's work. Also he had a significant career in America after the war and did not restrict himself to journalism. There are, however, some startling similarities in the early lives of both men. Godkin was born in October 1831 at the home of his maternal grandparents in Moyne, Co. Wicklow. Like Russell he spent the early years of his life in the home of his grandparents; cared for by his mother, Sarah Lawrence, and his maternal grandmother while his father was away working. His father, James Godkin (1806–79), was a Presbyterian minister and writer who founded *The Christian Patriot* in Belfast in 1849, was editor of the *Derry Standard* and later a Dublin correspondent for *The Times*. James Godkin was also politically active and was involved with the Tenant League in the 1850s. His journalistic talent and political views had an influence on the career of his son. In 1838 Edwin Lawrence Godkin went to Armagh, where his father was then living, before

2 While at Trinity College, Dublin, Russell lived in No. 17 in Botany Bay, on the third floor.
3 John B. Atkins, *The life of Sir William Howard Russell* (2 volumes, London, 1911).

attending a school for congregational ministers near Wakefield, in Yorkshire (1841–6). He entered Queen's College, Belfast, graduating in 1851.

Like Russell, he then went to London and studied for the bar at Lincoln's Inn but was never called to the bar. His interest in legal studies waned and he decided to earn a living through writing. In 1853 he published *The history of Hungary and the Magyars from the earliest period to the close of the late war*. This was published by Cassell's, his father's publisher. He had also written occasional articles for the *Daily News* and, as was the case with Russell, the Crimean war provided him with a focus for his life and confirmed in him a desire to pursue a journalistic career.[4] Godkin was actually sent to the East before Russell as the *Daily News* sent him to Turkey in October 1853. Attaching himself to the army of Omar Pasha, he witnessed the outbreak of the war and was, therefore, in the East before the allies had declared war.

James Carlile McCoan has also been given very little attention and has never been the subject of a biography. Born in Dunlow, Co. Tyrone, in July 1829, he went to school in Dungannon and later attended Homerton College, London. He matriculated at London University in 1848 and, like both Russell and Godkin, studied for the bar. In 1856 he was called to the bar but never practised. He travelled to the Crimea and worked as a correspondent for the *Daily News* during the final months of the war.[5] While McCoan's career as a Crimean correspondent was short, and perhaps not very significant, it is interesting that three of the correspondents that worked in the Crimea were Irish.[6]

Russell's dispatches from the Crimea

The use of steamships and the electric telegraph meant that the dispatches sent by Russell and Godkin from the Crimea could arrive in London within days, often arriving before the official dispatches from headquarters. Indeed some of the dispatches sent from the Crimea arrived in London more quickly than dispatches sent to London during the Falklands war in 1982. The use of the telegraph also allowed Russell and Godkin to send very long dispatches; 6,000 -word dispatches were not uncommon; and working without any kind of censorship they could report the war in detail.

Russell's dispatches from the Crimea had several serious results, ensuring his place in the history of war-journalism. The effect that his writings had on

4 Rollo Ogden, *The life and letters of Edwin Lawrence Godkin* (New York, 1911). See also *DNB*. **5** *Northern Whig*, 23 Jan. 1904. See also *DNB*. **6** Sir Joseph Archer Crowe (1825–96), correspondent for the *Illustrated London News* in the Crimea, also had Irish connections. His father, Eyre Evans Crowe, was a descendent of the Very Revd William Crowe, dean of Clonfert (1745–66), and he was educated in Carlow and Trinity College, Dublin. His mother was Margaret

the reputation of Lord Raglan was significant and it is no exaggeration to state that Russell effectively destroyed Raglan's reputation, setting the precedent for later historians of the war. Raglan did not trust Russell, or any other corre-spondents for that matter, and did his best to discourage them. The duke of Wellington had once accused the press of always getting its facts wrong and also of giving vital information to the enemy, which would seem to be something of a contradiction. Raglan held a similar view and gave Russell no assistance, even refusing to allow him to draw army rations. When some junior officers cut down Russell's tent, forcing him to move outside the main camp and to live with the camp followers, Raglan turned a blind eye. From early October 1854, Russell's dispatches began to include references that were damaging not only to Raglan but to the entire British staff. His dispatch of 13 October 1854 accused the British staff of being indifferent to the plight of the sick, concluding that 'the manner in which the sick are treated is worthy only of the savages of Dahomey'. Such attacks began to focus on Raglan in particular and in a private letter of 8 November 1854, Russell wrote to Delane, 'I am convinced that Lord Raglan is utterly incompetent to lead an army through any arduous task.' Comments regarding Raglan's ability soon began to appear in his public dispatches in *The Times*. In his dispatch of 25 November 1854, Russell described the condition of the men as winter set in and then went on to make a veiled suggestion that Raglan was responsible. It was a significant dispatch as it marked the beginning of Russell's public attacks on Raglan:

> It is now pouring rain, the skies are black as ink, the wind is howling over the staggering tents, the trenches are turned into dykes, in the tents the water is sometimes a foot deep, our men have not either warm or waterproof clothing, they are out for twelve hours at a time in the trenches, they are plunged into the inevitable miseries of a winter campaign, and not a soul seems to care for their comfort or even their lives.[7]

From this time onwards Russell suggested that the misfortunes of the army could be directly traced to Raglan's incompetence and insensitivity. Using a series of public dispatches and private letters to Delane, Russell effectively destroyed Raglan's reputation. It has since been shown by Raglan's biographers that he was a sensitive and humane man. Also he had pointed out the various shortcomings in the army supply system in his letters to Lord Hardinge. Yet Russell's dispatches, and indeed his post-war writings, served to cast Raglan in the role of a bungling, callous general. Raglan's reputation has never recovered from this assault. Russell also later wrote a two-volume history of the war, *The war with Russia*, updating this work as *The great war with Russia* in 1895. In

Archer of Kiltimon, Co. Wicklow.   **7** Christopher Hibbert, *The destruction of Lord Raglan: a tragedy of the Crimean war* (London, 1961), p. 218.

these books he still criticized Lord Raglan and many of his criticisms most definitely had the benefit of hindsight. Writing of the charge of the Light Brigade forty-one years after the event, Russell wrote:

> I am persuaded that whatever there was of disaster and misfortune on 25th October 1854 was due, first, to the distance of Lord Raglan from the field and secondly, to his failure to understand that he saw more than his generals below could see; therefore he did not take pains in wording his orders to make it plain to them that explanation of his meaning was not needed.[8]

While this comment contained a certain amount of truth, Russell's tone suggested that he had realized these facts during the actual event and that he had not been as much in the dark as everyone else at the time. By 1895, when he wrote these comments, he had the advantage of having read the numerous accounts of the charge that had been published. His habit of writing such negative comments about Lord Raglan at such late date is often viewed by historians of the war as being unfair.

There were also serious questions raised regarding the possibility of Russell's dispatches providing information to the Russians. Russell dismissed this after the war, saying the Prince Gorchakov, commander of the Russian 6th Corps, had told him after the war that *The Times* had provided him with no new information.[9] Prince Menshikov, commander-in-chief of the Russian forces in the Crimea, later stated that he did obtain information from British newspapers and that one copy of *Illustrated London News* provided more intelligence than a dozen spies.[10] Russell excused himself by stating that it was up to his editor, Delane, to delete any sensitive material from his dispatches. This was a somewhat lame defence as he knew that Delane was desperate for new information and that he would publish his dispatches in their entirety. Raglan and his staff, and other officers were not convinced that Russell's writings were not of major use to the enemy. Tsar Nicholas I had once stated, 'We have no need of spies; we have *The Times*', and this was foremost in Raglan's mind when he considered Russell's dispatch of 23 October 1854, which contained accurate details of the dispositions of the army and also told of the army's shortage of ammunition, engineering equipment and even gave the exact location of Raglan's, headquarters and the gunpowder mill. *The Times* editorial of 7 December 1854 admitted that the dispatches had 'gone to the verge of prudence'.

In another dispatch of early November, Russell pointed out that the army's weakest point was its thinly defended Eastern flank. Lord Burghersh stated,

---

8 W.H. Russell, *The great war with Russia* (London, 1895), p. 136.   9 Hibbert, *The destruction of Lord Raglan*, p. 160. Gorchakov replaced Menshikov as the Russian commander-in-chief in February 1855.   10 Some of the maps in the *Illustrated London News* showed the exact positions

'This infernal *Times* is inviting the Russians to attack our weakest point!'[11] Russell was obviously going too far and, on 13 November 1854, Raglan wrote to Lord Newcastle stating that Russell's October dispatch was 'invaluable to the Russians and to the same degree detrimental to Her Majesty's troops'. Raglan continued 'the innocency of his intention does not diminish the evil he inflicts, and something should be done to check so pernicious a system at once'.[12] He concluded: 'I do not propose to take any violent step, though perhaps I should be justified in doing so.'[13] Raglan did ask the deputy judge advocate, William G. Romaine, to approach the various correspondents then in the Crimea and:

> Quietly point out to them the necessity of greater prudence in future; and I have no doubt that they will at once see that I am right in so warning them.[14]

Newcastle was also asked to approach Delane and the editors of other London papers and ask then to 'expunge from their papers any information that might prove valuable to the enemy'. From this time Russell tried to include less military information in his dispatches and he was indeed lucky that Raglan did not deal with him more severely. Sidney Herbert, secretary of state at war, wrote: 'I trust the Army will lynch *The Times* correspondent'. An officer in the Crimea echoed this statement and was heard to say, 'That blackguard Mr Russell of *The Times* ought to be hung.' Another officer, Paymaster Henry Dixon, wrote of the effects he felt that Russell's disclosures in The Times brought about:

> The Russians left off from shooting at our camp entirely but Mr Russell must needs go put in his paper that the balls had reached us. We saw it in *The Times* a fortnight ago and at the moment I saw it I said as soon as the Russians heard it we should be shot at again, and sure enough the night before last, just as we were at dinner, they commenced their evening's performance. Russell takes precious care to live about a mile out of range.[15]

Russell had, however, developed a very accurate style of reporting by 1855 and also showed great literary skill. Despite establishment disapproval, his reports of the war achieved great notoriety and served to inform the public of the poor leadership, the lack of supplies, food and medical facilities. Indeed he has been identified as the 'whistle-blower' of the Crimean war. His reports of the battles of the Alma, Balaclava and Inkerman were written in a very patriotic and emotive style. At no time did Russell cast any doubt on the fighting abilities

of allied batteries.   **11** Lieutenant-Colonel Francis W.H. Fane, Lord Burghersh, ADC to Lord Raglan in the Crimea. Trevor Royle, *Crimea: the great Crimean war, 1854–1856* (London, 1999), p. 132.   **12** John Sweetman, *Raglan: from the Peninsula to the Crimea* (London, 1993), p. 263. **13** Ibid.   **14** Ibid.   **15** Hibbert, *The destruction of Lord Raglan*, p. 160.

and bravery of the British soldier. His account of the charge of the Light Brigade was read with keen interest in Britain and was the subject of much comment. Russell's Balaclava dispatch is still regarded as a classic example of the work of one of the early war correspondents. The following excerpt illustrates the style of his writing of actual battles:

> At ten minutes past eleven, our Light Cavalry Brigade advanced. The whole brigade scarcely made one effective regiment, according to the numbers of European armies; yet it was more than we could spare. As they rushed towards the front, the Russians opened on them from the guns in the redoubt on the right, with volleys of musketry and rifles. They swept proudly past, glittering in the morning sun in all the pride and splendour of war. We could scarcely believe the evidence of our senses! Surely that handful of men are not going to charge an enemy in position? Alas! it was but too true – their desperate valour knew no bounds, and far indeed it was removed from its so-called better part: discretion. They advanced in two lines, quickening their pace as they closed towards the enemy. A more fearful spectacle was never witnessed than by those who, without the power to aid, beheld their heroic countrymen rushing to the arms of death. At a distance of 1,200 yards the whole line of the enemy belched forth, from thirty iron mouths, a flood of smoke and flame, through which hissed the deadly balls. Their flight was marked by instant gaps in our ranks, by dead men and horses, by steeds flying wounded or riderless across the plain. The first line is broken, it is joined by the second, they never halt or check their speed an instant, with diminished ranks, thinned by those thirty guns, which the Russians had laid with most deadly accuracy, with a halo of flashing steel above their heads, and with a cheer that was many a noble fellow's death-cry, they flew into the smoke of the batteries, but ere they were lost from view, the plain was strewed with their bodies and the carcasses of horses.[16]

Had Russell only written this type of dispatch, Lord Raglan would have indeed been happy. His dispatch on the charge of the Light Brigade was perhaps his most influential of the war and it he who coined the phrase 'the thin red line' when describing the stand of the 93rd Highlanders. His accounts of the other battles of the war were written in a similar patriotic and moving style. Yet, when there were no battles to write of, Russell turned his attention towards the disorganized medical and supply services. He soon became the scourge of the numerous incompetent officers in the Crimea, shocking people at home with his accounts of inefficiency. It was not so much that Russell wrote of the horror of war, but rather that he wrote of the horrors of a war that was being badly managed. His reports from the Crimea were to have major implications as they stirred up such public indignation and anti-government feeling. Perhaps more important, however, were the private letters that he sent to Delane, letters that Delane then passed on to friends in the Commons to read. The following latter was written to Delane soon after his arrival in the Crimea in September 1854:

16 *The Times*, 14 Nov. 1854.

> The management is infamous and the contrast offered by our proceedings to the conduct of the French most painful. Could you believe it: the sick have not a bed to lie upon? They are landed and thrown into a rickety hut without a chair or a table in it. The French with their ambulances, excellent commissariat staff and boulangerie etc., in every respect are immeasurably our superiors. While these things go on, Sir George Brown only seems anxious about the men being clean-shaved, their necks well stiffened and waist belts tight.[17]

Russell concluded by asking Delane 'Am I to tell these things, or hold my tongue?' Delane told him to go on writing about what he saw but did not publish some reports as he considered them too critical. Yet he did find a use for these and began to circulate them among cabinet ministers.

Some of the dispatches that were published in *The Times* were shocking and painted a grim picture of life in the Crimea. It is impossible in the space of this study to go into great detail regarding Russell's dispatches. Nicholas Bentley's *Russell's dispatches from the Crimea* (London, 1966) and Andrew Lambert and Stephen Badsey's *The war correspondents: the Crimean war* (London, 1997) are well-edited and comprehensive collections of his Crimean dispatches. The following three excerpts give a good indication of his writings regarding the shortcomings of the army. On 4 December 1854 he wrote a dispatch describing the conditions the men had to endure as winter set in.

> Men wade and plunge about, and stumble through the mud with muttered imprecations, or sit down on a projecting stone, exhausted, pictures of dirt and woe unutterable. Sometimes on the route the overworked and sickly soldier is seized with illness, and the sad aspect of a fellow-countryman dying before his eyes shocks the passer-by, the more because aid is all but hopeless and impossible. Officers in huge sailors' boots, purchased at Balaclava for about five times their proper price, trudge on earnestly in the expectation of being able to carry back to their tents the pot of preserved meat or the fowl, bought at a fabulous cost in that model city of usurydom, ere the allotted portion of wood under the cooking tins has been consumed. It requires a soldier's eye to tell captains from corporals now, mounted on draggle-tailed and unkempt ragged ponies, covered with mud.[18]

On January 1855 he wrote of the lack of proper shelter and clothing for the men.

> Winter is setting upon us, and we are already in a position to form an opinion of its possible results. I cannot conceal my impression that our army is likely to suffer severely unless instant and most energetic measures be taken to place it in a position to resist the inclemency of the weather. We have no means of getting up the huts, all our army can do is to feed itself. Captain Keen, RE, is here in charge of 4,000 tons of wood for hutting, but he cannot get anyone to take charge

17 Philip Knightley, *The first casualty. From the Crimea to Vietnam: the war correspondent as hero, propagandist and myth maker* (London, 1978), p. 7.   **18** Andrew Lambert and Stephen Badsey, *The war correspondents. The Crimean war* (London, 1997), pp 150–1.

of it, or unload it out of the ships. Each hut weighs more than two tons, and somehow or other, I fear that it will so happen that no effort will be used to get them until men are found frozen to death in their tents. As to the 'warm clothing' the very words immediately suggest to us all some extraordinary fatality. Some went down with the ill-fated and ill-treated *Prince*, some has been lost, and now we hear that a ship with clothing for the officers has been burnt off Constantinople; that some of it has been saturated with water; and I had an opportunity of seeing several lighters full of warm great coats etc., for the men, lying a whole day in the harbour of Balaclava beneath a determined fall of rain and snow. There was no one to receive them when they were sent to the shore, or rather no one would receive them without orders. In fact, we are ruined by etiquette and 'service' regulations. No one will take responsibility upon himself if it were to save the lives of hundreds.[19]

His dispatch of 25 January 1855 described the fussy bureaucracy that was costing men's lives.

The *Charity* an iron screw steamer, is at present in the harbour for the reception of sick British soldiers, who are under the charge of a British medical officer. That officer went on shore today and made an application to the officer in charge of the Government stoves for two or three to put on board the ship to warm the men. 'Three of my men' said he, 'died last night from choleric symptoms brought on in their present state from the extreme cold of the ship; and I fear more will follow them from the same cause.'

'Oh!' said the guardian of the stoves, 'you must make your requisition in due form, send it up to headquarters, and get it signed properly, and returned, and then I will let you have the stoves.'

'But my men may die meantime.'

'I can't help that; I must have the requisition'. 'It is my firm belief that there are men now in a dangerous state whom another night will certainly kill'. 'I really can do nothing: I must have the requisition properly signed before I can give one of these stoves away.' 'For God's sake, then, lend me some; I'll be responsible for their safety'. 'I really can do nothing of the kind'. 'But, consider this requisition will take time to be filled up and signed, and meantime the poor fellows will go'. 'I cannot help that'. 'I'll be responsible for anything you do'. 'Oh no, that can't be done!' 'Will a requisition signed by the PMO of this place be any use?' 'No.' 'Will it answer if he takes on himself the responsibility?' 'Certainly not'. The surgeon went off in sorrow and disgust. Such are the 'rules' of the service in the hands of incapable and callous men.[20]

Russell became the scourge of army inefficiency and it was following such reports that the army was forced to act and organise better supplies of food, clothing and medical supplies. Not only did the army react but the public, shocked by such dispatches, formed groups to raise the money for food, warm clothing and 'comforts' for the soldiers in the Crimea.

---

19 Ibid. pp 155–6. The *Prince* transport ship had sunk during the hurricane of 14 November 1854. She had been carrying a cargo of 40,000 greatcoats and boots for the army.   **20** Ibid., pp 164–5.

It has often been suggested in biographies of Russell that his dispatches from the Crimea led directly to the fall of Lord Aberdeen's administration in January 1855. This is only partly true and, while Russell's dispatches and private letters to Delane undermined Aberdeen's position, they represented just one of several problems facing his administration. Aberdeen, patently not a 'war leader', was a victim of the machinations of Lord John Russell. As Lucille Iremonger put it in her biography of Aberdeen: 'He was to be beset by a Russell abroad as well as a Russell at home. Both would do him unparalleled damage.'[21] Delane had taken up Lord John Russell's campaign for the reform of the various government departments that controlled army supplies and backed William Howard Russell's dispatches from the Crimea by writing leading articles which criticised Aberdeen. Delane also continued to circulate Russell's private letters among cabinet members. Palmerston, who had made such impressive speeches throughout 1854, appeared to the public as being imbued with the right kind of fighting spirit. It is ironic indeed, however, that Aberdeen took the ultimate blame for the disorganization in the Crimea as he was a prime minister who had inherited forty years of neglect of the army when he took office. While it is untrue to claim that Russell's dispatches brought the government down, he did play a major part in Aberdeen's fall. Aberdeen became associated with failure and the public clamoured for his resignation while his cabinet colleagues looked for a new leader. While it is incorrect to state that Russell was wholly responsible for the fall of Aberdeen's administration in January 1855, his dispatches from the Crimea provided ammunition for men such as Lord John Russell and even his own editor, Delane, who were manoeuvring to oust him.

There is also a common misconception that Russell was responsible for Florence Nightingale's medical mission at Scutari. It is true that his dispatches often described the plight of the sick and wounded and the almost total lack of medical services. It was Thomas Chenery, however, *The Times* correspondent at Constantinople, who went to Scutari and wrote of the dreadful hospital conditions. This is a common mistake and still occurs in modern of histories of the war where the writer assumes that Russell was the only *Times* correspondent to cover the war.

Russell was directly responsible, however, for the arrival of Roger Fenton, the first war photographer, in the Crimea. The public reaction to Russell's dispatches was so extreme that Prince Albert suggested that a photographer be sent in the Crimea in the hope that some of his images would boost public morale. Fenton had been commissioned by a Manchester print-dealer, Thomas Agnew, to go to the Crimea and produce a series of photographs. Due to the

'PMO' = Principal Medical Officer.   **21** Lucille Iremonger, *Lord Aberdeen* (London, 1978), p. 243.

interest of Prince Albert in this project he was granted passage on HMS *Hecla* and even carried letters of introduction from Prince Albert to the divisional commanders. Arriving with his mobile darkroom in March 1855, Thomas Agnew had asked him to avoid photographing anything unpleasant and, as a result, his photographs show happy, well-fed and well-clothed soldiers. Many of his photographs show a mixed groups of French and British soldiers in domestic poses around camp fires. Some of Fenton's best known photographs are of the men of the 8th King's Royal Irish Hussars. He also took photographs of the railway navvies and, as has been previously mentioned, the Irish railway engineer James Beatty. Great care was taken to ensure that Fenton's photographs contained no disturbing images; he was only allowed photograph the interior of the Redan after it had been cleared of bodies. His mission in the Crimea can be seen as an effort to play down some of the work of Russell. The photographs Fenton took during the Crimean war were totally different to those taken during the American Civil war. While Fenton deliberately avoided photographing dead bodies, American Civil war photographers used their work to support newspaper reports of the horror of the war.[22]

It must be said, however, that Russell's dispatches from the Crimea had one great positive effect – the improvement of the conditions in the army. By the beginning of 1855 the army realized that all their shortcomings would be detailed in the pages of *The Times* and massive efforts were made to improve the supply situation and medical services. Perhaps the best tribute paid to Russell came from his fellow-Irishman and war correspondent, Edwin Lawrence Godkin. Godkin later wrote in his memoirs:

> If I were asked now what I thought the most important result of the Crimean war, I should say the creation and development of the 'special correspondents' of the newspapers. The real beginning of newspaper correspondence was the arrival of 'Billy' Russell with the English Army in the Crimea. He was then a man of mature age, had had a long newspaper experience, and possessed just the social qualities that were needed for the place. In his hands correspondence from the field really became a power before which generals began to quail.[23]

The dispatches of Edwin Lawrence Godkin

Godkin played a significant part in this new form of journalism himself. He displayed a keen awareness of conditions in the army and predicted many of the problems that had developed by the end of 1854. As early as January 1854 he predicted the difficulties that the medical services would later face and wrote

22 Lawrence James, *Crimea 1854–6. The war with Russia from contemporary photographs* (London, 1991).   **23** Rollo Ogden, *The life and letters of Edwin Lawrence Godkin* (New York,

that he could not understand why surgeons were not being recruited. In a dispatch of January 1854 he wrote:

> One would imagine that thousands of young surgeons who are starving in England and France would flock here to fill up the vacancies which exist in every regiment.[24]

While still in Varna he predicted the breakdown of the supply services and wrote some damning reports regarding the practices of the Commissariat Department:

> I do not know whether the British Commissariat officers know exactly what difficulties they will have to contend with, but certainly from what I heard and saw at Scutari, I rather think not. I am supported in my conclusions on this point by a piece of folly committed the other day in sending an officer to travel Romania and Bulgaria with a view to ascertaining what facilities there existed in them for supplying the English cavalry with horses. The ignorance which dictated this step is hardly conceivable. A single interrogatory addressed to the consul here at Varna, for example, would have elicited the fact that there are not 500 horses in all European Turkey fit to mount an English dragoon. When mistakes such as these are made regarding matters in which information lies within the reach of the most careless observer, one is naturally led to fear that many blunders and oversights may at first be committed in departments where knowledge is more difficult to assess.[25]

Also Godkin's accounts of actual battles tended to describe the effects of war on individuals, and in this way often had greater impact, while Russell often tended to write on the war in more general terms. Godkin's dispatches always displayed a sound knowledge of how the war was progressing. His dispatch of 18 October 1854 dismissed the reports in British newspapers predicting the imminent fall of Sevastapol. He wrote:

> Your readers must by this time have become aware of the utter groundlessness of the reports which represented Sevastapol as conquered by the allied armies, one half of the garrison killed, and the other half trembling on the brink of a very heroic and, what is more, melodramatic death. Sevastapol holds out, although there can be no doubt of our taking it when the time is come. That fortress is not such an easy prey as many people at home and on foreign stations seem to believe.[26]

In concluding this dispatch, he rightly predicted that artillery bombardment alone would not be enough to make Sevastapol surrender. He wrote:

1907), pp 102–3.   **24** Knightley, *The first casualty,* p. 13.   **25** Ibid., p. 8. See also Ogden, *Life and letters of E.L. Godkin*, p. 66.   **26** *Daily News*, 8 Nov. 1854, p. 2. There was a delay of a number of days from the time Godkin wrote his dispatches as they travelled by telegraph and steamer to London for publication.

We cannot expect to reduce the town by our cannonade; even the shells, red-hot shot, carcasses and rockets; which we have thrown for the last two days will not compel the garrison to abandon their post or offer to come to terms. Our regiments will have to fling their bayonets onto the scale, before it inclines to our side.[27]

Godkin's accounts of the lack of supplies and medicines were just as damning as Russell's. His dispatch of 25 December 1854 described the conditions in the army as winter approached.

Of the men, both of cavalry and infantry, I can only repeat my former assertion, that very large numbers of them fall victims to the climate, the fatigues of the siege, and the want of the most common means of comfort and cure, when suffering from complaints which, under our peculiar circumstances alone, are malignant and incurable. Of the hardships to which our troops are exposed I have often complained, not because I wanted an adequate appreciation of the straits of war, but because, with the means at our command and the generous disposition of the nation to do all and everything for the army, I consider one half of the hardships unnecessary. With common care our troops might have been hutted before the setting in of the rainy season. With common care, field hospitals of wood and straw work might have been erected for the reception of the wounded. With common care, medicines would not be allowed to rot in bulk in Constantinople, while brave men die and doctors despair for the want of them.[28]

His dispatches also realistically described the grim realities of combat and he frequently wrote of the lives wasted in the unsuccessful attacks on Sevastapol. His dispatch of 11 September 1855, described the aftermath of the unsuccessful British attack on the Redan on 8 September 1855.

Those who had died within the Redan had also been gathered into the ditch; so that I looked upon nearly all the British who had fallen in this last scene of an eleven month's tragedy. The first fact which struck the observer was, that nearly all who lay there were old soldiers, who had borne the heat and burthen of the day, hardly a beardless face was to be seen; the second, the calmness which appeared on almost every countenance, even where the death-wounds had been severe. Some, whose death must have been instantaneous, lay with unclosed eyes 'gazing upon the sky', and but for the glazed pupils and ghastly countenance, might have been supposed basking for pleasure in the sun; whilst others again were stretched out in all the seeming composure of a calm sleep.[29]

Godkin's dispatches were far more personal, describing his conversations with French and Turkish soldiers and he regarded the soldiers of Britain's allies highly. His accounts of some of the battles, particularly the battle of Balaclava, described the battle as he saw it and did not, unlike some of Russell's dispatches, rely on second-hand information. He also had a keen eye for the

27 Ibid.   **28** *Daily News*, 25 Dec. 1854, p. 5.   **29** *Daily News*, 26 Sept. 1855, p. 5.

bizarre and humorous and occasionally tried to add some light relief in his dispatches. Godkin took an interest in the Irish troops in the Crimea and included stories relating to them in his dispatches. The following excerpt from his dispatch of 11 September 1855 describes a confrontation between an Irish and a French soldier and is a fine example of his more humorous writing.

> More than one lament on our failure at the Redan was also uttered, and in one case in which reproach was thrown into the teeth of a brawny Irish Grenadier by a diminutive Chasseur with more impudence than discretion, I take to myself the credit of having saved a subject of the Emperor from summary annihilation. Pat had laid his hands on a bundle of crockery-ware, and was proceeding comfortably along under the influence of a double allowance of rum, when the Frenchman, still worse-off for liquor, came reeling by with a looking-glass under one arm and a couple of ducks under the other. 'Ha! Redan No!, Malakoff Yes!; Ingelese no bono!' spirited out the son of France, tapping the Irishman with impudent familiarity on the elbow. The 'whiroo' that followed was worthy of Donnybrook, and in an instant, dashing his crockery to the ground, Paddy grasped the Frenchman by the most capacious portion of his pantaloons, sent the looking-glass to shivers, and would have made work for the doctor of its owner if I had not at that moment come up to the rescue. Seeing Frenchmen hurrying to the scene of this tragi-comedy from all points, I deemed it best, for my country-man's own sake, to prevent his administering a chastisement which, however well-deserved, might have endangered the safety of its bestower, and so liberated the frightened impudent, and endeavoured to calm down the wrath of the infuriated Kerryman. This, however, was no easy task, but by endorsing his declaration of being able to beat ten Frenchmen any day, I finally reduced the storm and sent him on his way to the outskirts of the town.[30]

There were, therefore fundamental differences in the writing styles and, indeed the attitudes of these two men. While Russell attacked incompetence wherever he saw it, he still saw himself as being part of the establishment. He wrote of the shortcomings of the staff and the difficulties of the common soldier but did not attack the phenomenon of war itself. Godkin on the other hand showed a more developed social conscience and wrote increasingly against the war. Of his own work in the Crimea he wrote:

> I cannot help thinking in that the appearance of the special correspondent in the Crimea led to a real awaking of the official mind. It brought home to the War Office the fact that the public had something to say about the conduct of wars and that they are not the concern exclusively of sovereigns and statesmen.[31]

The later careers of Russell, Godkin, and McCoan

The differences in attitude of these two men can also be seen in how their careers developed after the Crimea. Russell continued to work for *The Times*

30 Ibid.   **31** Ogden, Op. cit., pp 102–3.

and his name became synonymous with war-reporting. On his return from the Crimea, he was given an honorary doctorate by Trinity College, Dublin, and later covered the Indian Mutiny, the American Civil war, the Austro-Prussian war, the Franco-Prussian war and the Zulu war. He also transformed himself from being the scourge of the establishment into being an accepted figure in political and military circles. He stood as a Conservative candidate for Chelsea in 1869 and, although defeated remained a supporter of the party. A friend of the prince of Wales, the future Edward VII, he accompanied him during his tour of the Near East and India in 1875–6. Russell also maintained contacts with the military, founding the *Army and Navy Gazette* in 1860. He was keenly interested in the Volunteer Rifle Corps, which were raised in 1859 due to the mounting fears of French invasion. Russell wrote a training booklet for these corps, *Rifle clubs and volunteer corps* (London, 1859), and was one of the first officers of the 28th Middlesex (London Irish) Rifle Volunteer Corps when it was formed in 1860.[32]

A friend of Thackeray and Dickens he was knighted in 1895 and made a CVO in 1902. He died in 1907 and was buried in Brompton cemetery. Two years after his death, a memorial bust was unveiled in the crypt of St Paul's Cathedral. The plaque on the memorial described him as 'the first and greatest of War Correspondents'. By the end of his life, therefore, he had changed his position in society entirely. In 1856 he returned from the Crimea a figure hated by the military and political establishment. By the time of his death he was accepted in both military and political circles. Fundamentally Russell was not a revolutionary but a reformer who wished to work within the system of his day.

Godkin, on the other hand, was a totally different type of person. After a period writing for the *Northern Whig* in Belfast, he went to America in late 1856, initially touring in the south and studying the effects of slavery. He still wrote occasional pieces for the *Daily News* and was admitted to the bar of New York in February 1858. During the American Civil war he did not work as a war correspondent although he did write for the *Daily News* and condemned Britain's support of the Confederate States. In July 1865 he founded a New York weekly, *The Nation*, which he hoped could operate free of any political allegiances. In its first issue the editorial stated that it 'would not be the organ of any party, sect or body'. In 1881 *The Nation* was sold to the *Evening Post*, due to financial difficulties, but in 1883 he became editor of both papers. During his time as editor he denounced political and municipal corruption and, in 1875, became a member of a commission appointed to reform the administration

---

32 Asquith, Stuart, 'D (London Irish Rifles) Company' in *Regiment*, no. 35, March 1999, p. 50. This battalion was renumbered as 16th Middlesex in 1880, becoming a battalion if the Rifle Brigade in 1881. In 1908 the London Irish transferred to the Territorial Force and were retitled the 18th (County of London) Battalion the London Regiment (London Irish Rifles). Since 1993: D

of New York. He later denounced the Spanish-American war and Britain's behaviour in South Africa during the second Boer war. Godkin remained interested in Irish politics and published, in 1887, his *Handbook of Home Rule*. In 1897 he was given an honorary doctorate by Oxford University. He died during a visit to Devonshire in May 1902 and was buried in Hazelbeach cemetery, Northamptonshire. His gravestone described him as a 'Publicist, economist and moralist'. A series of lectures, the 'Godkin lectures on the essentials of free government and the duties of the citizen', was later established at Harvard University. Godkin was totally different to Russell in terms of his political and social thought. His experiences in the Crimea had made him vehemently anti-war and he remained a thorn in the side of corrupt and inefficient politicians for the rest of his life, an advocate of fair and good government.[33]

James Carlile McCoan settled in Constantinople after the war and later founded an English language newspaper, the *Levant Herald*. He returned to England in 1870 and published several books detailing his travels in Circassia, Turkey and Egypt. In 1880, he entered parliament as a Home Rule MP for Co. Wicklow (1880–5) and was one of the Irish MPs suspended from the Commons in February 1881 for defying the authority of the Speaker. He subsequently disassociated himself from the methods employed by the Land League and supported the Land Act of 1881. He was an unsuccessful Liberal candidate in elections in Lancaster (1885), Southampton (1886) and Macclesfield (1892). He died in London, 13 January 1904, and was buried at Kensal Green cemetery.[34]

It is significant that of the handful of special correspondents who covered the Crimean war, three of them should be Irish. Russell, Godkin and McCoan were examples of a new type of correspondent. In some ways the Crimean correspondents were a unique group as they operated without being under any form of government control or censorship. Despite the efforts of Lord Raglan to curb their activities, they were, in reality, only answerable to their respective editors. General Sir William Codrington, who succeeded General Sir James Simpson as commander of the British army in the Crimea, consulted Lord Panmure, the new secretary of state for war, regarding methods of restraining the press. Panmure, rather weakly, suggested that they should:

> Put it to their patriotism and honour whether they would endanger the success of the army by premature and improper publication of its number, conditions etc.[35]

Codrington was prepared to go somewhat further and, in February 1855, issued an order which authorised the removal of a correspondent who had published

(London Irish Rifles) Company of the London Regiment.   **33** Ogden, op. cit. See also *The Annual Register* (1902), p. 127, *The Times*, 23 May 1902 and *DNB*.   **34** *Northern Whig*, 23 Jan. 1904.   **35** Knightley, op. cit., p. 16.

information that could have been useful to the Russians. This order also authorised the removal of any other correspondents who published sensitive information and it marked the beginning of military censorship. While the Crimean war was effectively over at this stage, Codrington's order served as a precedent and the press was strictly controlled in subsequent wars, especially the Boer war and the First World War. Russell and Godkin had operated free from such restraints and this is reflected in the graphic way in which they described the short-comings of the army's administration in the Crimea.

Irish newspaper coverage of the war

No Irish newspapers sent correspondents to the Crimea, presumably due to the cost of funding such an expedition. They relied heavily on the official dispatches and in many cases printed these dispatches in their entirety. Several newspapers, such as the *Dublin Evening Post*, the *Belfast Newsletter* and the *Cork Examiner* also published excerpts from Russell's dispatches in *The Times* and Godkin's dispatches in the *Daily News*. Most of the Irish newspapers also occasionally published letters that had been posted to Ireland by Irish officers and men in the Crimea. These letters were usually published without including the name of the man who had set them. On some occasions, where a particular regiment or battle was referred to, it is possible to make some effort to identify the writer.

The *Belfast Newsletter* provided very good coverage of the Crimean war and published excerpts from official dispatches, Russell's dispatches and also excerpts from Godkin's dispatches in the *Daily News*. The *Belfast Newsletter* also published letters from the Crimea on a much more frequent basis. Several of the Irish newspapers also published excerpts from French and Sardinian newspapers and journals. The *Cork Examiner* made the most use of foreign newspapers and journals, publishing excerpts from *Siecle, Moniteur, Courier de Marseilles, Gazette Piedmontese* and *Piedmont*. Indeed the *Cork Examiner* also frequently published excerpts from a Russian journal, the *Invalide Russe*.

Yet, while the Irish newspapers did not publish any war news that had not appeared previously in some other newspaper, they did publish reports about the Irish public's attitude to the war. An examination of Irish newspaper coverage indicates that the Irish public remained interested in the progress of the war and that they maintained a high level of enthusiasm for the war. It has already been shown in Chapter 1 that the Irish public were enthusiastic when war was declared and displayed this enthusiasm in the towns and cities of Ireland as the troops left for the Crimea. It would also seem that troops who left for the Crimea late in the war were still given similar send-offs. The *Dublin*

Evening Post of 8 September 1855 reported that 200 men from the 40th Foot and forty-one men from the Royal Artillery had boarded the steamer *Sylph* at the North Wall in Dublin two days previously. The report concluded by remarking that 'the quay was crowded with hundreds of persons who loudly cheered as the soldiers departed'. Such a public display of enthusiasm is perhaps surprising so late in 1855 but it is another indication that the Irish were still profoundly interested in events in the Crimea.

Irish newspapers also frequently referred to the success of recruiting parties and it would appear from their reports that men were still enlisting late in the war. The *Cork Examiner* of 3 September 1855 reported that 200 men form the South Cork Militia had volunteered to serve in a regular regiment while the *Dublin Evening Post* of 8 September 1855 reported that a further thirty-five men from the South Cork Militia had followed their comrades example and volunteered. Indeed the militia would appear to have become the main target of recruiting parities by late 1855. The *Wexford Independent* of 7 September 1855 reported a review of the Wexford Militia. The review attracted:

> The largest assemblage of the nobility and gentry of the country that we have seen collected together for many years.[36]

When the Wexford Militia had been assembled they were addressed by Lieutenant-Colonel Richard Waddy of the 50th Foot, a Wexfordman, who encouraged them to join a regular regiment:

> Being anxious to have as many Wexford men as I can procure in my regiment, I hope when next called on to volunteer, that you will not forget that your countyman commands a regiment before Sevastapol and that he would be proud to be your leader and promises to be your friend.[37]

The response to Lieutenant-Colonel Waddy's call for recruits was not indicated in the report. Yet men from the militia regiments continued to enlist in 1855. In October 1855 twelve men of the Westmeath Militia volunteered to serve with the Connaught Rangers in the Crimea.[38]

News of the Russian evacuation of Sevastapol south of the bay, described as the 'fall of Sevastapol', following the assault of the 8 September 1855 began to appear in Irish newspapers on the 10 September 1855. This news was greeted with a series of public celebrations all over Ireland. In a number of successive issues the *Belfast Newsletter* had a special column describing the celebrations in Belfast, and in other towns in Ulster, and also in Dublin and England. The

---

36 *Wexford Independent*, 7 Sept. 1855. Lieutenant-Colonel Richard Waddy commanded the 50th Foot when it left Dublin in February 1854. The 50th Foot was the first regiment to leave Ireland for the Crimea.   37 Ibid.   38 *Dublin Evening Post*, 2 Oct. 1855.

Belfast Newsletter of 13 September 1855 remarked that the celebrations on the previous evening had not been as intense as on the first two nights but that still large crowds had gathered. The Belfast celebrations were described:

> In various parts of the town, tar-barrels blazed and fireworks were discharged despite the drizzling shower. The sound of guns was heard at intervals. A van was driven through the streets accompanied by a band of music, on which were exhibited figures of Davis, the Life Guardsman, and Corporal Quinn, the latter being designated by the inscription as a 'Son of the Sod'.[39]

The Belfast celebrations finished with a 'splendid pyrotechnic display opposite Messrs John McGee & Co. in High Street'. The *Belfast Newsletter* then described the celebrations in Ballymacarret:

> The Police Barracks, the premises of Mr Jones, and the adjoining houses were illuminated, and upwards of 5,000 persons paraded in the thoroughfare.[40]

The celebrations in Ardoyne were begun with a fireworks display:

> A beautiful pyrotechnic display took place in the village square. A number of tar-barrels were lighted and several kegs of ale having been broached by the fitful glare of the ruddy flames, the hearty followers, quaffed the inspiring liquor, and in the true spirit of Irish hospitality, freely entertained all comers.[41]

At Ardoyne the evening ended with Joseph Carson, described as 'an intelligent workman' from Michael Andrews Royal Damask Factory, giving an address to his fellow employees on the importance of the victory.

The *Belfast Newsletter* described similar scenes all over the province. At Lisburn there was an 'outburst of popular enthusiasm' while at Cotton Mount tar-barrels were lit, several hundred gathered and 'the Cotton Mount Amateur Band attended and played several popular tunes in good style'. In Londonderry the bells were rung, ships were decorated and crowds gathered and cheered the queen, the emperor and the French. The lord mayor proposed a general illumination and French tricolours and the Union Jacks were hung from the city walls. The report concluded:

> The Apprentice Boys turned out in large force and fired several discharges of cannon from the walls.

The *Belfast Newsletter* of 14 September 1855 described the continued celebrations in Ulster. In Holywood there had been a 'grand pyrotechnic display' the previous evening, the funds for the display being raised by public subscription.

---

39 *Belfast Newsletter*, 13 Sept. 1855. Corporal Quinn of the 47th Foot had killed two Russians and captured a Russian officer during the final assault on Sevastapol. **40** Ibid. **41** Ibid.

At 9 p.m. a gun was fired by the Coast Guard Station and the entertainment was opened by a grand discharge of rockets, the burning of blue lights and beautiful devices. The fireworks were very fine and the night being favourable, the amusements passed off in the most satisfactory manner.[42]

The same report also told that the bells in Christ Church Cathedral, Dublin, had been rung during the previous nights in celebration.

The 20th of September 1855 was also the first anniversary of the battle of the Alma. Many of the towns and cities in Ireland held a dual celebration and the account of the Dublin event, recorded in the *Dublin Evening Post*, is worth quoting at length.

Thursday being the anniversary of the battle of the Alma, several of the public buildings, the establishments of respectable traders, and the residences of private citizens were brilliantly illuminated, not only in honour of the victory gained on that day twelvemonths on the banks of the Alma, but also to commemorate the signal victory recently achieved in the capture of Sevastapol. The line of streets leading to the places illuminated were densely crowded by all classes, from the humble citizen up to the most opulent citizen. From Carlisle Bridge up to the furthermost end of Grafton Street was almost impassable; and the northern side of St Stephen's Green presented, in front of the Hibernia United Service Club, one vast crowd who seemed highly to enjoy the scene before them. This vast assemblage was attracted by the brilliant illuminations which decorated the front of the club. On the upper section of the building the illuminated word 'Alma' extended from one side to the other. Under this device at either side the letters 'V' and 'N', each surmounted by the royal and imperial crowns. Beneath these blazed the word 'Sevastapol'. From the windows on the front story the flags of Sardinia, Turkey, France and Britain were suspended. On the steps of the club some of its principal members were collected; and in the balconies and windows a large number of ladies (the friends and relatives of the members) were assembled. The band of the 16th Lancers was stationed within the enclosed ground on the Green, and the band of the Cambridgeshire Militia was placed in the immediate neighbourhood of the club. Both bands performed a series of French, English and Scotch airs during the evening. On the bands striking up the French national air of 'Partant pour la Syrie' the cheering of the people became most vehement, and also when 'Rule Britannia' and 'St Patrick's Day' were given. The members entertained as guests the Consuls of Sardinia, Turkey and France and the lady visitors partook of tea and coffee in the drawing room. The police under the command of Inspectors Walpole, Finnamore and Lowry and Mr Guy, acting Chief-Superintendent, kept admirable order. The rejoicings commenced shortly after 11 o'clock with a well arranged display of fireworks, under the direction of Mr Bruce. All kinds of pyrotechnic contrivances were brought forward on the occasion and we have seldom seen anything more effective than those presented last night. The finale was exceedingly good. After all that could be devised in the form of rockets, Catherine wheels etc., were exhausted, a grand explosion took place and, out of the ignited materials the word

'Alma' arose in the most brilliant colours amidst the enthusiastic cheering of the vast crowds assembled.[43]

The *Dublin Evening Post* also added that the ships in the harbour joined in by firing fireworks and signal rockets while several businesses premises had been illuminated. Celebrations continued throughout the country during the next number of days. As late as early October 1855 there was a celebratory dinner held in the Curragh.

The reception of the news of the fall of Sevastapol would appear to have been greeted with more restraint in Cork. The *Cork Examiner* reported that a military review was held in Victoria Barracks while the *Cork Constitution* reported that the guardship at Queenstown (Cobh) had flown the French and Turkish flags and fired a twenty-one gun salute. Preparations then began for a formal reception and dinner for the French Emperor, Louis Napoleon, who was returning to France and whose ship was expected to stop at Queenstown. After the preparations had gone on for two days it was announced that the Emperor would not stop at Queenstown as he wished to return to Paris for the celebrations there.[44] The *Cork Examiner* was not enthusiastic when reporting the news of the fall of Sevastapol and rightly pointed out that the Russians had only evacuated from the south side of the bay and were still firmly entrenched on the northside. The editorial of 12 September 1855 remarked:

> Then we are told that the British have lost about 2,000 men in their attack on the Redan. This is as much as to say that 1,000 Irish men have been killed or wounded, for now, as from the first hour that blood was shed on the soil of the Crimea, Ireland has more than satisfied the national co-partnership by her share of the loss; whatever may become of her share of the profit.[45]

Bearing this in mind, and also that the north side of Sevastapol still held out, the *Cork Examiner* stated that it would keep its 'exultation within the limits of sobriety'. In a similar vein it was reported that a meeting of the residents of Skibbereen had decided not to illuminate the town in celebration of the victory:

> When it considers the affliction and mourning which that success has brought to so many homes and families.[46]

It would appear, therefore, that the reception of the news of the fall of Sevastapol was met with much less enthusiasm in Cork, if the reports of the *Cork Examiner* are to be believed. It is also possible that the *Cork Examiner* was printing negative reports only and not reporting on any celebrations in the

43 *Dublin Evening Post*, 22 Sept. 1855.   44 *Cork Examiner* and *Cork Constitution*, 12–14 Sept. 1855.   45 *Cork Examiner*, 12 Sept. 1855.   46 Ibid.

Cork area. It seems unlikely, in light of the crowds that regularly turned out to cheer troops who were leaving Queenstown for the Crimea, that there were no public celebrations of any kind, after the dinner for the Emperor was cancelled. On 20 September 1855, Lieutenant-Colonel Richard Waddy, who was still on a recruiting tour of Ireland, was honoured with a formal dinner at the Assembly Rooms in Cork and was warmly welcomed by the 'nobility, gentry and inhabitants of Cork' on his arrival in the city.[47] Again this would indicate that the people of Cork had maintained an interest in the war and it seems highly likely that there was some form of public celebration in Cork when Sevastapol fell, and that this was not reported in the local newspapers.

While the Irish newspapers did not send correspondents of their own to the Crimea, their reports of events in Ireland give a good indication of the public's attitude to the war. Their reports of the celebrations of September 1855 indicate that the enthusiasm of the early months of the war had not diminished and that the Irish public were still profoundly interested in events in the Crimea.

Irish Crimean war ballads

The war ballads published during this period represent another manifestation of the interest shown by the Irish public in the Crimean war. There are about fifty of these Crimean war ballads in the White Ballad Collection in Trinity College, Dublin, and their various themes suggests that the Irish public was keenly interested in the war and also appreciated hearing news of the war in ballad form. Many more Crimean ballads were probably published but, due to the difficulty of collecting and preserving printed ballads, they do not survive in any ballad collections. While the ballads in the White Ballad Collection no doubt represent only a small proportion of what was published, they cover a number of different themes and can be categorised into separate types.

Firstly there are some ballads which are very patriotic, if not over-excited, in tone but which do not supply any real information. They appear to have been written early in 1854 when war was declared and, while they are in support of the war, they display a lack of knowledge of the exact details of what was going on. Examples of this type of ballad are 'The Russians are coming', 'A new song on the Russian war' and 'A new hunting song on the Eastern Question'. These ballads are very enthusiastic in tone but often display a total ignorance of the actual details of the war. For example 'A new song on the Russian war' states:

> For to oppose bold Nicholas the Austrians have declared,
> The valiant Cuirassiers of France will prove his downfall

47 *Cork Examiner*, 21 Sept. 1855.

> And Paddie's sons with Britain's guns will make him pay for all,
> The forty second highlanders and Faugh a Ballaghs too,
> Likewise the Connaught Rangers and Enniskillens true.[48]

This ballad, while no doubt merely trying to entertain, makes a number of fundamental mistakes. The most glaring error in this quote is the statement that the Austrians had declared war on Russia, something that they refused to do despite the pressure being put on them by Britain and France. Also, while the 42nd Highlanders and the Connaught Rangers served in the war, the 87th Foot (Royal Irish Fusiliers), referred to here by their regimental motto, 'Faugh a Ballagh', did not.[49] The 'Enniskillens' mentioned in the ballad could be a reference to the 6th (Inniskilling) Dragoons. This regiment served in the Crimea while the 27th (Inniskilling) Foot was not in the Crimea.

   There are also ballads in the collection which emphasise the concept of unity among the allies. There are several ballads which centre on the fact that Britain and France had joined forces, despite enmity after the Napoleonic wars, to fight the Russians. Turkey, perhaps surprisingly, is not mentioned often in these ballads. Typical of this type of ballad are 'The allied volunteers', 'The young soldier's letter to his mother' and 'A new song on the Russian war'. (This is a different ballad from the one previously mentioned. Several titles are repeated in the collection.) 'The young soldier's letter to his mother', obviously written after the fall of Sevastapol in September 1855, stated:

> The batteries of Sevastapol, the world did surprise,
> And it was hard to take it, the enemy were so wise,
> But Paddy's sons, with British guns, their valour did display,
> Together with the men of France, thank God, they gained the day.[50]

Some of these ballads also concentrate on the French participation in the war but do not mention the British army. 'Napoleon will muzzle the Bear' is a prime example of this type of ballad which tells of French and Irish co-operation in the fight against Russia.

> Our valiant troops from Dublin and other parts of Ireland
> They have embarked for Turkey the sons of France to join.[51]

'A new song on the Russian war' follows the same theme, ignoring British participation and suggesting that the Irish and French would somehow unite and defeat Russia.

48 White Ballad Collection, OLS/X/1/531, ballad no. 260.   **49** Lieutenant-Colonel R.J. Dickinson, *Officers mess* (London, 1973), p. 112.   **50** White Ballad Collection, OLS/X/1/530, ballad no. 60.   **51** Ibid. ballad no. 262.

When he heard that our brave Irish boys were going o'er
It grieved the old monster and tortured him some
By the brave sons of France he's completely baulk'd
To take Europe, the reptile, he's in the wrong box.
Our brave Irish soldiers for me.[52]

The ballad 'Napoleon's visit' states ' Hurrah for Louis Napoleon and the Irish Volunteers' while 'The hero of war' is basically a tribute to Louis Napoleon. Both are typical of this type of ballad which is pro-French while at the same time not making any references to the British army.

There are ballads which refer to militia regiments, usually putting forward the view that the Irish militia regiments, if unleashed upon the Russians, would soon end the war. 'The militia train', 'The Donegal Militia' and 'The poor militia boy' are typical of these militia ballads. A good example of this type of ballad is 'The Tipperary Militia' and it is interesting in a number of different ways. 'The Tipperary Militia' is very patriotic and aggressive in tone. Verse seven and the chorus read:

To see them parading it would you delight,
With their coats trimmed with scarlet so neat and so tight.
If they were in Russia I'd venture to say
They would muzzle the bear without any delay.

Chorus.
Hurragh for the Tipp boys, firm and sound,
The bear and his cubs they will help to put down.
If only we could catch him we would chase him to morn.
We would dance Garryowen on the monster's breast bone.[53]

The extremely aggressive tone of this ballad is somewhat ironic when one considers that the 2nd, or North Tipperary, Militia mutinied in July 1856.[54] The ballad also refers to specific officers; 'Mr Quinn' was Captain William Quinn, 'Demster' was either Lieutenant Thomas C. Dempster or Surgeon James Dempster. There is also a reference in the ballad to a Captain Massy who was Captain (later Major) Henry William Massy, of Grantstown, Co. Tipperary, and father of William Godfrey Dunham Massy, known as 'Redan Massy'.[55] All of

52 Ibid. ballad no. 268.   53 White Ballad Collection, OLS/X/1/531, ballad no. 272.   54 The reasons for this mutiny will be outlined in Chapter VII.   55 William Godfrey Dunham Massy, born in Rathfarnham, Co. Dublin, in November 1838, entered Trinity College, Dublin, in June 1854 but left in October to join the army. A lieutenant in the 19th Foot, he took command of his regiment's grenadier company during an attack on Sevastapol on 8 September 1855. Badly wounded in the legs he lay in the trenches before Sevastapol all night, keeping up the spirits of the other wounded. He became known as 'Redan Massy' and returned to TCD. In July 1856, he was presented with a commemorative sword in TCD and graduated in 1859. He was subsequently awarded an honorary doctorate (1873). He served in the Second Afghan war (1878–80) and

these officers served with the 1st, or South Tipperary Militia and the ballad was written specifically with that regiment in mind.[56] The ballad 'War song of the Tipperary Light Infantry' refers to the 2nd, or North Tipperary Militia. Also 'The waggoners' was written about the Land Transport Corps, verse nine referring to the Irishmen who served with that corps:

> But Sevastapol is standing up still.
> We'll tear it asunder, let him talk as he will.
> Long life to Napoleon and the lads wears the blue,
> Hurrah for our brave Irish waggoners too.[57]

There are also ballads which are far more sentimental, if not depressing, in tone. Typical of these are 'The mother's lament' and 'Marlow's farewell to Erin'. 'Marlow's farewell to Erin' was written on the outbreak of the Indian Mutiny in 1857 but begins with references to the Crimea:

> Now India's on fire, your aid is required
> At John Bull's desire, go lay down your life,
> As you did at Alma, Inkerman and the Redan.
> Which caused many an orphan and wife to mourn.
> March off to the slaughter without any falter,
> If you fall in the struggle, no more is about you.
> Don't talk of Erin, her sad habitation,
> But win all the laurels for England you can.[58]

Perhaps the most interesting type of ballad are those which refer to specific battles or incidents. Ballads such as 'Lines on the battle of Alma', 'The battle of Alma', 'A new song on the siege of Sevastapol' and 'Inkerman' tell of specific battles, often highlighting the part of Irish soldiers in these battles. 'The battle of Alma' was printed by Haly's printers in Hanover Street in Cork, one of the more prolific printers of Crimean ballads. A prime example of this heroic type of ballad, it states:

> The 33rd, the 7th and Fusiliers
> Then climbed the hill and gave three cheers,
> While 'Faugh-a-ballagh' did rend our ears,
> From Hibernia's sons at Alma.
> And the Highland lads in kilt and hose,

---

finished his career as a lieutenant-general. In 1856 he was one of the best-known soldiers in the British army. Mark Marsay, 'The stirring tale of Redan Massy' in *Newsletter of the Friends of the Green Howards Regimental Museum* (Sept., 1997), pp 16–8. See also the *Illustrated London News*, 5 July 1855, p. 11. **56** Hart's *Army List* (1855). The full regimental title of the South Tipperary Militia was the Duke of Clarence's Munster Artillery or 1st, or South Tipperary Militia. **57** White Ballad Collection, OLS/X/1/532, ballad no. 51. **58** Ibid. ballad no. 4.

> They were not last, you may suppose,
> But boldly faced the Russian foes,
> And gained the heights at Alma.[59]

Another ballad which refers to a specific incident is 'The gallant escape of Pat McCarthy from the Russians' and, indeed, this is perhaps one of the most interesting Crimean ballads in the White Collection. William Howard Russell of *The Times* included a piece in one of his dispatches on a Sergeant Patrick McGuire who had managed to escape from his Russian guards after being captured in an attack on Sevastapol. McGuire was being led away between two Russians and noticed that the man on his right had his rifle cocked and his finger inside the trigger guard. McGuire recognized an opportunity and seized hold of the barrel of the Russian's rifle, causing him to fire the weapon. The shot killed the Russian to McGuire's left and he then wrenched the rifle from the first guard and clubbed him to the ground with the butt. A third Russian approached and he chased him away at bayonet point. This action was witnessed by one of McGuire's officers and he was later commended for his quick thinking.[60] 'The gallant escape of Pat McCarthy from the Russians' was obviously based on this event. It was also printed by Haly's of Cork and this no doubt explains why the name of the main protagonist was changed from McGuire to McCarthy, a more common name in Co. Cork.

> It was life and death to draw his breath
> While he was in their clutches,
> He ran the chance and made them dance
> Like billy goats on crutches.
> He shot down one upon the ground,
> With just two once of powder,
> He gave the other a mortal wound,
> That flattened him like a flounder.[61]

A common theme in many of these ballads was the emphasis put on the past services of Irishmen in the Napoleonic wars and the Sikh wars of the 1840s. 'The Russians are coming' states:

> For our locals are waiting to give you some play,
> Under Moore Abercromby and brave Wellington,
> We fought and we bled and the laurels had won.
> At famed Salamanca and Badajoz too,
> Triumphant we were at famed Waterloo.

---

59 Ibid. ballad no. 44.   **60** W.H. Russell, *The war. From the landing at Gallipoli to the death of Lord Raglan* (London, 1855), pp 240–1.   **61** White Ballad Collection, OLS/X/1/532, ballad no. 45. Sergeant McGrath also retrieved his own rifle and brought back the two rifles of the Russians he had killed.

We will blow everyone to death away,
Old England with Scotland and Irishmen too.[62]

The Crimean ballads in the White Collection are an interesting indication of the level of interest that the Irish public showed in the war. The various different themes indicates a desire on the part of the ballad writers to reach as wide an audience as possible. While some of the ballads are vague in terms of detail, others indicate that the writers were following the course of the war closely, perhaps using the dispatches appearing in newspapers for information. The militia ballads are interesting in that they show that the writers of these ballads had a high level of local knowledge and could even refer to specific officers in their work. The ballads that refer to specific battles and incidents also show that the ballad writers were obtaining information on the war, probably from newspapers. The detail in some of these descriptions indicates that Irish ballad writers had more than just a passing interest in the Crimean war, and that they were trying to cater to the demands for more information about the war and they provided this information in ballad form.

62 White Ballad Collection, OLS/X/1/531, ballad no. 258.

7

Ireland in 1856: the Nenagh mutiny and the Crimean banquet. Irish Crimean veterans and memorials

The end of the Crimean war in 1856 had several consequences for Ireland. When the ratification of the peace settlement was announced in April 1856, the Irish public was relieved and there was a period of celebration as the troops returning from the Crimea were warmly welcomed. The end of the war had, however, negative consequences for the men of the militia of Ireland and also for many veterans of the war. 1856 became a year of both celebration and protest.

The Nenagh mutiny

The militia mutiny at Nenagh, Co. Tipperary, in July 1856 occurred due to the end of the Crimean war and the announcement of plans to disembody the militia of Ireland. There had been a number of disturbances connected with the militia since it had been embodied in January 1855, but the Nenagh mutiny was by far the most serious incident. When war was declared in 1854 both the government and the army commanders thought that the war would be a short one, as was the case in 1914. By the end of 1854, however, it was obvious that the war was going to continue for some time. The battles of the Alma, Balaclava and Inkerman had resulted in serious losses for the British army and replacements had to be sent from garrisons at home. In light of this reduction of the strength of the regular army, it was decided that the militia should be embodied. On 1 January 1855, the forty-five regiments of the militia of Ireland were embodied and it was hoped that a force of 30,000 would be raised (see Appendix D).

There was some difficulty in raising the militia quotas in Cork and in Ulster. In Cork men of military age had already joined the Royal Navy or the regular army. Many Ulstermen had also enlisted in the regular army or were in secure employment and were not particularly tempted by the prospect of militia bounties and pay. The enlistment bounty of £6, payable in £1 instalments at the end of each period of annual training, was raised to £7.15s. and then to £10 by the end of 1855, in the hope of attracting more recruits. There was also a £1 grant for clothing and a daily rate of pay of 1*s*.1*d*. per day.[1] There were, however, a number of deductions from each militiaman's pay for 'necessaries'; mess charges, blankets, sheets, hair cuts etc. These deductions reduced the amount of actual pay that each militiaman received per month. Private Joseph Moore, for example, of the Louth Rifles, was charged over 20*s*. in February 1856 for 'necessaries', leaving him only 3*s*. 7*d*. In January 1856, Moore had been left with only 7*d*. pay after purchasing his kit![2] Also, the enlistment bounty was paid out in an initial instalment of 10*s*. when the recruit volunteered and then, as has been previously stated, in £1 instalments at the end of each period of annual training. Any remaining bounty money should have been paid when the militia regiments were disembodied. As a result of this system, the men of the militia of Ireland had received virtually none of their promised enlistment bounty when rumours began to circulate in 1856 that they were about to be disembodied.

There had been a series of problems with the militia, however, both in England and Ireland, during 1855. Few, if any, militia regiments reached full strength. Yet despite this the ballot act, which allowed for conscription into the militia by parish ballot, was not invoked. Also, as the war had been dragging on for nearly a year, it was difficult to find recruits with any military experience as the majority of such men had already rejoined the regular army. The Louth Rifles found it difficult to raise recruits and could not get any experienced NCOs; Sergeant-Majors Patrick Lanning and Thomas Odell came from England to begin training the recruits. The Louth Rifles, initially based at Millmount Barracks, Drogheda, had begun recruiting on 20 January 1855 and the *Newry Examiner* of 24 January 1855 described their rather unimpressive recruiting party:

> Recruiting for the Louth Rifles. On Monday last a drummer and a fifer, both in coloured clothes and rather gloomy looking wights, treated our denizens to a few tunes invitive of recruits. 'The tune the old cow died of' would have suited the exhibition made by the musicians and a small juvenile attendant mob. The ensemble looked like a burlesque on former recruiting displays, and we were accordingly gratified as Sir J. Robinson, on seeing the awkward squad, at once dismissed them, headed as they were by an 'old fogy' wearing ribbons very like in hue to a faded rose in a Covent-Garden basket-woman's Sunday cap.[3]

An examination of the nominal list of the Louth Rifles for the period 1855 to 1856 shows that 38% of those who enlisted were described as labourers. Other

---

1 Rod Robinson, 'The Nenagh mutiny' in *The War Correspondent*, xviii, no. 4 (January 2001), 14–8.   2 Brendan Hall, *Officers and recruits of the Louth Rifles, 1854–1876* (Dun Laoghaire, 1999), p. 27.   3 Ibid. p. 13. Lieutenant-Colonel Sir John S. Robinson, officer commanding the Louth Rifles. He had previously served in the 60th Rifles.

occupations mentioned included shoemaker, tailor, weaver, carpenter and baker. By May 1855 the Louth Rifles had reached a strength of 300 and had been trained to a good standard of drill. The *Newry Examiner* of 2 May 1855 described an inspection:

> The Louth Rifles were inspected on Wednesday last in the large Market Square, Fair Street, Drogheda. The soldier-like bearing and perfect discipline of the men, now raised to nearly their full complement, was the surprise of many who remembered the mirth exuded by the awkward appearance as new recruits a few months ago.[4]

As mentioned in Chapter 6, the militia regiments became the main source of recruits for the regular army during 1855. Recruiting parties concentrated on trying to attract men from the militia regiments as the rush of civilian recruits began to dwindle and many militia regiments, having struggled to find recruits themselves, lost trained men to the regular regiments throughout 1855. The Louth Rifles, having reached a strength of 300 in May 1855, lost eighty-seven men to recruiting parties from the 2nd Dragoon Guards, 88th Foot (Connaught Rangers) and the 47th Foot. More men later volunteered to serve with the 5th Dragoon Guards, the 6th Dragoon Guards and the Rifle Brigade. This pattern was repeated in militia regiments all over Ireland and the numbers of militia-men were constantly reduced by opportunistic recruiting parties. It was not until 1860 that legislation was passed restricting this form of recruiting.[5]

Breaches of discipline were also a major problem; they took several forms. The nominal list of the Louth Rifles shows that there were numerous cases of desertion during 1855, men being absent without leave and men being confined in the guard-house. Yet such problems were common in all regular and militia regiments. There were also numerous affrays between militiamen and members of the constabulary. A typical example took place in Cork in September 1855 when a group of some fifty men of the South Cork Militia pursued two con-stables who had arrested one of their comrades for being drunk and disorderly. The two constables took their prisoner to the Cork Bridewell and the crowd of militiamen laid siege to the building. It was only when Head Constable Crowley handed over the prisoner to a corporal of the South Cork Militia that the men agreed to disperse.[6] There were also cases of militiamen assaulting civilians in the towns where they were stationed. In August 1855 the Louth Rifles moved to the Cavalry Barracks in Dundalk and a series of clashes with the local population followed.

> Courts Martial began to be frequent & Patrols commanded by Officers were constantly required to patrol the streets. The County people had little respect for

---

4 Ibid. p. 14.   **5** Ibid.   **6** *Cork Examiner*, 3 Sept. 1855.

their County force, which presented themselves in bad clothing & with a less military air than the Cavalry they were accustomed to. Serious fighting often occurred and loaded whip handles and other dangerous weapons were often taken from the County people & shown in Barracks.[7]

There were also more serious disturbances where militia officers were defied by their men. In September 1855 there was a confrontation between the officers and men of the Clare Militia, then stationed at the Curragh Camp. The men had taken offence when they were refused permission to use the regimental band for mass parade. The *Munster News* of 3 September 1855 reported that the men had gathered on the parade ground and 'shouted the officers off the square. The adjutant got a blow across the face that knocked him down'. The ringleaders of this protest were arrested and later court-martialled.[8]

The most serious disturbance that took place during this period of embodiment of the militia of Ireland occurred in Nenagh in July 1856 and concerned the 2nd, or North Tipperary Militia. Following the peace in April 1856, the North Tipperary Militia were moved from Tralee, Co. Kerry, to Nenagh, Co. Tipperary. In Nenagh they were billeted in temporary barracks in Pound Street and at the main barracks at Summerhill. The Summerhill barracks also held a magazine. It would appear that the majority of these militiamen had received very little of their enlistment bounty and, as rumours spread that they were about to be disembodied, the relationship between officers and men became tense. It would also appear that the regiment's officers were conscious of the fact that they had a potential mutiny of their hands, as all ammunition had been taken from the militiamen when they left Tralee.

In early July 1856 a number of events occurred in rapid succession which transformed this simmering discontent in the ranks into open mutiny. Firstly, it was announced that any militiaman who wished could present himself to his colonel and gain his discharge, apparently without any of the bounty money due to him. Secondly, it was then announced that the remaining bounty money would be paid at a rate of 5s. per quarter but only while the militia remained embodied. As disembodiment seemed imminent it seemed fairly certain that the best the militiamen could hope for was a further 5s. of their bounty money.

The final spark that ignited the Nenagh mutiny came on Monday, 7 July 1856. The militia had been issued in April with new parade uniforms; boots, trousers, tunic and shako. As this uniform was considered to be only part-worn, orders were given to take back into store the newly issued trousers, tunics and shakos. At the Summerhill barracks in Nenagh, one of the sergeants went around collecting this uniform, ordering men to strip off there and then. Many militiamen obeyed but one man of No. 4 Company refused to give up his trousers and was

7 Hall, Op. cit., p. 14.   8 *Munster News*, 3 Sept. 1855.

sent under arrest to the guard-house. As the parish priest of Nenagh, Fr Scanlon, later stated that it was unreasonable to ask the men to hand over their trousers and then go 'half-naked upon the country, a source of jest to all unthinking boys, in their rags'.[9] The Nenagh mutiny was later christened the 'Battle of the Breeches' by some Irish newspapers. When other members of No. 4 Company came to the barracks for drill, things very quickly got out of hand. *The Reporter* of 8 July 1856 described the outbreak of the mutiny.

> An order also having been received to take up the new clothing issued to the Militia in April last, yesterday morning a sergeant commenced to take up the clothing from the men, when some few quietly gave it up. One man refused to give away his black trousers, whereupon he was sent to the guardhouse. In a very short time afterward the company to which he belonged came down to the guardhouse to rescue him. The guard was ordered to fire, which they did not owing to their having no ammunition. The men, however, desisted, but in a very short time after, the five companies quartered in Pound Street Barracks, came to Summerhill Barracks, as is their custom every day for the purpose of being drilled. Hearing that the man was confined, they fixed bayonets and rushed at the guardroom, flinging the guard away, and with their guns and stones they broke open the cell doors, and let out all the prisoners, at the same time demolishing the windows, doors, seats etc.[10]

Lieutenant-Colonel Francis Cornwallis-Maude, the officer commanding the North Tipperary Militia, and Major George Frend then tried to calm the militiamen and succeeded in getting them to form up in companies at Summerhill Barracks. *The Reporter* stated that 'the greatest excitement prevailed' and the colonel lectured them on the possible consequences of their actions. Fr Scanlon also arrived and tried to convince the militiamen to give up their protest. They in turn declared that they would not give up their arms until they had received the balance of their bounty money and were allowed to keep their clothes. They then agreed to return to their quarters in Pound Street.

At 10 p.m., however, they came out of their quarters and charged through the town, causing a great commotion. The local constabulary barracks was attacked and the militiamen then stormed the Summerhill Barracks in the hope of getting ammunition from the barracks' magazine. The officers, and the majority of NCOs, had emptied the magazine and moved all the ammunition to the gaol on the outskirts of Nenagh and remained there until help arrived. Sergeant Cole was attacked in Pound Street and a pouch of ammunition was taken from him. It would also appear that some local shopkeepers had actually sold some powder and ball to the mutineers during the day. The mutineers forced the band to turn out and to play them around the town and they later roamed around in groups, occasionally firing shots into the air. The house of the petty

9 Robinson, 'The Nenagh mutiny'.   10 *The Reporter*, 8 July 1856.

sessions clerk, William Bull, was attacked and had its windows smashed. The house of John Kennedy in Silver Street received similar treatment and a crowd of militiamen gathered outside the gaol and pelted it with stones before returning to their quarters around midnight.

On the morning of 8 July 1856 they left their quarters again and spent the early part of the day rampaging around the town. During the day the local magistrates and others such as Lord Dunally attempted to negotiate with the mutineers. Also Lieutenant William Godfrey Dunham Massy of the 19th Foot, the 'Redan' Massy referred to in Chapter 6, tried to pacify the mutineers. His father, Henry William Massy, was then a captain in the 1st, South Tipperary Militia and the two men had travelled form the family home at Grantstown, Co. Tipperary in order to try to convince the militiamen to give up their protest. 'Redan' Massy was still on crutches due to his wounds in the Crimea but, as a Tipperary man and a known Crimean veteran and hero, he was no doubt asked to make some representation to the men. The best that he could achieve, however, was to persuade the mutineers to unfix their bayonets.[11]

Lieutenant-Colonel Henry George Hart, officer commanding the depot at Templemore received a dispatch on the morning of 8 July 1856 telling him of the mutiny at Nenagh. There were depot companies of the 13th Foot, 41st Foot, 47th Foot and 55th Foot at Templemore and he assembled a force of 574 men of all ranks.[12] At 4.30 p.m. on the afternoon of 8 July 1856, Major-General Sir James Chatterton received a message in Limerick telling him of the mutiny and also informing him, incorrectly, that eleven police constables had been shot by the mutineers. He immediately dispatched a squadron of the 17th Lancers, who had just returned from the Crimea and later sent 200 men of the 21st Foot. Hart's force reached Nenagh first, having made a forced march of some twenty-three miles, arriving in the town at around 4 p.m. The *Nenagh Guardian* of 9 July 1856 described Hart's arrival but overestimated the size of his force.

> At about 4 o'clock the military, consisting of 1,000 soldiers of the 13th, 41st, 47th, and 55th depots, under the command of Lieutenant-Colonel Hart, entered Barrack Street from Templemore, and were halted opposite the church. Here they received instructions to fix bayonets and load with ball cartridge, to march on the barrack of Nenagh and take possession of it.[13]

The account continues:

11 Robinson, op. cit. 12 H.G. Hart, *New Annual Army List* (1860), p. 56, p. 70. Lieutenant-Colonel Henry George Hart was the publisher of Hart's *Annual Army List*. His actions in July 1856 represented the only active service of his career and he devoted no less than nineteen lines in subsequent editions of the *New Annual Army List* to describing his part in the Nenagh mutiny. In contrast, the entries for the officers on either side of his own entry, veterans of the Sikh wars and the Crimean war, were only allocated seven-line entries! 13 *Nenagh Guardian*, 9 July 1856.

> On reaching the barrack gate the Colonel demanded admittance. There was no reply … it was a moment of dread suspense! He placed his hand on the gate and it opened to his touch. He advanced, followed by his men, who opened into single file and surrounded the barrack walls.[14]

The militiamen inside the barracks surrendered rather meekly but there were other smaller groups roaming around the town and some of these men gathered outside the barracks. Private Stephen Burns of the North Tipperary Militia and another unknown private each fired a shot through an open side-gate when the regular troops assembled inside. Private Curley of the 41st Foot was hit and killed while Private Patrick Reilly of the 47th Foot was hit in the hip. Both were Crimean veterans, Private Reilly had been wounded in his other leg during the final assault on the Redan.

Hart then set out to subdue the remainder of the mutineers who were believed to be in the Pound Street Barracks. A group of mutineers had gathered at the Market Cross and when Hart and his men arrived there several volleys were exchanged. The mutineers were short of ammunition and it was later claimed that they fired pebbles, marbles and even tunic buttons at the regulars. The regulars for their part would appear to have tried not to inflict serious casualties on the mutineers, whether they had been ordered not to do so is not known. When one considers that the regulars were armed with minié rifles, extremely accurate rifles that had inflicted serious casualties on the Russians in the Crimea, the death-toll appears amazingly small. Despite the fact that this exchange of fire took place at short-range and in a confined area, only two militiamen were killed and six wounded. Eight regulars were also wounded. The rest of the mutineers then fled back to the Pound Street Barracks and after a brief fight, in which another nine militiamen were wounded, the majority of them threw down their weapons.[15]

Some militiamen had managed to get away and on the next day, 9 July 1856, men of the 21st Foot, under the command of Colonel Charles Crutchley, and assisted by John Stephen Dwyer JP, rooted the mutineers out of houses in Peter Street and then in the fields around the town. The pursuit of the last of the mutineers went on for the rest of the week, the 17th Lancers patrolling the area around the town and taking militiamen prisoner. There were also some Crimean veterans among the mutineers. The *Nenagh Guardian* described the capture of one such man who had served with the Land Transport Corps in the Crimea.

> Constable Aubrey, of the Nenagh Station, apprehended in a cornfield at Annebrook, Thomas Cawley, of the Tipperary Militia, who took a most prominent part in the encounter between that corps and the regulars, his wrist was

---

14 Ibid.   **15** Robinson, op. cit. See also *Nenagh Guardian* 9–10 July 1856.

broken by a gunshot wound received on that occasion. When arrested he wore a straw hat and outside coat. Cawley formerly served in the line, and was more recently employed in the Commissariat during the Crimean Campaign.[16]

Several civilians had also been wounded during the fighting and one Nenagh man, Peter Gibbons of Pound Street, had been killed when a bullet hit him in the head as he stood in his doorway watching the fighting. Gibbons was an army pensioner. Private Curly of the 41st Foot, who had been killed in Summerhill Barracks, was buried with full military honours in the Roman Catholic graveyard in Nenagh. He was only nineteen and had fought in the battles of Alma and Inkerman, had survived the first winter in the Crimea and had served during the siege of Sevastapol. At his graveside Lieutenant-Colonel Hart paid him tribute, describing him as a man who had 'done honour to himself and his country, in gallantly assisting to uphold the glory of the nation against its enemies in the Crimea'.

The official reaction to this mutiny was surprisingly lenient. On 15 July 1856 the men of the Tipperary Militia were paraded and informed that they would be disembodied and that each man would receive ten shillings and fourteen day's pay. There were some ninety courts-martial, however, for the ring-leaders of the mutiny. Private Burns, who was positively identified as the man who had killed Curley, was sentenced to death. His sentence was commuted to transportation for life and he was in fact released in 1876. Five other ring-leaders, Privates Gleeson, Devereux, Tumpane, Cawley and Skelton were sentenced to transportation for life but their sentences were again reduced to ten years which they served in Mountjoy Gaol. Three other men also served four years in gaol.[17]

The newspaper coverage of the mutiny in local newspapers, such as *The Reporter*, *Nenagh Guardian* and *Limerick Observer*, was quite sympathetic. This is perhaps surprising, when one considers the terror of the local inhabitants and the damage caused in the town. These newspapers pointed out that it was the shoddy way in which the militiamen had been treated which had caused the mutiny. Had the Government paid the bounty in full, the problem would never have arisen. The demand that the newly issued uniforms be returned to store only served to add insult to injury. Perhaps it is more surprising that *The Times* took a very similar line and placed the blame for this mutiny firmly at the Government's door. *The Times* also published large extracts form the Irish newspapers which followed this line.

On 1 September 1856 the militiamen assembled and were read an address from General Lord Seaton, the commander-in-chief in Ireland. They were then paid and sent home. Despite the fact that the other regiments of the militia of

16 *Nenagh Guardian*, 10 July 1856.   17 Robinson, op. cit. See also E.H. Sheehan, *Nenagh and its neighbourhood* (Ormond Historical Society, 1976), pp 91–7.

Ireland remained embodied due to the shortage of soldiers caused by the Indian Mutiny, the North Tipperary Militia was not re-embodied. The officers were later criticized by Lord Seaton for failing to deal with the mutiny promptly. In October 1856, Lieutenant-Colonel Cornwallis-Maude demanded a court-martial to clear the names of the regiment's officers but this was refused. One officer, Captain Josiah G. Hort, from Co. Kilkenny, resigned due to the criticism levelled at him by Major Frend and went to India.[18] It must be said, however, that the actions of the officers in emptying the magazine probably prevented the mutiny form becoming a much more serious event.

The Nenagh mutiny of July 1856 was a most interesting event as it outlines the potential disciplinary problems inherent in the regiments of the militia of Ireland. One can only assume that morale in all these regiments was low after this event. What is certain that the men of the North Tipperary Militia were very poorly treated. The penny-pinching attitude of the government was caused directly by the end of the Crimean war and a desire to save some money now that the militia was perceived to be no longer needed. The outbreak of the Indian mutiny ensured that the majority of militia regiments remained embodied in both England and Ireland.

The indiscipline of some of the regiments of the militia of Ireland remained a problem. In December 1857 and January 1858 the Royal Dublin City Militia was stationed in Lancashire and there were a number of disturbances at Bradford, Burnley and Ashton-under-Lyne where companies of the regiment were stationed. The worst disorder was at Burnley on New Year's Eve 1857 when groups of the Dublin City Militia got drunk and became violent 'striking with their belts all who came within reach'. The behaviour of the regimental picket, which turned out to deal with this problem, was as bad as that of the original offenders', if not worse! There were numerous violent assaults in the town and also much damage caused. The inquiry that followed decided to send the regiment to Aldershot.[19]

The history of the regiments of the militia of Ireland was indeed a chequered one during this period. There had been an initial difficulty in actually finding enough recruits and also NCOs to train them. Thereafter there had been numerous cases of indiscipline and insubordination in the regiments of the militia of Ireland. What makes such breaches of discipline more interesting is the fact that they often involved large groups of men from the militia regiments. When faced with a perceived injustice, Irish militiamen would appear to have engaged in collective protests, and even mutiny, rather than individually trying

---

18 Sheehan, *Nenagh and its neighbourhood,* p. 93. See also David Murphy, 'The Battle of the Breeches: the Nenagh mutiny, July 1856' in *Tipperary Historical Journal* (2001), 139–45. 19 Robert J. Williams, 'Royal Dublin City Militia riots in Lancashire' in *Irish Sword,* xiv, no. 55 (Winter 1980), pp 195–6.

to gain some form of redress. The Nenagh mutiny of July 1856 illustrates the potentially disastrous result of treating Irish militiamen badly. The whole event could have been avoided if the government had acted honourably towards these men when the Crimean war ended.

The Crimean banquet

Following the ratification of the Peace Treaty between the allies and Russia in April 1856, the regiments still stationed in the Crimea received orders to return to their home stations. As the regiments arrived in various towns and cities of the British Isles in the summer of 1856, they were greeted warmly by the local population. In London a dinner was held in honour of the men of the Guards Division and similar dinners were held in Edinburgh, Folkestone and Portsmouth. In August 1856 the lord lieutenant of Ireland, the earl of Carlisle, wrote to the lord mayor of Dublin, Fergus Farrell, suggesting that a reception be organised in Dublin for the troops then in Ireland who had served in the war. A meeting was held in the Mansion House on 19 August 1856, the lord mayor presiding, and it was decided that a banquet should be organised in honour of Irish Crimean veterans. A committee was subsequently elected and among the committee members were Isaac Butt MP, Captain John Esmonde MP, Patrick O'Brien MP, and the Hon. John P. Vereker. The Hon. John Butler and the high sheriff of Dublin, James West, were also present and the latter proposed that a public meeting be held and a call be made for public subscriptions.

Advertisements were placed in Irish newspapers and a public meeting was duly held on 21 August 1856. Included among those at this second, and public meeting, were the marquess of Kildare, the earl of Bandon, the earl of Bessborough, the earl of Howth, Lord Dunally and Lord Talbot de Malahide. There were also several aldermen of the city of Dublin, members of the legal profession, army officers and tradesmen. The high sheriff proposed a resolution:

> This meeting is of the opinion that the presence in Ireland of so many of the troops who have returned from the Crimea, demands from the Irish nation that we should accord, both to our gallant countrymen who have gloriously returned to their native land, and to their brave companions in honour and danger, a reception worthy of their merits.[20]

Field-Marshal Viscount Gough was elected as chairman of the committee and a national subscription fund was organised, the Bank of Ireland acting as treasurer. The lord mayor donated the first £50 and by 19 September 1856, £2,000 had been

20 *History of the great national banquet given to the victorious soldiers returned from the Crimean war and stationed in Irish garrisons by the people of Ireland in the city of Dublin,*

raised by public subscription, the banquet fund finally reaching £3,634 14s. 2d. Twenty-one meetings of the committee took place to organize the banquet and the date of 22 October 1856 was decided for the event.[21]

At the meeting of 21 August 1856 it had been decided that all 'who are wearers of Crimean Medals' should be entitled to invitations. Inquiries were addressed to Lord Seaton, commander-in-chief in Ireland, as to how many troops in Ireland were entitled to the Crimean Medal and were thus eligible to attend. A brief survey of those entitled to the Crimean Medal then stationed in Ireland indicated that there were about 10,000 troops in Ireland who had served in the Crimea. Admiral Chads, officer commanding the Royal Naval base at Queenstown, also wrote to inform the committee that he had a large number of seamen and marines under his command who had served in the Crimea. HMS *Hogue* alone had 85 seamen and 25 marines who were entitled to wear the Crimean Medal. It was then made clear to the committee that there were also men in the Irish Constabulary, Dublin Metropolitan Police and HM Coast Guard who were eligible to attend. It was ultimately decided that 1,500 men from the Dublin Garrison, 1,000 men from the Curragh and Newbridge and 500 men from other garrisons would be given invitations. The commanding officers of the various regiments were asked to choose a party of their men to represent their regiment at the banquet. Crimean veterans from the Royal Navy and the Irish Constabulary would also receive invitations. It was also decided that some of the in-pensioners from the Royal Hospital Kilmainham, both Crimean invalids and some described as 'Peninsular and Indian veterans', would be given invitations. One thousand members of the general public were allowed to apply for tickets at a price of 10s. for gentlemen and 5s. for ladies. These tickets were first sold to members of the committee who wised to bring guests and the remainder was sold to members of the public. It was estimated that around 5,000, including sixty 'gentlemen of the press' would eventually attend.[22]

The first priority of the committee was to find a venue where such a multitude could actually be accommodated. John Harris, proprietor of the Theatre Royal in Hawkins Street, offered his premises but it was decided that these were too small. The open area in front of the Leinster House, the Rotunda and the Upper Castle Yard were also considered. Henry Scovell, a customs official, suggested that the bonding warehouse at the Custom House Docks (Stack A) could provide a suitable venue for the banquet, if the warehouse was cleared of bonded goods. William P. Gardner, collector of customs for the port of Dublin, agreed and preparations began under the supervision of James H. Owen CE, Architect of the Board of Works.

October 22, 1856 (Dublin, 1858), p. 9.   **21** Ibid. See also *The Times*, 22 and 24 Oct. 1856, *Dublin Evening Mail*, 22 Oct. 1856.   **22** *Freeman's Journal*, 16 Oct. 1856.

Stack A, a warehouse of some 70,000 square feet, is a most interesting and historic building and is classed as a listed building. It was designed by the Scottish engineer, John Rennie, and it was built between 1818 and 1821. Stack A first appears on a Dublin map in 1821 but is believed that construction had been completed in 1820.[23] In 1821, when George's Dock was officially opened, Stack A had been used as the venue for a celebratory breakfast and in 1856 it was used again as the venue for the Crimean banquet. The metal pillars that divided the interior of the warehouse into aisles were painted in brilliant colours; red, cobalt blue and yellow. The walls were painted white. Numerous signalling and national flags, supplied by the Royal Navy at Queenstown and the Royal Western Yacht Club, were hung around the walls. The Union Flag and the flags of France, Sardinia and Turkey were given prominence in the decorations and dedications were painted on the walls to Lord Raglan, Maréchal St. Arnaud, Maréchal Pélissier, Lord Codrington and Florence Nightingale. The names of the significant battles, Alma, Balaclava, Inkerman, were also painted on the walls. Around the pillars in the warehouse stands of muskets, swords and cutlasses were stacked and two six-pounder cannons were placed on a platform. There were also two triumphal arches built beside the top table, surmounted by busts of Queen Victoria and Prince Albert and Louis Napoleon and the Empress Eugénie. A gallery was built for the members of the public who had bought tickets.[24]

Several tradesmen supplied goods for the banquet free of charge. Henry Brennan, wine-merchant, offered to provide one pint of port or sherry-wine for each soldier and only asked that the duty on this wine be paid. Messers Martin & Sons supplied all the timber for tables and platforms while Messers Todd Burns & Co. of Mary Street supplied all the linen required. Messers Spadaccini & Murphy won the contract to carry out the catering while Joseph Farley, of 8 South Great George's Street, and Mrs Ledwidge, of 15 William Street, won the contracts to supply the meat and fowl. The Lord Lieutenant offered the use of his servants to work as waiters on the day of the banquet. The rail companies were asked to transport the troops and sailors from their various barracks free of charge and agreed to do so. The district inspectors of the Irish Constabulary and the commissioners of Dublin Metropolitan Police were also asked to help in any way that they could.[25]

Due to the efforts of the committee and the co-operation of the Board of Works, the rail companies and the constabulary all was ready for the banquet by the morning of 22 October 1856. The banquet was due to start at 1 p.m. and was to be presided over by the lord mayor. The lord lieutenant was the guest of

23 Derval O'Carroll and Sean Fitzpatrick (eds), *Hoggers, lords and railwaymen. A history of the Custom House Docks, Dublin* (Dublin, 1996), pp 73–9. **24** *History of the great national banquet*, p. 27. **25** Ibid. pp 20–2.

honour and the French consul also attended while one member of the committee sat at each table with the soldiers and guests.

Due to the large number of soldiers in Ireland who had served in the Crimea, the officers of each regiment had to nominate men to go to the banquet. Most of the regiments sent men who had seen service in the Crimea. The 8th Royal Irish Hussars, 13th Light Dragoons and the 17th Lancers sent a half troop each, all three regiments had taken part in the charge of the Light Brigade. The Scots Greys and the 1st Royal Dragoons also sent a half-troop each, both regiments had been in the charge of the Heavy Brigade. The list of regiments represented at the banquet is too long to include here but it included the 18th Foot (Royal Irish), the 88th Foot (Connaught Rangers), the 14th Foot, the 28th Foot, the 63rd Foot and the 95th Foot. The men came not only from the Dublin barracks and the Curragh camp but also from the barracks at Templemore, Birr, Cahir, Limerick, Fermoy, Kilkenny, Dundalk and Belfast. Some regiments sent quite large parties to the banquet. The 4th Foot sent 333 men while the 46th Foot, then with its depot at Enniskillen, sent one officer and nineteen men. There were also 115 men from the Royal Artillery, who had come from the artillery barracks in Dublin, Ballincollig and Charleville. The bands of the 2nd and 3rd Dragoon Guards and the Rifle Brigade were positioned in the hall to provide the music. The final list of those who attended the banquet included 3,000 NCOs and privates, 50 petty officers, seamen and marines, 50 Royal Hospital, Kilmainham pensioners (Crimean), 20 Royal Hospital, Kilmainham pensioners (Peninsular and Sikh Wars), 50 Irish Constabulary, 25 HM Coast Guard, 5 Dublin Metropolitan Police and one man from the Land Transport Corps.[26]

The men began arriving in Dublin early on the morning of 22 October 1856, much to the excitement of the local population:

> From early in the morning the neighbourhood of Sackville Street, the entire length of the quays from Kingsbridge terminus to the Custom House and the various streets leading towards the scene of the coming banquet, were thronged with groups of people, awaiting the first arrival of the military guests.[27]

As the troops marched down the quays it was noted that certain things caught their attention, especially the officers and men who wore foreign decorations:

> Wherever the cross of the Legion of Honour was seen appended to the uniform of a British officer or soldier, the wearer was enthusiastically cheered.[28]

The mass of people who lined the quays and streets were not insensitive to the signs of suffering and hardship that were obvious on the faces of some of those

---

26 Ibid. p. 41. See also *Irish Sword*, iv, no. 14 (Summer 1959), pp 73–4.   27 *History of the great national banquet*, p. 40.   28 Ibid. p. 39.

who paraded past. Others showed the signs of serious wounds that they had received in the Crimea and these were also noticed:

> But many an ejaculation of pity escaped from the crowd, as some splendid young fellows, officers of the 88th and the 33rd, were seen with the right sleeve of the gorgeous uniform coat hanging empty from their breasts. Nothing could equal the warm and enthusiastic feeling of admiration manifested by all present towards these noble fellows.[29]

All morning the troops arrived and marched down to the area of the Bonded Warehouse where they assembled in the yard outside before going in to take their seats. The mass of assembled men, all wearing the Crimean Medal, made an impressive sight:

> The animation of the men, the long and endless lines of red coats, the ladies in the gallery, the flags, and decorations, all combined to form a gorgeous *coup d'eoil*.[30]

As further groups of men arrived in the hall, they were cheered in by those already seated. It was noted that the Peninsular and India veterans from the Royal Hospital, Kilmainham were 'judiciously introduced' by members of the committee: 'Their appearance was cordially hailed by their more numerous and younger competitors in the paths of glory'.[31]

Despite the mass of men who had to arrive and be seated in the hall, all was ready to proceed at 1 p.m. but the beginning of the banquet was delayed as the guest of honour, the Lord Lieutenant, did not arrive until 1.15 p.m. The arrival of the food was an event in itself. Spadaccini & Murphy kept the potatoes at their premises until the banquet was about to begin, in an effort to keep them hot.[32] Three tons of hot potatoes were then sent in four vans which pulled up to the hall 'steaming like locomotives'. The drivers of these vans were 'literally enveloped in clouds of steam', much to the delight of the small children who were looking on. A vast amount of food and drink was consumed which included 250 hams, 230 legs of mutton, 500 meat pies, 100 venison pasties, 100 rice puddings, 260 plum puddings, 200 turkeys, 200 geese, 250 joints of beef, 100 capons and chickens and 2,000 two-pound loaves. Each soldier was given a quart of porter and a pint of port or sherry.[33]

The bands played throughout the dinner and it would appear to have been a lively event.

29 Ibid. p. 38.   **30** Ibid. p. 45.   **31** Ibid. p. 26.   **32** Carlo Spadaccini was the proprietor of Anderson's Royal Arcade Hotel, at 32–33 College Green, and it would appear that the food for the banquet was prepared in the hotel's kitchens.   **33** *Freeman's Journal*, 23 Oct. 1856.

During the dinner the proceedings were agreeably and characteristically interrupted by the Irish soldiers rising as if with one impulse when the Irish airs 'Patrick's Day' and 'Savoureen Deelish' were struck up, and cheering enthusiastically, others kept the time to the refrain with the knives and forks.[34]

There then followed speeches and toasts, each toast being announced by four trumpeters. The toasts included the queen, the lord lieutenant, the emperor of the French and 'our French allies'. Isaac Butt proposed the 'Heroes of the Crimea' while Lord Talbot de Malahide 'the Fallen', which was drunk in silence. A toast was also drunk to the 'illustrious ladies who nobly ministered to the sick and wounded in the Crimea'. Florence Nightingale and the Irish Sisters of Mercy were mentioned.[35] The lord lieutenant's speech was quite emotional and obviously meant to set the tone for the banquet:

We are here on Irish ground and Ireland has a right to give a welcome to heroes, because many and many she has sent forward to every grade of your ranks (loud cheering, which continued for several minutes). But Irish hospitality is not stinted to her own children, as it was not asked, when the cheer rose loudest in your charge, whether it had most of the English, or Scotch or Irish accent, as it was not asked, when the red blood from the field or from the trench, whether the warm tide gushed from English, or Scotch, or Irish veins (cheers).[36]

The banquet ended at 4.15 p.m. when the soldiers mustered again in the Custom House Yard and began to march to their Dublin barracks or to the various railway stations. Many had taken some piece of the laurel or paper decorations in the hall as a memento. All would appear to have been in high spirits, perhaps due to the amount of drink consumed. Masses of people had remained in the vicinity to see them off and the area became quite congested.

As the troops passed along the quays, the crowds began to pour in from every side, and at one time Carlisle Bridge was entirely blocked up, and continued so for nearly half an hour. Notwithstanding the crushing and squeezing, and the inconvenience that persons on business had to endure, the utmost goodhumour prevailed, and during the day or evening we could not hear of the slightest indication of disorder or disturbance.[37]

On Monday 27 October 1856 there was a further public meeting to thank all those who had helped organize the banquet. It was decided that the 'substantial fragments' left over from the banquet should be divided among the workhouses of Dublin.[38] The total cost of the banquet came to just over £2,600, the most expensive item on the list of expenses being the bill for the caterers, Spadaccini

34 *History of the great national banquet*, p. 45.   35 *Dublin Evening Mail*, 22 Oct. 1856.
36 *History of the great national banquet*, p. 47.   37 *Freeman's Journal*, 23 Oct. 1856.
38 *Dublin Evening Mail*, 24 Oct. 1856.

& Murphy. There was, therefore, just over £1,000 pounds remaining from the funds collected by public subscription for the banquet. The members of the committee called for suggestions as to how this money could be best used and further meetings were held. Ultimately the committee had to choose from three suggestions. Firstly it was suggested that the money could be used to apprentice 100 Crimean orphans to various trades. Secondly, it was suggested that the money be used to build a Crimean memorial in Dublin. It was the third suggestion that was agreed on, however. This was that the £1,000 should be invested in shares whose annual interest should be awarded to the students of the Royal Hibernian Military School who had displayed the most effort during the year. The final act of the committee was to organize for the publication of a history of the event. This was finally published in 1858, delayed due to the committee being preoccupied in organising the fund for the Royal Hibernian Military School.[39] The Royal Hibernian Military School was still awarding 'Crimean banquet fund prizes' until 1924 when the school closed and the students transferred to the Duke of York's Royal Military School in Dover.[40]

Stack A has survived the extensive developments in the Custom House Dock area so far. Until the 1980s dockworkers and locals still referred to it as the 'Banquet Hall' due to the various entertainments that had taken place there. As late as the 1950s the decorations painted on the walls and pillars were still visible. During a recent tour of the warehouse, I found that all that remains of the banquet decorations is the bright coloured paint on the metal support pillars, some traces of blue and red paint. The neighbouring Stack C was demolished in 1990 during the construction of the Irish Financial Services Centre but Stack A, a fine example of early nineteenth-century industrial architecture, was preserved.[41]

The Crimean Banquet of October 1856 was obviously one of the major social events of that year. It is significant that the event was supported by all sections of Dublin and Irish society. The generosity of the railway companies, the tradesmen and the general public who subscribed to the banquet fund, indicates once again that the Irish public was profoundly interested in the war. The scenes that met the troops as they marched through Dublin to the banquet would also indicate that the Irish public was proud of their fellow-countrymen who had served in the war.

---

39 *History of the great national banquet*, p. 79.   **40** G.H. Reilly, *History of the Royal Hibernian Military School, Dublin* (Genealogical Society of Ireland, 2001), p. 164.   **41** There have been various proposals as to how Stack A could be used. In 1986 a proposal from the Department of the Taoiseach suggested that it be used as a gallery of contemporary art, a folk museum and a museum of science and technology. In 1987, Taoiseach Charles J. Haughey suggested that the National Museum should move its collection of silver and glass to Stack A. There was also some suggestion that it could be used to house a national transport museum and that the National Print Museum at Beggars Bush could move there. It was used as a location during the filming of Neil Jordan's *Michael Collins*. In March 1995, Professor Dervilla Donnelly, chairperson of the Dublin

Irish Crimean veterans

What became of the thousands of Irish Crimean war veterans who returned to England and Ireland after the war? The later careers of some of those who served in the war have been outlined in previous chapters. Also, it is impossible in the space of this study to give details of the lives of a large number of Crimean veterans. It is possible, however, to show that the these men's lives followed a number of broad patterns.

It was not uncommon for Irish Crimean veterans to emigrate and then serve in foreign armies. A large number of Crimean veterans served during the American Civil war. These men were often prominent in the volunteer regiments raised by the Union army in the early months of the war. In June 1861 the adjutant of the New York Irish Brigade was Lieutenant James F. Cosgrove who had served with the 62nd Foot during the Crimean war and had been present at the siege of Sevastapol.[42] Cosgrove wore the Crimean Medal with Sevastapol clasp, on his Union Army tunic, as many veterans of the war did in the hope that it would boost the morale of their recruits. He served with the Union Army until June 1865.

Another Irish Crimean veteran who served in the American Civil war was Henry James Nowlan. Nowlan was born in Corfu but his parents were from Co. Carlow and he returned to Ireland as a child. He had served in the Crimea with the 41st Foot and had also been at the siege of Sevastapol. In 1861 he resigned his commission and went to America, joining a cavalry regiment in the Union Army at the outbreak of the Civil War. He fought in several battles, including Gettysburg, was promoted to major and remained in the army after the war. Nowlan was reduced in rank, due to post-war reductions in the size of the army, and transferred as a lieutenant to the newly raised 7th US Cavalry, where he became a close friend of Captain (Brevet Colonel) Myles Walter Keogh, a fellow Carlowman. Nowlan subsequently fought in the Sioux war of 1866–8. During the Sioux War of 1876 he was posted as acting quartermaster to Brigadier-General Terry's Dakota Column and, as a result of this posting, was not at the Little Big Horn on 25 June 1876 when Custer and his command were wiped out. He was, however, with the troops who discovered the remains of Custer and his men and also found the body of his friend, Myles Walter Keogh. He later accompanied Keogh's remains to Auburn, New York, where they were re-interred.[43] It is

Docklands Development Authority stated that there were 'numerous proposals' for Stack A. Stack A is currently being managed by Hardwicke Properties Ltd and it would seem that the latest proposal is to develop Stack A and transform it into a complex incorporating shops, bars, restaurants and a night-club. O'Carroll and Fitzpatrick, *Hoggers, lords and railwaymen*, pp 79–81.
42 Maurice Hennessy, *The Wild Geese. The Irish soldier in exile* (London, 1973), p. 179. The New York Irish Brigade consisted of the 63rd, 69th and 88th New York Volunteers.   **43** G.A. Hayes-

interesting that this Irish officer, who began his career in the British army, later
fought against Sioux Indians on the plains of Montana. Yet it was not uncommon for Irish Crimean veterans to emigrate. As previously stated, Chartres
Brew who had served with the Irish Constabulary contingent in the Crimea,
went to British Columbia while Private James Bourke of the 18th (Royal Irish)
Foot emigrated to Australia.

Many Irish Crimean veterans later served in the Irish Constabulary, the Dublin
Metropolitan Police and police forces abroad. Lieutenant (later Lieutenant-
Colonel) John Augustus Conolly, born in Ballyshannon, Co. Donegal, won the
Victoria Cross for his actions on 26 October 1854. Serving with the 49th Foot,
he was prominent in the repulse of the Russian attack of that day and later
served in the Coldstream Guards. In 1877 he was appointed as an assistant
commissioner of the Dublin Metropolitan Police, retiring from this office in
1883. He died in December 1888.[44] Lieutenant (later Lieutenant-Colonel) Thomas
Esmonde also won the Victoria Cross during the war while serving with the 18th
(Royal Irish) Foot. He was awarded his VC for his bravery during the assaults
on Sevastapol in June 1855. Esmonde, who was from Pembrokestown, Co.
Waterford, joined the officer corps of the Irish Constabulary in November 1859
as an assistant inspector general. Promoted to the rank of deputy inspector
general in May 1865, he served in Belfast until his retirement in July 1867 and
died January 1873.[45] Sergeant John Mulcahy, a survivor of the charge of the
Light Brigade who had served with the 13th Light Dragoons, joined the Irish
Constabulary in January 1858. Appointed as a 1st class head constable in July
1858, he was promoted to 3rd class sub-inspector and riding master at the
Constabulary Depot in June 1866. Mulcahy was the first riding master of the
Royal Irish Constabulary and died in Dublin in 1872.[46] He is buried in Glasnevin
Cemetery. Private Samuel Wilson, an Ulsterman and another survivor of the
charge of the Light Brigade, emigrated to New Zealand on being discharged from
the 8th Royal Irish Hussars. He joined the Otago Mounted Police and was
promoted to sergeant. He died in Christchurch, New Zealand, in August 1884.[47]
Private John Bevin, from Bandon, Co. Cork, went to Australia on being
discharged from the 8th Royal Irish Hussars. He went to New Zealand in 1861
and also joined the Otago Mounted Police. It must be safe to assume that both
Wilson and Bevin knew each other and perhaps emigrated together. Bevin
finished his career as a sergeant-major and was presented with an engraved

McCoy, *Captain Myles Walter Keogh, United States Army, 1840–76* (Dublin, 1965).   **44** Garda
Siochana Archives, Dublin Castle, 'Chief and assistant commissioners of the DMP since 1836'.
See also *Ireland's VCs*.   **45** *Proceedings of the Royal Ulster Constabulary historical society*
(Winter 1998), p. 7. See also Ireland's VC's.   **46** Jim Herlihy, *The Royal Irish Constabulary. A
short history and genealogical guide* (Dublin, 1997), p. 55.   **47** W.M. Lummis and K.G. Wynn,
Honour the Light Brigade (London, 1973), p. 122.

silver cup on the twenty-eighth anniversary of the charge of the Light Brigade. He died in Dunedin in May 1892.[48]

Many Irish Crimean veterans finished their days as in-pensioners in the Royal Hospitals at Kilmainham and Chelsea. Private Robert Moneypenny, who had served with the 8th Royal Irish Hussars in the Crimea, had won the DCM and survived the charge of the Light Brigade, became an in-pensioner of the Royal Hospital, Kilmainham in the 1870s. Moneypenny was something of a character and was also a tough man, perhaps brutalized by the war. He served a period in Mountjoy Gaol for a serious assault on his wife. At his trial he excused his behaviour by saying that she had 'nagged' him. Nevertheless, he was a popular figure in the Kilmainham area and was often seen out walking his bulldog. When he died in 1906, he was buried with full honours in the hospital graveyard.[49] Another Light Brigade veteran who was a in-pensioner in Kilmainham was Private Christopher E. Hanlon of the 13th Light Dragoons. During the charge he had received a lance wound to the neck and was captured by the Russians. He died in the Royal Hospital, Kilmainham on 15 February 1890 at the age of sixty-three. Some Crimean veterans were still living in the Royal Hospital, Kilmainham at a surprisingly late date. As late as 1921 there were still Crimean veterans at the Royal Hospital, Kilmainham, John McGrath of the 18th (Royal Irish) Regiment and Anthony McCormack of the Welsh Regiment.[50]

Other veterans experienced difficulties in their later lives due to the wounds they suffered in the Crimea. Private Thomas Keefe, of the 20th Foot, lost his right arm in the Crimea and also suffered a wound to his shoulder. He was discharged in 1855 and was living in Cork on a pension of 1s.2d. per day.[51] Hundreds of Irish soldiers had suffered similar wounds. During an inspection of Crimean invalids, Queen Victoria noticed a young gunner who had lost both arms. This was Gunner Davis, an Irishman. The Queen enquired as to whether he had anyone to look after him to which he replied, 'Haven't I the best friend in the country when I have yourself'. The Queen ordered that Davis be given a pair of false arms and a pension of 2s. a day.[52] This rather pathetic story illustrates the point that there were probably hundreds of Irish Crimean veterans who lived out their lives suffering from the effects of dreadful wounds. While many of these men were cared for in military hospitals, there must have been hundreds more who returned home to be cared for by their families. There were probably examples of such invalids living in every town and village in Ireland during the late nineteenth century.

There were also thousands more Irish Crimean veterans who left the army at the end of their service and did not receive any pension whatsoever. Pensions

48 Ibid. p. 88.   **49** Ibid. p. 110.   **50** Major E.S.E. Childers and R. Stewart, *The story of the Royal Hospital, Kilmainham* (London, 1923), pp 68–9.   **51** *Cork Examiner*, 19 Sept. 1855. **52** *Kilmarnock Journal*, 6 Sept. 1855.

were only awarded at that time to soldiers who had been wounded or had completed twenty-one years service. If these men were in good health and of good character they had some chance of finding some form of employment. Richard Lucas, for example, of St James Parish in Dublin, became a commissionaire at the Army and Navy Club in London on being discharged from the 4th Light Dragoons in 1859. On the other hand there were many cases of Irish veterans who, for various reasons, fell on hard times but were not eligible for an army pension. Many of these men depended on charity to survive and received support from the Patriotic Fund or other veteran's help groups. In 1897 the publisher Thomas Harrison Roberts organized a relief fund for survivors of the charge of the Light Brigade. In May 1897 he had published an announcement inviting surviving 'Chargers' to come and watch the Queen's Jubilee procession from the windows of his offices in Fleet Street. Disgusted at the conditions that some of these men were living in, he issued an appeal to his readers for funds and also made sizeable donations himself. The T.H. Roberts Fund provided some financial support for charge veterans and also paid the funeral expenses of many men. In September 1920, when the last charge veteran who was receiving support from the fund died, it was wound up having paid out many thousands of pounds.[53]

Several of those who received support from this fund were Irish. In August 1897 Roberts found out that Private John Smith, a Dublinman, had fallen on hard times and was in Edmonton Workhouse. Smith, who had served with the 17th Lancers, was also known as 'Blood Smith' or 'Fighting Smith' due to his fighting spirit. Roberts took Smith out of the workhouse and gave him employment as a caretaker in his Fleet Street offices and also arranged for him to receive payments from the relief fund. Despite Roberts' efforts Smith ended his days in St Pancras Workhouse, perhaps due to heavy drinking. He died in the workhouse in January 1899 and was buried in the Roman Catholic portion of the St Pancras Cemetery, East Finchley. The T.H. Roberts Fund paid his burial expenses.[54] Private Patrick Doolan, who had served with the 8th Royal Irish Hussars, also received support from the T.H. Roberts Fund. A native of Nenagh, Co. Tipperary, he had been wounded in the charge and was rescued by Major De Salis who found him lying wounded while returning from the Russian batteries. Doolan died in Dublin in August 1907. His Crimean Medal, with Alma, Balaclava and Sevastopol clasps, was sold by Sotheby's in April 1996, realizing £5,290.[55] It is ironic indeed that the medal of a man who died in poverty should realize what was then a record price for a 'Charger's' medal.

53 Lummis and Wynn, *Honour the Light Brigade*, pp 313–14. T.H. Roberts best known publication was *Illustrated Bits*. Between July 1897 and December 1911, the T.H. Roberts Fund paid over £7,800 to fifty-nine pensioners at a rate of seven to 15s. a week. Several funerals were also paid for.   54 Ibid. p. 296.   55 *Irish Times*, 12 Apr. 1996.

The number of Irish veterans who ended their lives as charity cases is far too numerous to mention but is a sad fact that many men, who had been lauded for their bravery in the war, ended their lives living in dire poverty.

Efforts were also made to help the hundreds of Irish Crimean war widows and orphans. Archbishop Cullen organized a diocesan collection in an effort to help them and also encouraged Irish priests working abroad to collect donations for this fund. A Carmelite priest, J.M. Percival, who was working in Sydney, collected over £470 and sent this money to Dublin as 'an act of Charity towards relieving the widows and orphans of the soldiers and sailors who fell during the present war'.[56] In a letter to Archbishop Cullen in January 1856, Canon Searle in London mentioned the money collected in Sydney and also money that had been collected in Venezuela.[57] In February 1856, Cullen received a letter from Fr Mauricastro, writing on the behalf of Archbishop Sant of Malta, about an Irish Crimean widow, Mary Ann McDonald (*née* Kearney). This woman's husband had been killed in the war and in his letter Mauricastro stated that she had been saved by some good people from 'going astray'. Mauricastro asked Cullen to contact her family who were living in St James Parish in Dublin.[58] The Society of St Vincent de Paul also made a special effort to help Crimean widows and orphans and St Vincent's School in Glasnevin was originally built to provide a school for Crimean orphans. In 1856 the Seaton Needlework Fund was founded in Dublin, under the patronage of General Lord Seaton. This fund was also organized to assist Irish Crimean war widows and raised funds by establishing a needlework co-operative, the widows producing garments that were later sold to pay for their support.[59]

Many Irish veterans suffered physical and financial hardships, some ending their days dependent on charity or living in the workhouse. Some, however, still suffered due to their traumatic experiences in the war. It was not uncommon for Crimean veterans to go insane and several Irish veterans were later confined in mental asylums. An obvious example of an Irish veteran who suffered mental torments after the war was Private Dennis Connor of the 4th Light Dragoons. A survivor of the charge of the Light Brigade, he was discharged on a pension in August 1866 and was admitted as an in-pensioner of the Royal Hospital, Chelsea, in February 1875. The other in-pensioners later remarked that he was somewhat withdrawn and seemed to live in a world of quiet reflection. In October 1875 he attended the first Balaclava banquet and was interviewed by the correspondent of the *Illustrated London News*. (An excerpt from this interview is included in Chapter 2.) By January 1876 he had ceased to talk at all and seems to have been suffered from, what was termed in World War I, as

56 Cullen Papers, 332/5/II, 24 Jan. 1855. 57 Ibid. 4 Jan. 1856. 58 Ibid. 6 Feb. 1856.
59 PRONI, Belfast, Ms: T164–7, 'Documents relating to the foundation of the Seaton Needlework Fund'.

'muteism'. Connor was handed over to the parish authorities and became a mental patient at St Luke's, Chelsea, where he eventually died. It is not unreasonable to assume that he was suffering from post-traumatic stress disorder and that, due to recounting his Crimean experiences for the *Illustrated London News* correspondent, that his mind became totally unhinged.[60]

There were several cases of suicide among Crimean war veterans and there were examples of Irish veterans taking their own lives. John Sullivan from Bantry, Co. Cork, and who had been awarded the Victoria Cross for his bravery with the Naval Brigade in the Crimea, came to a particularly tragic end (see Chapter 3). Sullivan spent thirty-seven years in the Royal Navy, the last ten spent as boatswain of Portsmouth Dockyard. In April 1884 he retired as a chief boatswain's mate with a pension of £150 a year and returned to Ireland where he bought a small farm near Kinsale, Co. Cork. In early June 1884 he began to complain of headaches but the local doctor could find no cause and could offer no cure. On 28 June 1884 he suffered another headache and went out into the garden of his house. He was found there later in the day having cut his own throat with a sailor's knife. This was a particularly tragic case. Sullivan was well known and liked while in the Royal Navy and also in his native Cork.[61]

The case of Private John Byrne of the 68th Foot was equally tragic. Byrne, from Castlecomer, Co. Kilkenny, had also been awarded the Victoria Cross for his bravery at the battle of Inkerman. He later served in the Maori War of 1860–6 and as a sergeant of the Queen's Co. Militia in 1869. He re-joined the 68th Foot in October 1869 and was finally discharged, as a sergeant, in May 1872. In the same year he joined the North Durham Militia as a colour-sergeant but was discharged 'for insubordination and highly improper conduct'. His military career had come to an inglorious end. Apart from his VC he had been awarded a DCM, the Crimean Medal with all four clasps, the Turkish Crimean Medal, the New Zealand Medal and three good conduct badges. Nothing is known of what he did for the next number of years but, in 1878, he obtained employment in Bristol as a labourer with the Ordnance Survey. On 10 July 1879 he was working for the Ordnance Survey at Caerleon, Monmouthshire, when a fellow worker, John Watts, insulted his Victoria Cross.[62] Byrne drew a revolver from under his jacket and fired at Watts but missed. A constable (rather bravely) later called to Byrne's lodgings at 7 Crown Street, Maindee, to investigate the shooting. When the constable entered Byrne's room he again drew the revolver but this time he put the barrel in his mouth and fired. He died instantly. The coroner's inquest returned a verdict of suicide 'whilst of unsound mind'.

---

60 Lummis and Wynn, *Honour the Light Brigade*, p. 40.   61 John Winton, *The Victoria Cross at sea* (London, 1978), pp 35–6.   62 It is believed that Watts claimed that Byrne's commanding officer had been allocated a certain number of VCs to award and that Byrne had won his by

Byrne is buried in St Woolo's Cemetery, Newport, in an unmarked grave.[63] It cannot be coincidental that so many Irish Crimean veterans later suffered from mental illnesses and that some even took their own lives.

Other Crimean veterans became involved in criminal activities and one of the most infamous murders of the late nineteenth century was carried out by an Irish veteran, Philip Henry Eustace Cross. Cross was born in Cork and educated at Trinity College, Dublin, joining the army as an assistant surgeon in April 1849. He served in the Crimean war, retiring from the army as a surgeon-major in April 1875 and settled at Shandy Hall, near Coachford in Co. Cork. On 2 June 1887 his wife, Mary Laura Cross (*née* Marriott) died at the family home. Shortly after his wife's death, Cross married his children's governess, a Miss Skinner. The police were naturally suspicious and, following an investigation, he was charged with his first wife's murder. He was tried in Cork in December 1887 and at the trial it was revealed that he had been having an affair with Miss Skinner for some time. Evidence was also put before the court which proved that he had bought arsenic in a Cork chemist's shop in September 1886. The prosecution maintained that he had slowly poisoned his wife over a period of several months. Found guilty, he was hanged at Cork gaol on 10 January 1888.[64]

Many Irish veterans were also the victims of serious crime. Lieutenant-Colonel Hugh Denis Crofton, of the Crofton family of Mohill, Co. Leitrim, was born in Dublin in January 1814. Entering the army, he served in the Crimea, commanding the 20th Foot at the battle of the Alma and one wing of the army at the battle of Inkerman. In September 1861, he was serving at Fulwood Barracks, Preston, and ordered that a Private Patrick McCafferay of the 32nd Foot be punished for neglect of duty. On 14 September McCafferay shot Crofton and another officer in retaliation and both officers died, Crofton dying of his wound on 15 September. Tried at Liverpool assizes in December 1861, McCafferay was hanged at Kirkdale prison on 12 January 1862.[65] While these two cases were quite sensational, it was not uncommon for Irish Crimean veterans to be involved in serious crimes, either as perpetrators or as victims.

The vast majority of Irish Crimean veterans no doubt returned to their previous lives, taking up their trades again or perhaps working in agriculture. Those of the officer class were usually from the upper classes and returned from the Crimea and took up their 'place' again in society. Many men chose to remain in the army and went on to serve in further campaigns while others emigrated or joined various police forces. It is also true to state, however, that

drawing lots. **63** W. A. Williams, *The VC's of Wales and the Welsh Regiments* (Clwyd, 1984), pp 19–20. Byrne's regiment, the 68th Foot, the Durham Light Infantry, had been raised as the 23rd Royal Welch Fusiliers in 1756. The regiment was redesignated the 68th Foot in 1758. **64** Boase. See also the *Irish Times* for December 1887 and January 1888. **65** Boase supplement. See also Burke, *Peerage* (1912), 527.

a disturbingly large number of Irish Crimean veterans suffered due to financial hardship and, in some cases, continued to re-live the horrors of the war in their minds.

Crimean guns and monuments in Ireland

We are surrounded with physical reminders of the Crimean war in Ireland. There are people who go about their everyday business in the towns and cities of Ireland, unaware that they are passing relics of the war, in the shape of trophy guns, memorials and gravestones. The most obvious relics of the war are the trophy guns which are placed in prominent positions around Ireland. After the fall of Sevastapol in September 1855, the allies formed a commission to decide what to do with the Russian cannons and mortars that had been captured in the city. It was decided that these cannons and mortars be classed as 'trophy' guns and they were divided up among the allied armies. This was a rather cynical manoeuvre as the Russians had only 172 cannons in batteries defending Sevastapol when the siege began. By September 1855, the Russians had 1,497 cannons in batteries around the city. The allies had captured, however, a total of 3,839 guns when the city fell. As Sevastapol was the main base for the Russian Black Sea Fleet, the allies found over 2,000 cannons in naval storerooms and workshops. Most of these were mounted on naval gun carriages and could not have been used to defend the town. Also many others were so old, having been cast in the 1790s, that they could no longer have been used with any degree of safety. The Russian gun on the Promenade at Cobh was cast in 1794 and is a typical example of one of those guns which were no longer serviceable but were still classed as 'trophy' guns.

Due to the public discontent over the way the war had been mismanaged it was decided to give the impression that all these guns had been in batteries defending the city, in the hope that the public would believe that this was why the siege had been so prolonged. 964 of these guns were assigned to Britain in accordance with Item 1 of the Paris Declaration of 1856. During the summer of 1856 trophy guns were presented to the town councils and city corporations around the British Isles. Some were shipped to the colonies. Canada received twenty while four were sent to Australia.[66]

Over twenty trophy guns were presented to town councils and city corporations in Ireland (see Appendix E). N. St John Hennessy of the Irish Military History Society, has carried out comprehensive research on these guns.[67] It is

---

66 Norman Jones, 'Russian guns: Research at the PRO' in *The War Correspondent*, xvi, no. 3 (October 1998), pp 36–40.   67 St John Hennessy's findings were published in an article in *Irish*

not my intention to repeat St John Hennessy's work in this book but there are some points regarding these guns that should be clarified.

Firstly the two 36-pounder cannons and the two 13-inch mortars that he lists as being in Collins Barracks in Dublin have been moved since 1995 to Cathal Brugha Barracks in Rathmines. All the Crimean guns in Dublin, four 36-pounders and two 13-inch mortars, are now in Cathal Brugha Barracks and are maintained by the Irish Army. This move occurred due to the National Museum of Ireland taking over Collins Barracks. This was actually the second move for the guns because, when they were first presented to the city of Dublin in 1857, they were placed in the small public park on the Esplanade in front of the Royal Barracks, now Collins Barracks. In fact the four cannons and two mortars presented to Dublin Corporation were all originally at this site. This was in keeping with the policy of placing these guns in prominent positions. It is interesting that when this park was being renovated in the 1970s a letter appeared in the *Irish Times* suggesting that the guns also be renovated. Dublin Corporation rather tartly announced that the guns were the property of the Irish Army and not their responsibility. An Irish Army spokesman immediately refuted this claim and a brief search in the Dublin City Archives revealed that these guns had indeed been presented to the city of Dublin.

At a meeting of the Dublin Municipal Council on 20 July 1857 the lord mayor, Fergus Ferrall:

> Called the attention of the Council to the fact that portions of the Trophies taken from the Russians in the recent War had, upon the application of the Municipal Authorities of several Cities and Towns in the United Kingdom, been granted to be deposited in such Cities and Towns, and His Lordship sought the instruction of the Council whether application should be made for any portion of the Trophies for this city.[68]

The members of the municipal council agreed with this proposal and a request for some of the trophy guns was duly sent to the lord lieutenant. In August 1857, Colonel Thomas Larcom acknowledged receipt of this request and wrote that the secretary of state for war, Lord Panmure, had 'expressed his readiness to supply the trophies applied for'. In a further letter of 11 August 1857, Larcom notified the lord mayor of the trophies that would be presented to the city.

> I am directed by the Lord Lieutenant to acquaint you that a communication has been received from Lord Panmure stating that His Lordship has much pleasure in presenting the City of Dublin four Russian iron guns with carriages, two

---

Sword in 1995 and he gives comprehensive information regarding the calibres, weights and places of manufacture of these guns. N. St John Hennessy, 'Crimean-war guns in Ireland' in *Irish Sword*, xix, no. 78 (Winter 1995), pp 333–344. **68** Dublin City Archives: C2/A1/19. 'Minutes of the Municipal Council of Dublin City, 18 February 1856 to 3 December 1857', p. 370.

mortars, and a supply of shot and shell to be piled near them, as a trophy of the late War, trusting that His Excellency will cause this memorial to be placed in an appropriate and conspicuous situation and relying for its careful preservation upon the public spirit of the Corporation and the Inhabitants of Dublin.[69]

In September 1857 Captain Henry William Gordon, officer commanding the Military Store Office in Dublin, wrote to say that the guns had arrived and also listed the shot and shell that had been sent to be piled around them: 280 32-pounder shot, 280 8-inch mortar shot and 55 10-inch shells.[70] It is interesting to note that, as the guns presented to the City of Dublin were 36-pounders and 13-inch mortars, none of this shot and shell was of the correct calibre for any of the trophy guns. Perhaps it was deemed to be unwise to place both guns and shot in a public place and this could have been a security precaution.

There was a considerable delay as the 'Trophy Committee' of the Municipal Council tried to decide on a site to place the guns. In February 1858 they recommended using the vacant plot 'north of the Mansion House and parallel with Dawson Street'. By May 1858 they were recommending a totally different site.

> Your Committee are of the opinion that the place best suited for the grouping of the Crimean Trophies is the small piece of ground beyond the Esplanade opposite the Royal Barracks, near the King's Bridge. This ground is at present planted with evergreens and enclosed with iron railings.[71]

The guns were not finally placed at this site until June 1859 and they lay in the Pigeon House Fort in Ringsend, causing Captain Gordon to write in exasperation to the lord mayor asking 'how soon it may be expected that they will be required for removal from the Military Stores'. At the end of June 1859 these six guns were formally presented to the city of Dublin and, despite of the delay, it was decided that the chosen site was an excellent one. Positioning the guns on the Esplanade so near Kingsbridge Station and on the busy quayside guaranteed that they would be seen by many people as they travelled into Dublin. These guns are now on the main square of Cathal Brugha Barracks; it has been arranged for the Irish Army to maintain them and the Ordnance Corps now takes care of all the Crimean guns in Dublin. There is another Crimean gun in the army's care. This is listed by St John Hennessy as being in Devoy Barracks in Naas but was moved in 1998 to the Curragh Camp when Devoy Barracks was closed. While the Ordnance Corps keeps these guns in excellent condition, it is a pity that they are no longer on public display.

The two guns on the courthouse steps in Tralee, Co. Kerry, are also worth mentioning as the plinths they are placed on have memorial plaques to local

69 Ibid. p. 392.   **70** Ibid. p. 423.   **71** Dublin City Archives: C2/A1/20. 'Minutes of the Municipal Council of Dublin City, 21 December 1857 to 5 September 1859', p. 142.

men who were killed in the Crimea and the Indian Mutiny. The pair of guns that appear on St John Hennessy's list as being outside the Harbour Office in Limerick were originally placed on Wellesley Bridge (now Sarsfield Bridge) on either side of the memorial to Viscount Fitzgibbon.[72] St John Hennessy's article also only covers the twenty-one guns placed in positions around the Republic of Ireland. There is another 36-pounder cannon on the Armaghdown Bridge in Newry, Co. Down, outside the courthouse. There would also appear to have been one in Coleraine but this was moved to make way for the town's World War II memorial and has since disappeared. This is not unusual. Several guns have disappeared from town squares in England over the years, in some cases stolen by unscrupulous scrap metal merchants. Also during World War II many Crimean guns were melted down so that their metal could be used in new guns. There would also appear to have been a pair of guns in Dawson Square in Monaghan town on either side of the Dawson monument. These also have been moved but the large retaining rings that secured them to the monument can still be seen. Perhaps these were moved as a security measure sometime during this century. Crimean guns have been moved and stored in the past for similar reasons. In 1866 the *Westmeath Independent* carried the following announcement: The old Russian guns presented to the Corporation of Galway, and for some years mounted in Eyre Square, have been removed by order of the Government and taken into store in Athlone Barracks.[73] This action was taken due to concerns regarding Fenian activity. While the guns had been spiked, an experienced armourer could have bored out the touch-holes and converted the guns into serviceable weapons once gain. Did similar concerns result in the Monaghan guns being moved? Finally St John Hennessy's article does not mention the 9-pounder howitzer in Clancy Barracks in Islandbridge. While not a Russian trophy gun, it is a Royal Naval Brigade howitzer and was cast in the early 1850s. It could conceivably been used by the Naval Brigade in the Crimea. There are, therefore, twenty-one Russian guns in the Republic and another gun in Newry. Counting the guns that were once in Coleraine and Monaghan, this would mean that at least twenty-five were presented to Irish towns and cities.

There are other monuments around Ireland to those who died in the Crimea. As previously mentioned there is one in Tralee. There is also an impressive monument in Dawson Square in Monaghan, dedicated to Lieutenant-Colonel Thomas Vesey Dawson, Coldstream Guards, who was killed at the battle of Inkerman. An unusual monument was the tree planted in Pettigo, Co. Donegal with a commemorative plaque to the men from the locality who had died in the war. Perhaps the most impressive monument was the one built at Ferrycarrig,

---

72 John, Viscount Fitzgibbon (1829–1854), only legitimate son of Richard Hobart Fitzgibbon, 3rd earl of Clare.   **73** *Irish Sword*, iii, no. 11 (Winter, 1957), p. 87.

Co. Wexford. A replica round tower was built, overlooking the River Slaney, to commemorate Wexfordmen who had died in the war. There is also a memorial plaque in McKee barracks which is a very interesting and unusual monument. It is dedicated to troop horse B7, 'Dickie Bird' of the 5th Dragoon Guards who had served throughout the Crimean campaign with his regiment. He was shot, 'by special authority from the Horse Guards', to stop him being sold by public auction and buried under a flower bed in front of the cavalry officers mess. 'Dickie Bird' also passed into barrack folklore. It was the practice of NCOs, when drilling men on the square, to chastise men who anticipated their commands by shouting 'Wait for the Dickie Bird!' rather than 'Wait for the word!'.

There are also numerous memorial plaques in churches around Ireland to men who died in the war. There are in fact too many of these to go into in great detail here but a fine example of these Crimean war plaques would be the memorial to William Young Johnston in the Church of Ireland at Donagh, Co. Donegal. There is also a memorial to Captain John Pratt Winter, 17th Lancers, in the Church of Ireland at Agher, Co. Meath. Winter was killed in the charge of the Light Brigade.[74]

There are also a vast number of Crimean veterans buried in Ireland. Six Irish Victoria Cross winners, who were awarded their VC's for bravery in the Crimea, died and were buried in Ireland.[75] There are also a further two Crimean Victoria Cross winners, one Englishman and one Scot, who died and were buried in Ireland.[76] A particularly fine gravestone with a Crimean war connection is the gravestone of Private John Duggan in St Peter's Church of Ireland in Drogheda. Duggan, a survivor of the charge of the Light Brigade, had returned to Drogheda and become sexton of St. Peter's. His gravestone has the badge of the 17th Lancers, a skull and crossbones, and 'Balaclava, 25 October 1854' inscribed upon it.[77] There are also two streets in Dublin, Raglan Road and Raglan Lane, named after the British commander, Lord Raglan. There a number of streets in Belfast named after the Crimean battles of Alma, Balaclava and Inkerman.

Some monuments have also been lost. The fine monument to Viscount Fitzgibbon on Wellesley Bridge in Limerick was dynamited in 1930. There was also another monument to a horse, 'Crimean Bob' of the 11th Hussars, who died at Wellington Barracks in Cahir, Co. Tipperary, in 1862. 'Crimean Bob' was buried with full honours and a memorial plaque was placed above his

---

74 It is also interesting to note that the Crimean Memorial Church in Constantinople was designed by George Edmund Street who later planned the restorations of Christ Church Cathedral, Dublin, and the Cathedral Church of St Bridgid in Kildare.   75 John Augustus Conolly (Mount Jerome Cemetry, Dublin), George Gardiner (Lifford, Co. Donegal), John Sullivan (Kinsale, Co. Cork), John Lyons (Naas, Co. Kildare), Joseph Prosser (Tipperary town), Philip Smith (Harold's Cross cemetery, Dublin).   76 Edward W.D. Bell (Belfast), Henry Ramage (Newbridge, Co. Kildare).   77 There are also numerous Irish graves in the Haydar Pasha cemetery, beside the Scutari hospital,

grave. It was thought that the plaque had been destroyed when the barracks was burned down during the Irish Civil war. When the road near the remains of the barracks was widened in the 1940s the plaque was found and is now in the mess of the King's Royal Hussars in Pensinula Barracks,Winchester. The Cahir Historical Society have had a replica of the plaque made, using illustrations of the original, and it has been placed in the town square.[78]

One can also assume that, in light of constant reports of graveyard vandalism, that Crimean headstones are being destroyed every year. Some members of the CWRS came to Dublin in April 1999 and we made a visit to the Royal Hospital, Kilmainham, to see Private Robert Moneypenny's grave. The enlisted men's graveyard has suffered a considerable amount of vandalism, gravestones being smashed by cider-drinking parties who use the graveyard at night.

Irish Crimean veterans also appear in a large number of photographs taken after the war. Photographing Crimean veterans became something of a craze in 1856 and many photographic studios asked soldiers to pose in their uniforms with their medals and while still sporting their Crimean beards. Inevitably a large number of Irishmen were photographed on their return from the war in 1856. Some photographers also had a rather gruesome practice of photographing soldiers who had been wounded in the war. Numerous photographs survive of Crimean soldiers displaying their wounds and occasionally holding the bullet, shell fragment or cannon ball that crippled them. One of the most bizarre photographs of an Irish Crimean veteran is the study of Corporal John Lyons of the 19th Foot. Lyons, a native of Carlow, won the Victoria Cross for his bravery on 10 June 1855 and returned to Ireland after the war.[79] He died at Naas in April 1867 and his relatives dressed him in his uniform, attached his medals and prepared him for burial. They then decided that, as Lyons looked so spruce, to have his photograph taken and propped his body in a chair for the local photographer.[80] This photograph has been used in works on the Victoria Cross such as *The register of the Victoria Cross and Ireland's VCs* but usually only the head and shoulders of the study is used. The full photograph is pretty macabre.

Two Irish officers, Oliver Matthew Latham (48th Foot) and Robert Charles Goff (50th Foot) both pursued artistic careers after the war, Latham exhibiting some of his Crimean drawings in Dublin. Goff later travelled extensively and the majority of his paintings are of foreign landscapes. Also the Irish artist Lady Butler, wife of General the Rt. Hon. Sir William Butler, painted some Crimean scenes including *After the charge and Calling the roll after an*

---

in Constantinople/Istanbul.   **78** Information kindly supplied by Mrs Dymphna Moore, Cahir Historical Society.   **79** During a bombardment of the British trenches, Lyons picked up an unexploded shell and threw it out of the trench where it had landed. It exploded just a few seconds later. He was also awarded the French Legion of Honour.   **80** *Newsletter of the Friends of the Green Howards Regimental Museum*, no. 3 (September, 1997), p. 11.

engagement. There are also some oil paintings of Irish Crimean subjects. Troop Sergeant-Major Dennis O'Hara, who rallied the remnants of the 17th Lancers after the charge of the Light Brigade, is the subject of an oil painting by Orlando Norrie which hangs in 17th Lancers Museum. There is a painting of 'Crimean Bob', by the Irish artist William Osborne, in the mess of the King's Royal Hussars in Pensinula Barracks, Winchester.[81] A painting entitled *Storming the Redan* hangs in the Green Howards Museum in Richmond, Yorkshire depicting Lieutenant William Godfrey Dunham Massy leading his men. One of the VC paintings of Chevalier W. Desanges depicts Sergeant (later Major-General Sir) Luke O'Connor winning his VC at the battle of the Alma. This particularly fine painting is in the Royal Welch Fusiliers Museum. There is also an oil painting entitled *The charger of Captain Nolan carrying his dead master* by Thomas Jones Baker in the National Gallery of Ireland. It is the only painting with a Crimean theme in the National Gallery of Ireland's collection and recent research by Adrian Le Harivel of the National Gallery would indicate that it is actually a preparatory work for a bigger painting. It is believed that a larger version of the painting is held in a private collection in England or Ireland. Ireland is, therefore, quite rich in terms of Crimean memorials and Irish subjects appear frequently in paintings and photographs. The part that Irish soldiers and sailors played in the war is reflected in the large number of photographs of Irish veterans.

The end of the Crimean war in 1856 triggered a series of greatly contrasting events in Ireland. The Nenagh mutiny of July 1856 was a manifestation of the discontent of the men of the North Tipperary Militia. Militiamen serving in different regiments in Ireland and England no doubt sympathized with the Nenagh mutineers. The Crimean banquet of October 1856 was an impressive display of the support of the Irish public for those who had served in the war. The later lives of Irish Crimean veterans were varied. Some men enjoyed prosperity and success while others languished in poverty. The great longevity of some of these men, many of whom survived until the 1920s, ensured that there were people who could testify as to the part that Ireland played in the war living around the country in the early twentieth century.[82] The number of Crimean guns and memorials must have served a similar purpose and probably the majority of Irish towns have some relic of the war, if not a Crimean gun then at least a gravestone or memorial of some kind. It is perhaps surprising, therefore, that the public's awareness of Ireland's part in the war is so totally lacking.

81 William Osborne (1823–1901), portraitist, animal painter and father of Walter Frederick Osborne.   **82** *Porter's Directory* (1911) notes that the occupant of 15 Northumberland Avenue, Kingstown, was one Laurence Redmond, described as a 'Crimean pensioner'. There were probably many of these veterans in the towns and cities of Ireland.

Conclusion

The Crimean war was one of the most important international events of the nineteenth century and it had a major effect on all the countries involved. The Treaty of Paris put an end to Russian expansionism in the short term and it was not until after France's defeat in the Franco-Prussian war of 1870–1 that Russia re-fortified Sevastapol and manifested territorial designs in the East once again. Turkey was content with the treaty as it was protected by a clause which stipulated that the shores of the Black Sea should be demilitarised. There were further assurances for Turkey in the form of promises of protection from Britain and France in the face of future aggression from Russia. Louis Napoleon found that France's international prestige was restored and a period of re-militarization followed, viewed with great alarm in Britain. Sardinia-Piedmont gained perhaps most from the war and, assured of a place at the peace negociations in Paris, had managed to establish itself as a European power. The Crimean war is seen as a major step on the road to Italian unification. For Britain, the major lesson of the war was that the army needed to be reformed. The failings of the supply and medical services in the Crimea showed that such reforms were now urgently necessary. Indeed, there had been calls for such reforms before the war. Now, with its shortcomings reported across the pages of *The Times*, the Horse Guards instigated major reforms and, while there would be serious failings again in campaigns in India, Afghanistan and South Africa, the British army would never be quite so ill-prepared again.

What then was the effect of the Crimean war on Ireland? For two hectic years the war had been the main focus of attention in Ireland. Contemporary newspaper reports and broadsheet ballads show that the progress of the war was followed with great interest and that the public supported the war. This is perhaps not all that surprising considering the large number of Irish men and women involved, both in military and civilian capacities. This book has tried to outline the level of Irish involvement in the war. It has shown that there was a large Irish contingent in the British army and the Royal Navy and, when one considers the large number of VCs awarded to Irishmen in the war, the commitment and bravery of the Irish contingent cannot be doubted. Also, generals Sir

George De Lacy Evans and Sir John Lysaght Pennefather both played a significant role in the war, especially at the battles of the Alma and Inkerman. These two Irish generals were perhaps the only generals to emerge from the war with their reputations intact. Some of the most prominent soldiers in the war, such as Lieutenant William Godfrey Dunham Massy ('Redan Massy'), were also Irish and performed exceptionable acts of bravery. The Irish contingent in the Royal Navy was equally important and Irish seamen served in the campaigns in the Baltic, the Black Sea, the Azov and also with the Naval Brigade on land.

The Irish civilians who went to the Crimea represent an even more interesting aspect of this Irish involvement in the war. The involvement of Irish doctors, Catholic priests, Sisters of Mercy, engineers and navvies serves to illustrate the wider level of Irish interest in the war and these men and women made an important contribution. The contribution of James Beatty, the Enniskillen-born railway engineer, was extremely important and one could well argue that no other single individual made such an impact on the outcome of the war. War correspondents were used for the first time during the Crimean war and three of these, W.H. Russell, Edwin Lawrence Godkin and James Carlile McCoan, were Irish. W.H. Russell is often seen as the father of war-journalism yet the work of Edwin Lawrence Godkin was equally important and, on occasion, even more shocking.

The reaction of the Irish public to the outbreak of the war and the support they showed to the troops leaving for the war, is of interest. This reaction was no doubt due to the fact that so many families in Ireland had men serving in the war. The Irish public's interest is reflected in the large number of Crimean ballads that survive in the White Ballad Collection in Trinity College, Dublin. The Crimean banquet, held in Dublin in October 1856, illustrates the level of Irish public interest. When one considers that 5,000 soldiers and guests arrived at Stack A for the banquet, while thousands more gathered outside, the Crimean banquet must have been the major social event of 1856.

There was, however, one very negative effect on Ireland that cannot be overlooked. If Irish troops made up at least one-third of the army, is it not reasonable to assume that their casualties were proportionate? The British army suffered 21,097 fatal casualties.[1] It is quite possible that over 7,000 Irishmen died in the campaign. The official casualty figure does not include Irish women who travelled as camp-followers and died in the Crimea. Nor does it include the death-toll amongst the navvies, muleteers and other civilian workers. It is probable that the number of Irish dead was in fact higher. These deaths must have had an impact on Irish society. We have already seen how Royal Navy

1 John Sweetman, *The Crimean war*, p. 89. The breakdown of British army casualties was 2,755 killed in action, 2,019 died of wounds, 16,323 died of disease.

casualties in just a few Co. Cork parishes greatly reduced the male population of the area. In a country already suffering from the effects of famine and mass-emigration, the high-death toll in the Crimea must have had drastic conse-quences for many communities.

Yet, perhaps surprisingly, there is no large body of literature on the Irish in the Crimean war. With the exception of Evelyn Bolster's *The Irish Sisters of Mercy in the Crimean war* (Cork, 1964), there have been no comprehensive histories written on any aspect of the Irish involvement in the war. Despite the fact that there are Russian trophy guns, memorials, headstones and numerous photographs of Irish Crimean veterans which serve as reminders of this Irish involvement, there has never been any serious research carried out on the subject of the Irish in the Crimean war. There were even Crimean veterans still alive in Ireland in the 1920s, yet no-one seems to have thought of recording their experiences. There has, in short, never been any sustained historical interest in the Irish involvement in the Crimea.

This is due to a number of reasons. Firstly, one must look at how the war has been addressed by historians. The major histories of the Crimean war, such as A.W. Kinglake's *The invasion of the Crimea* (8 volumes, London, 1868–87) and E.H. Nolan's *Illustrated history of the war against Russia* (2 volumes, London, 1856–7) focused on the major events and battles of the war. As John Keegan has pointed out in his book *The face of battle* (London, 1976), military historians are often more interested in the strategic-thinking behind campaigns than in the experience of the men who actually fought in them. Most histories of the Crimean war follow this rule and focus on the strategic thinking of the British, French and Russian generals. The contemporary histories of the war, such as those written by Nolan and Kinglake, tended to focus on certain major events. Crimean war historians have tended to concentrate on subjects such as the work of Florence Nightingale and the charge of the Light Brigade. The battles of the Alma and Inkerman were covered in detail and there have been numerous biographies of the well-known figures of the war. Indeed both Florence Nightingale and Lord Cardigan have, despite their relative lack of success, taken on an almost iconic status and this creates an imbalance in the historiography of the war.

Secondly, the contemporary histories relied on the accounts of officers and did not refer to the experiences of the enlisted men in great detail. While there were many Irish officers in the Crimea, the Irish were at their most numerous in the ranks and their experiences have never been the focus of serious historical research. Many officers, including Irish officers, later wrote accounts of their experiences in the Crimea but this is not true of the most successful of the Irish officers, Sir George De Lacy Evans and Sir John Lysaght Pennefather. This was in marked contrast to the behaviour of Lord Cardigan who toured the

British Isles, giving interviews and delivering speeches, in spite of his disastrous war-record. One could account for this lack of historical interest in the war in Ireland by arguing that the Irish enlisted men, who formed such a large part of the army in the Crimea, did not write many accounts of their experiences. Yet some Irish enlisted men's accounts do exist, such as John Doyle's *A descriptive account of the famous charge of the Light Brigade at Balaclava* (London, 1877), James O'Malley's, *The life of James O'Malley* (Montreal, 1893) and Philip O'Flaherty's, *Philip O'Flaherty, the young soldier: containing interesting particulars of the war in the Crimea* (Edinburgh, 1855). Indeed one of the most popular accounts of the war was written by an Irishman: Lieutenant-Colonel Anthony Sterling's *The Highland Brigade in the Crimea* (London, 1895). While such accounts were comparatively few in number there were of a very high quality indeed. Yet, three of these accounts have something in common; they were both written many years after the war by which time the attention of the Irish public, and Irish historians, was focused on the political events unfolding in Ireland.

Also, the Irish public had demonstrated a profound interest in the Crimean war but this interest was not maintained later in the century. The outbreak of the Indian Mutiny in 1857 moved the focus of Irish public interest and, while the accounts of the hardships and battles of the Crimean war had occupied the public's attention for two years, events such as the Cawnpore massacre and the siege of Lucknow became the new focus of public interest. The stories of the dreadful atrocities being committed in India soon filled the daily newspapers and, to a great extent, the Crimean war simply became old news in Ireland. In the same way the major political and social events in Ireland in the late nineteenth century, such as the Land War and the Home Rule campaign, moved the focus of Irish public interest to more immediate and domestic matters.

Another reason for the lack of interest in the Irish involvement in the Crimean war was the way military history was approached in Ireland in the twentieth century. It is no exaggeration to state that, in the Irish Republic at least, military history has been something of a non-subject for the past sixty years as Irish historians have devoted their energies to studying the great political events of the late nineteenth and early twentieth centuries. One can qualify this statement even further. In the field of Irish military history there have been researches and publications on subjects such as the Irish in the French service in the eighteenth century, the Irish in the Union Army of the American Civil war and the Irish in the Papal Army of 1860. Yet the subject of the Irish in the campaigns of the British army in the nineteenth century has remained almost a taboo subject. While these other aspects of Ireland's military history were important, it was in the British army that the Irish were at their most numerous and, for many years, there was a lack of will on the part of Irish historians to address this subject.

This trend has been most obvious in the way the subject of the Irish who served in the British army in World War I has been treated. While the 36th (Ulster) Division has been the subject of Cyril Fall's *History of the Ulster Division* (Belfast, 1922), there have been no comprehensive histories written of the 10th (Irish) and 16th (Irish) Divisions. The whole episode of Irish involvement in the First World War has been relegated for many years to a few lines in Leaving Certificate history books. It has only been in recent years that research has begun again on this subject and that books such as Bryan Cooper's *The Tenth (Irish) Division in Gallipoli* (London, 1918) and Rudyard Kipling's *The Irish Guards in the Great War* (2 volumes, London, 1923) have been re-printed. In this context it is perhaps less surprising that the Crimean war has never been the focus of serious research in Ireland. If the part played by over 200,000 Irish men in World War I was not seen as being of historical interest for the best part of the twentieth century, it is not surprising the Irish in the military campaigns of the nineteenth century have been forgotten.

The Crimean war was just one of many wars that have never been the focus of research in Ireland. Throughout the reign of Queen Victoria, there were numerous wars and, what the UN would now term, 'police actions'. Indeed, scarcely a year passed in which British soldiers were not involved in a war somewhere in the world.[2] There were Irish soldiers in all of these wars. Many soldiers had only returned home from the Crimea when their regiments received orders to depart for India and thousands of Irish Crimean veterans later helped suppress the Indian Mutiny. At the outbreak of the Ashantee war of 1873, there were 42,284 Irish soldiers in the British Army.[3] Many of these served in West Africa with General Sir Garnet Wolseley. At the outbreak of the Second Afghan war in November 1878, there were 39,121 Irish men in the British army and thousands of these served in the war.[4] During the Zulu war of 1879, there were 36, 871 Irish soldiers in the army and again thousands of these served in South Africa. Five Irishmen were awarded the Victoria Cross during the Zulu war, perhaps the most famous being Surgeon James Henry Reynolds (1844–1932), who won a VC for his bravery during the defence of Rorke's Drift.[5]

The subject of Irish involvement in the British army during the nineteenth century has, therefore, been largely ignored and the Crimean war is just one instance of this lack of interest. This book has tried to outline level of Irish involvement in the Crimean war and it has shown that the Irish were repre-

---

2 Byron Farwell, *Queen Victoria's little wars* (London, 1973).   3 H.J. Hanham, 'Religion and nationality in the mid-Victorian army' in M.R.D. Foot (ed.), *War and society* (London, 1973), p. 176.   4 Ibid.   5 David Murphy, '"They poured on us a continuous fire." Surgeon James Henry Reynolds and the Defence of Rorke's Drift, 22nd to 23rd January 1879' in *Journal of the Dun Laoghaire Borough Historical Society*, no. 8 (1999), pp 43–55.

sented at every level. The Irish public was intensely interested in the war and showed their support for the troops in the Crimea. There can be no real doubt that the Crimean war was one of the major events in Ireland in the nineteenth century but has been overshadowed by the fact that historical attention has remained focused on the major domestic events of that century.

In the late-1970s, however, the Irish public came close to being gripped with 'Crimean Fever' for the first time since 1856. During 1977 several scenes for the film *The first great train robbery* were filmed in Ireland. The film was based on Michael Crichton's *The great train robbery* (London, 1975), an historical novel based on a daring gold bullion robbery of May 1855.[6] In both the novel and the film, the main characters steal a shipment of gold that is being sent to the Crimea to pay the troops. As the film-crew shot several scenes in locations such as Kingsbridge Station, Parliament Street and Trinity College, Dublin, large crowds gathered to try and catch a glimpse of the film's leading men, Sean Connery and Donald Sutherland. It is ironic indeed that, in 1854, large crowds gathered at the same locations to see the troops as they marched through Dublin at the beginning of their journey to the Crimea.

6 On 15 May 1855, around £12,000 worth of gold was stolen from a shipment of bullion being sent by Messrs Thomas, Bult & Spielman to bullion dealers in Paris. It was later discovered that the gold had been taken from the Chubb safes in the guard-wagon of the South Eastern Railway's Londonbridge to Folkestone train. Four men, William Pierce, Robert Agar, James Burgess and William Tester were later tried and convicted for the crime. Both Burgess and Tester were employees of the South Eastern Railway. Pierce had been dismissed from his job with the South Eastern Railway in 1850. Agar was the only 'professional' criminal in the group.

Appendices

A. Irish recipients of the Victoria Cross in the Crimean war[1]

The Victoria Cross was instituted by royal warrant on 29 January 1856 and the first recipients were men who had served in the Crimean war. The medals were cast from the metal of Russian guns taken at Sevastapol. The first VC investiture took place in Hyde Park on 26 June 1857, Queen Victoria presenting the medals to those present. Originally the ribbon of the VC was crimson for the army and dark blue for the Royal Navy. Following the formation of the RAF in 1918, the crimson ribbon was awarded to all recipients.

Rank/Name: Private John Alexander
Born: Mullingar, Co. Westmeath
Regiment: 90th Foot (Perthshire Volunteers)
VC Deed: Awarded for actions on 18 June and 6 September 1855
London Gazette **Citation**: 24 February 1857
Died: Lucknow, India, 24 September 1857

Rank/Name: Private (later Corporal) Joseph Bradshaw
Born: Dromkeen, Co. Limerick, 1835
Regiment: 2nd Bn., The Rifle Brigade (Prince Consort's Own)
VC Deed: 22 April 1855
London Gazette **Citation**: 24 February 1857
Died: Woolwich, 21 March 1855

Rank/Name: Lieutenant (later Captain) Hugh Talbot Burgoyne
Born: Dublin, 17 July 1833
Service: Royal Navy, HMS *Swallow*
VC Deed: 29 May 1855

London Gazette **Citation**: 24 February 1857
Died: At sea, near Finisterre, 7 September 1870

Rank/Name: Private (later Corporal) John Byrne
Born: Castlecomer, Co. Kilkenny, September 1832
Regiment: 68th Foot (The Durham Light Infantry)
VC Deed: Awarded for actions on 5 November 1854 and 11 May 1855
London Gazette **Citation**: 24 February 1857
Died: Caerleon, Monmouthshire, 10 July 1879

Rank/Name: Sergeant (later Master Gunner) Daniel Cambridge
Born: Carrickfergus, Co. Antrim, 1820
Regiment: Royal Regiment of Artillery
VC Deed: 8 September 1855
London Gazette **Citation**: 23 June 1857
Died: London, 12 June 1882

---

1 Compiled from *The London Gazette, Ireland's VCs, The Register of the Victoria Cross,* Winton's *The Victoria Cross at Sea* and Doherty and Truesdale's *Irish Winners of the Victoria Cross.*

Rank/Name: Private (later Sergeant) William Coffey
Born: Knocklong, Co. Limerick, 5 August 1829
Regiment: 34th Foot (The Cumberland Regiment)
VC Deed: 29 March 1855
London Gazette **Citation**: 24 February 1857
Died: Chesterfield, Derbyshire, 13 July 1875

Rank/Name: Lieutenant (later Lieutenant-Colonel) John Augustus Conolly
Born: Cliff, Ballyshannon, Co. Donegal, 30 May 1829
Regiment: 49th Foot (Princess Charlotte of Wales's, or the Hertfordshire Regiment)
VC Deed: 26 October 1854
London Gazette **Citation**: 5 May 1857
Died: Curragh, Co. Kildare, 23 December 1888

Rank/Name: Private (later Corporal) Joseph Connors
Born: Davaugh, Listowel, Co. Kerry, October 1830
Regiment: 3rd East Kent (The Buffs)
VC Deed: 8 September 1855
London Gazette **Citation**: 24 February 1857
Died: Corfu, 22 August 1858

Rank/ Name: Captain (later Lieutenant-Colonel) Thomas Esmonde
Born: Pembrokestown, Co. Waterford, 25 May 1829
Regiment: 18th (Royal Irish) Foot
VC Deed: Awarded for actions on 18 and 20 June 1855
London Gazette **Citation**: 25 September 1857
Died: Bruges, Belgium, 14 January 1873 [2]

Rank/Name: Quartermaster-Sergeant John Farrell
Born: Dublin, March 1826
Regiment: 17th Lancers
VC Deed: 25 October 1854
London Gazette **Citation**: 20 November 1857
Died: Secunderabad, India, 31 August 1865

Rank/Name: Sergeant (later Colour-Sergeant) George Gardiner
Born: Glenwallen, Warrenpoint, 1821
Regiment: 57th Foot (The West Middlesex)
VC Deed: Awarded for actions on 22 March and 18 June 1855
London Gazette **Citation**: 2 June 1858
Died: Lifford, Co. Donegal, 17 November 1891

Rank/Name: Private (later Sergeant) Thomas Grady
Born: Cheddah, Co. Galway, 18 September 1835
Regiment: 4th Foot (The King's Own)
VC Deed: Awarded for actions on 18 October and 22 November 1854
London Gazette **Citation**: 20 November 1857
Died: Victoria, New South Wales, 18 May 1891

Rank/Name: Captain Henry Mitchell Jones
Born: Dublin, 11 February 1831
Regiment: 7th Foot (Royal Fusiliers)
VC Deed: 7 June 1855
London Gazette **Citation**: 25 September 1857
Died: Eastbourne, Sussex, 18 December 1916

Rank/Name: Corporal (later Sergeant-Major) William James Lendrim
Born: Ireland, 1 January 1830
Regiment: Corps of Sappers and Miners
VC Deed: Awarded for actions on 14 February, 11 and 20 April 1855

---

2 Thomas Esmonde was the great-uncle of Lieutenant-Commander Eugene K. Esmonde, 825 Squadron, Fleet Air Arm, who was killed leading the Swordfish attack on the German battle cruisers *Scharnhorst*, *Gneisenau* and *Prinz Eugen* in the Straits of Dover, 12 February 1942. Lieutenant-Commander Esmonde was posthumously awarded the Victoria Cross.

London Gazette **Citation**: 24 February 1857
Died: Camberley, Surrey, 28 November 1891

Rank/Name: Master's-Mate (later Rear-Admiral) Charles Davis Lucas
Born: Druminargale House, Poyntzpass, Co. Armagh, 19 February 1834
Service: Royal Navy, HMS *Hecla*
VC Deed: 21 June 1854.
London Gazette **Citation**: (First recipient of the Victoria Cross): 24 February 1857
Died: Great Culverden, Kent, 7 August 1914

Rank/Name: Private (later Corporal) John Lyons
Born: Carlow, 1823
Regiment; 19th Foot (1st Yorkshire, North Riding)
VC Deed: 10 June 1855
London Gazette **Citation**: 24 February 1857
Died: Naas, Co. Kildare, 20 April 1867

Rank/Name: Private Charles McCorrie
Born: Killeard, Co. Antrim, 1830
Regiment: 57th Foot (The West Middlesex)
VC Deed: 23 June 1855
London Gazette **Citation**: 24 February 1857
Died: Malta, 9 April 1857

Rank/Name: Sergeant William McWheeney
Born: Bangor, Co. Down, 1837
Regiment: 44th Foot (The East Essex)
VC Deed: Awarded for actions of 20 October, 5 December 1854 and 18 June 1855
London Gazette **Citation**: 24 February 1857
Died: Dover, Kent, 17 May 1866

Rank/Name: Sergeant (later Lieutenant) Ambrose Madden
Born: Cork, 1820
Regiment: 41st Foot (The Welsh Regiment)
VC Deed: 5 November 1854
London Gazette **Citation**: 24 February 1857
Died: Jamaica, 1 January 1863

Rank/Name: Lieutenant-Colonel (later General) Francis Frederick Maude
Born: Lisnadill, Co. Armagh, 20 December 1821
Regiment: 3rd East Kent (The Buffs)
VC Deed: 5 September 1855
London Gazette **Citation**: 24 February 1857
Died: Torquay, Devon, 20 June 1897

Rank/Name: Sergeant (later Major-General Sir) Luke O'Connor
Born: Elphin, Co. Roscommon, 21 January 1831
Regiment: 23rd Foot (The Royal Welsh Fusiliers)
VC Deed: Awarded for actions on 20 September 1854 and 8 September 1855.
London Gazette **Citation** (First award of the Victoria Cross to a member of the British Army): 24 February 1857
Died: London, 1 February 1915

Rank/Name: Corporal (later Sergeant) James Owens
Born: Killane, Baileyboro, 1829
Regiment: 49th Foot (Princess Charlotte of Wales's, or the Hertfordshire)
VC Deed: 30 October 1854
London Gazette **Citation**: 24 February 1857
Died: Romford, Essex, 20 August 1901

Rank/Name: Sergeant John Park
Born: Londonderry, February 1835
Regiment: 77th Foot (The East Middlesex)
VC Deed: 20 September, 5 November 1854 and 19 April 1855
London Gazette **Citation**: 24 February 1857
Died: Allahabad, India, 18 May 1863

Rank/Name: Private Joseph Prosser
Born: Monegal, King's Co., 1828
Regiment: 2nd Bn., 1st Foot (The Royal Regiment)
VC Deed: 16 June and 11 August 1855
London Gazette **Citation**: 24 February 1857
Died: Tipperary, 1869

Rank/Name: Corporal (later Sergeant) Philip Smith
Born: Lurgan, Armagh, 1825
Regiment: 17th Foot (The Leicestershire)
VC Deed: 18 June 1855
London Gazette **Citation**: 24 February 1857
Died: Harold's Cross, Dublin, 16 January 1906

Rank/Name: Lieutenant (later General) Mark Walker
Born: Gore Port, Finca, Co. Westmeath, 24 November 1827
Regiment: 30th Foot (The Cambridgeshire)
VC Deed: 5 November 1854
London Gazette **Citation**: 2 June 1858
Died: Arlington, Devon, 18 July 1902

Rank/Name: Petty Officer (later Chief Boatswain's Mate) John Sullivan
Born: Bantry, Co. Cork, 10 April 1830
Service: Royal Navy (Royal Naval Brigade)
VC Deed: 10 April 1855
London Gazette **Citation**: 24 February 1857
Died: Kinsale, Co. Cork, 28 June 1884

Rank/Name: Private Alexander Wright
Born: Ballymena, Co. Antrim, 1826
Regiment: 77th Foot (The East Middlesex)
VC Deed: Awarded for actions on 22 March, 19 April and 30 August 1855.
London Gazette **Citation**: 24 February 1857
Died: Calcutta, India, 28 July 1858

Recipients of the Victoria Cross born in England of Irish parents

Rank/Name: Sergeant (later Captain and Riding Master) Joseph Malone
Born: Eccles, Lancashire, 11 January 1833
Regiment: 13th Light Dragoons
VC Deed: 25 October 1854
London Gazette **Citation**: 20 November 1857
Died: Pinetown, Natal, South Africa, 28 June 1883

Rank/Name: Seaman (later Able Seaman) James Gorman
Born: London, 1832, parents from Waterford
Service: Royal Navy (Royal Naval Brigade)
VC Deed: 5 November 1854
London Gazette **Citation**: 24 February 1857
Died: New South Wales, Australia, 18 October 1882[3]

A Crimean Victorian Cross recipient who served in an Irish Regiment

Rank/Name: Surgeon (later Surgeon General Sir) James Mouat
Born: Chatham, Kent, 14 April 1815
Regiment: 6th (Inniskilling) Dragoons
VC Deed: 26 October 1854
London Gazette **Citation**: 2 June 1858
Died: London, 4 January 1899

3 Several works on the Victoria Cross, including *The Register of the Victoria Cross and Ireland's VCs*, state that Gorman died in Southwark, London, 27 December 1889. This was due to the fact that an impostor, James Devereux, who called himself 'James Gorman Devereux, VC', had been masquerading as James Gorman for years and had died in London in 1889. Recent research by John Winton, author of *The Victoria Cross at Sea*, has discovered that the real James Gorman, VC, went to Australia in 1863 and died in New South Wales in 1882. John Winton, 'Was Gorman VC an Aussie?' in *The war correspondent*, xvi, no. 2 (July 1998), pp 22–6.

B. Irish commissioned officers in the Army Medical Service in the Crimean war

Rank/Name[4]	Place of Birth
A.S. Fred T. Abbott	Nenagh, Co. Tipperary
A.S. Robert F. Andrews	Co. Offaly
A.S.Thomas J. Atkinson	Ballina, Co. Mayo
S. Daniel P. Barry	Dundalk, Co. Louth
A.S. Thomas S. Barry	Coolmain, Co. Cork
S. Francis H. Baxter	Enniskillen, Co. Fermanagh
A.S. Robert H. Beale	Cahir, Co. Tipperary
S. James H. Bews	Athlone
A.S.Thomas McDoughall Bleckley	Monaghan (TCD) [5]
A.S. Henry C. Boate	Dungarvan, Co. Waterford
A.S. William Bradshaw, VC	Thurles, Co. Tipperary
A.S. Thomas C. Brady	Co. Donegal
A.S. William H. Brice	Co. Cavan
A.S. Allen Bryson	Carrickfergus, Co. Antrim (UG)
A.S. William R. Burkitt	New Ross, Co. Wexford
A.S. Robert A. Chapple	Limerick
S. Patrick J. Clarke	Edgeworthstown, Co. Longford
A.S. George C. Clery	Cork
S. Philip H.E. Cross	Co. Cork, (TCD)
S. O'Connor D'Arcy	Ennis, Co. Clare (UG)
A. S. George F. Davis	Dublin
A.S. Charles C. Dempster	Nenagh, Co. Tipperary
S. Daniel J. Doherty	Kilkenny
A.S. John Duffin	Ballymena, Co. Antrim
A.S. James Ekin	Dungannon, Co. Tyrone
S. Usher Williamson Evans	Mallow, Co. Cork
A.S. Robert L. Ferguson	Dublin
A.S. James H. Finnemore	Dublin.
P. David Fitzgerald	Ireland
A.S. William Fletcher	Dublin
S. John S. Furlong	Enniscorthy, Co. Wexford (KCA)
S. William J. Fyffe	Baronscourt, Co. Tyrone (TCD)
A.S. John Gibbons	Co. Westmeath,
S. Richard Gilborne	Danesfort, Co. Kilkenny
A.S. Henry Grange	Portarlington, Co. Laois
A.S. Arthur J. Greer	Co. Tyrone
A.S. Michael J. Griffin	Co. Mayo

→

4 All ranks given are those held during Crimean war. A.S.=Assistant Surgeon; S.=Surgeon; S.M.=Surgeon-Major; P.=Purveyor. **5** Details of colleges attended included: TCD=Trinity College, Dublin; UG=University of Glasgow ; KCA=King's College, Aberdeen; QCB=Queen's College, Belfast.

Rank/Name	Place of Birth
A.S. Frederick G. Hamilton	Co. Kildare,
A.S. James Hannan	Dublin
A.S. William Haughton	Rathgar, Co. Dublin (TCD)
S. John C. Haverty	Co. Galway
A.S. John H. Hearn	Belturbet, Co. Cavan
A.S. Exham L. Hiffernan	Aglish, Co. Kilkenny
A.S.William Hemphill	Castlederg, Co. Tyrone (UG)
A.S. Francis Holton	Edgeworthstown, Co. Longford (TCD)
A.S. Alexander Humfrey	Co. Donegal
A.S. Richard Hungerford	Clonakilty, Co. Cork
S. George Hyde	Longford (KCA)
A.S. Sir Robert W. Jackson	Edenderry, Co. Offaly
A.S. Edward Y. Kellet	Clones, Co. Monaghan
S. George S. King	Dublin (TCD)
A.S. Francis W. Knox	Ballina, Co. Mayo,
A.S. Digby W. Lawlor	Co. Laois
A.S. James H. Lewis	Co Clare
A.S. Edward L. Lundy	Cork
S. Alexander MacArthur	Co Offaly (UG)
A.S. Patrick McDermott	Co. Longford (TCD)
A.S. John A. McMunn	Dublin (TCD)
A.S. William McNamara	Ennis. Co. Clare (UG)
A.S. Thomas McSheehy	Limerick (QCB)
A.S. Charles D. Madden	Kilkenny
A.S. Richard W. Meade	Kinsale, Co. Cork
S. James Mee	Tynan, Co. Armagh
A.S. Ormsby B. Miller	Dublin
A.S. William W. Mills	Slane, Co. Meath,
A.S. Hamilton Mitchell	Co. Londonderry
S.M. James Guy P. Moore	Dublin (TCD)
A.S. Stuart Moore	Co. Tyrone
S. Thomas Moorhead	Co. Monaghan
A.S. John J. Mulock	Dublin
S. Nicholas O'Connor	Co. Cork (TCD)
A.S. Francis Odell	Dublin
A.S. John F. O'Leary	Cork
S. Thomas Connor O'Leary	Tralee, Co. Kerry (TCD)
A.S. John C. Owens	Killaghtee, Co. Donegal
A.S. Joshua H. Porter	Dublin
A.S. Willaim Ramsay	Strabane, Co. Tyrone
A.S. Alexander Reid	Dublin
P.-in-Chief James S. Roberts	Co. Wicklow
A.S. Sampson Roch	Youghal, Co. Cork
A.S. Samuel B. Roe	Cavan
A.S. William C. Roe	Borris-in-Ossory, Co. Laois
A.S. Henry J. Rose	Dalkey, Co. Dublin

→

Rank/Name	Place of Birth
A.S. Edward C. Ryall	Ennis, Co. Clare
S. George Saunders	Co. Cork
S. James E. Scott	Co. Down (TCD)
A.S. John J. Scott	Aughnacloy, Co. Tyrone
A.S. Ralph R. Scott	Kiltegan, Co. Wicklow
S. George A. Shelton	Limerick (TCD)
A.S. Thomas W. Shiell	Rathkeale, Co. Limerick (TCD)
A.S. Robert B. Smyth	Co. Dublin
S. Henry Somers	Dublin (UG)
A.S. David Stranaghan	Rathfriland, Co. Down
S. Thomas M. Sunter	Co.Meath (TCD)
A.S. Thomas Tarrant	Cobh, Co. Cork
A.S. Arthur H. Taylor	Belfast
A.S. Thomas Teevan	Co. Fermanagh
A.S. Richard C. Todd	Dublin
A.S. Benjamin Tydd	Ennis, Co. Clare,
S. Thomas F. Wall	Arclough, Co. Kildare,
S. William P. Ward	Dublin
A.S. John H. West	Enniskillen, Co. Fermanagh (UG)
A.S. Richard Wolsey	Co. Dublin (UG)
A.S. Thomas Wright	Kilkenny
A.S. John E. Young	Co. Meath (UG)

C. Members of the Irish Constabulary who served in the Crimea

Mounted Staff Corps

Home Station	Rank	Name
East Cork	SC	Edward Costello
East Cork	SC	James Bunter
East Cork	SC	Thomas Mullen
Cork City	SC	Francis Carty
Down	SC	Edward Beacon
Down	AC	John Walsh
Kerry	AC	Daniel Leary
Kerry	SC	Denis Kelly
Kerry	SC	Thomas Abernethy
Kildare	SC	Thomas Madigan
Kilkenny	SC	John Enright
Kilkenny	SC	John Kelly
Kilkenny City	SC	Richard Bradshaw
Limerick	SC	Michael Mannion

→

Home Station	Rank	Name
Limerick City	SC	Bernard Gordon
Limerick City	SC	William Moynihan
Meath	C	Patrick Duffy
Meath	AC	John Kelly
Meath	SC	Charles Leslie
Queen's Co.	C	Samuel Croker
Queen's Co.	C	Peter Pender
Queen's Co.	AC	Peter Coogan
Waterford	C	John Stoddart
Waterford	SC	William Maguire
Waterford	SC	James Cotter
Wexford	C	John Enright
Wexford	C	John Mack

Officers seconded to the Commissariat Department

Home Station	Rank	Name
Reserve	1st SI	E.J. Banon
Reserve	2nd SI	T.C. Anderson
Reserve	3rd SI	J.F. Studdert
Reserve	2nd SI	W.P. Coppinger
Reserve	3rd SI	R.J. Reamsbottom
Antrim	1st SI	C.J. Gernon
Carlow	2nd SI	J.S. Watkins
Carlow	2nd SI	H. Bindon
West Galway	2nd SI	V. Goold
Kilkenny	3rd SI	T.P. Carr
Mayo	3rd SI	H.B. Thornhill
Mayo	3rd SI	W.H.S. Hemsworth
South Tipperary	1st SI	C. Brew
South Tipperary	2nd SI	W. Fosberry
South Tipperary	3rd SI	W.S. Keogh
Waterford	2nd SI	G. Du Bourdieu

Other ranks seconded to the Commissariat Department

Home Station	Rank	Name
Reserve	Sub-C	Thomas Gildea
Reserve	AC	Richard Roynane
Reserve	C	James Hobson
Reserve	C	Nicholas Carden
Reserve	2nd HC	James Ross
Reserve	C	Adam McClelland

Home Station	Rank	Name
Reserve	C	Henry Reynolds
Armagh	C	W.G. Moran
East Cork	C	Donal McMahon
East Cork	C	Redmond Walker
Cork City	C	James Vickers
West Cork	C	John McCarthy
Dublin	C	Henry Clinton
Dublin	C	Robert Lalor
Dublin	C	Andrew Menahan
Dublin	C	Thomas Talbot
Dublin	AC	John Rock
West Galway	HC	John Reilly
Mayo	C	Joseph Cue
Monaghan	C	James Miller
Roscommon	C	James Vaughan
Roscommon	C	Martin Hanly
South Tipperary	C	William Stack
Waterford	HC	John Power
Westmeath	C	Martin Meagher
Wexford	C	Thomas Maunsell[6]

D. Regiments of the Militia of Ireland: Embodied January 1855

Antrim Militia (The Queen's Royal Rifles)
Royal Antrim Artillery
Armagh Light Infantry
Armagh Artillery
Carlow Rifles
Cavan Militia
Clare Militia
North Cork Rifles
87th, or South Cork Light Infantry
Royal Cork City Artillery
West Cork Artillery
Donegal Militia (102nd, or Prince
   of Wales's)
Donegal Artillery
Royal North Down Rifles
Royal South Down Light Infantry

Royal Dublin City Militia (Queen's Own
   Royal Regiment)
Dublin City Artillery
Dublin County Light Infantry
Fermanagh Light Infantry
Galway Militia
Kerry Militia
Kildare Rifles
Kilkenny Fusiliers
King's County Royal Rifles
Leitrim Rifles
Royal Limerick County Militia
Limerick Artillery
Londonderry Artillery Company
Longford Rifles
Louth Rifles

                                      ⟶

6 Compiled from *Constabulary List and Directory,* no. 27 (Dublin, 1855), pp 149–51 and *Constabulary List and Directory*, no. 28 (Dublin, 1855), pp 150–2. SI= Sub-Inspector; HC= Head Constable; C= Constable; SC= Sub-Constable; AC= Acting Constable.

North Mayo Militia
South Mayo Rifles
Royal Meath Militia
Monaghan Militia
Queen's County Royal Rifles
Roscommon Militia
Sligo Rifles
The Duke of Clarence's Munster

Artillery, or 1st, or South Tipperary Militia
2nd, or North Tipperary Light Infantry
Royal Tyrone Fusiliers
Tyrone Artillery
Waterford Artillery
Westmeath Rifles
Wexford Militia
Wicklow Rifles[7]

E. Russian trophy guns in Ireland

Town	Place	Year	Calibre/Shot weight
Birr	Heritage Centre	1827	18-pounder
Bunratty	Bunratty Castle		24/30-pounder
Cobh	The Promenade	1794	36-pounder
Dublin	Cathal Brugha Bks	1835	36-pounder
Dublin	Cathal Brugha Bks	1836	36-pounder
Dublin	Cathal Brugha Bks	1847	36-pounder
Dublin	Cathal Brugha Bks	1847	36-pounder
Dublin	Cathal Brugha Bks	1807	13-inch mortar
Dublin	Cathal Brugha Bks	1811	13-inch mortar
Dun Laoghaire	Park at Pier		24-pounder
Ennis	Courthouse	1837	36-pounder
Galway	Eyre Square	1824	36-pounder
Galway	Eyre Square	1826	36-pounder
Kildare	Curragh Camp	1831	24-pounder
Limerick	Harbour Office		36-pounder
Limerick	Harbour Office		36-pounder
Newry	Courthouse		36-pounder
Tralee	Courthouse	1801	30-pounder
Tralee	Courthouse	1802	30-pounder
Trim	Trim Castle	1845	24-pounder
Waterford	Peoples Park	1828	24-pounder
Waterford	Peoples Park	1828	24-pounder[8]

7 Compiled from 1855 *Army List*.   **8** Note. In some cases the markings on these guns are illegible and the date of casting cannot be ascertained. There would also appear to have been a pair of guns in Monaghan and another gun in Coleraine but these have been moved. In Clancy Barracks, Dublin, there is a 9-pounder Royal Naval Division howitzer, dating from the Crimean period.

Bibliography

PRIMARY SOURCES

1. MANUSCRIPT MATERIAL

National Archives, Dublin
Browne (Lieutenant C. Wade Browne, letters from Balaclava). MS 2092.
Lists of men from Aghada and Whitegate parishes, Co. Cork serving in the Royal Navy. MS 6077.
Chief Secretary's Office; Registered Papers, 1854–6.
National Library of Ireland
Fortescue (Captain John Charles William Fortescue, Royal Artillery, of Stephenstown, Co. Louth. Dispatches and orders, February 1854 to March 1856). MS 19,360.
Fortescue (Captain John Charles William Fortescue RA. Account of his voyage to the Crimea). MS 19,462.
Fortescue (Captain John Charles William Fortescue RA. Crimean diary, September 1854 to June 1855). MS 19,459.
McDonnell (Robert McDonnell FRCSI, of Dublin and Kilsharvan, Co. Meath. Letters from the Crimea). MS 18,491.
Dublin Diocesan Archives
Cullen (Archbishop Paul Cullen, files of letters received from Irish priests and nuns serving abroad and also from foreign priests and bishops). MS Volumes 332/5/II; 332/7/I; 332/7/II; 339/1/II.
Irish Jesuit Archives, Leeson Street, Dublin
Menologies, ii.
Memorials of the Irish Province SJ, viii.
Duffy (Patrick Duffy SJ, letters covering the period 1873–1904). MS J.457.
Ronan (William Ronan SJ, file of material relating to his life as a Jesuit priest, including references to his services in the Crimea).
Dublin City Archives
Minutes of the Municipal Council of Dublin City, 18 February 1856 to 3 December 1857. C2/A1/19.
Minutes of the Municipal Council of Dublin City, 21 December 1857 to 5 September 1859. C2/A1/20.
Private Collection (Ireland)
Montgomery (Regimental Sergeant-Major Edward Montgomery, Royal Engineers, unpublished memoir detailing his experiences in the British army, including his service in the Crimean war).

Public Record Office, Kew

Azoff [*sic*] Clasp Roll. ADM 171.25.

Muster Rolls of the 4th Light Dragoons.

W.O. 12/659 (1854–5), W.O. 12/660 (1855–6), W.O. 12/661 (1856–7).

Muster Rolls of the 8th (Royal Irish) Hussars.

W.O. 12/844 (1854–5), W.O. 12/845 (1855–6), W.O. 12/846 (1856–7).

Muster Rolls of the 11th Hussars.

W.O. 12/1012 (1854–5), W.O. 12/1013 (1855–6), W.O. 12/1014 (1856–7).

Muster Rolls of the 13th Light Dragoons.

W.O. 12/1118 (1854–5), W.O. 12/1119 (1855–6), W.O. 12/1120 (1856–7).

Muster Rolls of the 17th Lancers.

W.O. 12/1339 (1854–5), W.O. 12/1340 (1855–6), W.O. 12/1341 (1856–7).

National Army Museum, Chelsea

Bourke (Private Daniel Bourke, an account, written in 1910, of his experiences with the 18th (Royal Irish) Regiment in the Crimea). MS 6807/152.

Cattell (Assistant-Surgeon William Cattell, 5th Dragoon Guards, account of his experiences in the Crimea).

Connaught Rangers (Account of the Light Division's service in Bulgaria, written in 1871 by an unknown Connaught Ranger). MS 6501–183–8.

Esmonde (Captain Thomas Esmonde VC, file containing press cuttings relating to his service with the 18th (Royal Irish) Regiment). 5904/131.

Fitzgerald (Donation of C.F. Fitzgerald. An account of the charge of the Heavy Brigade, written by an unknown trooper of the 6th (Inniskilling) Dragoons). MS 7703/52.

Percival (Captain E.A. Percival, Connaught Rangers, letters written during his service in the Crimean war and the Indian Mutiny, includes some captured Russian documents). MS 6509/139.

Pine (Surgeon C. Pine, 4th (Royal Irish) Dragoons Guards, letters from the Crimea). MS 6807/262.

Seager (Captain Edward Seager, 8th (Royal Irish) Hussars, two manuscript volumes containing copies of letters written to members of his family, June 1854 to August 1855). MS 8311–9.

Timson (Henry Timson, 6th (Inniskilling) Dragoons, copies of letters written from the Crimea, including an account of the charge of the Heavy Brigade). MS 6807/244.

The Royal Scots Dragoon Guards (Carabiniers and Greys) Museum, the Castle, Edinburgh

Nominal Roll of the service squadron that sailed for the Crimea in 1854. MS GB46 G176.

Nominal Roll of the replacement draft that sailed for the Crimea in 1855. MS GB46 G179.

Troop Roll Book, 'D' Troop 1857.

2. BRITISH PARLIAMENTARY PAPERS

Return of the number of English, Scotch and Irish non-commissioned officers and privates in the British army, in each of the years on the 1st day of January 1830 and 1840, HC 1841 (307), xiv, 93.

Report showing total number of recruits for the British army admitted from 1844 to 1847, HC 1847–8 (228), xli, 23.

A return of the number and names of the surgeons, assistant-surgeons and dressers, HC 1854–5 (293), xxxiv, 197.

Annual report of the commissioners for administering the laws for the relief of the poor in Ireland, [1945], HC 1855, xxiv, 523.

Annual report of the commissioners for administering the laws for the relief of the poor in Ireland, [2105], HC 1856, xxviii, 415.

Return of all vessels and goods taken at sea as prize during the late war, either by revenue cutters or vessels attached to the coast guard service, HC 1856 (325), xli, 247–59.

Statistical abstract of education and religious denomination in the Royal Navy, HC 1866 (45), xlvi, 57.

Returns of the religious persuasions of the seamen of the Royal navy, and also of the Royal Marines, and of the chaplains, HC 1876 (132), xlv, 169.

Report of the royal commissioners appointed to inquire into the granting of medical degrees, with evidence, appendices and index, [C 3259], HC 1882, xxix, 489.

3. CONTEMPORARY NEWSPAPERS AND JOURNALS

Annual Register
Belfast Newsletter
Cork Constitution
Cork Examiner
Daily News
Dublin Evening Mail
Dublin Evening Post
Freeman's Journal
Illustrated London News
London Gazette

Minutes of the Proceedings of the Institute of Civil Engineers
Munster News
Nenagh Guardian
Newry Examiner
The Reporter
Sligo Journal
The Times
United Service Journal
Wexford Independent

4. CONTEMPORARY WORKS OF REFERENCE

Constabulary list and directory, nos. 27 and 28 (Dublin, 1855).

Corpo Reale Di Stato Maggiore, Annuerio Militare Ufficiale dello Stato Sardo l'Anno 1854 (Turin, 1854).

Dublin directory

Hart, Henry George, *Annual Army List* (London, 1854 etc.).

Lodge's, *Peerage* (1859).

Thom's Irish almanac and official directory for the year 1854

5. CONTEMPORARY WORKS

Calthorpe, J. Gough, *Letters from headquarters* (London, 1857).

Cameron, Sir Charles, *History of the Royal College of Surgeons in Ireland* (Dublin, 1886).

Colborne, the Hon. John, and Brine, Frederic, *Memorials of the brave: or resting places of our fallen heroes in the Crimea and at Scutari* (London, 1858).

Corpo Reale di Stato Maggiore, *Riccordo Pittorico Militare della Spedizione Sarda in Oriente, 1855–56* (Turin, 1857).

Doyle, Sr Aloysius, *Memories of the Crimea* (Dublin, 1897).

Doyle, John, *A descriptive account of the famous charge of the Light Brigade at Balaclava* (London, 1877).

Duberly, F., *Journal kept during the Russian war* (London, 1855).

Fitzpatrick, W.J., *Secret service under Pitt* (1892).

Gadsby, John, *A trip to Sebastapol in 1857* (London, 1884).

History of the great national banquet given to the victorious soldiers returned from the Crimean war and stationed in Irish garrisons by the people of Ireland in the city of Dublin, October 22, 1856 (Dublin, 1858).

Helps, Arthur, *The Life and labours of Mr Brassey, 1805–70* (London, 1872).

HMSO, *Grand annual return of the British army* (London, 1868).

Kinglake, A.W., *The invasion of the Crimea*, (8 volumes, London, 1868–87).

Manfredi, Cristoforo, *La Spedizione Sarda in Crimea, 1855–56* (Rome, 1896).

Martineau, Harriet, *England and her soldiers* (London, 1859).

Nolan, Captain Louis Edward, *Cavalry: its history and tactics* (London, 1853).

— *The training of cavalry remount horses* (London, 1861).

Nolan, E.H., *The illustrated history of the war against Russia* (2 volumes, London, 1856–7).

O'Flaherty, Philip, *Philip O'Flaherty, the young soldier. Containing interesting particulars of the war in the Crimea* (Edinburgh, 1855).

O'Malley, James, *The life of James O'Malley, late corporal of the 17th Leicestershire Regiment, 'Royal Bengal Tigers'* (Montreal, 1893).

Paget, Lord George, *The Light Cavalry Brigade in the Crimea* (London, 1861).

Portal, Captain Robert, *Letters from the Crimea* (London, 1900).

Russell, William Howard, *The war: from the landing at Gallipoli to the death of Lord Raglan* (London, 1855).

— *The war: from the death of Lord Raglan to the evacuation of the Crimea* (London, 1856).

Small, Edward (ed.), *Told from the ranks* (London, 1898), p. 39.

Sterling, Lieutenant-Colonel Anthony, *The Highland Brigade in the Crimea* (London, 1895).

Vicars, Hedley, *Memorials to Captain Hedley Vicars, 97th Regiment* (London, 1863).

Wrottlesley, Lieutenant-Colonel the Hon. George, *The life and correspondence of Field Marshal Sir John Fox Burgoyne, Bart.* (2 volumes, London, 1873).

6. PRINTED BROADSHEET BALLADS

White Ballad Collection (John Davis White,1820–93, antiquary, solicitor and editor of the *Cashel Gazette*), Early Printed Books Department, Trinity College, Dublin, Volumes OLS/X/1/530; OLS/X/1/531; OLS/X/1/532.

SECONDARY WORKS

1. MODERN WORKS OF REFERENCE

Australian dictionary of biography.

Belchem, John, Price, Richard and Evans, Richard J. (eds), *The Penguin dictionary of nineteenth-century history* (London, 1996).

Boase, Frederic, *Modern English biography* (London, 1892–1901).

Burtchaell, G.D., and Sadleir, T.U., *Alumni Dublinenses* (2nd edn, Dublin, 1935).

Burke, *Landed gentry of Ireland* (London, 1912).

Buzzell, Nora (ed.), *The register of the Victoria Cross* (Cheltenham, 1981).

Coakley, Davis, *Irish masters of medicine* (Dublin, 1992).

Dictionary of Canadian biography.

Dictionary of national biography.

Dickinson, Lieutenant-Colonel R.J., *Officers' mess* (London, 1973).

Doherty, Richard, and Truesdale, David, *Irish winners of the Victoria Cross* (Dublin, 2000).

Drew, Robert (ed.), *Commissioned officers in the medical services of the British army 1660–1960*, (Wellcome Historical Medical Library, 1968).

Farset Youth Project, *Ireland's VCs* (Belfast, 1996).

Makepeace-Warne, Anthony, *Brassey's companion to the British army* (London, 1995).

Stenton, Michael, and Lees, Stephen, *Who's who of the British members of Parliament, 1832–1885* (London, 1976), i.

Walker, Brian M., *Parliamentary election results in Ireland, 1801–1922* (Dublin, 1978),

Williams, W.A., *The VCs of Wales and the Welsh regiments* (Clwyd, 1984).

Windrow, Martin, and Mason, Francis K., *The Wordsworth dictionary of military biography* (London, 1990), pp 177–9.

Winton, John, *The Victoria Cross at sea* (London, 1978).

2. MODERN WORKS

Adkin, Mark, *The charge* (London, 1996).

Allendorfer, F. von, 'Irish Officers in the Turkish Service' in *Irish Sword*, ii, no. 9 (Winter 1956), p. 377.

Asquith, Stuart, 'D (London Irish Rifles) Company' in *Regiment*, no. 35, March 1999, pp 50–60.

Atkins, John B., *The life of Sir William Howard Russell* (2 volumes, London, 1911).

Barthorp, Michael, and Turner, Pierre, *The British army on campaign, 1816–1902* (2): *The Crimea 1854–56* (London, 1987).

Barthorp, Michael, *Heroes of the Crimea: the battles of Balaclava and Inkerman* (London, 1991).

Bentley, Nicholas (ed.), *Russell's dispatches from the Crimea: 1854–6* (London, 1966).

Bolster, Evelyn, *A history of the diocese of Cork: the episcopate of William Delany: 1847–86* (Cork, 1993).

—— *The Irish Sisters of Mercy in the Crimean war* (Cork, 1964).

Bonner-Smith, D., and Dewar, Captain A.C. (eds), 'Russian war 1854. Baltic and Black Sea: Official Correspondence' in *Journal of the Navy Records Society*, lxxxiii (London, 1943).

Brunicardi, Lt-Commander D. Niall, 'A letter from Varna' in *Irish Sword*, xiv, no. 57 (Winter, 1981), pp 316–20.

Butler, General Sir William, *Sir William Butler: an autobiography* (London, 1911).

Chappell, Michael, *Redcaps: Britain's military police* (London, 1997).

Childers, Major E.S.E., and Stewart, R., *The story of the Royal Hospital, Kilmainham* (London, 1921).

Coleman, Terry, *The railway navvies* (2nd edn, London, 1981)

Comerford, R.V., 'Conspiring brotherhoods and contending élites, 1857–63' in W.E. Vaughan (ed.), *A New History of Ireland*, v (Oxford, 1989), pp 415–30.

Compton, Piers, *Cardigan of Balaclava* (London, 1972).

Cook, Frank and Andrea, *Casualty roll for the Crimea* (London, 1976).

Cook, Hugh, *The Sikh wars: the British army in the Punjab 1845–49* (London, 1975).

Cooke, Brian, *The Grand Crimean Railway: the railway that won a war* (2nd edn, Cheshire, 1997).

Cunliffe, Marcus, *The Royal Irish Fusiliers, 1793–1968* (London, 1970).

Crew, Graeme, *The Royal Army Service Corps* (London, 1970).

Dillon, Viscount, 'Irishmen in the Light Brigade, Balaclava, 1854' in *Irish Sword*, xii, no. 48 (Summer 1976), 254–6.

Doyle, Arthur H., *A hundred years of conflict: being some records of six generals of the Doyle family, 1756–1856* (Dublin, 1911).

Duckers, Peter, and Mitchell, Neill, *The Azoff campaign, 1855* (Shrewsbury, 1996).

Farewell, Byron, *Queen Victoria's little wars* (London, 1973).

Fitzpatrick, David, 'A Peculiar Tramping People' in W.E. Vaughan (ed.), *A new history of Ireland*, v (Oxford, 1989), pp 623–61.

Fleetwood, John, 'An Irish field-ambulance in the Franco-Prussian war' in *Irish Sword*, vi, no. 24 (Summer, 1964), pp 137–48.

Fortescue, Sir John, *The early history of transport and supply* (London, 1928).

Fosten, Bryan, *Wellington's light cavalry* (London, 1982).

Friendly, Alfred, *Beaufort of the Admiralty: the life of Sir Francis Beaufort, 1774–1857* (London, 1977).

Fry, William H.P. (ed.), *Annals of the Late Major Oliver Fry, RA* (London, 1909).

Furneaux, Rupert, *The first war correspondent: William Howard Russell* (London, 1944).

Garland, J.L, 'Irish Officers in the Turkish Service' in *Irish Sword*, iii, no. 11 (Winter 1957), p. 132.

Gibbs, Peter, *The battle of the Alma* (London, 1963).

Giddings, Robert, *Imperial echoes: eye-witness accounts of Victoria's little wars* (London, 1996).

Goldfrank, David M., *The origins of the Crimean war* (London, 1994).

Goldie, Sue M., *Florence Nightingale: letters from the Crimea* (London, 1997).

Greenhill, Basil, and Giffard, Ann, *The British assault on Finland, 1854–55: a forgotten naval war* (London, 1998).

Hall, Brendan, *Officers and recruits of the Louth Rifles, 1854–76* (Dun Laoghaire Genealogical Society, 1999).

Hanham, H.J., 'Religion and nationality in the mid-Victorian army' in M.R.D. Foot (ed.), *War and society* (London, 1973), pp 159–83, notes 318–320.

Hankinson, Alan, *Man of wars: William Howard Russell of The Times* (London, 1982).

Hannon, Kevin, 'Limerick: The garrison town' in *An Cosantóir* (November 1989), pp 33–4.

Harries-Jenkins, Gwyn, *The army in Victorian society* (University of Hull Press, 1993).

Hayes-McCoy, G.A., *Captain Myles Walter Keogh, United States Army, 1840–76* (Dublin, 1965).

— 'The Irish Company in the Franco-Prussian War' in *Irish Sword*, i, no. 4 (1952–3), pp 275–83.

Hennessy, Maurice, *The Wild Geese. The Irish soldier in exile* (London, 1973).

Herlihy, Jim, *The Royal Irish Constabulary: A short history and genealogical guide* (Dublin, 1997).

Hibbert, Christopher, *The destruction of Lord Raglan: a tragedy of the Crimean war* (London, 1961).

Hinton, Mike, 'Sardinians who charged' in *The war correspondent*, xvii, no. 4 (January 2000), pp 42–4.

Holt, Edgar, *The Carlist wars in Spain* (London, 1967).

Iremonger, Lucille, *Lord Aberdeen* (London, 1978).

James, Lawrence, *Crimea 1854–6: the war with Russia from contemporary photographs* (London, 1981).

Johnstone, Tom, and Hagerty, James, *The cross on the sword: Catholic chaplains in the forces* (London, 1996).

Jones, Norman, 'Russian guns: research at the PRO' in *The war correspondent*, xvi, no. 3 (October 1998), pp 36–40.

Knightley, Phillip, *The first casualty. From the Crimea to Vietnam: The war correspondent as hero, propagandist and myth maker* (London, 1978).

Lalumia, Matthew Paul, *Realism and politics in Victorian art of the Crimean war* (Epping, 1984).

Lambert, Andrew, and Badsey, Stephen, *The war correspondents: the Crimean war* (2nd edn, London, 1997).

Lummis, Canon William, and Wynn, Kenneth, *Honour the Light Brigade: a record of the services of officers, non-commissioned officers and men of the five light cavalry regiments* (London, 1973).

McArdle, Joseph, *Irish legal anecdotes* (Dublin, 1995).

McLaughlin, R., *The Royal Army Medical Corps* (London, 1972).

Mallinson, Colonel Allan, *Light Dragoons: the origins of a regiment* (London, 1993).

Marsay, Mark, 'The stirring tale of Redan Massy' in *Newsletter of the friends of the Green Howards Regimental Museum*, no. 3 (September, 1997), pp 16–18.

— 'One woman's story. With the 19th Foot by Margaret Kirwin' in *Newsletter of the friends of the Green Howards Regimental Museum*, no. 3 (September, 1997), pp 14–15.

Martin, Kingsley, *The triumph of Lord Palmerston: a study of public opinion before the Crimean war* (London, 1963).

Mercer, Lieutenant-Colonel Patrick, *Inkerman 1854* (London, 1998).

Mollo, John and Boris, *Into the valley of death: the British Cavalry Division at Balaclava, 1854* (London, 1991).

Moyse-Bartlett, Lt-Col. H., *Nolan of Balaclava: Louis Edward Nolan and his influence on the British cavalry* (London, 1971).

Murphy, David, '"As if hell's gulph was opened". The letters of Robert McDonnell, a volunteer surgeon in the Crimean war' in *Soldiers of the Queen*, no. 96, March 1999, pp 6–10.

—— 'Irish Jesuit Chaplains in the Crimea' in *The war correspondent*, xvii, no. 1 (April 1999), pp 42–7.

—— '"The Battle of the Breeches": the Nenagh mutiny, July 1856' in *Tipperary Historical Journal* (2001), 139–45.

Murphy, J.J.W., 'An Irish Sister of Mercy in the Crimean War' in *Irish Sword*, v, no. 21 (Winter 1962), p.251.

Murray, R.H., *The history of the VIII's King's Royal Irish Hussars* (2 volumes, London, 1928).

Nicholson, J.B.R., *The British army of the Crimea* (London, 1974).

O'Brien, Eoin, Browne, Lorna, and O'Malley, Kevin, *The House of Industry hospitals, 1772–1987* (Dublin, 1988).

Ó Gráda, Cormac, *Ireland before and after the Famine: explorations in economic history, 1800–1925* (Manchester University Press, 1988).

O'Carroll, Derval, and Fitzpatrick, Sean, *Hoggers, lords and railwaymen: a history of the Custom House Docks, Dublin* (Dublin, 1996).

Ogden, Rollo, *The life and letters of Edwin Lawrence Godkin* (New York, 1911).

Paget, George Charles Henry Victor (7th marquess of Anglesey), *A history of the British Cavalry*, i, 1816–50 (London, 1973).

—— *A History of the British cavalry*, ii, 1851–71 (London, 1975).

Patterson, T. G. F., 'A letter from the Crimea' in *Irish Sword*, vi, no. 25 (Winter 1964), pp 283–7.

Pickles, Tim, *New Orleans 1815* (London, 1993).

Radford, Mark, 'Thomas Esmonde, VC. Constabulary of Ireland 1859–1867' in *Proceedings of the Royal Ulster Constabulary Historical Society* (Winter 1998), p. 7.

Ricks, Christopher (ed.), *The poems of Tennyson* (London, 1969).

Robinson, Rod, 'The Nenagh mutiny' in *The war correspondent*, xviii, no. 4 (January 2001), 14–18.

Seaton, Albert, *The Russian army of the Crimea* (London, 1973).

Sheehan, E.H., *Nenagh and its neighbourhood* (Ormond Historical Society, 1976).

Sheffield, G.D., *The Redcaps* (London, 1994).

Shephard, John, *The Crimean doctors: a history of the British medical services in the Crimean war* (2 volumes, Liverpool, 1991).

Simms, J.G., 'The Irish on the Continent, 1691–1800' in T.W. Moody and W.E. Vaughan (eds), *A new history of Ireland*, iv (Oxford, 1986), pp 629–54.

Sinclair, R.J.K., and Scully, F.J.M., *Arresting memories* (Belfast, 1982).

Smith, George Loy, *A Victorian regimental sergeant–major: from India to the Crimea* (Tunbridge Wells, 1987).

Smyth, Hazel P., *The B+I Line* (Dublin, 1984).

Smyth, Sir John, *In this sign conquer: the story of the army chaplains* (London, 1968).

Spiers, Edward M., *Radical general. Sir George De Lacy Evans. 1787–1870* (Manchester 1983).

St. John Hennessy, N., 'Crimean-war guns in Ireland' in *Irish Sword*, xix, no. 78 (Winter 1995), pp 333–44.

Starling, Peter Captain, 'Queen Victoria's visits to the hospitals at Fort Pitt and Chatham, 1855–6' in *The war correspondent*, xvi, no. 1, (April, 1998), pp 36–9.

Sweetman, John, *Balaclava 1854* (London, 1993).

—— *Lord Raglan: from the Peninsula to the Crimea* (London, 1993).

—— *The Crimean war* (Essential Histories Series, London, 2001).

Tisdall, E.E.P., *Mrs Duberly campaigns: an Englishwoman's experiences in the Crimean war and the Indian mutiny* (London, 1963).

Vaughan, W.E., *Sin, sheep and Scotsmen: John George Adair and the Derryveagh evictions, 1861* (Belfast, 1983).

—— 'Ireland c.1870' in W.E. Vaughan (ed.), *A new history of Ireland*, v (Oxford, 1989), pp 726–800.

Warner, Philip, *The Crimean war – a reappraisal* (London, 1972).

—— *The fields of war: a young cavalryman's Crimea campaign* (London, 1977).

Watts, Anthony J., *The Royal Navy: an illustrated history* (London, 1994).

Wells, Captain John, *The Royal Navy: an illustrated social history, 1870–1982* (London, 1994).

Williams, Godfrey T., *The historical records of the 11th Hussars:'Prince Albert's Own'* (London, 1908).

Williams, Robert J., 'An Irish Brigade for the Crimea' in *Irish Sword*, xiv, no. 55 (Winter, 1980), p. 195.

— 'Royal Dublin City Militia riots in Lancashire' in *Irish Sword*, xiv, no. 55 (Winter 1980), pp 195–6.

Winton, John, 'Was Able Seaman James Gorman, VC, an Aussie?' in *The war correspondent*, xvi, no. 2 (July 1998), pp 22–5.

Woodham-Smith, Cecil, *The reason why: the story of the fatal charge of the Light Brigade* (London, 1953).

—— *Florence Nightingale* (London, 1958).

Index